LOVE FOR SALE

GENDER AND AMERICAN CULTURE

love for sale

COURTING, TREATING, AND PROSTITUTION IN NEW YORK CITY, 1900-1945

ELIZABETH ALICE CLEMENT

THE UNIVERSITY OF NORTH CAROLINA PRESS Chapel Hill

Set in Arnhem and Eagle Bold types
by Tseng Information Systems, Inc.
Manufactured in the United States of America

The paper in this book meets the guidelines for
permanence and durability of the Committee on
Production Guidelines for Book Longevity of the
Council on Library Resources.

Library of Congress Cataloging-in-Publication Data
Clement, Elizabeth Alice.
Love for sale : courting, treating, and prostitution in
New York City, 1900–1945 / Elizabeth Alice Clement.
    p. cm. — (Gender and American culture)
Originally presented as the author's thesis (Ph. D.)—
Univ. of Pennsylvania, 1998, under the title: Trick or
treat: prostitution and working-class women's
sexuality in New York City, 1900–1932.
Includes bibliographical references and index.
ISBN-13: 978-0-8078-3026-0 (cloth : alk. paper)
ISBN-10: 0-8078-3026-7 (cloth : alk. paper)
ISBN-13: 978-0-8078-5690-1 (pbk. : alk. paper)
ISBN-10: 0-8078-5690-8 (pbk. : alk. paper)
1. Prostitution—New York (State)—New York—
History—20th century. 2. Sex customs—New York
(State)—New York—History—20th century.
3. Courtship—New York (State)—New York—
History—20th century. I. Title. II. Gender & American
culture.
HQ146.N7C55 2006
306.7409747′1—dc22   2005037961

cloth   10 09 08 07 06   5 4 3 2 1
paper   10 09 08 07 06   5 4 3 2 1

For my mother,
Alice Regina Meehan Clement,
and my aunt,
Marguerite Therèse Meehan Wallace,
who grew up on and
love the sidewalks of New York
like I do

East side, west side, all around the town

The tots sang "Ring-a-rosy, London Bridge is falling down"

Boys and girls together, me and Mamie O'Rourke

Trip the light fantastic on the sidewalks of New York

Down in front of Casey's old grey wooden stoop

On a summer's evening we formed a merry group

Boys and girls together, we would sing and waltz

While Tony played the organ on the sidewalks of New York

—"Sidewalks of New York,"

    by James Blake and Charles Lawler, 1894

CONTENTS

ILLUSTRATIONS

ACKNOWLEDGMENTS

I owe an enormous debt to the many people and institutions who supported me through the writing and research of this book, though it should go without saying that only I can be held responsible for the way it turned out. I was very fortunate to attend the University of Pennsylvania's history department, which, with the help of the Mellon Foundation, provided five years of full funding for my graduate training. The research and writing of the dissertation was assisted by a Sexuality Research Fellowship from the Social Science Research Council with funds provided by the Ford Foundation. The Society for the Scientific Study of Sex also provided a grant for dissertation research. For the arduous process of turning the dissertation into a book, I received the Larry J. Hackman Research in Residence Award from the New York State Archives. I also had extensive support from the University of Utah, including a Faculty Fellow Research Leave and a University of Utah Research Committee Grant. The Undergraduate Research Opportunities Program at the University of Utah funded several undergraduate research assistants, which allowed me to deepen my source base and complete the project more quickly. I am particularly proud of the work done by Katrina Paxton, Jane McBroom, Elizabeth Toscano, Mary Toscano, Yana Walton, and Michaele Smith. The Social Science Research Council and the Kinsey Institute for Sex Research provided support for a seminar in the history of sexuality that produced invaluable evidence for the final chapters of this book. Many archivists and librarians guided my research, but Melanie Yolles of the New York Public Library deserves special thanks for all she did to steer me towards rich material and for sponsoring me in my fights to gain access to it.

I have been very lucky in the guidance I have received and the mentorship I have experienced throughout my entire career. My adviser, Carroll Smith-Rosenberg, encouraged me to think more theoretically but also gave me the freedom to chose my own topics and go my own way. She gave me fine lessons in the importance of agency and resistance. Drew Faust supported me in every aspect of this dissertation and my larger project of being a graduate student and assistant professor, and for that I am eternally grateful. She also proved to be an excellent model for how to gracefully balance teaching, scholarship, and service. Lori Ginzberg and Kathy Brown have provided invaluable assistance in the writing of the dissertation and the book, giving insightful, incisive comments that pushed me to explore the implications of my findings and to write about them clearly.

Numerous scholars have read this work in its myriad of drafts. I am particularly grateful to Timothy Gilfoyle and Leisa Meyers who provided excellent critical response at crucial stages of the manuscript's completion. I must also thank several anonymous readers who read and commented on the manuscript. I am also grateful to Kathryn Jay, Bruce Lenthall, Michael Kahan, Kirsten Wood, Ellen Amster, and Dan Wadhwani, who continued the work they began in graduate school of shaping me and my manuscript. Though we scattered across the country to jobs inside and outside of the academy, they are, and hopefully always will be, my good friends and colleagues. I would also like to thank Chad Heap, with whom I swapped both ideas and sources. Sharing primary sources is rare among historians, and Chad's willingness to send me anything he thought I needed to see strengthened this book significantly.

Like the University of Pennsylvania, the University of Utah is teeming with wonderful colleagues, both in and out of the History Department, who have provided crucial support. I am particularly grateful to Kathryn Stockton and Gerda Saunders of Gender Studies, Larry Gerlach, Ron Coleman, and Peggy Pasco in History, and the vice president of diversity, Karen Dace, for their mentorship. I am even more grateful for the battles they fought to make Utah a place where women's history, and the history of America's diverse peoples, can be researched and taught so effectively. Our government documents librarian, Peter Krauss, arrived in Utah the year after I did, fresh from New York Public Library, and his knowledge of the New York City collections, along with his enthusiasm for this project, has been invaluable. My colleagues Lisa Diamond, Erin O'Connell, Tracy McDonald, Chris Talbot, Margaret Toscano, Martha Ertman, Megan Armstrong, Anne Keary, Raul Ramos, David Igler, Eric Hinderaker, Bradley Parker, Susie Porter, MaryAnn Villarreal, Matt Basso, Bob Goldberg, and Wes Sasaki-Uemura have all read various bits of this project and through their critical responses have made it better. Nadja Durbach and Janet Theiss deserve combat pay for reading an infinite number of drafts; I expect they are as relieved as I am that this book is finally done.

Finally, I would like to thank my family, biological, extended, and chosen. My mother and father, Alice and David Clement, have had their own struggles with academia, and I'm glad that the third generation of Clement Ph.D.'s finally produced someone tenurable. More important, they raised me to believe in justice and in the hope and potential of all people. They also advised me to choose my work based on what I loved and what I thought would be useful, rather than on how much money I could make. I hope they're not regretting that now. My sister Alexandra, my Aunt Margie and Uncle Gerry, and my cousin Joy have always been important fans of me and my work. I would also like to thank Carol and Peter Wallin; Maryellen, Mickey, and Colin Boyle (and Yami); Joan Reitzel; Nancy, Sheldon, and Rebecca Jane Jaffe; Gayle Gullet and Ed Escobar; Anna and Ernie; and Auntie Pam. Laurie Drummond deserves special praise for enduring me as I wrote all of the dissertation and much of the book. Kellie Custen made the last few months as I completed the manuscript far more entertaining than I ever could have imagined, and I hope she will stick around for the second project. Without the love, kindness, and enduring faith of my family, broadly defined, I would not be the person I am today.

LOVE FOR SALE

Introduction

THE EVOLUTION OF "NEAR WHORES" AND "WHORES IN THE MAKING"

Charles Briggs worked as an undercover investigator for New York's preeminent private vice society, the Committee of Fourteen, and filed a written report in the spring of 1913 that described the women frequenting a popular working-class club. Classifying them into four distinct "moral" categories, he identified the largest group as "store employees, telephone girls, stenographers, etc." These women's "morals are loose and there is no question that they are on terms of sexual intimacy with their male companions," he commented with distaste. Another group consisted of what he called "'near whores' or 'whores in the making.'" He also found "kept women" and "professional prostitutes," though he admitted that "the latter do not ply their trade in this rear room." However, they presented a serious danger to the other girls, because "from their example and conversation, the 'near whores' . . . gain further impetus in their downward spiral."[1] Although other observers at the time might have lumped all of these together as "immoral" women, a term the white middle class equated with prostitution, Briggs carefully acknowledged a new spectrum of women's sexual activities and identities. The emergence of these categories, which contemporary historians might be more likely to refer to as "courting couples," "charity girls" (also known as "treating girls"), "mistresses," and "professional prostitutes," marks the profound shift in sexual norms that was occurring in New York and other American cities in the late nineteenth century. As working-class youth moved away from supervised courtships and into commercial amusements, premarital intercourse rates rose dramatically.[2] At the same time, a new kind of sexual actor stepped onto the stage, the charity girl. Charity girls engaged in "treating," exchanging sexual activities (sometimes including sexual intercourse) for entertainment expenses like theater tickets, dance hall admissions, and late-night dinners at the automat.[3] "Kept" women formed more long-term relationships of sexual exchange, while professional prostitutes demanded cash for their services. As Briggs's report makes clear, all of these women overlapped in new and frightening ways in the exciting world of New York's commercial amusements. This book explores the historical relationships between different kinds of sexual intimacy and exchange in American history, culture, and social practice. Focusing on New York City from 1900 through 1945, I trace the interactions among courtship, treating, and prostitution.

Demographically, New York's working class in the early twentieth century changed constantly as waves of immigrants from eastern and southern Europe and steady streams of African Americans from the South and black immigrants from the West Indies flowed into the city.* Once there, they combined (often uneasily) with a working class that was composed of the descendants of the Irish and German immigrants of the mid-nineteenth century. This segment of the working class spoke English, possessed a strong identity as native New Yorkers, and dominated the skilled trades and municipal employment of the labor aristocracy. Native-born African Americans, though less than 2 percent of the population in 1900, made up a small but significant segment of New York's working class and lived in pockets scattered throughout the poorer districts of the city.[4]

Rather than assume that these different communities shared a common set of ideas about gender and sexuality, I have paid careful attention to ethnicity, religion, and race as I traced the development of new sexual norms. Italians did not approach sexuality or "Americanization" in the same way that eastern European Jews did, nor can West Indians comfortably be folded into a broader "African American" cultural framework. For the purposes of this book, I have defined "the working class" largely in terms of economic status and occupation. While this may seem like a crude set of indicators of social class, it has allowed me to address the ethnic and racial diversity of the city and to make comparisons within segments of the working class rather than solely between monolithic "working" and "middle" classes. By the late 1920s, New York had developed a broad working-class culture in which many different ethnic and racial groups participated. While ethnic and racial distinctions remained important, broadly speaking, Italians and Jews had become white New Yorkers, and West Indians and southern African Americans had become black New Yorkers. The pan-working-class culture that these groups developed became one of the driving forces behind

*Because my sources (particularly in chapters 6 and 7 and the conclusion) relate both to African Americans and to West Indians who have African heritage and "look" black by American standards, I have chosen to use the term "black" when referring to community practices, standards, and institutions. When discussing specific individuals whose backgrounds are identified in the sources, I use either "African American" or "West Indian" as appropriate.

the radical changes in sexual norms witnessed by all Americans during the first half of the twentieth century.[5]

In the 1890s, the children of New York's working class began venturing into the city's new "cheap amusements." For girls, at least, the question of how to pay their way loomed large, and treating provided a solution. From its beginnings in America's dance halls and cabarets, treating existed on a continuum between courtship and prostitution. In experimenting with sexual barter, young working-class women forged a new category of sexual identity that allowed them to profit from sex without completely abandoning their particular culture's conceptions of female respectability. Like most compromises driven by need and desire, treating blurred lines and crossed boundaries. Aware that this new practice violated working-class conceptions of morality, working-class women constructed linguistic and behavioral boundaries between themselves and prostitutes. Charity girls policed their sexual and social exchanges fiercely, denouncing those women whose bartering too closely resembled prostitution. The effect of these new identities and practices changed ideas about courtship and notions of sexual morality and disturbed the place that prostitution held in American urban culture.

The emergence of treating had a profound impact on both courtship and prostitution and set the trajectory for the development of modern American sexual values and behaviors. Although working-class courtship had always contained sexual activity, experience with treating accelerated the widespread inclusion of heterosexual intercourse into modern American courtship, which approached the level of 50 percent for white American women by the mid-1930s.[6] Furthermore, treating also introduced a pattern of sexual exchange into dating relationships that remains embedded in the practice today. While few men assume that buying dinner for a woman will automatically lead to sexual intercourse with her, both sexes agree that monetary payments sometimes leave the recipient with a sexual debt.[7]

Because it made sexual intercourse outside of marriage more available to men, treating also had a profound impact on prostitution. At the end of the nineteenth century, prostitution was an important sexual outlet for American men in both the working and middle classes, and prostitutes were well integrated into New York's working-class neighborhoods.[8] When combined with the pressure of the new sex industry that developed in America's large cities in the 1920s, treating forced prostitution to the margins of American sexual culture. While treating provided a brief and tenuous compromise between prostitution and courtship in the early twentieth century, its development led to the wide divergence between these two heterosexual practices.

By the 1930s, the specific language of treating began to disappear as it was absorbed into the newly developing "dating system." With both economic exchange and noncommercial intercourse embedded in dating, prostitution became a far less common element of American sexual culture. With treating gone, the gulf between courtship and prostitution had become so wide that few in the early twenty-first century can even imagine a relationship between the two. But as the evidence from the early twentieth century indicates, all three practices existed on a continuum of sexual behaviors paralleled by a system of corresponding sexual values. The marginalization of prostitution as a stigmatized and illegal economic and sexual practice by midcentury masked how well-integrated it had been in working-class communities and how close it was to other, more "respectable" forms of sexual barter and exchange in the early twentieth century.

Prostitution, treating, and courtship occurred side by side in working-class neighborhoods, bars, and dance halls at the turn of the century. While they were distinct practices, they also interacted with each other and at times overlapped, both in participants and in behaviors. Charity girls denounced prostitutes for their depravity, but it would be a mistake to take their word that the sexual and economic negotiations they engaged in differed as radically from prostitution as they claimed. I have tried to separate their voices for the sake of clarity, but readers should keep in mind that while these practices may have differed significantly in their relative respectability, they often were quite similar in their daily expressions. Profoundly shaped by women's economic inequality and insecurities, all three practices—courtship, treating, and prostitution—reflected the negotiations in which women and men engaged over the economic and social value of sex.

Developing as they did in the context of New York's ethnically and racially diverse working class, these changes in morality and sexual practice always had ethnic, religious, and racial inflections. As a result, this study also examines the ways in which race and ethnicity as well as gender and class shaped modern courtship and the modern sex industry. Courtship practices and popular culture played a crucial role in the process of "Americanization" and the creation of white working-class ethnic identities. For the first generation of European immigrant women, courtship usually took place in community venues. These settings tended to limit interethnic, interfaith, and interracial relationships because families exercised control over the process of meeting and courting appropriate mates. As they grew accustomed to America, the children of immigrants in the 1920s moved "dating" into commercial amusements, and parents lost their authority over the process of courtship itself. However, parents did not give up entirely on shaping their children's marriage choices. As they became "white," many immigrants accepted marriages involving members of other ethnic groups (Italians intermarrying with the Irish, for example), at the same time that they vigorously opposed interfaith and interracial matches. Even as they lost control over the practical realities of courting, race and religion became the dividing line between appropriate and inappropriate matches as immigrants and the children of immigrants strove to influence the creation of new families. "Becoming white" involved immigrants' accepting white supremacy. Even in a northern city like New York, a white-dominated racial hierarchy forced African Americans into the poorest, most overcrowded neighborhoods, severely restricted their occupational and class mobility, and labeled their sexuality and family structure deviant and pathological. New York's criminal justice system also supported this hierarchy, reinforcing the importance of racism in the Americanization of working-class immigrants. Bedford Hills, New York State's reformatory for women, began segregating white and African American inmates in 1914, and courts often interpreted interracial sociability and sexuality as a evidence of a white woman's immorality and likelihood to engage in prostitution.[9] Sexual practices formed the backbone of the process of assimilation, particularly for women, and changes in courtship shaped emerging understandings of race, class, and "Americanness."

Working-class African Americans also participated in the moral and sexual changes associated with treating, much to the consternation of middle-class "race" leaders who promoted what Evelyn Brooks Higginbotham has termed the "politics of respectability."[10] Looking for ways to stem the tide of racism and segregation that threatened to engulf the nation, middle-class African Americans embraced a bourgeois respectability that included, among other things, a strict standard of female chastity. Because white men used stereotypes of African American women as morally "loose" to justify their own sexual aggression, the politics of respectability also addressed the very real problems of sexual exploitation that working-class African American women faced. However, working-class African Americans had their own standards of respectability. Historian Victoria Wolcott's research in Detroit indicates that working-class African American women embraced a complicated vision of respectability that encouraged sexual chastity but also demanded economic independence and self-reliance.[11] Similarly, my research shows that some working-class African American women in New York participated in treating and the attendant expansion of women's sexual choices. They often preferred treating with white men because they believed those men had more money and would be unlikely to harbor any expectations of engagement or marriage (white women made similar evaluations of older men).[12] But African American women's treating with white men some-times affirmed white supremacy. When they accompanied white men to the Cotton Club, for example, they patronized an establishment that made enormous profits affirming white men's access to African American women while excluding African American men altogether. Cross-racial treating at times supported commercial entertainment venues that actively promoted whites' vision of the proper racial hierarchy of the city.[13]

The "politics of respectability" also played out in the shifts in African American courtship practices. As in white ethnic families, by the 1920s, Afri-can American parents exercised little control over their children's courtship. However, class politics rather than race politics determined the lines they drew over inappropriate choices. While white ethnic working-class families intervened when their children engaged in interfaith or interracial court-ship, middle-class African American parents opposed dating across class lines. Similarly, contemporary scholarly assumptions that African Ameri-cans tolerated premarital pregnancy, and thus premarital intercourse, are not borne out by the responses of individual families. Instead, families re-acted in ways similar to white families, often according to either the class status or the class aspirations of the families in question. The politics of re-spectability did not just represent a strategy of empowerment imposed by middle-class African Americans on the rest of the community. Some African Americans of the working class saw female chastity as an important com-ponent of their family's respectability and social mobility.

Just as the shifts in courtship and treating were racialized, so were the shifts in prostitution. Race shaped both the practice of prostitution and the emerging sex industry. Beginning in the 1920s, prostitution began to lose ground to other forms of sex work, such as taxi dancing, stripping, and erotic dancing.[14] These sorts of jobs appealed to some working-class women be-cause they paid better than most women's work and because they were not technically illegal. However, not all women had equal access to this work, as most clubs refused to hire black women. The discrimination against black women benefited white women both materially, in terms of artificially re-ducing competition for high-paying jobs, and morally, as they became a separate and more respectable class of sex worker.[15] These developments created a racial hierarchy in the American sex industry that has persisted into the twenty-first century. While white and Asian women dominate the higher-status, higher-paying, and more "respectable" job categories such as stripping and call prostitution, African American women and Latinas are overrepresented in streetwalking, the lowest paid and most dangerous form of sex work.[16] While this racialization initially mimicked and reinforced the racial hierarchy of the "legitimate" economy, it persists in the sex industry despite forty years of civil rights law that makes it illegal for employers to classify workers by race.

Focusing as it does on questions of morality, sociability, and sexuality, this book exposes the crucial importance of prostitution, sexual exchange, and courtship to the modern constructions of class, race, and gender in America. Where people go and with whom they socialize shape everyday understandings of these fundamental categories. Sociability and courtship therefore constitute a crucial site of identity construction and an important place to study how people experience and contribute to racial, class, and gender hierarchies.

This project owes a great deal to the work of other historians, particularly those writing about working-class women's culture and work life. Most obviously, it builds on the work of Kathy Peiss and Joanne Meyerowitz, who first identified the practice of treating in their explorations of working-class women's social and economic lives at the turn of the century.[17] Their brief but cogent discussions of this activity provided a framework for thinking about how changing sexual identities might interact with existing commercial, social, and cultural practices. More broadly, this project relies on the rich historical literature on young girls and sexual delinquency. Historians have traced the development of institutions such as sex-segregated reformatories for wayward girls, homes for unwed mothers, and juvenile courts. Scholars have shown how emerging professions like social work and psychiatry interpreted young women's sexual agency and, at times, used their newfound "expertise" to build careers and bodies of "knowledge" on the backs of working-class women caught up in the institutions they directed. Other scholars have addressed the changing laws that accompanied these institutions, showing how legal definitions of "wayward minors" were gendered and sexualized, and how "age of consent laws" sought to protect young girls by putting forward narratives of female innocence and male depravity at the same time that they brought young working-class women under the maternal control of middle-class social workers.[18] In analyzing both the institutions and the young women they held, these historians have presented working-class women in dialogue with the middle class. While this is a valuable strategy and one that exposes the difficulties of using evidence produced in these contexts, it also tends to skew the narrative, making it appear that the working class engaged in a constant conversation with the middle class about sexual behaviors and the definitions of respectability. I place working-class activities and worldviews at the center of analysis. Such an approach, though difficult, reveals the arguments that went on within the working class over the meaning of emerging sexual practices and the negotiations among women occupying these different social and identity categories. Middle-class reform women strove to have an impact on the sexual behaviors and values of their working-class charges; however, in reformatory records the working-class girls appear more engaged in debates within their own community than with the ideologies and values introduced by middle-class women. Arguments with parents, siblings, and neighbors dominate these conversations, even as some girls attempted to shape what they said to please the middle-class women who decided when they had been "reformed" and could go home.

Historical analyses of immigrant and African American women's gender identities have also informed this work. Addressing the importance of gender and generation, scholars such as Elizabeth Ewen, Susan Glenn, and Donna Gabaccia have complicated the narratives of immigration and assimilation.[19] While much of the work on immigration at the turn of the century focuses on men and identifies the shop floor as the most important location for absorbing American values, these historians have convincingly argued that women assimilated differently than men and that generation mattered more in women's engagement with Americanization. This project pushes their analyses further by arguing that while assimilation may have occurred outside the home, the most important battles over which aspects of "Americanness" to accept occurred within the home and over issues of family formation; that is, courtship, engagements, and marriage.

Focused as it is on the practical considerations of how ideals of sexual chastity changed over time and varied by ethnicity and race within the working class, the work of Evelyn Brooks Higginbotham provided an invaluable starting place for analyzing African Americans' reactions to shifting sexual practices.[20] The strong arguments that middle-class African Americans made for embracing the politics of respectability have, at times, overshadowed the opinions of working-class African Americans who embraced their own understanding of sexual "respectability." But of course, it was largely working-class African Americans who participated in the changes in sexual norms addressed in this study. Victoria Wolcott's analysis of Detroit's working-class and middle-class women's engagement with the politics of respectability provided a crucial example of how to address these class-based arguments.[21] New York's working-class African American women balanced the ideal of sexual chastity with the reality of sexual exploitation in all forms of employment. They also valued economic self-sufficiency, which led many of them to temper their condemnations of sexual barter and, at times, even of prostitution. During the Great Depression, many working-class African Americans saw prostitution as a practical and self-reliant alternative to charity. Their engagement with treating and with changes in courtship must be seen in the light of these debates over racial uplift, as well as the appalling economic conditions that racism in New York forced upon their community.

The extensive literature on prostitution also informs this study. Historians of prostitution have analyzed the place that prostitution has held in the American imagination, the structures of prostitution, its relationship to urban development and to other kinds of vice, and the importance of prostitution as both a symbol and subject of sexual, political, and health reforms.[22] Timothy Gilfoyle's work on prostitution in nineteenth-century New York City proved particularly helpful, as he created the framework for understanding the relationship between prostitution and commercial and urban development in the city that this study addresses.[23] Although I pay careful attention to changes in the forms prostitution took in the first four decades of the twentieth century, I focus more on the place that prostitution held in the moral world of working-class New Yorkers. Following the lead of Christine Stansell, who analyzes poor women's networks and alliances in antebellum New York City, I bring similar attention to the changes that young girl's extensive participation in wage labor and the commercialization of entertainment brought to working-class families in the early twentieth century.[24] Treating, which emerged in this context, can clearly be seen as an attempt by young working-class women to grapple with the problem of how to participate in the exciting world of commercial amusements without either resorting to prostitution or being mistaken for prostitutes. In addition, taking this study through World War II allows for a long-range plotting of these developments. No previous study has fully evaluated the significance of the emergence of the larger sex industry in the 1920s, an enormous quasi-legal business that began selling sex as entertainment in the form of striptease, taxi dancing, and burlesque. This industry had a profound impact on prostitution and the racial and ethnic patterns of commercialized sex in modern America.

There has also been excellent work done by historians on courtship, particularly in the nineteenth and early twentieth centuries. Scholars like Beth Bailey, Ellen Rothman, and Karen Lystra have addressed the changes in courtship practices in the middle class from the colonial period through the 1950s. They have evaluated the meaning of romantic love and analyzed its effects on courtship patterns and changes in attitudes toward sex and marriage. Addressing the emergence of dating culture, they have traced the changes in advice manuals and in behaviors among high school and college students from the 1920s through the 1950s.[25] However, all of these projects have focused exclusively on the white middle class. To date, no study has adequately traced the changes in working-class courtship practices or explored the racial and ethnic nuances of working-class understandings of appropriate behavior for young men and young women involved in courting relationships. Scholars of the working class have long hypothesized that middle-class "dating" emerged from earlier working-class experiments. This project is the first to deeply explore this contention and examine how working-class social and sexual experimentation led to much larger changes in American sexual behavior and conceptions of morality.

This book grows out of the gaps in these literatures, taking as its premise that practices emerging from the urban working class should be studied, to the degree possible, from its perspectives. Focusing specifically on working-class conceptions of sexual norms and sexual morality, it analyzes how the innovations in those sexual practices and norms shaped wider American definitions of appropriate sexual behavior and values. It addresses how these three activities—courtship, treating, and prostitution—interacted in the neighborhoods and commercial spaces of New York's working class during the first four decades of the twentieth century. By the 1920s, many sexual practices in America's cities took place in a profoundly commercial context. To see prostitution as unique misses the point that sexual barter occurred extensively in places where women lacked economic independence, and it distorts the profound transformation that advanced capitalism wrought on twentieth-century social and sexual relationships.

Studying and writing about America's working-class people has never been easy, because they so rarely speak to us in their own voices. Addressing issues of sexuality, often taboo in public discussions for all classes, compounds these problems of evidence. Forced to rely heavily on sources produced by non-working-class people, I, like many before me, have had to read across the sources, interpreting them carefully and using them against each other to paint a larger portrait of working-class sexual behavior and morality. However, New York City is a particularly good place to study developments in entertainment and sexual culture. Rivaled perhaps only by Chicago in the materials both collected and preserved by contemporary researchers and reformers, New York's numerous archives contain a treasure trove of data about both the working class and urban sexual activities. The reports of New York's various vice societies proved invaluable for tracking interactions between the different kinds of amusements and commercial spaces and changes in sexual behaviors and identities.[26]

The Committee of Fourteen, the longest running of these societies, was organized by members of the city's charitable elite and initially attempted to use its board members to explore vice in New York.[27] However, they quickly found that they could not pass in working-class neighborhoods. One African American proprietor made this problem clear when he commented in September 1915 that "Mr. Whitin who is the Executive Chairman of the Committee of Fourteen . . . generally drops in Saturday Nights."[28] Instead, the committee began hiring working-class white ethnic (that is, not Anglo-Saxon Protestant) and African Americans to investigate the city's working-class precincts. The committee instructed these men to find out which establishments tolerated prostitution so that it could pressure the owners and managers through threats made to their brewers and insurance providers. This strategy neatly sidestepped the police, who were often in the business of protecting "vice," because it used bureaucratic and economic means to convince proprietors that tolerating prostitution would hurt their business. For a historian, this approach also had the benefit of largely ignoring the activities of individual prostitutes, who in turn did not have to add the Committee of Fourteen to the list of dangers that made their daily lives so difficult; if the committee had targeted prostitutes, they would have avoided it and thus disappeared from the historical record. The reports these investigators generated provide us with a precious window into the lives of people who did not often leave records of their lives and stories, and who, for the most part, did not know that their activities and conversations were being observed, much less recorded. This perhaps accounts for the sometimes outrageous comments, jokes, and diatribes investigators recorded and the resulting vividness of their accounts of life in New York City's working-class districts.

In addition to vice reports, this project also relies heavily on case records produced by some of New York's penal and social work agencies. New York's Women's Prison Association provided housing as well as psychological, educational, and occupational counseling for women caught up in the criminal justice system. These case files have the benefit of following women during their probationary periods and after their release. As a result, they contain information about women's lives outside the reformatories as they tried to reestablish relationships disrupted by the heavy-handed intervention of the state. Both the Women's Prison Association records and the Bedford reformatory inmate case files provide summaries of interviews with and correspondence from friends, families, community members, and the young women themselves. Though mediated by the social workers, judges, and prison officials who created them, these records still contain the voices of young women caught in the state's correctional apparatus. When read carefully, they provide invaluable information about the lives, choices, and moral views of young working-class women, their families, and their communities.

The records of vice societies and prisons have been augmented with extensive research into oral histories, particularly those with New York's immigrant women. The "World of Our Mothers" interviews, conducted with Jewish and Italian immigrant women by Rose Coser and her associates, and Herbert Gutman's New York City Immigrant Labor History Project have provided crucial perspectives, particularly on courtship practices, popular entertainments, and broader working-class definitions of virtue and vice. Finally, memoirs, autobiographical novels, sociological studies, and newspapers have rounded out the evidence collected from archival sources.

Reading these sources together and against each other has made a study of New York working-class sexual practices and values possible. Without the meticulous record keeping of a variety of agencies and the interest of professions such as social work and criminology, this world would have been lost to us, and with it, important evidence about a driving force of change in American sexual practices and values. As Americans begin a new century confronted by profound disagreements over social, cultural, and sexual values, it is crucial that we understand just how the world we live in and the values we embrace came to be. The interactions among courtship, treating, and prostitution that occurred between the turn of the century and World War II provide an important framework for understanding both the development of modern heterosexual practice and its relationship to changes in the economy, social structure, and popular culture. Without this history, privileged sexual values can always be labeled "traditional," denying us vital information on the way sexual practices and the meanings ascribed to them have changed over time and in relation to larger forces in American community and life.

Chapter One

TODAY'S CHILDREN

COURTSHIP, AMERICANIZATION, AND MODERNITY

Francie Nolan, fictional heroine of Betty Smith's *A Tree Grows in Brooklyn*, loved to sit on the fire escape of her family's tiny third-floor apartment. Taking a pillow, a book, and some ribbon candy, she would carefully observe her immigrant neighborhood. One late Saturday afternoon as the sun filtered through the leaves of the tree of heaven, she watched the community's young women getting ready for their dates. Smith wrote: "Francie saw young girls making preparations to go out with their fellers. Since none of the flats had bathrooms, the girls stood before the kitchen sinks in their camisoles and petticoats, and the line the arm made, curved over the head while they washed under the arm, was very beautiful. There were so many girls in so many windows washing this way that it seemed a kind of hushed and expectant ritual."[1]

Smith's lyrical description highlights many aspects of courtship in working-class New York at the turn of the century. Living in crowded tenements, the daughters of New York's poor had no privacy and few amenities. "Going out" both with girlfriends and with "fellers" was an established tradition among the working classes, but these girls had new places to choose from in New York's vibrant world of working-class amusements. Perhaps they would go to a nickelodeon, a theater, or a dance. Just as likely, they might indulge in older and cheaper forms of entertainment, such as a walk in Prospect Park or a party held by a friend in the neighborhood. Where couples "kept company" involved not just choices about the various amusements they could attend, or the cost of those entertainments, but also the level of supervision their activities received. Moving toward a more individualistic model of family creation, the young people of New York's working classes struggled for autonomy against the older, more family-directed marital choices. Parents, in turn, at times rejected and at other times embraced newer ideas about love in courtship but always kept a careful eye on the effects such changes had on reputation, family, and community. While many of them approved of the increasing importance of love as a prerequisite to marriage, they did not relinquish control over courtship without a fight. The emergence of dating culture in the 1920s would move toward settling this debate, but in the years before World War I, much of courtship's logic, purpose, and practice remained in flux.

Courtship has always served a multiplicity of purposes for both couples and their families. Marriage makes new families and establishes connections between existing ones. It sometimes serves to solidify economic relationships and can create and continue dynasties in professions, politics, and trade. In the modern Western tradition, marriage has also become an important place for expressing romantic love and for nurturing the extended dependencies of modern childhood. In this study, I examine courtship in relation to changing understandings of sexual practices, economic concerns, and moral beliefs.

Courtship existed as part of a paradigm of sexual morality and sexual norms that incorporated interconnected understandings of women's virtue, premarital sexuality, promiscuity, and prostitution. Both white and black working-class families considered engagement to be a part of a long negotiation over marriage and, with the exception of Italians, many expected there would be a high level of sexual expression in these relationships. They understood that a young man might demand sexual intercourse once he had publicly stated his intention to marry, and some parents tolerated premarital intercourse for women in this context. In this respect, they differed significantly from the middle class, which placed a far higher value on virginity. But New York's working class also censured casual sex. As the next chapter will show, parents and other adults resisted the development of treating because it often involved sexual intercourse between couples who had no intention of marrying. It was, in essence, promiscuous, and promiscuity for women could lead to ruin. Prostitution, illicit and despised, was the fear that lurked in the minds of working-class parents (and, at times, young women themselves) when they contemplated premarital intercourse either in courtship or outside of it. In America's brutal working-class labor market, prostitution represented a very real threat to the virtue of women and girls, and premarital intercourse seemingly opened up that road to ruin, making it if not a likely, at least a possible, outcome. Thus, while the working-class parents might tolerate sexual intercourse in courtship, they could not imagine it without the long shadow cast by the specter of prostitution.

This chapter traces the arguments over premarital intercourse and the meaning of courtship through the trails of evidence left in prison records, court cases, memoirs, and oral histories. Beginning with a discussion of the arguments about sexuality articulated in the Bedford Hills State Reformatory inmate files and "seduction under promise of marriage" cases, I evaluate the meaning of premarital sex and premarital intercourse in working-class understandings of sexual norms and sexual morality in the early twentieth century. These cases reveal a vigorous debate over premarital intercourse among New York's racially and ethnically diverse working-class communities as love increasingly encroached on both sexual and economic considerations in working-class courtship. The gradual incorporation of commercial amusements into courtship practices accelerated these changes, because the shift from neighborhood spaces (unlike middle-class courtship, working-class courtship rarely took place in "homes") prevented the extensive supervision by families, making sexual activities far more likely. Older women took an active role in this debate, and while they often doubted the wisdom of giving in to sexual desires in courtship, many of them also vigorously defended the young women who did.

Finally, this chapter addresses the role of immigration and ethnicity in shaping courtship practices and the importance of courtship as a site of assimilation to American values and identity. In this period, New York's working class was made up largely of the children and grandchildren of the Irish and Germans who had flooded into the city from the early nineteenth century onward.[2] But the future of New York's working-class culture lay in the negotiations between these native-born ethnic groups and the tide of late nineteenth-century immigrants from eastern and southern Europe. As a result, I have chosen to look forward, comparing the experiences of Italian and Jewish families in their confrontations with American sexual culture and values. Oral histories, memoirs, and newspaper accounts all indicate that Italian and Jewish families experienced very similar changes in courtship but responded in ways that had very different implications for young women, the choices they made, and the battles they fought. In general, Italians saw courtship as a place to defend the purity of the Italian community against what they saw as an onslaught of inferior and immoral American practices. In contrast, Jews largely embraced Americanization, viewing it as one link in a chain of positive changes they linguistically referred to as "modern" that stretched back across the Atlantic. Like Italians, Jews valued chastity before marriage, but they also approved of many of the changes in courtship that made chastity more difficult to regulate among their daughters. Taking the opportunities presented by the upheaval of immigration, both Jewish and Italian girls fought for love matches and less supervised and more commercially and sexually oriented courtships. Their experiences uncover the diversity of opinions in New York's ethnically mixed working class, highlighting both the strengths and weaknesses of Americanization as an agent for change in immigrant families.

Trying Virtue: Working-Class Attitudes about Premarital Sex as Seen through Reformatory Records and Court Cases

Although she admitted to prostituting periodically to pay for drugs, May Lewin resented her 1917 stay at Bedford, New York State's primary reformatory for women. "I don't think I got a square deal at all," she complained to her social worker. "I have not committed murder that I should . . . [be] locked up in a room."[3] Most girls hated their stay at Bedford, but like Lewin, their commitment has left a crucial record of working-class sexual values. Filtered through the exasperated musings of social workers, inmate case files still echo with the voices of working-class families who articulated their own vision of sexual norms and sexual morality. Like all legal documents about personal and domestic disputes, reformatory files and court cases are both personalized and contested. Witnesses often disagree with each other or offer completely contradictory evidence on the same events. For example, a mother might insist that a girl was "good," while a social worker might call her a "thoroughly bad girl."[4] But unlike the social workers bent on reforming girls, or the jury asked to judge a case, the historian need not sort out who is lying and who is telling the truth. Instead, we use these documents to establish the boundaries of accepted behavior by focusing on what claims the individuals involved thought were reasonable to make. As Nancy Cott has persuasively argued, such cases force their participants to articulate their values and their understandings of community standards and traditions.[5] While perhaps not typical of working-class courtships, when read carefully, these cases reflect the participants' perceptions of the boundaries of acceptable behavior and thus illuminate the rules surrounding premarital intercourse, courtship, and marriage.

May Lewin's file from Bedford reformatory and Yetta Lvofsky's prosecution of Samuel Rosen for seduction both highlight the boundaries of acceptable sexual behavior for young unmarried women. Unlike the middle class, which saw any breach of chastity as ruining a young woman, these cases make clear that working-class New Yorkers were more willing to accept premarital intercourse during engagement but also condemned it between couples without such bonds. Promiscuity, that is, sexual intercourse with more than one man, and not sex itself, marked the difference between good and bad girls. In addition, all community members acknowledged the risks young women took when they had premarital intercourse. As always, the specter of prostitution, that harbinger of moral and economic disaster, loomed large in people's minds. Most attuned to the dangers of sex for younger women, older women tried to dissuade them from sexual intercourse with their fiancés. At the same time, when things went wrong, older women were young women's staunchest allies, arguing on their behalf with recalcitrant men. Premarital intercourse may have been an accepted part of courtship, but it was also one whose dangers for women were well understood. For them, the gradual shift from parental to peer supervision and from family to commercial space represented both new freedoms and a devastating loss of older protections. Still vulnerable to the very real and very gendered consequences of loss of reputation and premarital pregnancy, young women struggled with the changing sexual norms. Even as premarital intercourse became more common, the sexual double standard held only women responsible for the serious consequences of intercourse.

National studies that estimated the rates of premarital sex provide an important backdrop for the discussion of these two cases. Summarizing data from national surveys done on premarital intercourse among whites by the researchers Lewis Terman (1938) and Alfred Kinsey (1953), historical demographer Daniel Scott Smith reports that premarital sex rates among white women rose rapidly between the turn of the century and the 1920s and then leveled off in the 1930s. For young white women of courting age between 1900 and 1910, Terman found self-reported rates of premarital intercourse to be 13.5 percent. In the 1910s, Terman and Kinsey both saw that percentage double to 26 percent, and by the 1920s, that percentage nearly doubled again, to an astounding 48 percent (Terman) or 51 percent (Kinsey).[6] While the number of women having intercourse with men they did not intend to marry rose, most young women who engaged in premarital sex did so with their fiancés, that is, within the parameters of courtship and engagement.[7] Sexual intercourse within committed relationships increased far more quickly than promiscuity. Finally, both researchers identified higher levels of premarital intercourse among the working class. Summarizing both Kinsey's and Terman's findings, Scott comments that white "college-educated women, largely of the middle- and upper-middle-class backgrounds, maintained conservative sexual standards longer than the remainder of the population."[8] Or, for the purposes of this study, we might say that working-class women like May Lewin and Yetta Lvofsky pioneered the inclusion of premarital intercourse into courtship rituals.

May Lewin's records come from the Bedford reformatory case files. Founded in 1901 to house wayward minors and other women whom magistrates deemed salvageable, Bedford initially functioned as a reformatory in the true sense of the word, that is, a place bent on reforming women who had strayed but were not yet committed to a life of crime. Most of the women incarcerated there had been convicted either as wayward minors or as prostitutes, though a significant minority had been charged with other crimes like burglary and petty theft. Most of Bedford's "wayward minors" had been brought before the courts either by the police or by their parents because of their sexual behavior. For boys, "wayward" usually meant stealing or being involved in gangs, but for girls, the term invariably involved sexual activities (and, at times, sexual intercourse) outside of marriage. These girls had not prostituted themselves, but the officers of the court and sometimes their own parents feared they might come to that and sent them to Bedford where, it was hoped, they would be redeemed by strict moral guidance and instruction in the "domestic arts." Bedford housed few women who had been in prostitution for long, because the courts usually sent unrepentant "recidivists" to the workhouse for punishment.[9]

May Lewin's story reflects the debates over premarital intercourse among women in New York's multiethnic working class. The child of a Polish Catholic father and a German Protestant mother, Lewin had been keeping company with a man named Joe Daly before her arrest.[10] Lewin's mother described Lewin and Daly's courtship as typical, with trips to the movies and other commercial amusements, as well as time spent in the neighborhood and at home. May, she asserted, was a good girl who led a quiet life, "going out only occasionally with girl friends or Joe Daly . . . never stay[ing] out late at night." When asked by the social worker whether she thought her daughter had had "sexual relations with Joe Daly," Lewin's mother said "she did not know for sure but did not think she had because of the fact that he was willing to marry the girl." The social worker continued in her summary, stating that the mother "thinks that if she had lowered herself to have relations with him he would have lost respect for her."[11] The term "lowering" implies that Lewin's mother saw premarital intercourse primarily in moral terms, though she also obviously understood the practical problems as well, namely the loss of respect. Other female relatives of Bedford inmates proved more flexible in their attitudes about premarital intercourse. Hetty Feder, a young Russian Jewish woman incarcerated for burglary, "overheard [a] conversation while her mother was entertaining women in the home that the mother knew of married women in Russia, who had been immoral prior to their marriage and yet settled down and became good wives and mothers." According to the social worker's report, this girl "therefore, felt that if women could do such things and settle down, and that her mother did not condemn them for their actions, that she too could go out and act as she did and then settle down and become a good wife and mother."[12] As these cases suggest, while some mothers focused on the still very real problems that accompanied premarital intercourse, others did not see it as permanently endangering a girl's chances at marrying and having a family.

Ironically, May Lewin's fiancé proved far more "forgiving" than her mother. Joe Daly admitted that they had been having intercourse, but this did not interfere with his desire to marry her. Furthermore, not only did Daly accept their premarital intercourse as normal, he also knew about her occasional prostitution and still expressed a willingness to marry her if "she intends to reform." Neither virginity nor monogamy seemed to matter a great deal to Daly, although he did expect that, once they married, she would be faithful to him. His attitude of forgiveness was tempered slightly by his (perhaps justifiable) sense that May needed supervision. He told the social worker that because he was likely to be drafted, he "thinks her commitment to Bedford is the best thing that could have happened to her. . . . Says she always behaved herself well when out with him and he cannot understand why she should associate with Italians."[13] If anything, it was Lewin's lack of ethnic discrimination, and not her promiscuity, that damned her in Daly's eyes.[14] Prostitution may have been bad, but associating with Italians was worse. Daly was not alone in his relaxed attitude toward premarital intercourse both within courtship and outside of it. Although several young men broke off their engagements after their fiancées had been sent to Bedford,[15] others still wanted to marry their inmate girlfriends even when these girls had had intercourse with other men. One young American-born Austrian's fiancé told the social worker that "She had something to do with another feller, this I am willing to prove, and by the way, I can show you I am doing what is right by marrying her. I love her and nothing can make me break with her."[16] While this young man may have taken faith in love a step further than most when he argued that love could solve problems caused by infidelity, his general belief in the power of love echoed the testimonies of young men and women from a variety of New York's ethnic communities. As understandings of the relationship between sexuality and morality shifted, young people began to see love as not just an essential component to marriage but one that could outweigh previous obstacles like a young woman's promiscuity.

May did not comment on the moral problems of premarital sex, but she understood some of the risks. When asked about venereal disease, she explained that she felt "sure that she never had a bad disease" because she examined men before she had sex with them and "always had a douche bag."[17] Lewin's knowledge of venereal diseases probably came from her experience in prostitution. Many of the women committed for prostitution provided similar descriptions. In contrast, while some of Bedford's wayward minors had heard of venereal diseases, none could explain how to prevent them.[18] However, wayward minors did know about pregnancy. One white inmate said that the dangers of premarital sex involved "being sent here, getting pregnant, getting a baby."[19] An American-born Austrian girl committed for petty larceny described the consequences of associating with men as a slippery slope of certain disaster. As she explained to her social worker, "They may have intercourse with you, then you may give birth to a child and then they wont [sic] marry you, and they may have certain diseases that girls may catch. I have heard girls and women talk about it. When they see a girl pass they think she isn't good they say: 'There goes a bum.'"[20] Incarcerated for stealing and not for sex, this young woman's attitude may have been fairly typical of working-class girls in general. Wayward minors had an investment in viewing their sexual behavior as normal and acceptable, but their very presence at Bedford indicated that they were wrong in this assessment.

Just as May Lewin's inmate case file reveals the conflicted attitude of working-class communities toward premarital sex, Yetta Lvofsky's "seduction under promise of marriage" case against Samuel Rosen in 1917 reflects the acceptance of premarital sex between engaged couples but also speaks to the risks for young women. In this period, New York defined the crime of "seduction under promise of marriage" as intercourse with an "unmarried female of previous chaste character" whom the perpetrator seduces with a promise of marriage.[21] Seduction under promise of marriage cases changed significantly over the course of the nineteenth century. Under common law in the colonial period, these cases protected the father's rights to lost labor and also provided compensation for the possibility that a daughter might not marry and would remain a burden on her family. As legal scholar Jane Larson explains, "As a result, working class and poor families brought the greater number of seduction actions. Nineteenth century seduction plaintiffs thus sought both a remedy for economic loss and recompense for injured social status."[22] According to Larson, these cases were among the most frequent type brought and were usually successful because all-male juries sympathized with fathers' economic problems and social fears. As the value of chastity for women rose in the late nineteenth century, however, women began to bring these cases themselves, and the "moral and emotional investment in sexual chastity was recognized as a legally protected interest."[23] Because of this shift, the issue of consent became more important, and pregnancy no longer mattered: "The wrong remedied by the tort was the woman's loss of sexual chastity per se, and the courts presumed that a sexually active woman had no virtue to lose."[24]

The state's regulation of these private behaviors tacitly acknowledged a commonly held community view that sexual activity in the context of courtship constituted a different sort of relationship than other kinds of premarital sexuality. Such laws anticipated, and thus validated, sexual expression between unmarried, affianced couples and lent weight to the argument that a promise of marriage allowed for sexual intercourse. They also reinforced the idea that a couple made a contractual agreement with each other when they promised to marry, and that a man wronged both the young woman and the state if he seduced a woman by promising to make her his future bride and then refused to marry her. In essence, these laws upheld the notion that premarital intercourse was an appropriate part of courtship, and that girls who engaged in such sexual behavior with fiancés were not without legal rights and protections. However, the importance of "previously chaste character" in these cases also reflected the belief that young women should not engage in premarital intercourse without such promises, affirming the commitment of the state to distinguish between "casual sex" and sexual behavior in committed relationships.[25]

Yetta Lvofsky brought her case against Samuel Rosen after a few months of courtship. A young Jewish woman from eastern Europe, she had been in the country four years when she met Rosen. As she had no relatives here, she lived with a landlady who took an active interest in her life. Like most of the young women who resorted to such prosecutions, Lvofsky seemed vulnerable both in her social class and immigration status. All of the young women who brought seduction under promise of marriage cases came from white working-class backgrounds and held poor-paying jobs in the needle trades, domestic service, or department stores.[26] In addition, immigrant women brought the majority of cases, probably because they lacked the family to support their claims or to coerce unwilling or deceitful suitors.[27] In her monograph on girls in Hell's Kitchen in the early twentieth century, settlement-house worker Ruth True noted several instances where working-class families forced young couples to marry.[28] Lacking family in the country, immigrant women had to rely on the courts for justice. In these cases, landladies played a crucial role in supporting young women's complaints.

Immigrant and American identity played a role in the way Yetta Lvofsky articulated her grievances against Samuel Rosen. Rosen does seem to have been a particularly despicable young man. As he explained in court, Rosen began courting Lvofsky because he wanted to make another girl jealous. He promised her marriage, and after a few months of "keeping company," they had intercourse. When his ploy succeeded and his other girlfriend came back to him, he refused to have anything to do with Lvofsky and called her "dirty" in front of her friends. In one confrontation, Lvofsky used her understanding of immigration and assimilation as a reason she should not tolerate his treatment. She testified that "I told him, 'Don't think that I am a greenhorn. I am green, and poor, but nobody will stand for that, what you done.'"[29] Here, Lvofsky offered a curious blend of immigrant and American identity in which she combined the idea of the vulnerability of a "greenhorn" with its contrast, an assertive American who could rely on a community that would not "stand for" what he did. American identity brought new rights to girls in the context of courtship and allowed young women like Yetta Lvofsky to demand justice.[30]

Seduction cases reveal that some members of New York's working class expected couples to engage in sexual activity and even gave tacit approval for sexual intercourse after a promise of marriage had been made. In all eleven of the seduction cases, the young women reported kissing or "spooning" (a contemporary term for petting), activities that often occurred at the girls' homes with family members nearby. A neighbor testified that he had seen Rosen and Lvofsky embracing on several occasions.[31] In another case, Fannie Salmanowitz kept company with Emanuel Millinger for six months in 1916. As Millinger himself testified, they spent time "in the sitting room at her house, and in an affectionate mood, spooning, we were disturbed a couple of times by other members of the family, and she said to me, 'I wish we were alone, alone where there would be no chance of being disturbed.'"[32] Clearly, Salmanowitz's family knew about their sex play and saw it as a normal part of courtship. Margaret Galvin's landlady even allowed her fiancé to spend the night after she had extracted a promise from him that he would marry Margaret in due time.[33]

Lvofsky's use of language in describing what happened between her and Rosen reveals the lingering importance of virginity in immigrant communities and the possibility that engaging in premarital intercourse may have been an American innovation for her. When pressed by the court to describe the sexual encounter she had with Rosen, she simply replied, "he ruined me." Nor was Lvofsky alone in her choice of words. Five out of the eleven women in the cases surveyed for this study used the phrases "ruined" or "spoiled" to describe their encounters.[34] The language implies both that a woman's worth was invested in her virginity and that that worth was somehow related to a purity that could not be restored. Being ruined damaged a young woman's prospects in marriage and threatened her place in respectable working-class society. In addition, it raised the specter of promiscuity and prostitution. As Christine Stansell has shown, in antebellum New York, the phrase "going to ruin" meant sliding into prostitution.[35] The active verb "going" implies a journey that could take some time and that was not inevitable. "Going to ruin" was a process, then, and one that could be arrested by the girl herself or by her community. Bringing a seduction case against a young man could be one way to avoid that road. The young women in these cases did not discuss prostitution, indicating that perhaps the term "ruin" now applied to a wider range of sexual behaviors. However, the taint of prostitution remained, clinging to the phrase and perhaps to the women forced to employ it.

Seduced young women also used passive language when describing their feelings about the act of sexual intercourse that brought them before the court. This passive language skirts the edges of admission of desire and suggests the difficult tightrope that young women walked when engaging in sexual activities with their young men. Sadie Cohen stated that "finally after his persuasion I yielded, and I had sexual inercourse [sic] with him while I was sitting on his lap." [36] Persuasion in this case involved repeated promises of marriage but also kissing and fondling. Sex did not occur in the missionary position, often thought to be the most passive for women, but instead occurred with her on his lap, an arrangement that might have given her more opportunity to resist. In this context, did she yield to him, to her own sexual desires, or, most likely, to some combination of the two? Margaret Galvin's testimony contains similar ambivalent language about desire. Describing the first time she had intercourse, she stated that "then we sat down on the couch, and in the fooling he pushed me over and then went over on me and picked up my dresses. Then he laid over on me, and under his repeated promises of getting married I weakened." [37] While the verb "weakened" reflects a similar passivity to Cohen's, the word "fooling" emphasizes Galvin's sense of their earlier activities as an acceptable and enjoyable form of play. And, as in Cohen's case, it is impossible to tell whether she gave in to his desires or to her own.

Regardless of whether Yetta Lvofsky enjoyed sex with Samuel Rosen, she certainly felt herself to be wronged when he refused to marry her, and she relied on help from older women in her community to force him to do the "right thing." Lacking family in New York, she turned to her landlady for help both before and after she took the case to trial. When Samuel Rosen called Yetta Lvofsky dirty, her landlady retorted, "Well, who made her dirty, if not you?" [38] The landlady confronted Rosen on the street several times and testified on Lvofsky's behalf in court. For young women without family, enlisting a landlady could prove helpful. In four cases, landladies intervened with the young men before the trial, scolding them and demanding that they make good on their promises. In three cases, landladies testified to the girls' good character and to their knowledge that a promise had been made. In those trials where landladies did not involve themselves, it was because the girls had parents who could help them.[39]

Landladies deployed a particular vision of masculinity in these encounters. According to Margaret Galvin, her landlady confronted her fiancé, Daniel Lynx, stating, "she hoped he would be man enough to carry out his promise and do his duty toward me."[40] Men often responded in kind if they admitted responsibility. Outraged by the seduction that had occurred under her roof, Katina Contogianni's landlady confronted Katina's fiancé, John Nicholas. As she later testified, "I said, 'you will make her your wife?' And he said, 'Sure. I wouldn't do that to a Greek girl,' and I said, 'Sure no one would let you.'"[41] Unsatisfied with just an admission of guilt, she pressed him, finally getting him to promise, "I will make good. I give you my word as a man."[42] Undoubtedly, these young men had several competing notions of masculinity to consider, and some may have felt more manly for having seduced and abandoned a girl. But in confrontations with outraged older women, most did admit that manhood required that they not dishonor young women by breaking their promises. They may not have liked being held to this particular standard of masculinity, but they did acknowledge its validity.[43]

Landladies allied themselves with girls for complicated reasons. While they may have been genuinely interested in the reputations of girls under their care, they also were interested in protecting their own reputations as virtuous women and law-abiding business people. Yetta Lvofsky's landlady testified that in her confrontation with Samuel Rosen, she said to him, "Yetta lives at my house about a year and a half, and she is a very nice girl. What do you say now. You make so much trouble, and you do not make it right."[44] Even more direct, Katina Contogianni's landlady began her confrontation with John Nicholas by asking him, "Why did you interfere with a woman, and dishonor a woman, in my home?"[45] As these cases suggest, landladies vigorously defended their space, arguing for the respectability of their homes and the women who lived in them. They did so because landladies occupied a precarious position in the economic and moral world of working-class New York City. Working-class communities saw boardinghouse keeping as respectable work for older women but also knew that it often shaded into brothel keeping. Improprieties in courtship could taint a boardinghouse keeper's reputation, endangering her business and bringing her to the attention of police.[46] Ruth True discussed just such a case in Hell's Kitchen where a young girl had run away from home after a fight with her mother about her late nights. "Mrs. Mullarkey's fears pointed to a certain house on Eleventh Avenue where a woman lived who had a reputation of harboring girls," True reported. Mrs. Mullarkey brought the police, who knocked down the door but did not find the girl on the premises.[47] Landladies most likely intervened in courtship practices both because they saw themselves in a parental role and because they needed to preserve their own fragile reputations as respectable businesswomen.

Both Yetta Lvofsky's and May Lewin's experiences provide a fascinating window into courtship patterns of working-class youth. In both cases, communities had tried to keep track of the activities of their young people and had intervened when they felt concerned about the turn events had taken. Most young women could rely on their families for help with reluctant suitors. When they lacked family, young women could count on some protection from landladies and other older women in the neighborhood. These cases, when seen in conjunction with the information gleaned from other trials and other prison records, indicate that communities did regulate courtship, and where promises had been made and then broken, older women stepped in to force young men to be "men" and meet their responsibilities. Finally, working-class New Yorkers of both sexes accepted premarital intercourse within courtship and viewed it as different from more casual, or "promiscuous," sexual encounters. However, many older women, like May Lewin's mother, feared the risk that young women took when they had sex with their fiancés. Advising against it, they stressed that intercourse outside of marriage could be a dangerous threat to respectability and to future marriage prospects. In many ways, their position on the issue was one of toleration, rather than acceptance, of premarital intercourse. Watching girls with keen eyes, they reminded them of the gendered dangers of sexual experimentation within courtship.

Reluctant Americans: Italians, Gender, Generation, and Courtship

When Angelina Toscano sailed to America, she met a young man on the boat, and "it was love at first sight." They talked for hours on the trip, but when they docked in New York, Toscano's family quickly put an end to the romance. "He wanted to see me all the time," she explained, "but my mother wouldn't let him. . . . At that time you had to marry who your parents wanted you to. I used to love him, but I couldn't see him, and I couldn't marry him."[48] Her plight reflected the tensions created within families over conflicting ideals of marriage as Italians moved from the countryside of southern Italy to New York.[49] Like Toscano, other Italian immigrant women quickly adopted the ideal of a companionate marriage and began to fight for the right to marry for love. But also like Toscano, many of them failed to win the mate of their choice. Courtship, which both created new families and perpetuated the larger *domus*, or extended family, of the southern Italian world, became a battleground in resisting Americanization.[50] Despite the work of other historians that has located the site of "Americanization" at work or school, fights over assimilation were most intense in the intimate setting of the Italian American family itself. Southern Italians rooted much of a family's honor in female chastity and reputation, and as a result, the "Italian girl" and her courtship became crucial sites to defend Italian cultural purity. Italian American courtship practices emerged as a compromise between daughters' demands for more freedom and parents' and brothers' hostility toward breaking down the gendered and generational hierarchies of the family. Italians may have moved to America, but they did not have to become Americans, especially not in the way they formed and managed their families.

In traditional southern Italian courtship, families tightly controlled marriage choices. Although Italians did not use matchmakers, as Jews sometimes did, Italian parents often arranged marriages for their daughters.[51] Twenty-six percent of the women interviewed by Rose Laub Coser for the World of Our Mothers oral history project said their families picked husbands for them.[52] Sons had more power to choose their mates, and they sometimes approached a girl's family for permission to marry, often without the knowledge of the girl in question. However, young men's initiative did not always result in extended contact between engaged couples. As one young man explained, "in Italy no one had a chance to talk things over with one's future wife, less so to have kissed her. Between the announcement of the betrothal and the marriage, a fellow could see his girl not more than three or four times."[53] Liciana Caputo's description of her courtship in Italy emphasized the lack of control young women had over their marital choices. She lived with an aunt and uncle, and her future husband "would come over, and not even talk to me, I didn't know why he was there." "Everybody, his father, my aunt and uncle, my brother and father," she continued, "everybody knew we were going to get married, but I didn't know." Her aunt and uncle consented to the match, but as she explained, "it wasn't like it is today[,] if you like somebody then you go out, you talk. We never even talked, we never went out, never!"[54]

The data about arranged marriages suggest that, though they were considered a traditional practice, by the early twentieth century most Italian women in both Europe and America chose their own mates (75 percent).[55] However, girls usually met boys under the watchful eye of parents at neighborhood parties, christenings, wedding, and religious festivals. Strictly supervised courtships, or even arranged marriages, did not preclude love as a motivation for marriage. A majority of the Italian women in Coser's study (63 percent) stated that they married for love. Although this number is lower than that for Jews (80 percent), it does show the increasing importance of love in Italian marriages and the acknowledgment of that importance both by girls and their families. When an interviewer asked Carolina Sansone why she married, she said, "Because I loved him. Ha, ha, why did I marry him. What a stupid question."[56] Instead of preventing love matches, Italian parents limited the choices a girl might have to those approved of by the family. In fact, the fear of the disruptive power of love may have driven the restrictions on girls. Discussing her father's attitudes in Italy, Rosa Vartone said, "He was very strict with me." "He was afraid," she explained. "Maybe I fall in love with somebody." Her father did not even allow her to go to the big church in Cosenza; instead, she attended the little church in her village with her mother because "he wanted me behind lock and key."[57] Vartone's analysis highlights both the importance Italians placed on controlling their daughters' marriages and the growing threat that love posed to that control.

According to oral histories and ethnographic studies, southern Italians provided dowries for their daughters, but this practice declined in America. In his book on the traditions of southern Italian families, Leonard Covello noted that dowries both gave women status in the family and preserved some independence for wives in what he identified as a profoundly patriarchal family. Although southern Italians believed that husbands should dominate their wives, tradition held that wives controlled their dowry and could take it with them if the marriage dissolved.[58] Italians who moved to America saw the decline in dowries as a weakening of the virtue and skill of women and thus of the family itself. As one young woman explained, "here in America, my mother insists, the dowry itself amounts to little since everything can be bought cheaply; many things even at Woolworth's. Yet when a girl works on her dowry, when she sews and crochets, when she acquires kitchen utensils and little things that make a home beautiful—she shows her serious disposition toward married life. Such a girl has reason to advertise her dowry for it characterizes her as a dependable wife and mother."[59] Commercially available goods disrupted this process, turning the skills that the dowry represented into something that could be bought for cash. This both literally and figuratively introduced an element of "America" into the very heart of the home. In the eyes of some Italian immigrants, this potentially corrupted the purity of women, their skills, their families, and by extension, the next generation.

In America, some Italian families continued the practice of arranged marriages.[60] When Regina Mazzi came to the United States, a man approached her father about marriage. "He was looking for a girl who was born and raised in Italy for a wife," she explained, "and they made the match (her father and the young man who later became her husband). I never met him before." But arranged marriages did not mean coerced marriages, and Mazzi's father did not marry her off against her will. Before agreeing to the match, Mazzi's father made sure that the man could afford marriage and asked Mazzi, "You like him? You want to marry him?" Her stepmother weighed in as well: " 'He's a very nice looking fella, but he's ten years older than you. Being as how I married your father, and he's twelve years older than me—I am happy in a way,' she used to say 'but twelve years more means a lot. Think about it, he's ten years older than you, do you wanna wait?' " Mazzi considered her options and agreed to marry.[61]

Italian parents in America also continued to supervise their daughters, but the availability of popular amusements began to shift Italian courtship patterns in subtle but important ways. One young woman said that she first went to the movies with her family when she was twelve. Her brothers gradually began to go on their own, but she always had to go with her mother: "love subjects were taboo and so much so that when hugging or kissing went on on the screen, it was automatically decreed that I look away."[62] Even the imagined sexuality of the silver screen could taint a young girl.

While most Italian American courtship occurred at home, some families allowed girls to go out with boys as long as they took a chaperone, usually a sibling, an aunt, or a cousin.[63] Graciella Filipelli's courtship was a typical mix of home and outings. She explained that "when I was keeping company with my husband we weren't allowed to go out[.] I kept company one year, I only went out three times and I had to have a chaperone."[64] Angelina Toscano had more freedom than Filipelli. Before she met her husband, she told an interviewer, "I used to go out with another fella. . . . We used to go with a chaperone, my aunt. . . . We used to go in the city to hear the music, the opera, and like that, you know."[65] In Italy, Toscano would not have had this opportunity because few entertainments existed, and even when they did, girls did not attend them.[66] Perhaps a more important change, though, was Toscano's going out with a man she did not marry. According to southern Italian custom, a girl could not go out with a young man she did not intend to marry because doing so threatened to taint the girl's reputation and the family's honor. As Carlotta Vina explained of her parents, "they were a little strict, like they believed that when you went out with anybody . . . that would be the one that you intended to marry."[67] In this, Italians differed significantly from other racial and ethnic groups in New York's working class, who tended to define "promiscuity" in sexual rather than social terms. Families of Jewish, Irish, German, and African American girls expressed little concern when their daughters courted different men. Toscano's ability to court a man she did not marry, even though it occurred under the sharp eye of a chaperone, indicated a real shift in Italian courtship practices.[68]

However, Italian families did not mind when their girls played together in New York's streets and parks, and daughters took advantage of this to evade familial supervision of their courtships. When a young man she met at the grocery store asked Martina Tosca to go out with him, she had to tell him that "I'm kept very strict from my father, ooh[,] my father won't let me go from here to there." However, Tosca and her girlfriends often walked in the park together, and she told her new beau to meet her there. "As soon he saw me going by with my girlfriend," she explained, "he took his friend and he follows, so when we got to the park we start talking, ooh[,] we had a wonderful time."[69] Sisters also helped each other out. Carlotta Vina stated, "we would make up excuses, like if my kid sister would have a date with somebody she would say that she went out with me or with the other one."[70] The very existence of unsupervised homosocial activities for girls in New York's working-class neighborhoods allowed Italian daughters more independence than they had experienced in Europe. As Sylvia Peluso stated in her interview, New York "was not like some part of Europa . . . [where] they don't have freedom."[71] America made a difference, and many young women took any opportunity they found to socialize on their own terms and to pick their own mates.

The increased freedom to socialize with men they might not marry endangered the honor of their family, though, and often brought about swift retribution. By definition, honor rests on reputation and is an external, and not internal, attribute.[72] In honor-bound societies, it is what others think that matters most, not what an individual actually does. Sexual reputation was crucial to Italian families, because honor was tied to female chastity. In America, where girls worked in factories rather than in the fields with their mothers, girls had the opportunity to mix with men in ways that often frightened their families. One young woman interviewed by Leonard Covello wanted to take a teaching job outside New York City, but her family refused. "The idea of a girl leaving home strikes terror in their hearts. It's not that they don't trust us or are afraid we will go wrong," she explained. "They are afraid of what the relatives and paesani will say about the girl."[73] While her family trusted her, they dared not risk the censure of community opinion. Honor and reputation, and not a lack of trust, constricted her choices.

The problem of public honor plagued girls not just by limiting their social and employment options but by disturbing relations within the family. In several families interviewed by Leonard Covello, both brothers and fathers beat girls for what they saw as breaches of honor. For example, one set of brothers beat their sister when she had an "unauthorized love affair with a son of a neighbor." The young woman went to the Girls' Service League for shelter when "although informed that the result of her physical examination was favorable to her character the parents would not accept her back into the home." It was the seeming impropriety, more than actual impropriety, that resulted in punishment. But of course, it was the freedoms that America introduced, with girls earning wages and tempted by the excitement of New York's streets and neighborhoods, that created these problems in Italian gender and generational dynamics. Whether their families wanted it or not, girls had more independence and sometimes rejected family pressure to conform to the norms of their parents' generation. The Girl's Service League report on this incident discussed the issue explicitly in these terms, commenting that the girl reacted "to the very rigid standards of a lower middle-class Italian family." "When she showed her self-assertion," the social worker continued, "reaching out after American social standards or any deviation from European standards[,] she was punished."[74]

Italian immigrant parents argued for the hierarchies they saw as essential to orderly family life, and as a result, debates over Americanization involved children of both sexes. Parents believed that children should obey their parents, and women should obey men. As Carolina Sansone said of her child rearing in America, "my children were taught to respect their father. Children were more respectful, not like today." She contrasted this with the American way: "They're too easy with them, because the mother can't scold them 'cause they'll leave."[75] To some, like Sansone, Americanization reflected a decline in the organization of families, because it shifted the balance of power, challenged the authority of parents, and threatened the disintegration of both family and community. Although young boys often ran into trouble with their parents for not being respectful or for participating in forbidden amusements like playing pool, girls bore the brunt of this conflict. Because Italian family honor required that girls remain chaste, even sons became involved in policing their sisters' activities. Restricting girls became a family affair, and, as we have seen, it sometimes resulted in violence. Beaten by fathers and brothers for even perceived infractions, Italian girls carried the weight of Italian values of marriage and family. Conflicts be-tween parents and children over the treatment of girls lingered into the sec-ond and third generations and linguistically always contrasted the purity of "Italian" with the corruption of "American." As Liciana Caputo explained in her interview, "my daughter, see, she's still mad at me and my husband be-cause we brought her up like Italian style. She was not allowed to go out. She was so mad at us."[76] Even as they resented these restrictions, young women also internalized these values, restricting their own daughters when they ap-proached adolescence. As one American-born Italian woman declared, "I was raised up strict by my mother and I am doing the same thing to my chil-dren—particularly my daughters. When I see so many girls running around loose, I am glad my mother was strict with me."[77]

Girls who wanted to organize their lives differently still acknowledged the linguistic significance of the categories of "Italian" and "American." Gloria Granato complained to an interviewer, "Sicilians are very strict . . . and that used to get my goat, I couldn't go out with my friends, my girlfriends say, 'how come you can't come out?' I says 'my parents are strict.'"[78] Resenting this aspect of her culture, Granato still granted that it was "Sicilian" and thus authentic and a force to be reckoned with. Like Granato, many girls resented the control parents tried to exert, and quite a few resisted it, but regardless of their responses, both parents and children identified the dif-ference in the essentialistic terms of "Italian" versus "American." Paulina Crupi said regretfully, "I couldn't go out, my father wouldn't let me go out—that was the Italian way."[79] Another young woman commented that "We are not like American girls. They can leave home, their mother and all the rest and think nothing of it. . . . It was knocked into us that a girl must stay with her family. We are doomed, I suppose."[80]

Italian immigrants' resistance to assimilation derived in part from their very strong sense of the virtue of both gender and generational hierarchies in family, but it also stemmed more generally from the shock of American difference. Migrating from rural areas in the south of Italy, with little experi-ence in either industrialization or urbanization, Italians expressed dismay at many aspects of American life. While they could not avoid their cramped apartments and their wage-labor jobs, they could protect what they saw as the core of their identity, the family, from a sinful, commercial, and indi-vidualistic American ethos. Courtship was a crucial battleground for the de-fense of the Italian family, and girls bore the brunt of the fight. But as the struggles of young Italian girls showed, at least some members of the Italian community did like the changes brought by Americanization. As individuals and, at times, in small alliances, Italian girls fought to have a say in their marital choices, and in so doing, moved their families closer to an American way of life, love, and family organization.

A Modern People: Jews, Courtship, and America

In Sholem Aleichem's story "Today's Children," Tevye, the poor dairyman, struggles to marry off his oldest daughter, Tsaytl. The first salvo in this particular battle comes when his wife tells him that the middle-aged butcher Layzer Wolf wants to talk to him. Waiving Tsaytl's dowry, Wolf promises to take care of the entire family, remarking, "you can also trust me to beef up your wallet while I'm at it." Tevye takes offense at this, retorting indignantly, "My Tsaytl, God forbid, is not up for sale to the highest bidder."[81] But Tevye agrees to the match under the condition that his wife approve of it. "I have to talk it over with the missus," he says, "because such things are her department. One doesn't give away one's eldest daughter every day." Staggering home drunk, Tevye tells his wife, Golde, about the match, and both of them are delighted.[82] Much to his surprise, Tevye's plans come crashing down when he meets Tsaytl on the road later in the week, and she bursts into tears. As it turns out, she does not want to marry the old, fat butcher Layzer Wolf. Tevye comforts her, saying, "but what is there to cry about silly? . . . we won't marry you off with a shotgun. We meant well. We thought it was all for the best. But if your heart tells you not to, what more can we do?"[83] Later in the day, Tevye receives another shock when Motl, the tailor boy, comes and asks for Tsaytl's hand. Motl explains that they love each other and had agreed to marry a year ago. "Are you crazy?" Tevye shouts. "Since when can you be the matchmaker, the father-in-law, and the groom all rolled into one. . . . I never in all my life heard of a young man making matches for himself."[84] However, Tevye's anger comes more from his sense that Motl has violated propriety than from any real objection, and he calms down and consents to the match. Motl and Tsaytl marry, Layzer Wolf presumably finds another bride, and Tevye and Golde muse over the habits of young people today and the way things change.

In each stage of this story, Sholem Aleichem highlights the shifts in Jewish courtship in the Russian pale at the end of the nineteenth century. In just a few vivid pages, he traces the decline of traditional practices like matchmakers, parental involvement in courtship, arranged marriages, and dowries. The story moves quickly through this process, beginning with the traditional offer of a prosperous husband to the father without the girl's knowledge or consent. Although Tevye does not particularly like Wolf, he does recognize that Tsaytl would have a comfortable life with him, and Golde agrees. Quickly Sholem Aleichem shifts the story to address the increasing role that children played in their own matches and then to the importance of independent courtship and love. The story details these changes in Russian Jewish courtship patterns, and at the same time, accurately predicts which patterns would survive in the New World. Jewish immigrant courtship in New York increasingly dispensed with arranged marriages and dowries, took place in a peer-centered and not parent-centered context, and stressed the importance of love. Unlike Italians, Jewish families embraced these changes. Referring to them linguistically as "modern," in contrast to Italians' use of the word "American," Jews saw shifts in courtship patterns and particularly love matches as developments that would strengthen rather than weaken the family.

As in Sholem Aleichem's story, Russian Jewish parents in the nineteenth century usually controlled their children's marriages. Some used professional matchmakers, while others relied on their own initiative to find appropriate mates. When they could, Jewish parents picked their daughters' partners based on family lineage (*yihkus*), scholarly prowess, and financial prosperity. The negotiations over marriage involved not just dowries but other guarantees of economic support for the newly wedded pair. Particularly among the wealthy, families could offer both a dowry and "*kest*," support for the couple to allow the husband to continue to study the Torah. As Rose Soskin explained in an interview, "In the Old Country, the first year of marriage, you lived with the parents of the bride—that goes in the dowry."[85] Poorer families could only offer small dowries, which affected the girl's marriage prospects.[86] Still, the use of dowries was so widespread among eastern European Jews that charitable societies established special funds to provide dowries for poor girls.[87]

By the end of the nineteenth century, these practices had begun to decline in Europe. The most important ideological critique of traditional marriage arrangements came from the Jewish enlightenment movement, or *Haskalah*. Pushing for modernity in all areas of Jewish life, proponents of the *Haskalah* argued vigorously that Jews should dispense with tradition and embrace modernity. Focused on the family as a crucial site of change, the enlightenment movement rejected practices like matchmaking, dowry, and *kest*. Young people, it believed, should choose marriages on the basis of love and compatibility.[88] At the same time, many Jews living under the oppressive Russian Empire joined resistance movements that offered deeply modern responses to modern conditions. Socialist and communist parties, while never dominated by Jews, did have significant Jewish membership and criticized contemporary society by looking forward to revolution, rather than backward to a romanticized and mythic past.[89] Jewish socialist movements like the Bund also gave young people new opportunities for less supervised interactions and introduced them to new attitudes about relationships between men and women and between parents and children.[90] Before moving to the United States, Jewish parents and children observed, and at times participated in critiques of, older Jewish practices. Courtship in the immigrant generation reflected these analyses and was a blend of traditional European, modern European, and distinctly American practices. The modernization of courtship in Europe affected the ways Jewish immigrants thought about Americanization and the new activities they encountered in New York.

Changes in courtship happened quickly, and in the case of matchmaking, clearly occurred in tandem on both sides of the Atlantic. Some immigrants arriving in America in the 1880s still relied on matchmakers. As one matchmaker lamented in an interview with the *New York Tribune* in 1898, "most marriageable men and women in the quarter depended on me to make them happy. Now they believe in love and all that rot. They are making their own marriages." He attributed this to their acculturation, arguing that "they learned how to start their own love affairs from the Americans."[91] However, evidence from oral histories with young Jewish immigrants, both those married in Europe and those married in the United States, indicate that such changes originated in Europe. Of the forty-four Jewish women interviewed for the World of Our Mothers oral history project, eight married in Europe, and none used a matchmaker. None of the women who married in the United States used a matchmaker either.[92] Nor did any of the forty-two Jewish women or men interviewed between 1973 and 1975 for the New York City Immigrant Labor History Project. For women and men coming to the United States, then, regardless of where their marriages took place, matchmaking had largely disappeared by the turn of the century. While the matchmaker quoted in the *Tribune* argued that exposure to American customs ended these practices, the evidence supports the conclusion that economic, social, and cultural changes in Europe had more of an impact.[93]

Dowries also quickly fell into disuse, and, as with matchmaking, its abandonment seems to have been underway in the Russian pale and may have been influenced by movements like the Bund. The World of Our Mothers interviewers asked about dowries, and only 7 percent of respondents said they had had one. Women's verbal responses to the questions about dowries are more telling than the actual numbers. Several women laughed when asked if they had had a dowry. Ida Greenberg expressed the typical sentiment, commenting, "No. Are you kidding?"[94] Although none of the women interviewed commented on why they did not have dowries, the decline in their use may have been influenced by ideas of socialism that criticized the involvement of cash in such an intimate transaction. Ella Safransky, reflecting newer ideas about companionate marriage, used the question to explain what she brought to the marriage instead of a dowry. She said, "the only dowry I gave is that I worked with him hand in hand." The new ideal of working "hand in hand" did not eliminate all traditions of material exchange in marriage, and some Jewish women had trousseaux, although even these underwent significant changes. Sonia Rosenthal explained that she brought her trousseau from Europe when she immigrated. "I had a beautiful trousseau. I had curtains, the drapes, everything." In contrast, Ella Safransky described how, before she married, she and her husband "saved the pennies to buy our . . . you know . . . things for the house, like linens." Safransky maintained the tradition of a trousseau, but instead of making the items, she worked for money and bought them.[95] This shift from traditional home production to the cash economy marked a significant facet of Jewish assimilation to urban American culture. Unlike Italians, Jews did not see this development as negative.

Even though Jews abandoned arranged marriages and dowries, families continued to play an important role in the selection and evaluation of mates. Women reported both deliberate introductions and accidental meetings at relatives' houses, parties, and events. When families tried to pressure girls into giving up undesirable boyfriends, it was usually because of financial considerations. Most often, families expressed concern that a man could not provide for a family. Bea Tannenbaum's aunt disapproved of her boyfriend because he had "no trade," while Sophie Meyer's family complained that her beau "wasn't a big money earner."[96] Becky Jaffe's mother tried to set her up with an older "rich man who was very much in love with me . . . so I told her that *she* should marry him." Laughing, she said, "I still married the one I wanted."[97] Although families mostly evaluated a young man's earning potential, a woman's earnings also mattered. Sarah Rothman told her interviewer, "I wouldn't mind not to marry at all, but I had my choice. It was because I used to make so much money."[98] In Marie Ganz's memoir of life on the Lower East Side, she described the luck one of her more shiftless relations had when he secured a hardworking young woman as a wife. As she commented acerbically, "The bride was Sadie Burick—a lucky match for Zalmon, for she could earn eight dollars a week in a skirt factory as she had done for years, and he had been out of a job for three months."[99]

After commenting on economic issues, most families left the choices up to the young women and increasingly accepted the idea that couples would marry for love. Bella Blackman's uncle helped her decide between two different men based on their temperament and character and not on their earning potential. Describing the arguments her uncle made on behalf of her future husband, she said, "So my uncle said to me he comes from a . . . very nice intelligent family . . . and he's such an intelligent person . . . and he's good natured and he cares so much for you."[100] In this case, the power to decide who to marry had shifted from the older male relative to the young girl herself. It also marked a significant development in what constituted a good partner. Blackman's uncle had clearly accepted the importance of compatibility and love in marriage.

If older relations began to see love as important, young people increasingly understood it as the most important factor in marital choice. When asked "Why did you marry your husband?" in the Coser study, thirty-five out of forty-four (80 percent) said they married for love. Laughing at such a preposterous question, Minnie Fox gave the typical answer. She married "because I was in love with him," she said, "why does anybody marry?"[101] As in the oral histories with Italian women, it is difficult to assess exactly what these women meant by "love" or whether the intervening years when love became more and more important in American marriages somehow affected their memories of their own courtships. Ella Safransky mentioned her own confusion over this, commenting, "I met him the day I came to this country [and] my father and the others said, 'Billy loves Ida. Ida loves Billy.' So I thought, 'This is love.'"[102] However, the numbers, especially for Jews, are convincing.

Courtship among Jewish immigrant groups took place in a number of different urban spaces, blending newer and older practices from Europe and America. Like other immigrant groups and the native-born working class, Jewish children loved New York's commercial amusements but only occasionally used these spaces for courtship. Ice-cream parlors and Yiddish theater drew some courting couples, but on the whole, young people relied more on activities in the neighborhood, peer social clubs, and dances sponsored by unions or *landsleit* organizations. For example, when relating how she and her future husband spent their time together, Esther Frankel stated that she "went visiting, went for walks, nothing exciting."[103] Perhaps courting couples preferred these activities because they were free, or maybe neighborhood and family events were more fun. Attending commercial amusements certainly could cut into the budget of working-class boys and girls. But the absence of Jewish couples from commercial dance halls is still puzzling, as many young Jewish women flocked to them in homosocial groups. Perhaps couples avoided commercial spaces like dance halls because in the early twentieth century they had a poor moral reputation. Social worker Ruth True described this when she commented that "The dance hall, with its air of license, its dark corners, and balconies, its tough dancing, and its heavy drinking, is becoming familiar to every reader of the newspapers." True took care to explain that girls of courting age rarely attended dance halls, explaining that "the most startling fact in this connection is that it is the little girls who are doing the dancing in the public places of amusement in New York. The young girl usually settles down to keeping steady company some time before her early marriage, and goes less to the dance halls."[104]

Courting couples may have avoided these amusements because they wished to disassociate themselves from activities like treating. Jews may have allowed more freedom in their children's courtship than Italians did, but issues of sexual reputation and sexual respectability still informed their choices. As the records of Bedford reformatory show, some young Jewish women did treat, and when they did so, they came into conflict with their parents and other authorities.[105] Even if the courting couples did not mind the presence of charity girls in their midst, they may have wished to avoid the association with overtly commercial spaces for fear that attending them might be construed as the young man "buying" the young woman's affection. Marie Ganz described one such problem when courted by Pincus Goldberg, a wealthy saloon owner. Dubious about her suitor, Ganz considered marrying Goldberg precisely because she and her mother needed financial help so badly. He took her to the Yiddish theater, where he took care to inform her that he had purchased "dollar seats." He presented her with candy. "'For you,' he said, 'and the candy ain't sweeter than your eyes.' I wondered how long it had taken him to compose that speech. It didn't sound like him at all, for he was a man of few, in fact of absolutely necessary words. . . . At the theatre door he bought a bag of peanuts. 'For you,' he said again, but this time without a compliment, though he seemed to be groping in his mind for one. Evidently he could find no inspiration from peanuts." He spent the evening bragging about his financial success, but Ganz finally lost her patience when, in the middle of the performance, another patron asked, "Who's the goil?" "'Mine!' my escort shouted back in a voice that nobody in the place could fail to hear. . . . I sprang up flushed with anger, left him, hurried home, and broke the news to mother that the courtship was over and that the way that had opened to us to a life of comfort was closed." Ganz clearly objected to his assumption that when she accepted his gifts, she had accepted his suit.[106]

Seen in the context of the development of treating, concerns about "being bought" were understandable, but they may also have had a particular resonance for Jewish immigrants. Like most immigrants, Jews engaged in what historians have referred to as "chain migration," meaning that those who came to America first sent money back for others to come.[107] Within families, such a strategy posed few problems. When combined with courtship, however, chain migration could force women into relationships they did not want. Sarah Rothman's sister accepted a ticket from a "suitor," but when she arrived, discovered that "he was so ugly. And then she told me that he's forcing her to marry him because he paid for the ticket second class. So I sat down and I wrote her a big letter and I says, 'What do you think, you're buying yourself a dress or a coat? No and no. If you have no love for him, if you have no feelings for him, wait until you start working. If you don't love him, don't you dare.'"[108] Rothman's story reflects fears many women harbored about "being bought," which might well have extended to young men paying for commercial amusements. During and after World War I, these fears waned. With the advent of dating culture in the 1920s, Jewish children joined the rest of New York's ethnic working class in commercial amusements.

One aspect of Jewish courtship that set them apart from other immigrant groups was their tendency to take political commitments into consideration when selecting a mate. Sonia Rosenthal told her interviewer that she liked "someone who fights for what he believes in.... he was a socialist."[109] Fannie Brode said, "I married him because we had so much in common. He was a big socialist and I was a very strong socialist."[110] Using political commitments as criteria for choosing appropriate mates demonstrated an understanding of modern conditions and modern values. Socialism itself was a modern movement, one that critiqued the modern system of industrial capitalism. Asking for such commitments in a mate reflected an embracing of modernity and a desire to establish a family in that context. Furthermore, while socialism focused on class issues, it also paid lip service to the very modern notion of gender equality, a position that appealed to many young women. In these marriages, partners could work together to bring about the changes they thought necessary to improve their lives and the modern world more generally. Marie Syrkin even used the tenets of gender equality as expressed in socialism in a generational and gendered battle with her socialist father over courtship practices. When she first began going out with young men, her father insisted that she take a chaperone. "Forgetting about the equality of sexes," she commented wryly, he "had decided that distinctions existed. . . . Yet after behaving briefly like a Victorian ogre he capitulated completely. Our debates on his bourgeois deviations from principle, plus counsel from Mrs. Katz, the unwilling chaperone who thought he was too strict, plus pointed reminders of what Mr. Barrett did to Elizabeth, proved too much."[111]

Jewish political activity did not begin in the United States, though the political freedoms of America when compared with conditions in Russia certainly helped. Participating in the Bund in Europe and other socialist or reform movements encouraged young women to join political or labor-related organizations in the United States.[112] Several women interviewed saw their political commitments as more European than American. Frieda Kaufman commented that "the youth at that time, especially the youth that came from the other side, were socially minded and thinking what to do with our lives." As such, she explained, we "need[ed] young men like we were ourselves."[113] Joining leftist movements in the United States, many young people envisioned these commitments as extensions of older European identities. Modernity did not begin in the United States, and neither did the fights to ensure that the poor and working classes would benefit from it.

Jewish immigrant courtship arched between Europe and America, with connections to both. On the whole, many of the changes that occurred in traditional courtship began in Europe, because for Jews, modernity itself began in Europe. Jewish couples certainly abandoned many of their marital traditions, and parents as well as children committed themselves to a new way of courting. America became an extension of these changes, not their origin. As a result, Jews looked on Americanization in family relations as the continuation of positive changes they already supported.[114] When describing the shifts in courtship patterns, Jews juxtaposed the word "modern" with "old-fashioned." This characterization emerged in Europe and involved far more than simply courtship. Bea Tannenbaum described how her future husband took her from Europe to the United States. "So when he came," she said, "he saw the way I was trying very hard to keep up a little modern and . . . and live like a human being, and . . . and I was a little oppressed by my existence." They first moved to Budapest and then to New York, where they married.[115] But what does "modern" mean in this context? Clearly, Jews associated modernity with more than marriage patterns. Tannenbaum was trying to be modern before she took the very modern step of moving to a large city without any supervision and with a man she would later marry. Modern certainly meant a shift in generational power that involved courtship but was not limited to it. Young Jews in eastern Europe began to strike out on their own and live life differently than their parents. This change was connected to changes in gender ideology. While some Jewish boys lived under the shadow of their parents, most Jewish girls certainly did. Modernity, then, also seemed to mean that girls as well as boys could live independently.

Changes in gender ideology for Jews did not mean a shift of Jewish women from unpaid domestic labor to paid work outside their homes. The European Jewish community valued men's scholarship and religiosity, and in this context, both married and unmarried women worked outside their homes to support their families.[116] Expectations that Jewish women would work also shaped Bea Tannenbaum's decision to leave home and her parents' decision to let her. When she proposed her move to Budapest, she thought her father might not approve. But he did, saying, "Yes. If you have a better opportunity there, go ahead." Whether "opportunity" might have meant a financial or marital one, Tannenbaum does not say, but it clearly involved independence for the young woman and the ability to move away from parental supervision. Such independence also extended to Jewish girls in America, but when discussing them, women emphasized both the European nature of these changes and the importance of generational power dynamics within them. When the male manager at her job invited her to go to the country for a week, Sonia Rosenthal refused, but not because her parents forbade it or because she saw it as unsafe. "At that time you didn't worry," she said, "but I didn't go. The Europeans always brought their kids up so that they were very independent. That was me."[117] Young Jewish women in America could make their own decisions about their sociability, and they attributed that independence to European training, even if it occurred in a new American context.

When Jewish families sent children to America first, they reinforced the growing independence of this generation. Such an experience would certainly increase independence in young people, as would either living with the extended family or boarding. As Trudy Rothman described, "I was only a young girl at that time and they didn't see it that it was fit for my parents, you know, to leave a young girl alone in the city[,] but believe me, my father always had good faith in me[,] he says 'I can always leave that girl of mine no matter where she is, she can take care of herself,' and I did. I worked hard[.] I didn't have time to fool around."[118]

Several Jewish women discussed how this independence extended to courtship. Jewish girls had a great deal of freedom and went on excursions that parents today might not allow. Chava Brier traveled from New York to Providence alone to meet a young man who expressed interest in her. "I says to my mother, 'if I like him, I'll stay there three days, and if I didn't like him, the next day I'll come home,'" she reported.[119] Lena Rubin often went out on her own to dances far from home. "I never allowed anybody to take me home because I lived so far away. . . . I used to say to my husband too, 'No, you're not going to take me home[.] It's miserable. It's far.' There was one night he insisted . . . then I got to sleep at his mother's house. He took me home and it was so bitter cold." Her sister did not like the idea of her being out late on the streets, so after this, she regularly arranged to sleep at his house.[120]

Jewish women also used the term "modern" to describe frank discussions about sex and reproduction. When asked how she learned about sexual intercourse, Zipporah Riegel explained that "When I was very, very young, my mother told me. . . . My mother and father did. Oh! They were very modern."[121] Anna Froelich also associated information about sexuality with modernity. Confronted with the same question put to Riegel, she said, "Yeah. Sure. My mother was a smart, modern woman." However, open discussions of sexuality did not translate into acceptance of premarital sex for this generation of Jewish women. Froelich's mother watched her carefully. "That's why she went with me dancing. Nobody should touch that daughter."[122] None of the women in either the Coser interviews or the Immigrant Labor History Project admitted to engaging in premarital intercourse, although, to be fair, they were not asked this question directly. The Bedford reformatory records do provide evidence that some Jewish girls engaged in premarital intercourse, but those activities were far more common among the children of immigrants than among immigrants themselves. Jewish girls committed to Bedford as wayward minors were mostly born in the United States.[123] Rose Chernin, whose memoir on her immigrant experience covers her courtship, did engage in premarital intercourse and even lived with a man without marrying him. However, she also knew that the rest of the immigrant community did not approve of such activities. When her new suitor, Paul Kusnitz, told his family that he wanted to marry her, they reacted badly. "You can imagine the objection they would have to me," she explained. "I was a woman living alone, going out with men and doing everything else they could imagine for a girl who lives in New York. I had a very bad reputation in Waterbury for living with David Thorne."[124] While Jewish parents gave their daughters more freedom than Italians did in this first generation, they did not approve of premarital intercourse. It would not be until the 1920s, with the development of dating culture, that Jewish children began to experiment in significant numbers with sexual intercourse before marriage.

In part, this ban on sexual intercourse before marriage stemmed from fears that such activities might lead to prostitution. In this, Jewish parents shared the concerns of the broader working class, which both understood and feared the economic circumstances that pushed women into prostitution. Premarital pregnancy, for example, could be resolved through marriage, but it could also lead to a loss of reputation and respectability. Loss of reputation and respectability damaged a young woman's marital prospects, which, with working-class women's wages being so low, could lead to a life of

FIGURE 1.1. *Samuel Zaget, "The First Step toward a Maiden's Downfall,"* Warheit, *n.d.*
(Tamiment Labor History Archives)

poverty. But for working-class parents, the most frightening outcome of pre-marital intercourse was single motherhood. Having a child without a man's financial support invariably led to the kind of poverty and family obligations that forced many women into prostitution. Samuel Zaget expressed these fears in a drawing for the Yiddish newspaper *Warheit* (Figure 1.1). Depicting two young women chatting on the street with two older men, the sketch could easily be a street scene on the Lower East Side. Zaget's choice for a title belies that innocent interpretation. He called the drawing "The First Step toward a Maiden's Downfall," which reframes the image as a caution-ary tale about the dangers Jewish girls faced when they explored New York's working-class neighborhoods. The freedoms Jewish girls enjoyed could lead to "downfall," that is, descent into prostitution. By titling the piece "The First Step *toward* a Maiden's Downfall," rather than "*in* a Maiden's Down-fall," however, Zaget implies that young women could still move back from the precipice of ruin. The dangers he portrayed were possible, but not inevitable. However, they were also very real and lay behind Jewish parents' concerns about premarital intercourse.

Despite these fears, Jewish parents embraced America and its freedoms. Although Jews tended to call changes in courtship "modern," they also acknowledged Americanization as a force, and unlike Italians, they saw that force as positive. When a young man from their town in Russia asked Anna Sach's father for her hand in marriage, he replied, "she lives in free country; she's got her own free will and she can marry whomever she pleases."[125] Coming from the extreme political and economic repression of the Russian Empire, Jews valued American freedom highly. American freedom could be about living where you wanted, working in a job you wanted, gaining an education, and participating in the cultural and political life of the community and country, all activities denied Jews by the laws of the Russian Empire. Sach's father obviously extended the general freedom of America to his daughter, reflecting changes both in generational and gender power in traditional Jewish families. In this, Jews differed significantly from Italians, who, as we have seen, viewed changes to family hierarchies as negative, a falling away from earlier purities.

Jews and Italians represented different responses to a very similar set of issues. Both groups of immigrants came to America from communities that valued chastity for unmarried women and saw courtship as properly conducted under the authority of parents and community. For them, the goal of courtship was the creation and continuation of economically, culturally, and socially stable families. But modernization—industrialization, urbanization, and the process of immigration itself—challenged these goals by upsetting family hierarchies of age and gender. America, as one of many places where such changes was underway, represented both a challenge and an opportunity. Marrying for love, a view of courtship that introduced an element of individualism into what had been a family concern, began to encroach on older practices both for Italians and for Jews. Despite the overwhelming differences in their responses to "American" or "modern" courtship and life, both Italians and Jews conceded that love should be a part of courtship, and thus something that should precede marriage, instead of something that would develop entirely out of the experience of marriage itself. Regardless of how they viewed this change in the motivations for marriage, such a shift represented a real accommodation with new ideas about family formation, structure, and relationships.

The shift to love matches emerged at the same time as commercial amusements, providing young people with different options for where and how they would court. Because of the expense and the dubious moral character of commercial amusements, immigrants and the working class incorporated them slowly into their courting, but the very existence of these spaces continued a revolution in sexual norms that love matches had begun. As the next chapter will show, family financial responsibilities and the lure of commercial amusements led to the development of treating, as some young working-class women sought to reconcile these competing demands and desires. While treating remained separate from courtship in the prewar period, its emergence as an intermediary moral space between chastity and prostitution gave young women new options for how to negotiate their poverty, their desire for amusements, and their new interest in exploring heterosocial and heterosexual activities. Treating existed in an uneasy tension between courtship and prostitution but in the end had a profound effect on both.

At J. J. Hym's Roadhouse in 1914, an undercover investigator for the New York vice society, the Committee of Fourteen, made the acquaintance of a young woman who was looking for a good time. He "learned that she was familiar with sexual intercourse and accustomed to practice the same with her gentlemen friends." After they had socialized for a while and he had paid for her drinks and food, "she offered to allow me to have intercourse with her in the grass if I should take her home after a few more dances and drinks." Hoping that she might offer to prostitute and thus provide him with information about the morals of the bar, he asked her "if we could not get a room in the premises." The young woman admitted that the bar did rent rooms, but she refused to get one with him. Only prostitutes rented rooms, she explained to him, and she was not a prostitute. As the investigator described, "she then pointed out two women in the room whom she said were prostitutes and would go to a room with any man who was willing to pay them."[1]

This incident reflected an important development in American sexual culture, values, and behavior. Beginning in the late 1890s, young women from New York's working class began to develop a new sexual practice they called "charity" or "treating." Treating emerged from the tension between girls' desire to participate in commercial amusements and the working-class community's condemnation of prostitution. Turning over their wages to their families, or living alone and in poverty, most working-class girls lacked even the meager finances that would buy them entry into New York's vibrant world of dance halls, movie palaces, and theaters. To gain this access, young women exchanged sexual favors in the form of kissing, fondling, and, at times, intercourse for dinner and the night's expenses or, more tangibly, for stockings, shoes, and other consumer goods. They used treating both to gain entry into the expensive world of urban amusements and to dis-

FIGURE 2.1. *Wladyslav Benda, "The Line at the Ticket Office" (first frame), Outlook, June 24, 1911. (New York Public Library)*

tinguish themselves from the prostitutes who lived and worked in the bars alongside them. Wladyslav Benda's sketch "The Line at the Ticket Office," published in the journal *Outlook* in 1911, shows what a treating exchange might have looked like (Figure 2.1). In the first frame, a young man leans in to talk with a young woman. Although she is surrounded by female friends, his body separates her from them visually. In the second frame, the young man buys tickets as the young women and some children look on.

Historian Kathy Peiss first identified the practice of treating in *Cheap Amusements*, her influential book on working-class girls' leisure in New York City. In it, she deftly describes how young women used treating to gain access to entertainments that would otherwise have been outside their grasp. Two years later, Joanne Meyerowitz, in *Women Adrift*, characterized treating as one way that working-class women stretched their meager wages. Unable to afford to eat every night, she argues, working-class women who lived independent of family treated to make up the gap between what they earned and what living in Chicago cost them.[2] Taking up where these historians left off, this chapter traces the development of treating in the context of working-class sexual norms and understandings of morality. Treating emerged as an intermediate category, lying somewhere in the morally gray area between prostitution and the premarital intercourse that often occurred in courtship. It allowed young women to avoid the label of prostitute but still engage in sexual exchange for material gain. Relying heavily on homosocial networks developed in schools, settlement clubs, and workplaces, young women in the generation that came of age between 1900 and World War I sought ways to explore public spaces while remaining within the boundaries of their own conception of virtue. The new category of the "charity girl" allowed for premarital sexual experimentation and the possibility of sexual barter between women and men. Evidence of treating can be found among young women from all of New York's working-class ethnic and racial communities and thus must be seen as a working-class, not an ethnic-specific, cultural innovation. By challenging traditional sexual norms of the broader working-class community, young women redefined the role of sexual exchange in modern heterosocial and heterosexual practices. Nineteenth-century notions of the meaning of "public" easily, and perhaps deliberately, conflated "women in public" with "public women," or prostitutes. Young women's creation of treating destabilized this assumption and made room for many more women in New York's vibrant world of public amusements.

As the next chapter will show, the new forms of prostitution in New York in this period provided women with very real economic choices. The decline of the brothel and the subsequent diffusion of prostitution into neighborhood bars and clubs removed some of the economic exploitation associated with nineteenth-century commercial sex. As a result, treating must be seen not just in light of prostitution in the abstract but in relation to new forms of prostitution in New York City that gave women more control over their work and their profits. Treating was thus a deliberate economic choice for young women who had other, more profitable, if less reputable, options for making ends meet. By bartering sex for commercial goods and services, these women removed their behavior from the realm of the cash economy and made real distinctions between themselves and the prostitutes who charged money for sex. Rather than identifying with the economic implications of their behavior or the services they performed, charity girls chose to focus on the company they provided. This allowed them to justify their new categories of respectability without wholly violating older rules governing acceptable sexual practices and the suspect nature of sexual barter. Treating was an ingenious compromise in a world where most women earned little but increasingly attempted to seize economic and social freedom.

Treating and Working-Class Culture

Sexual barter, like prostitution, exists in most cultures, but its meaning varies from community to community and often changes over time. In her now classic *City of Women*, Christine Stansell identifies the "Bowery Gal" of antebellum New York City as a young woman, interested in finery and entertainment, who sallied forth into the previously all-male public culture of the city. Stansell's Bowery Gals are an obvious precursor to the charity girl, even if they never articulated a specific language to describe their practices. Their existence indicates not the uniqueness of treating as a practice but instead its uniqueness as a language and an identity, that is, a behavior with a clearly articulated set of rules, assumptions, and vocabulary.[3]

At the turn of the century, working-class New Yorkers used two terms to describe this activity—"treating" and "charity"—both of which affirmed important gendered concepts in working-class communities. Kathy Peiss argues that the verb "treating" originated in working-class men's habit of "treating" each other to rounds of drinks in the homosocial space of saloons. When young women began to explore language for their heterosocial and heterosexual barter, they borrowed the verb "to treat" from this previously masculine and homosocial activity.[4] Reformer Belle Israels described young women's use of the term when she reported that being able to say "he treated" was the "acme of achievement in retelling experiences with the other sex."[5] As with men's homosocial activities, "to treat" was a verb, with men as the actors and women as the recipients of "treats." This use of "treat" as a verb reinforced gender identities for both men and women. In a community where even men's wage earning could be precarious, spending money on behalf of others played an important cultural role in defining masculinity. Men treated each other to drinks as a way of showing off their success and sharing it with each other. By treating, they were, in effect, saying, "I earn money, and I can choose to spend my money in this way." Such activities reified men's wage earning, declared their economic independence, and reaffirmed their manhood. Despite the fact that women might actively pursue treating partners, spending money on women emphasized men's masculinity, positioning men as active and women as passive. Conversely, even when they worked, women had little money to spend. Since they did not reciprocate, as men did for each other, their position of passivity highlighted both their own femininity and the masculinity of the men who paid. It also indicated their attractiveness and desirability; in essence, they were worth the money men spent on them. Thus, treating became a ritual of heterosexuality that symbolically reaffirmed the masculinity of men and the femininity of women.

The term "charity" reinforced similar gendered messages but revolved more around women's identities. The word "charity" functioned largely as an adjective, and both women and men used the word freely. Women used it to describe themselves, while men used it with other men to distinguish "charity girls" from prostitutes and from chaste working girls who attended popular entertainments in homosocial groups. Charity girls gave away for "free" something for which prostitutes charged cash. H. N. Cary emphasized this aspect of "charity" in his "Sexual Vocabulary" (1916) when he defined a "charity cunt" as "a woman who distributes her favors without a price."[6] Unlike the nuances of "treating," which placed women in the passive position relative to men, "charity" made them active but performed a crucial shift in the location of the exchange from the formal economy, where cash bought services, to an informal economy, where women could bestow gifts. "Charity" established women as generous and protected them from the assertion that they sold or even bartered things like sex and affection that should never be assigned monetary value. Like "treating," "charity" preserved important gendered meanings for working-class women, reinforcing both their femininity and their fictive distance from a cash economy.

Playing a crucial role in the gender economy of New York's working class, treating's emergence as a specific, named activity in the late nineteenth century resulted from a variety of trends that transformed the conditions of working-class family life, economy, and authority. Three factors — an increase in the cultural and economic freedom that working for wages gave young women, their substantial financial contributions to their families, and the rise of cheap popular amusements — combined to spur young women's experimentation with new forms of sexual barter. Walking a fine line between the working class's grudging acceptance of intercourse in courtship and its condemnations of women who had intercourse with multiple partners, charity girls pushed to expand the boundaries of acceptable activities for unmarried women to include more sexual intercourse and more sexual exchange. By the late 1890s, conditions were ripe for a revolution in working-class understandings of the appropriate sexual behavior for women.

The first of these factors, wage work by young unmarried women, had been increasing throughout the nineteenth century as working-class families drew on children's labor to supplement fathers' earnings. According to historian Lynn Weiner, 41 percent of all single women worked for wages in 1890. This rate remained steady in 1900, rose to 48 percent in 1910, and dropped slightly to 44 percent in 1920. These numbers represent national averages and not averages for only urban areas.[7] In cities like New York, that figure for single working women was much higher. Economist Claudia Goldin estimates that 55 percent of white single women in urban areas worked for pay in 1900; African American women undoubtedly performed wage work in even larger numbers.[8]

The shift in numbers that these statistics represent had a profound effect on attitudes about "public women." By 1900, a majority of New York City women between fifteen and twenty-nine years of age, coincidentally an age range that included most prostitutes, went to work outside their homes and used the streets, trolleys, and subways to get there. Their presence made it impractical for most observers to automatically associate women in public with prostitutes. Young women's legitimate employment gave all women, young and old, access to the streets and thoroughfares of the city without loss of reputation. Quite simply, by the turn of the century, their presence was commonplace. Working girls had replaced prostitutes as the symbol of working-class women's public face.

This public presence gave many women and girls both physical and psychological freedom. Not only did women have compelling reasons to be out on the streets, but their identities as wage earners gave them a feeling of self-confidence, which they exhibited by claiming streets, factories, and stores as legitimate places for them to be. In *Jews without Money*, Michael Gold explores the connection between wage earning and independence. He describes a young girl who broke free from parental control after years of doing piece work at home. "At the age of fifteen she rebelled," he wrote, "she went to work in a paper box factory. She began to wear long dresses, and put up her hair. She flirted with boys in the hallways; she went to dances and stayed out late at night. . . . Her parents scolded her; but she fought back, she was earning wages, she was free at last."[9] Working girls benefited from their culture's valorization of the independence and judgment of wage earners and used it to claim public space as their own.[10]

Young working women made explicit connections between their wage contributions and their right to go out unattended and enjoy the city's entertainments. When asked by her social worker at Bedford if her mother was right to restrict her attendance at popular amusements, a young southern African American inmate responded, "In some ways, but, why shouldn't I go out some times if I worked?"[11] An American-born Austrian echoed these sentiments, as her caseworker summarized: "She says she felt that she worked all day and could go out once in a while in the evening."[12] These young women clearly believed that wage earning gave them new freedom to explore other parts of the city and, refusing to provide accounts of their activities and whereabouts to frustrated parents, expected more privacy about their social and sexual lives. Working gave young women self-confidence, relatively free access to the streets, and a degree of anonymity few had enjoyed in the nineteenth century. They tended to use this newfound freedom to attend cheap amusements and participate in popular culture.[13]

Even though they gained a degree of independence through their wage earning, most young women did not get to keep their wages. According to Claudia Goldin, 86 percent of those who lived in their natal households gave their entire earnings to their family.[14] As Italian immigrant Carla Mastrionari described, "I gave the [pay] envelope to my mother—I wouldn't dare open it up, you know."[15] Unlike their brothers and fathers, only a small number received any spending money in return. Jewish immigrant Trudy Rothman gave her wages to her mother, "and if it was possible, I could get [an allowance], and if not I had to do without."[16] While young women had some freedom to move about the city, they had very little money with which to do so.

It was not just the contingencies of class that drove girls' interest in treating; ethnicity, race, and religion all shaped their involvement, although the paucity of sources make firm conclusions difficult. What evidence is available indicates that treating girls came from the most poverty stricken and marginalized communities in New York, that is, immigrant whites and southern African Americans. Most of the reports by investigators from New York's various vice societies did not report on the ethnicity of the women they encountered. In the cases where investigators for the Committee of Fourteen noted race or ethnicity, they identified one Jewish girl, one German, two Irish, and two African Americans clearly engaging in treating.[17] Records from Bedford Hills State Reformatory confirm this pattern. In my survey of over five hundred case files, first- and second-generation immigrants made up the largest group of girls involved in treating among whites, and children of the Great Migration among African Americans.[18] Katharine Bement Davis's survey of the background of women incarcerated at Bedford also supports this contention. Davis did not separate out wayward minors (the category most treating girls would fall into) from prostitutes, but her analysis of the broad outlines of Bedford's wards shows that the children of white immigrants and of African Americans made up the majority of the population.[19] The influence of religion on these young women is even more difficult to ascertain than their ethnic background. While Bedford reformatory and the Women's Prison Association carefully noted the faith of each of the girls who came into their care, social workers did not comment on their religion, nor did the girls themselves. Charity girls came from all the major religious faiths represented in working-class New York, and all of these faiths—Judaism, Catholicism, and various Protestant sects—disapproved of premarital sex. Unfortunately, even sources that indicate religious affiliation do not discuss religious convictions or the impact of religious teachings on young girls' decision making.[20]

Despite the radical differences in their cultures of origin, young white immigrant and African American women shared a very similar vision of treating, and by extension, of prostitution. Young women identified as "charity" consistently pointed to money as the most important difference between themselves and prostitutes. One Irish woman incarcerated at Bedford told her social worker that she was not a prostitute because she had "never taken money from men." The men took her to "Coney Island to dances and Picture Shows instead of giving her money."[21] Southern-born African American Maisie Andrews described her activities in an almost identical fashion, explaining that she had "sexual intercourse with three different friends but has never taken money from them." Instead, her men friends had "sent her presents and have taken her out to dinner and the theatre often."[22] The consistency with which both African American and white immigrant women described treating hints that it may have developed in the context of interracial discussions between girls. While it is impossible to verify this contention with the available sources, the similarities between white and black definitions of treating and prostitution are striking.[23] In addition, treating developed among working-class girls whose families were still adjusting to life in urban America. As such, it can be seen as an important part of Americanization or, in the case of young African American girls, of adjustment to a northern city.[24] For both economic and cultural reasons, these families would be the least likely to give their daughters allowances.[25]

Regardless of ethnicity or race, the shifts in women's employment and their loyalty to family obligations served as a crucial backdrop for the development of treating, but these did not provide the motive. Only the emergence and popularity of "cheap amusements" gave young women sufficient incentive to take advantage of their relative freedom, independence, and anonymity in ways that led them to explore sexual barter. The dramatic changes in the organization and price of popular entertainment in the late nineteenth century gave young girls a compelling reason, even a hunger, to go out on the town and to experiment with ways to pay for such excursions.

At the same time that women entered into the wage economy in large numbers, the number of public amusements in the United States increased significantly. The rapid expansion of cheap amusements just before

1900 transformed the nature of working-class entertainment. In the mid-nineteenth century, when theaters and other venues priced their tickets out of working-class range, these communities had created their own shows and amusements. The dramatic change in prices allowed New York's working class to participate in what were becoming new forms of mass entertainment and culture. Seeing the enormous profits to be made in penny entertainments, producers and petty entrepreneurs revolutionized both the content and format of entertainment.

In his work on urban amusements, historian David Nasaw has argued that vaudeville proprietors' exploration of cheap tickets required that they draw not just the men who had traditionally attended amusement halls but also women and families. To do so, however, they had to eliminate the nineteenth-century association of public amusements with prostitution and gambling. Instead of changing their acts and removing sexually explicit material, proprietors advertised their acts as respectable largely on the basis of their clientele. The presence of women and families signaled a proper venue, even though the entertainment they witnessed contained jokes about sex and differed little from the entertainment provided in clubs with all-male audiences. This sleight of hand drew working-class families to vaudeville without either significantly changing its content or endangering the respectability of the new patrons. Families and groups of young people began to frequent these establishments in large numbers.[26]

Cheap amusements expanded into other areas as well, and at the turn of the century, New York and other urban areas experienced a dance craze.[27] As Polly Adler described in her memoir, "Since no escorts were necessary, I began going there [a dance hall] Sunday afternoons with a girl from the factory, and before long we made friends with the 'regulars'—the kids who, like us, were dance mad." [28] Young men and women frequented dance halls in great numbers. In addition, bars and restaurants provided space for dancing to attract patrons. Settlement houses, noticing the draw of dance halls, decried their immoral influences and countered by providing chaperoned dances for the young people in their neighborhood.[29] For example, the *New York Times* reported the opening of a dance hall sponsored by "philanthropist women" that was intended to "strike a happy medium between the higher-priced 'palais' and the 'danses de' this and that and the cheaper type of dance hall where couples pay 5 or 10 cents for each dance." [30] Working-class organizations also noticed dancing's appeal, and ethnic societies and labor unions provided dances for their constituents.[31]

Cheap amusements encouraged treating among young women by connecting sexuality to popular amusements in several ways. First, cheap

FIGURE 2.2. *John Sloan, "Fun, One Cent," 1905, from the series* New York City Life. *(National Museum of American Art, Smithsonian Institution)*

amusements themselves, like other aspects of working-class culture, contained sexual content. Movie theaters, nickelodeons, and vaudeville used materials that discussed sexuality in a manner that reformers deemed inappropriate and ultimately corrupting.[32] The artist John Sloan's 1905 etching, "Fun, One Cent" captured exactly what frightened reformers about the content of popular culture (see Figure 2.2).[33] As he wrote in his notes, "The Nickelodeon (penny arcade), with its hand-cranked moving photographs, was one of the attractions preceding the moving-picture theaters. The one in which I garnered this bouquet of laughing girls was for many years on Fourteenth Street near Third Avenue."[34] His etching shows young girls watching the flickering images of the nickelodeon. Above their heads, an advertisement reads "Girls in Their Night Gowns, Spicy." The Society for the Prevention of Cruelty to Children used identical language in condemning sexualized content, complaining about "the 'spicy' pictures shown in many" nickelodeons.[35] Such displays, they argued, led to "improper relationships" that "were directly traceable to a first meeting at this resort."[36] Reformers often viewed the sexualized content of these shows as the direct cause of the downfall of good girls and boys.

As unsupervised spaces, commercial amusements also gave young people the opportunity to associate in mixed-sex groups. One investigator for the Community Service Society reported, "the arcades . . . provide not merely amusement but a place for standing and gathering informally, especially during the evenings." [37] The Society for the Prevention of Cruelty to Children also deplored the unsupervised aspects of these shows, arguing that they presented "a seductive form of entertainment for youths of both sexes." [38] It also disapproved of "the attendance of large numbers of young girls without escort," who could be led astray "by young men who lured them thence to improper resorts." [39] For reformers, at least, these new activities were dangerous because of their content and the unsupervised mingling of boys and girls. Just as clearly, these amusements had wide working-class appeal. As one field investigator for the Community Service Society explained, the people who found these new entertainments the most compelling were "children and immigrants—the formative and impressionable elements in our population." Penny arcades alone, he reported with distress, drew over three thousand patrons a week.[40]

But the real reason that commercial amusements encouraged treating lay in their commodification of entertainment. The popular turn-of-the-century song "Take Me Out to the Ball Game" exemplifies this argument by detailing a girl's obsession with a particular kind of nonsexual commercial amusement. The introduction to this song, rather than its better-known chorus, establishes the desirability of commercial amusements:

Katie Casey was baseball mad,
Had the fever and had it bad;
Just to root for the home town crew,
ev'ry sou Katie blew
On a Saturday, her young beau
called to see if she'd like to go,
To see a show but Miss Katie said "no,
I'll tell you what you can do":
   (Chorus:) "Take me out to the ball game." [41]

Baseball has little to do with sexuality and has no sexual content, yet here Katie Casey chose it over other forms of popular amusement that did. Although there is no evidence that Katie Casey was a charity girl, the song highlights the commercialization of leisure and girls' hunger for it. In this context, cheap amusements themselves became a crucial item of exchange regardless of their sexual content, something that young women wanted but could not afford. With little access to money, some young women made the obvious choice to exchange some kind of sexual favor to gain access to commercial entertainments. It was not the sexualized content of popular culture, as many conservatives then and now would argue, but the cost and commodification of popular entertainment that led young girls into what reformers despairingly called "sexual promiscuity."

As they entered the work force, young women increasingly attended public amusements with their families, by themselves, or in groups. Ironically, while women gained more freedom on the streets and in other public venues, they still lacked the ability to pay for urban amusements. After all, the entertainments were only relatively cheap, making them easily available only for those members of the working class whose wages could provide at least a small margin above bare survival. Turning over their wages to their families, most young girls had to find other ways to fund their growing desire for urban amusements. The lucky few who received allowances might have enough to pay for an evening's entertainment, but the majority who either received no pocket money or supported themselves on meager wages simply lacked the wherewithal to pay. Treating thus emerged as a dynamic interaction between women's economic options and their desire to participate in popular culture and amusements. It let young girls continue to turn over their much-needed wages to their families, while at the same time allowing them entrance into dance halls and penny arcades. As a result, treating can be seen as a radically new moral response to older and more traditional responsibilities. Rather than abandon family ties, as indeed some young women and men did, treating girls attempted to stretch the boundaries of sexual morality to include behavior that proved beneficial both to them and to their families.

The Homosocial Origins of Treating

As much as treating was a heterosexual behavior, it developed in homosocial settings and out of homosocial networks of friendship. Using settlement clubs, schools, and their workplaces, young women debated, defined, and policed the boundaries of this new sexual category. As a result, treating emerged from relationships between young women. Especially for young girls, treating was more about socializing with other girls than it was about meeting young men. Social workers noted the connection between homosocial and heterosexual behaviors. As the authors of *Young Working Girls* cautioned, "a practically overwhelming consciousness of sex, combined with a growing desire for companionship, leads the girl into short-lived and cliquey alliances with those of her own sex, and into various forms of adventure with members of the other sex."[42] In this analysis, an awareness of sex and a desire for company (or entertainment) led young women to band together to go out on the town. These homosocial nights then led to the heterosexual "adventures" that so distressed social workers.

Settlement workers often witnessed the homosocial side of treating, because girls used settlement-house events and clubs to discuss these issues. For example, Bedford inmate Gretta Froehlich identified the Columbia Girls Club held at the East Side Settlement House as the source of her information about entertainment, boys, and sexual exchange.[43] In their clubs, girls created forums for discussion of issues of propriety, entertainment, and sexuality, including treating practices. At the Rosebud Settlement Club, which drew from the neighborhood from 102nd through 105th Streets, the Italian and Jewish girls asked each other questions like "'Should a girl talk to a strange man?' 'Should a girl permit a stranger to treat her to the movies?' 'Is it advisable for girls to go out with boys?' 'How could one make one's parents reasonable, so that they would permit the girls to go out with boys? 'Was it all right for a girl to be kissed by the fellow who took her out?'"[44] Progressing from the propriety of talking to strangers through whether or not entertainment should be exchanged for kissing, these young girls debated the ethics and, to a degree, the necessity of sexual exchange in their lives.[45]

Using the all-female settlement club as a forum to work out their own ideas about sexuality, these girls explored whether it was proper for a girl to exchange a kiss for urban amusement. As they did so, they touched on the three crucial questions involved in treating: was it safe, could they maintain respectability, and would they get the entertainment they wanted at a price they felt they could afford? The assumptions underlying this debate reveal a great deal about the place that entertainment began to occupy in urban life and the role that young women, and even young girls, took in developing treating. Wishing to avoid not only prostitution but also ruined reputations, these girls looked to each other to define acceptable and unacceptable modes of exchange. Evaluating the sexual values of the world around them, they negotiated between their desire to be entertained, their understanding of what might constitute a fair exchange, and the more conservative views of their parents on this issue (how *does* one make one's parents reasonable?). Discussions of acceptable sexual behavior created feelings of camaraderie, and girls stuck together while treating, both for safety and because they grew accustomed to pursuing treating in homosocial groups.[46] The girls in the Rosebud Settlement Club were young enough that their discussions were largely theoretical. Most of the development of treating and the definitions and policing of its boundaries went on at work.

Young working women used their lunch hour in the same ways that other girls used the resources of the settlement clubs. Girls also talked about their evening's entertainments, and it is in these conversations that they developed treating as a new sexual category, creating a wedge that opened a space between respectability and prostitution. Because they were older, however, these young women had more experience in the dance halls and had moved from the hypothetical to the practical when evaluating their behavior and the behavior of the women around them. After all, many of them went out to nightclubs, and the question of how to pay for such excursions loomed large. Instead of asking each other what kinds of exchange were acceptable, young women at work evaluated each other and condemned those who fell short of the new balance that treating required. In these discussions, young women negotiated and renegotiated the boundaries of respectable behavior. The line between acceptable and unacceptable behavior was constantly in flux.

The "Department Store Investigation" conducted by the Committee of Fourteen in 1912 provides an excellent source for evaluating how young women used work time and work relationships to define and police this new behavior. The committee hired three white middle-class women to go undercover and determine whether department stores endangered the morals of their young women workers. The investigators found that the vast majority of girls clerking in stores attended dance halls and other popular amusements. Once there, however, young women clearly had varying standards for what constituted proper behavior. When discussing a particularly problematic dance hall, for example, one clerk remarked that "I know that it has a bad name, but I believe that if a girl is decent, nobody will touch her." Her companion disagreed, saying that "she would not go there."[47] Here, the two girls debated the strategic as opposed to the actual dangers of going to a questionable establishment. One was concerned with the danger that could befall a girl who goes to a "bad hall." She concluded that her reputation would protect her. Her companion saw women's reputations as more fragile things and refused to go to a hall that had a bad reputation.

Continuing the conversation, the two clerks evaluated the virtue of another girl in a similar fashion. "Rose told me that Margaret hangs out with a tough bunch," the undercover investigator reported, "and although a 'good girl' she had a poor reputation for this reason." Rose explained to the investigator that "I have never gone out with her and Kittie Tansey for this reason. They think that if they know they are all right, the rest can go to the devil, but I don't want to do anything that will spoil my 'rep.'"[48] For these young women, reputation was rapidly becoming divorced from actual behavior. The slippage between these two categories, reputation and behavior, was an old one, but the freedom that young women had to explore these previously all-male spaces and retain some of their "rep" was new. This conversation reflected treating's effect in expanding the meaning of women's presence in the public and, to an extent, others' judgments about their sexual behavior while there. At the same time, it also underlined the limitations of those new freedoms. Reputations still mattered, and young women used gossip to define new lines around what "good girls" could do.

While young women could be remarkably flexible in their judgments, most still had a strong investment in the boundaries of treating and guarded them ferociously. In the opinion of the clerks quoted above, girls who went out to "bad places" or with "bad crowds" were not in and of themselves bad.[49] This evaluation complicated working-class girls' understanding of sexual respectability. Sexual behavior existed on a spectrum that paralleled a similar spectrum of sexual respectability. Interacting in complicated ways, understandings of respectability shifted to accommodate changes in sexual behavior. The clerks discussing Kittie Tansey evaluated her respectability by observing her behavior and not her associations. From their point of view, Tansey was not immoral but was walking closer to the line that divided good girls from bad girls than they themselves cared to. This indicates a broad range of possible activities and an associated set of risks.[50]

Prostitution occupied one end of this moral spectrum, and the girls in this store disapproved of prostitution, in spite of the fact that they themselves often treated. In one instance, clerks expressed disgust for a girl they knew who went into prostitution. The investigator reported that "she got in with a very nice fellow, who used to sell automobiles and make good money. She is said to have corrupted him, for she is now hustling, and he is her pimp." Anna, another young woman who worked with the dismissed worker, stated that "She was a dangerous girl, for she could corrupt anyone. . . . I was always afraid that she might get hold of some girls . . . and start them off. She certainly ruined that fellow." Here, prostitution represented a moral contagion that could "ruin" and "corrupt" both men and women. According to the investigator's earlier reports, however, Anna herself engaged in treating. As the investigator described, Anna was "a plain girl to look at. She is a wonderful dancer and has a vivacious manner and a disregard for what she does and says which makes her popular among the 'fellows.' She has been going out with one man for two years, but he is always reproaching her for having other friends."[51] Although she occupied the new gray area of acceptable sexual behavior that treating introduced, Anna drew a firm line between prostitution, or going out for the money, and going out for fun. While treating girls might "profit" from their sexuality, they did not accept cash and, at least in these girls' minds, did not endanger others when they attempted to expand the range of sexually acceptable behavior.

Women testifying in court cases and incarcerated as wayward minors also made similar distinctions between treating and prostitution. Defining prostitution as the exchange of sex for money, these young women admitted to having intercourse with different men but vehemently denied any involvement in prostitution.[52] Prosecutors asked one woman if she considered herself to be "a good woman" after she admitted to having sexual intercourse with a man. "Why, I took no money off of him," she retorted.[53] Another young woman explained to her committing judge that she had never received any money but instead men "took her for motor cycle and automobile rides" and gave her birch beer.[54] While she clearly saw this behavior as very different from prostitution, her judge sentenced her to the reformatory anyway and described her as "just a little animal." Like Anna at the department store, these women condemned prostitution while at the same time admitted to engaging in sexual intercourse in exchange for entertainments and gifts. One young African American girl, committed for being a wayward minor, admitted that she had treated but volunteered in her interview that "One fellow asked me would I go out and make some money for him and I knew that is wrong, that is very wrong." The social worker then concluded, "so she did not do it."[55] Working-class attitudes toward prostitution, while more sympathetic than those of the middle class, still reflected the belief that prostitution was wrong because it placed intimate relations in the realm of the cash economy. These young women had internalized that message and sought other ways to pay for their entertainments.

The risks of reputation were not the only reasons these young women condemned prostitution. In one conversation between a social worker and a young southern African American wayward minor, the girl admitted that "she has had sexual intercourse with three different friends but has never taken money from them. They have sent her presents and have taken her out to dinner and the theatre often." When asked about prostitution, she commented that "in a way prostitution is the worst crime anybody can commit because you have to do things that take away your self respect."[56] For this girl, prostitution not only damaged reputations, it destroyed a girl's sense of self and her sense of her own respectability. Both external and internal respect governed the judgments young women made about their sexual choices.

Like the young women working in department stores and those meeting in settlement clubs, girls incarcerated at Bedford identified other young women as both the source of their information about and motivations for treating. The social worker interviewing Austrian immigrant Gretta Froehlich gave this explanation of Gretta's behavior: "She got in with a bad crowd."

Gretta met "girls who went with boys and introduced her to them and she went around with them to shows and dances." [57] Native-born white inmate Gladys Steele told her social worker that she "became acquainted with fast girls who were working in the factory and since then she has been going out with these girls very often." Steele denied prostituting "but has had sexual intercourse with five or six different men many times during the last year and a half. Took presents from the men but never received any money." [58] A young African American inmate reported a similar introduction to treating, reporting that she "was friendly with a girl who had also been in the Orphanage and who had a bad reputation." [59]

Of course, these young girls, incarcerated and under the power of social workers who wanted to reform them, had strong motives for denying any involvement in prostitution. And, in fact, most girls at Bedford denied that they were prostituting at the time of their arrest. However, a surprising number of inmates did acknowledge involvement in prostitution more generally. The young women discussed above consistently denied prostitution at any time, and their social workers seem to have believed them. Even the committing judge who called his ward "a little animal" admitted that while she "was promiscuous sexually [engaged in premarital intercourse] before her arrest," she had "probably received no money." [60] These young women's testimony about their lives, and in particular the attitudes working-class girls expressed about prostitution, should not merely be viewed as their attempts to justify their activities retrospectively. Rather, they provide a snapshot of young women's evaluations of their new sexual norms and the place they felt they should occupy in the sexual values of the larger working-class community. They drew firm lines between prostitution and sexual barter, because if treating were to be accepted as something that respectable girls could engage in, it had to be disassociated from the stigma of prostitution. Young women clearly defined prostitution and treating as different and condemned prostitution as wrong and, at times, as bad for a girl's self-respect. In the case of the girls incarcerated at Bedford, they made these judgments in their own defense. The department store girls, as we saw, used these discussions to regulate the sexual behavior of their peer group. This self-policing was just one aspect of treating's homosocial nature and development. Young women also went out and treated in single-sex groups. In this respect, treating girls used heterosexuality as a way to fund homosocial activities.

Young women often began their forays into treating by going out with friends from work. John Sloan captures the exuberance of girls just released from work in his 1915 etching "Return from Toil" (see Figure 2.3).[61] Taking

FIGURE 2.3. *John Sloan, "Return from Toil," 1919, from* New York Etchings (1905–1949), *ed. Helen Farr Sloan (New York: Dover, 1978).*

over the sidewalk, the girls walk five abreast, laughing uproariously and drawing the attention of passersby. A dance hall called the Strand Roof Garden provides a good example of a place where these young women might be headed. After grabbing a quick meal, youngsters who attended the Strand spent most of their time dancing and making each other's acquaintance. Used to large lunchtime crowds, the owners posted signs that stated, "no gentleman is permitted to ask a lady to dance unless he has been previously introduced to her." Theoretically, this eliminated indiscriminate mingling between the young patrons. However, the Strand employed older women as "matrons" who introduced young people to each other, thus fulfilling both the requirements of propriety and the demand of youngsters for relatively unsupervised entertainment.[62] Girls attended places like the Strand together and usually spent more time socializing with each other than they did with men. One investigator identified the young women patrons of a dance hall as "working girls" employed in department stores, factories, and telephone exchanges. Referring to them as "near whores," he described them as "sporty in appearance" and implied that they exchanged sexual favors with their male companions. But he also reported that "their favorite portion of the premises is the ladies toilet which is by far the busiest place in the room. There they smoke cigarettes and converse for long periods of time."[63] By his own description, this investigator revealed that the most morally suspect of the girls ("near whores") spent the majority of their time in the all-female environment of the ladies' toilet. Their main crime, besides "sporty" dress, was smoking and socializing together.

Some young women focused on each other, using their knowledge of the treating exchange to manipulate men into financing their evening without actually committing to sexual exchange. In May of 1914, one investigator paid for two girls' drinks and attempted to get a sexual promise from them: "both girls 'snickered' and looked at one another. AGNES HART, one of the girls, said, 'We don't understand just what you mean.'" Lillie, the other girl, took pity on his confusion and explained, "You can't be blamed for taking us for common women, any one of us or both of us together for that matter can entertain you any place not quite as public as this place is." Sparring with them, the investigator could not determine if they were the "charity" type or not. Pressing them for a price did no good, because "under no condition would they mention money directly but AGNES 'needed' $5 for one of the 'new style long corsets,' while LILLIE would 'love to get together about $7 more for an aigrette,' (this to one another)."[64] Agnes and Lillie understood the rules of treating, knew what the investigator wanted, and deftly avoided discussing it with him. In addition, although it became clear that they had no intention of actually treating with him, they had no problem accepting the drinks that he bought them. In refusing to discuss money with him, the two girls indicated their understanding of the line between treating and prostitution and their fear of crossing that line. Although the girls were willing to be perceived as charity girls, they had no desire to be taken for prostitutes. Items of clothing were the second most common currency of treating after the price of an evening's entertainment. Further, the two girls used the vocabulary of a treat. Speaking to each other, they mentioned things that they "wanted" or "needed" and named a cash-price equivalent, one that matched the current price for intercourse with a prostitute. In essence, the girls knew how much sex cost, what might be a likely treating substitute for cash, and the appropriate language to use when discussing a possible exchange with a man. Although they chose not to treat with him, they did gain from the encounter.

The use of treating for homosocial ends was possible because it was such a casual exchange. Relying on unspoken gestures and assumptions, men paid for a woman's expenses as a down payment on later activities. As Agnes and Lillie's activities attest, young women benefited from the new social space treating opened up and used it to finance their own socializing. Perhaps more crucial, however, was the ways in which treating changed cultural assumptions that equated women's presence in bars and cabarets with prostitution. The practice replaced this earlier assumption with one that posited most women as potential charity girls whose company could be won by promises of fun and not by offers of cash. This created a public space that was more affable and forgiving of women's sociability. As young women got closer to the age when they might want to marry, they began to treat in earnest and with more heterosexual intentions. The homosocial nature of young girls' participation in urban amusements, and the creation of an intermediate category such as treating, protected them as they moved on to explore sex and sexuality more fully.

The Treating Exchange

If treating developed in homosocial networks, it was, of course, still a heterosocial and heterosexual activity. Young women who engaged in the practice negotiated with men over what they wanted and what they were willing to provide in exchange. The vast majority of these young women treated with men for the cost of the evening's entertainment. By this, however, they meant not only the entertainment provided by the dance hall or movie theater but also that provided by the presence and companionship of the young man. In this way, the homosocial practice of treating shifted to a heterosexual one as girls grew older and as meeting and socializing with young men became one of their primary concerns. For these young women, treating served a number of purposes. Most obviously, they still expected men to pay for their meals and entertainment while avoiding the taint of prostitution. Young women wanted the men they met to provide good company, and some, though not all, wanted sexual intimacy and satisfaction. Obviously, however, these desires created problems of their own. Treating girls struggled to balance their hunger for entertainment, company, and sex with the dangers of ruined reputations, pregnancy, and disease. On the whole, the ambiguity of the treating exchange—the very vagueness of its negotiations and promises—allowed young women more room to choose what they would exchange and sometimes to cheat or manipulate men.

Women engaged in treating often discriminated against men whom they perceived as lacking the funds to take them out on the town. Their selectiveness functioned as a regulation within treating, a subsidiary set of rules that governed what was and was not a fair treat. In a sociological study of waitresses, for example, the author documented girls' preferences for older men and their view that older men were fair game for fleecing. One young woman explained that "I always keep two or three fellows on the string and I get all I can out of them. I never come through; unless I have to. . . . I have three now, this fellow I went out with last night (and I'm good to him) and John, he's a married man." Another girl was more explicit, stating, "I don't have nothing to do with no young fellow. . . . it isn't worth it. Now an old fellow is worth stringin' along, you can pull his leg and get somethin' out of him but these young fellows ain't got any money."[65] These young women gave financial reasons for going with older, more prosperous, men. Older men could pay more and thus made better companions. But the women may also have felt that it was unfair to take advantage of younger men, who might genuinely feel that they could court and fall in love with a young woman. Older men were themselves playing the entertainment con-game and thus could take care of themselves.[66]

African American women who treated expressed similar attitudes about white men. One young African American woman told an investigator that "she ain't out for the dollar but is as game as the rest of them, and if she likes a white man, she'd go the limit with him, she wouldn't expect any pay for it but if she needs a pair of shoes or waist she'd expect him to buy it for her."[67] Her silence on what she did with African American men and her emphasis on the whiteness of the men involved suggest that for this young woman white men made better treating partners. They had more money, and like older men, they understood that a relationship with her would not lead to something more. She may also have used this activity to protect herself, either from falling in love or from spoiling her reputation in her own community. Although I have no direct evidence that African American charity girls crossed race lines to shield their reputations, African American prostitutes sometimes limited their clients to white men because they wanted to marry within the black community. As one African American investigator reported of an encounter with an African American prostitute, "it developed that she does not solicit colored men as a general rule but operates among Chinese, Philipinos and Porto Ricans. She said she adopted this policy because some day she might decide to marry a negro man and no other negro man [would] be able to say anything about her that her husband might hear. She said if she should marry and pass some of the Chinese or Spanish fellows who know her they would talk their language and nothing would be understood."[68] Restricting themselves to white clients shielded African American women's activities from African American men and thus allowed them to maintain a level of respectability with potential marriage prospects. Using age and race to select treating partners allowed these young women to exploit those who were most likely out to exploit them and perhaps to protect the men who might mistake a treating exchange for a potential courtship encounter.

Although most young men probably hoped for sexual intercourse, some young women attempted to satisfy men without "going the limit." One disgruntled man told an investigator that he could "get all I want, but you know how these kids are. Some of them —— all right and like it, but a good many of them just give you a hallway rub and let you finger —— them. They're afraid of getting knocked up."[69] In another investigation conducted in May of 1916, a female undercover agent wrote that "there is dating up among the lunch crowd. . . . there are some boys . . . who are flush and who take girls out—meeting them after their work, then dancing through the evening with them, after which they sometimes spend the night together." Despite her obvious distaste for this group of youngsters and their socializing, she was forced to admit that "largely, however, the boys as well as the girls are 'salamanders'—they will go all the way up to the limit, but they do not often overstep that mark."[70] Young people consistently used the phrase "going the limit" in the prewar period to indicate intercourse. The use of the word "limit" as a noun in the expression emphasizes the importance of sexual boundaries. There were limits beyond which good girls should not go. It also highlights the important difference between all other kinds of sex play and intercourse. "Going all the way," of course, is the contemporary equivalent. Charity girls engaged in a wide range of sexual activities, and not all of them had sexual intercourse with the men they met.

Young women had very good reasons for avoiding intercourse and satisfying men through other means. Despite the availability of condoms, pessaries, and suppositories in many turn-of-the-century pharmacies, charity girls and other nonprostitutes rarely used contraception.[71] Although conversations with inmates who admitted to engaging in treating revealed that they understood that pregnancy was a risk, few of them could explain how to prevent it. White native-born Ethel Saunders's social worker noted, "When asked what the dangers are for sexual promiscuity it is found that she knows nothing of venereal diseases but cites as dangers only 'being sent here, getting pregnant, getting a baby.'"[72] Despite her understanding of the risks, Saunders offered no way to avoid them. Most charity girls risked pregnancy when they had sexual intercourse with men. An unwanted pregnancy would topple the precarious balance that treating provided for them. Many young women wanted to keep information about their sexual activities from parents and neighbors, and pregnancy made that impossible. Although some young women sought and obtained abortions, these could be difficult to find, dangerous, and expensive. One lucky girl had an aunt who helped her find a midwife willing to perform the procedure and kept the entire incident secret from her parents, but few young women had access to such resources.[73]

In addition to pregnancy, women who had sex with men they didn't know risked contracting sexually transmitted diseases. Both syphilis and gonorrhea had reached epidemic proportions among the working classes of cities like New York by the turn of the century. Not only were the diseases easily transmitted but there were few effective treatments for them. The introduction of salvarsan did help with the treatment of syphilis in the 1920s, but it was an expensive and long-term process that often proved ineffective. There were no effective treatments for gonorrhea. Until the development of penicillin in the 1940s, sexually transmitted diseases posed a serious risk.[74] Although they could not always prevent them, prostitutes knew a great deal about sexually transmitted diseases and willingly discussed condoms, douching, and inspection of partners. In contrast, the charity girls who found themselves at Bedford reformatory seemed largely ignorant about disease. When asked about the possible dangers of premarital sex, one southern African American teenager listed only getting pregnant. The social worker then reminded her of venereal diseases, to which she replied, "I have heard of them but never bothered about it."[75]

In this period, both prostitutes and treating girls usually refused to perform oral sex.[76] However, this does not mean that they all had intercourse with their partners; indeed, many relied on other forms of sexual activity, for example, kissing, fondling, and hand jobs, to keep their male companions happy. One man's reference in 1914 to girls' allowing only a "hallway rub and let you finger —— them" clearly referred to mutual masturbation and possibly ejaculation between the legs.[77] In another instance, an investigator reported on a game played by youngsters at "Goldberg's Farm" in Brooklyn. "After, we all went to the woods," he stated, "a kissing game started, we sit down in a bush and could go as far as we liked, but the girls skimmed, that they do anything we want except the right thing, because they were never touched yet, and trying to avoid it [sic]."[78] In this sex game, the young girls shunned sexual intercourse, though they seemed more concerned about reputation and the cultural and social importance of preserving virginity than about fears of pregnancy and sexually transmitted diseases.

Although some young women avoided intercourse, the material rewards for treating did not exclude sexual desire as one of many motivations. One group of white women told an investigator that they were not prostitutes but "would not be averse to sexual intercourse for the pleasure of the act."[79]

Another woman expressed interest in intercourse to an investigator who reported that she referred to the "great physical pleasure said to be [illegible] with the consummation of sexual intercourse." [80] Another young white woman had an almost identical conversation with her social worker at Bedford. As the social worker reported, "Patient admits having been immoral but denies ever having taken any money. When asked why she did it, she says: 'Nature'; and she frankly admits that she derived pleasure from the intercourse." [81] These women wanted to have intercourse and both experienced and expressed sexual desire. Treating for them involved both the fun of an evening on the town and the enjoyment of sexual intercourse afterward. The clearest indication that some women wanted and enjoyed intercourse came in reports where women berated men for not "putting out" after the men had paid for their entertainments. As one investigator reported, "she was very much offended" when he refused to have intercourse with her "and gave me considerable abuse [and] characterized me as 'a bum sport.'" [82] Another investigator witnessed an altercation in which a young man "was scolded several times by one young woman for not 'loving her up like the other fellows do.' [He] became disgusted and left premises." [83]

However open these women and girls seemed to be about intercourse, the issue of their public reputations still loomed large for them. Although they regulated each other's behavior and approved of treating within their peer group, most still had to confront other community values that disapproved of such expression. One investigator provided the perfect example of this phenomenon in his report concerning two young girls in a public park: "1 was willing to [illegible] up to the nooks and do some 'loving' while the last was very anxious 'to be loved' and stated plainly that she was desirous of intercourse as soon as darkness fell and detection was improbable." These young women expressed the balance that treating required of young women who wished to have intercourse while still maintaining public virtue. Although the second girl said she wanted to have intercourse with her new male friend, she was afraid that people from her neighborhood might see them. Just as important, however, the young girls did not hide their behavior from each other but instead picked up men together. Perhaps the most useful way to think about reputations in the context of treating is to realize that young girls maintained different reputations with different people. Young women might have one reputation with their female friends, another with their families or neighbors, and yet another with the boys they met. The kind of things they were willing to do depended largely on which reputation might be endangered by that activity and who was watching.

Fear of exposure shaped the geography of sex for treating girls. Where

they had sex made a difference to them, both because they feared exposure and because they avoided locations that implied prostitution. The anonymity of the city and the location of women's work away from their local
neighborhoods allowed them to attend urban amusements away from the
watchful eye of family and neighbors. This gave them much more sexual
freedom than they might otherwise have enjoyed. But even when they attended establishments far from home, young women routinely refused to
have sex in hotels. One young man informed an investigator that "some of
the women . . . are out for the coin but there is a lot that come in here that
are charity. One [man] told me that he has picked up many a girl in here,
he sometimes takes them to the hotels, but sometimes the girls wont [sic]
go to hotel to stay for the night, they are afraid of their mothers, so he gets
away with it in the hallway." [84] "Going to a hotel" implied prostitution, and
few treating girls would assent to that: spending the night with a man in a
hotel room both violated treating girls' sense of the important differences
between themselves and prostitutes and meant risking discovery by their
family.

This aspect of treating reflects the importance that most of these women
attached to the maintenance of an identity that was sexual but explicitly excluded prostitution. Although the anonymity of a large city like New York
could free women to engage in prostitution outside of their neighborhoods,
many women refused to prostitute but still held onto an exchange in which
they could turn a profit. Treating was thus not just about exchange but about
creating and maintaining a moral middle ground. Girls who could have accepted money often did not. This refusal indicates just how crucial their behavior was to their sense of self-worth and how much treating as a practice
had become part of their personal identity. In addition, as a sexual category,
treating stood on its own. Women could consider themselves "charity girls"
and claim the mantle of "good women" through an explicit comparison to
prostitutes.

For the most part, prostitutes before World War I ignored treating girls.
It was not until the more intense competition of the 1920s that prostitutes
began to complain that charity girls cut into their business. But even in this
period, some prostitutes noticed the treating that went on around them,
particularly when the women involved asked for material goods in addition
to a night on the town. One young African American woman told an investigator that the prostitutes she knew "get sore because they are out for the
dollar and they always blame her for stealing their men away." She identified herself as a charity girl, saying that she wasn't "out for the dollar" but
that she would ask men to pay for other items like shoes.[85]

Clothing and shoes were the most common items mentioned when a woman expected more than just entertainment. In addition, as this woman's explanation indicates, the exchange was not necessarily required in every encounter. Instead, her current situation dictated whether she asked for more than just paying her way. Treating was ultimately a very flexible system that women used to meet immediate needs. Although most women only required a man to foot the evening's bill, those who asked for more did so by defining their needs using the language of gifting. This language served the important psychological purpose of keeping treating in the realm of friendship and courtship for the women who practiced it. For example, an investigator "was told by one of them that I could have intercourse with her provided that I buy her a 'nice little present.'"[86] The language of gifting further removed treating from prostitution in the minds of the women who practiced it. Not only did they not accept cash, they did not really exchange sexual services for material goods. Instead, they received presents from their friends. This language also reaffirmed important gender identities, with women shielded from the cash economy and in the passive position of receiving gifts. In contrast, men took the active role in giving gifts and treating young women to things they "needed."

Some women went to ridiculous lengths to avoid accepting cash, which suggests both their desperate need and the real moral line they refused to cross. One woman demanded that the investigator pay her butcher bill. He reported that he bought the woman drinks and then asked where they could go: "She then asked me to buy pack of cigarettes also bottle of whiskey to take with us. Then asked me to go to butcher store with her, she wanted me to pay her butcher bill, I told her all butcher shops were closed now, and I didn't care to travel around from store to store, she got sore at me and called me a piker and told me to beat it."[87] While this woman could have asked for cash directly, she did not. Instead, she requested that her companion pay for something that she needed, but when he refused, she did not take the logical step of asking for cash to pay the bill herself. Rather than accept money and cross over the line into prostitution, she terminated the relationship.

Although the vast majority of women identified as charity girls in the Committee of Fourteen investigations did not accept material goods for sex when they treated, the fact that some women did was important. Occupying the extreme border of the treat, the ways they justified their actions and the manner in which they separated themselves from prostitutes demonstrate the extent to which treating was becoming a form of sexual barter distinct from prostitution. Although not thoroughly respectable, charity girls carefully avoided the label of prostitute. Treating thus provided a buffer between chastity and prostitution in a world in which women's small wages (and desire for entertainment) forced them to use their sexuality to meet their material needs.

Men and Treating

Men made up the other half of a treating exchange and, of course, had their own views about the relative merits of treating versus prostitution. When evaluating the two practices, men tended to express the difference in terms of what they could expect sexually and emotionally and how much they might have to pay for it. Prostitution was a sure thing, and a man could negotiate over prices and services. Treating proved more difficult, with uncertain expenditures and uncertain payoffs. As reflected in the Committee of Fourteen investigations, men's comparisons of treating and prostitution most often reflected a pragmatic vision, a cost-benefit analysis of what they might expend and what they might receive in return. The investigators' reports also show that, for the time being at least, men felt that they lost considerable power in their negotiations with women over what they would receive and how much they would pay. Between the turn of the century and World War I, young women held the upper hand in the treating exchange, and men's attitudes reflected this fact.

Men rarely made judgmental comments about women who treated, and they did not support as complicated a view of women's sexuality as the women themselves did. Rather, their focus remained on what a girl could give them and how much they would have to pay for it. One investigator reported that "I started a conversation with the young man sitting nearest to me. He said that only a portion of the girls 'were out for the money'; some of them were 'straight,' by which he meant that the girls had sexual relations only with one man at a time. The three girls sitting to my right, he said, were not in the business at all, but came only because they were good dancers. The professional prostitutes were taken, at the close of the evening, to a hotel on 116th St. and Eighth Avenue, he said."[88] This young man had three separate categories for women: the prostitutes who "were out for the money," the "straight" girls who were serially monogamous, and the good girls who attended public amusements for their own purposes, in this case dancing. One of the most interesting aspects of this man's commentary lay in his arrangement of the women in descending order of how willing they might be to have sex. His assessment contained far less moral judgment of women's behavior than did the women's evaluations of each other. He also employed metaphors to describe, and apparently mask, the sexual nature of their actions. Instead of describing them as loose or bad, as other women might, he stated that some were "in the business" and others were not.

Understandably, men often resented the uncertainty of treating. One disgruntled young man assessed the character of the women in the room and stated that "there is a lot of charity here but there is also a lot of teasers here too, they'll sit and drink with you and then all of a sudden beat it."[89] In this case, the man made a distinction between treating girls who actually would have sex to pay for their evening and girls who posed as charity but then skipped out on their end of the bargain. Warning other men about the intentions of women became an important part of male culture at the turn of the century. Mirroring the entrenched homosociality of treating for women, men discussed the character of the female patrons of particular bars and, at times, informed each other about the likelihood that an individual woman would make good on her promises.

Some women did cheat men in the treating exchange, either by pretending to be charity or simply by avoiding having sex when they felt they could. A young white woman in Bedford for being a wayward minor reported to her social worker that "she made him drink a great deal more and drank none herself. He was so intoxicated that he could not undress—simply lay on the bed and 'did not bother me at all.'"[90] "Teasers" might sneak out the bathroom window or, less dramatically, a side door, but many women simply put off sex for long periods of time. One investigator complained to a bartender about a girl he had been seeing. The bartender listened sympathetically and countered with a story of his own. According to the investigator, the bartender "remarked 'Still after her, eh! You must like her,' and to which I replied in affirmative, adding that she was a fine 'chicken,' that I had spent all kinds of money on her and would get her in a hotel do or die. I said further that I would take her to Palsto's in Harlem some night, get her under the influence of liquor, take a taxi and rush her into a hotel before she would realize it." The bartender told him that he "had a girl on his staff and took her out fully twenty times before he could have intercourse with her."[91] The casual way in which the bartender responded to this complaint indicates that it must have been a common, or at least not unheard of, experience.

In addition to men's complaints about "teasers," the Committee of Fourteen's use of female undercover agents inadvertently provided evidence that women, and not men, usually controlled the treating exchange. Posing as prostitutes, the middle-class women who worked for the committee attempted to obtain information about where prostitution might be tolerated.

However, the communities that they observed often mistook these women for charity, as none reported any direct solicitation. Furthermore, several of them consistently strung along their male friends for months at a time without suffering any serious repercussions. In one case, a female investigator named Natalie De Borgey picked up and strung along a suitor for over four months. Apparently, he didn't find this extended pursuit unusual. On August 14, 1912, she reported that "Tom Burns tried to make a date with me. . . . I told him to go to Daisy [a 'fairy,' or effeminate homosexual friend of theirs][92] for what he desired. 'No,' he answered, 'I must pay Daisy, while here I know that there is a little girl who will give free.'" Later that evening, she described Burns's frustration with her, and it is clear that his patience was wearing thin. She commented that "Mr. Burns had warned me that he would get my promise as he would not be kept on the string any longer."[93] In this case and in the others involving female investigators, the women clearly had the upper hand in the treating exchange. While men might threaten, bluster, or simply refuse to participate, there is little evidence that they did anything more.

Women's control over the treating exchange sprang from the location of these negotiations in a public space. As long as men had to pay for entertainment expenses first and receive sex later at a different location, they had difficulty enforcing the woman's end of the bargain. Furthermore, the very existence of treating girls confused older sexual categories, opening up room for many young women to take advantage of men's confusion and relative prosperity. Treating made "teasers" possible, because their presence as quasi-respectable women legitimated the presence of all nonprostitute women in the public sphere. Martina Tosca, a young, married Italian immigrant, reported attending public amusements with her married friends. Citing a very strict Italian American upbringing, she said that marriage marked the first time she could go out unsupervised. She and her friends went to the Roseland, one of New York's largest and most glamorous dance halls, where "[we] took our wedding rings off . . . and we start dancing and some boys dated up. . . . we give them the wrong address. . . . we had a wonderful time." When asked what their husbands thought of these activities, she replied, "well, we didn't tell them. . . . we were so young. . . . we didn't do nothing wrong. . . . we gave [the boys we met] some kind of different names . . . and then we wouldn't see them no more."[94] Conversely, the existence of teasers also made it possible for many treating girls to withhold sex, if they chose. The severing of the link between practicing prostitution and just being in public opened up room for many women to pursue different sorts of relationships in the public spaces of New York City. There was little men could do to reverse the trend, and, as I have shown, they responded instead by trying to sort women into categories of relative cost.

Of course, some men preferred treating girls for the same reasons that girls liked to treat. Filling an intermediate stage between prostitution and the forms of courtship that eschewed sexual interactions, treating provided men with companionship, entertainment, and, occasionally, sex. For their part, many prostitutes also drank with men before taking them to a hotel and expected them to pick up the tab. Given this practice, charity girls probably did cost men less, even if they required dinner and dance hall admission from their dates. That might prove less expensive than going to a prostitute, especially if the prostitute required similar advance spending and then also demanded additional cash for her services.

Men's opinions about treating offer interesting insight into the ways in which the new system functioned and how people outside it evaluated its characteristics. The young men cited above clearly understood the treating exchange and the difference between treating and prostitution. More prosaic than working-class young women in their evaluations of treating girls, they tended to focus on what they could get and what they would have to pay for it. They did not acknowledge treating girls' meticulous avoidance of participation in a cash economy. For them, spending money was spending money, and therefore both treating and prostitution remained within the cash economy of market capitalism. The fact that women did not accept money from them directly did not appear to matter much in their evaluation.

The blindness of men to the distinction that women drew between accepting cash and accepting an evening's entertainment highlights the different relationship that women and men had to the cash economy. Although both groups now actively participated in that economy as workers, women were still judged more by their sexual behavior than by any other criteria. As a result, they had to draw a firm line between the acceptance of cash and the acceptance of goods bought on their behalf. While treating functioned as a wedge to open up space for women in the public, "respectable" women still had to distinguish themselves from prostitutes. In that way, treating girls succeeded in reconfiguring sexual exchange and sexual morality. Men, for whom the cash economy proved far less problematic, continued to evaluate women according to how much they might have to pay, in essence, their worth or cost in the cash economy.

As a sexual practice, treating opened up new realms of sexual and economic possibilities for women. In the process, it transformed the ways men and women negotiated over sex and ultimately the practices of casual and professional prostitution. Prior to World War I, young women used homo-sociality as a bridge to straddle the divide between chaste and unchaste women. Treating and the new moral economy it represented allowed for far more social and sexual flexibility for women. By enabling young women to participate in a cash economy without accepting cash for their sexual favors, treating gave women the opportunity to expand their own respectable presence in the public. For the time being, at least, treating opened up real possibilities for many women to participate in New York's vibrant public spaces. However, the onset of the war, soldiers' sense of sexual entitlement, and young women's association of treating with patriotism began to tip the balance in men's favor. By the end of the war, young men had a great deal more to say about young women's sexual barter.

Chapter Three

THESE ARE THE PEOPLE IN YOUR NEIGHBORHOOD

PROSTITUTION, COMMERCE, AND COMMUNITY IN TURN-OF-THE-CENTURY NEW YORK CITY

In early 1901, an undercover investigator for the new vice society, the Committee of Fifteen, encountered a woman in a poor section of lower Manhattan who confided in him her rather startling commercial ambitions. A recent immigrant from St. Louis, Missouri, she supported her teenage son with her earnings. The investigator reported that "this woman . . . said if she could find somebody who would be willing to furnished [*sic*] the amount that is needed there would be plenty of money in this business; she said to us 'With the help of God I think we should make a success by opening a whore house.'"[1] Admitting previous experience in running a brothel in St. Louis, the woman lacked the capital to establish a place on her own. Driven by family responsibilities, she sought to parlay her expertise and ambition into a business.

While this woman expressed unusual ambition in the difficult world of sex work, her motivations were typical and reflect the importance of prostitution as an economic solution and occasional career path for some working-class women. Seeking to replace the wages of either dead or missing male breadwinners and to support children, widowed or invalid parents, and younger siblings, most women entered prostitution to provide for family members and maintain family ties. In a frightening and uncertain job market, prostitution could serve both personal and familial financial needs. Working women's wages were extremely low, even by working-class standards, and unemployment often struck women and their families especially hard. For the lucky few who could save their wages, prostitution made excellent business sense.

This chapter is about these women and how they negotiated a marketplace characterized by profound changes in the social organization, law, culture, and economics of prostitution between the turn of the century and World War I. While the century opened with the brothels firmly in control of most of the sex trade, within a few years, brothel prostitution slid into a precipitous decline. The disorganization of the industry gave individual women unprecedented opportunities to set the terms and conditions of their work. Prostitution has always generated significant profits, but in choosing the profession, women also risked a loss of their reputation and respectability in the eyes of their families and communities. The structural changes that prostitution underwent in this period allowed women to strike new balances between material profits and social costs.

The decline of the brothel and the diffusion of prostitution into residential working-class neighborhoods led women in two different directions. One group of women explored the entrepreneurial possibilities that non-brothel prostitution offered. Keeping an unprecedented proportion of their wages, these women participated in and helped develop small commercial networks. As women freed themselves from brothels, they embarked on careers as small business people. In the neighborhood setting of local bars and dance halls, these prostitutes developed client bases, entered into partnership with other local proprietors, and helped each other handle difficult patrons. In essence, they created small-scale commercial communities that revolved around the selling of drinks, company, and sex to neighborhood clients.

At the same time, other women took advantage of the new residential patterns in the city to practice prostitution in secret. New York, like all large American cities in the nineteenth century, always had women who used casual prostitution to augment other sources of income.[2] The development of rooming-house districts allowed women to live independent of family and periodically enter the sex trade without being detected by family members, friends, and prospective spouses. These women supplemented meager wages even while they limited the social cost that usually accompanied the choice to sell sex. In so doing, they blurred the line between respectable and disreputable women for their communities. Just who was a prostitute was no longer obviously revealed by clothing, behavior, or location. By hiding their activities, women who prostituted clandestinely, like the charity girls discussed in the previous chapter, began to unravel older understandings that automatically associated sexually promiscuous women with prostitution.

Exploring the development of independent prostitution, I examine the ways women made difficult choices about money, commercialism, business, and reputation. Women who chose to prostitute openly exercised greater control over the shape of prostitution as a profession, their working conditions, and their wages. These women favored economic considerations in their decision to prostitute. Other women prostituted casually and clandestinely, valuing their reputations higher than the profits they could make in the new sexual marketplace. Prostitution underwent enormous changes at the turn of the century in New York City that ultimately gave women more autonomy in their decisions and more freedom to exchange sex for money, if they chose to do so.

The Demographics of Prostitution in New York City in the Early Twentieth Century

Before I begin my discussion of how prostitution changed in the city between 1900 and 1917, it is important to address the aspects of prostitution that did not change in this period. The most significant of these aspects involves identifying which women prostituted in the city. Determining who sold sex for cash in New York City at the turn of the century can be difficult, as statistics on prostitution are notoriously fraught with problems of reliability and representativeness. But creating a "face" for prostitutes in this period is essential for understanding the patterns of prostitution and its relationship to other historical trends such as industrialization, migration and immigration, and urban development.

Most data on prostitutes are based on records of arrests and convictions for prostitution or of populations of women incarcerated for practicing it. Such data pose problems for a variety of reasons, most stemming from the representativeness of those women arrested. First, arrest statistics usually overrepresent certain kinds of prostitutes over others. For example, streetwalkers are more visible and thus are more likely to be arrested than brothel prostitutes. As a result, arrest statistics oversample one kind of prostitution that does not represent experiences or conditions for the profession as a whole. This proves particularly problematic in America's racially and ethnically stratified economy of sex. Some forms of prostitution, like brothel prostitution, discriminate against racial or ethnic minorities. African American women and some white ethnic minorities in the period under study worked as streetwalkers because they lacked safer options.[3] Arrests for streetwalking overestimate the number of African American women or other ethnic or racial minorities in the trade.

In addition, prostitution as a visible sign of the "morality" of a city was vulnerable to the vicissitudes of local and national politics. Local and state election campaigns periodically wrought havoc on business as candidates scrambled to "clean up the city." During the cleanup campaigns, statistics on prostitution fluctuated wildly as politicians pressured the police departments to make spectacular raids. Officers ignored previous agreements based on bribes, and large numbers of prostitutes found themselves temporarily dumped into the criminal justice system. What happened to them there depended on their connections, their wealth, and the degree to which the "cleanup" really mattered in the election. Thus, these and many other factors, such as public health campaigns, venereal disease scares, and wars, make arrest statistics an unreliable measure of who actually sold sex. Keeping these problems in mind, however, data on arrests and convictions can still give us some insight into the demographics of the sex trade.

Turn-of-the-century New York City had its share of experts who studied prostitution, and it is to them that we turn for our statistical profile of prostitution in the city. Katharine Bement Davis, the director of New York's Bedford Hills State Reformatory for Women, wrote one of the most useful of these reports for George Kneeland's *Commercialized Prostitution in New York City*. In this essay, her most reliable data address social class. Prostitution in New York City in this period drew overwhelmingly from the working class and the poor. Based on an analysis of the occupation of their fathers, Davis found that only 16 percent of prostitute inmates came from families that could be considered middle-class.[4] The other women in the group (84 percent) came from families whose fathers had working-class occupations from unskilled day laborers to the skilled stonemasons and cabinetmakers of the labor aristocracy. Even this number overestimates the class status of most prostitutes. Fifty-two percent came from families whose fathers worked in jobs that would not pay enough to keep a family together, requiring that women or children work as well.[5] Another sign of the overall poverty of Bedford's prostitutes emerges in her statistics on literacy. Seven percent could not read or write in any language, and over 45 percent never finished grade school.[6] Overall, Davis's survey of Bedford's prostitutes indicates that most came from working-class backgrounds and that a majority could be designated as poor and undereducated.

Statistics on ethnicity and race support the findings on class. Most of the prostitutes of New York City came from those groups most likely to be poor, namely the children of immigrants (eastern European Jews, Austro-Hungarians, and the Irish) and native-born African Americans.[7] Finding prostitutes from all different ethnic groups, Davis noted that their numbers reflected the proportion of their ethnic community in the city. Immigrants themselves provided less than their share, contributing 24 percent of all prostitutes while making up 40 percent of the population in the city. Their children, on the other hand, were overrepresented. "This is not surprising," Davis commented, because "the children, native-born Americans with American companions and American schooling, adopt American ideals often not of the highest and are apt, even when quite young, to feel that they know more than their parents."[8] From Davis's perspective, the children of immigrants learned to prostitute from their working-class, native-born American peers. Instead of viewing immigrants as racially or culturally inferior, as many middle-class white Americans did in this period, Davis emphasized "Americanization" as an explanation for their behavior. To her, prostitution reflected an adaptation to America, albeit a bad one, and not something inherent in either immigrants or their cultures.

Immigrants and their daughters made up the majority of prostitutes in New York City. Davis's numerical ordering of prostitutes ranked Russians first (95 percent of whom were Jewish),[9] followed by Germans (about 12 percent of whom were Jewish), Irish, English, French, and Italians. The percentage of Italian prostitutes did not match their proportion of the population, but, as Davis explains, "it is a well-known fact that Italy sends to the United States every year, many hundred unmarried men or men without their families" and therefore could hardly contribute much to the number of immigrant women involved in prostitution.[10] Furthermore, as I and other historians have found, Italians closely supervised their daughters, making it difficult for them to participate in many aspects of city life. Undoubtedly this had some effect on their number in the trade.

While Davis did not speculate why some immigrant groups provided more prostitutes than others, the congressional Immigration Commission's investigation into "white slavery" in 1907 provides a fascinating glimpse into the links between prostitution and immigration. Despite popular hysteria both nationally and internationally, the commission found little evidence of an organized traffic in women, or what contemporaries referred to as "white slavery." Although a few young women might be lured to the United States under false pretenses and then "betrayed into slavery," the commission stated that "the much greater number . . . have already been living an immoral life abroad . . . and come to the United States willingly to continue the practices of their former life."[11] These experienced prostitutes primarily came from France and did so because they wanted to "secure higher wages, often profits ten times as great as those they have received in Europe."[12] French women made up 7 percent of the women seen in New York's night court for soliciting, despite the fact that the French made up a tiny proportion of the immigration population.[13] Apparently, these prostitutes immigrated to the United States from France's regulated system of brothels and found conditions here more to their liking.[14]

Finally, several sources indicate that New York's small African American population contributed more than its fair share to prostitution in the city. Davis mentions that native-born "colored" made up 13 percent of prostitutes in Bedford, only briefly noting the percentage despite the attention she pays to other less statistically significant ethnic differences in prostitution.[15] Since blacks made up 2 percent of the population in 1910,[16] their overrepresentation at Bedford is startling, as is Davis's lack of interest. When she took over management of Bedford reformatory, Davis insisted that its inmates be racially integrated, indicating that her own racial politics were far more liberal than those of most of her peers.[17] Given her sympathetic discussion of prostitution among immigrants, she was unlikely to have assumed, as many middle-class whites did, that African Americans were inherently immoral and thus drawn to prostitution. Historian Linda Gordon has found that both African American and white women worked in Progressive-era reform organizations but that their networks remained segregated.[18] Perhaps Davis saw prostitution in the African American community as a problem best addressed by African Americans themselves.

Davis's failure to comment on the overrepresentation of African American women incarcerated at Bedford may also have reflected the lack of interest New York's reform organizations paid to prostitution in the African American community. Kevin Mumford makes this argument in his work on the development of interracial sex districts in New York City and Chicago in this period. Racism and concerns about the effects of prostitution on white women and in white communities, he argues, led organizations like the Committee of Fourteen to overlook vice in African American neighborhoods. When it did pay attention to African American participation in prostitution, the committee targeted interracial vice, which, of course, also involved the white working-class New Yorkers the committee really cared about.[19] My own work in the Committee of Fourteen records confirms Mumford's contention. The committee did periodically investigate Africa American clubs, but it focused more on interracial clubs, despite the fact that New York had never formally criminalized interracial sociability or sexuality. Because the committee did not go through the police or the courts but relied instead on pressuring brewers and surety companies, it could suppress a legal activity it defined as immoral.[20]

However, the committee's lack of interest in suppressing African American prostitution did not simply result from racism. It also derived from the difficulties it encountered in making alliances with leaders of the African American community. At the turn of the century, many members of the African American middle class began to promulgate what historian Evelyn Brooks Higginbotham described as "the politics of respectability."[21] They argued that adhering to bourgeois respectability would convince whites of African Americans' worthiness for citizenship and thus their basic rights to political and economic equality. In their attempts to reform the African American masses, these leaders exhorted working-class African Americans to embrace more restrained styles of dress, behavior, and personal expression and placed heavy emphasis on sexual chastity for women. As a result, African American organizations like the Urban League vigorously policed their own communities, chastising those who spoke too loudly on streetcars, spat in public, attended commercial amusements, or wore flashy clothing. As historian Victoria Wolcott has found, the Urban League of Detroit willingly cooperated with vice societies and the police, reporting businesses and individuals whom they suspected of participating in prostitution and gambling.[22] In New York, the Committee of Fourteen found a valuable African American ally in the city's most important African American newspaper, the *New York Age*. Frederick Moore, the paper's editor, sat on the Committee of Fourteen's advisory board, recommended African American investigators to the committee, and defended it against charges of racism and unfair targeting of black-owned businesses in articles and editorials.[23] He also used the paper to exhort his community to uphold the politics of respectability. For example, in an editorial published in 1911, the author fumed that "a new generation have come upon the scene in New York, many of whom have a notion that loud, boisterous and vulgar conversation, indelicately suggestive dress, dances in which the proprieties are whistled down the winds, and drinking to excess, are the things most approved to be done." [24]

However, other middle-class African Americans resisted the committee's policing of their community, revealing a competing vision of African American success grounded in economic self-help. David Elliot Tobias, a college-educated African American printer, spent over a decade battling the committee when it attempted to close various black-owned bars and clubs. He began his crusade in 1907 when he defended Baron Wilkins's Little Savoy Club in Hell's Kitchen from the committee's accusations that it tolerated prostitution and interracial mixing.[25] In a series of letters, Tobias excoriated the committee for attacking black-owned clubs while allowing white-owned clubs to flourish. However, Tobias took his analysis a step further, calculating the economic losses to the black community when such businesses closed. As he pointed out, the white men who ran black resorts, "for the most part, employ white people to wait on and serve colored people," which denied the black community needed jobs and revenue. He estimated that closing Edmund Johnson's club cost "Harlem families $7,967 a year" and the federal government $205 in taxes.[26] Tobias's emphasis on economics reveals divisions among middle-class African Americans of how best to promote the community's economic and political advancement. While Frederick Moore and others supported the politics of respectability, Tobias focused on economic self-sufficiency. Not only did these businesses bring needed revenues but African Americans were more likely to hire their own, which kept that money circulating in the community.

A final factor that limited the Committee of Fourteen's ability to police prostitution in the African American community emerged when national race leaders accused the committee of promoting racial segregation in New York City. In 1911, W. E. B. Du Bois, editor of the NAACP's journal *Crisis*, directly challenged the committee's right to interfere in African American affairs when it attempted to close a black-owned club called the Marshall in midtown Manhattan. Located on Fifty-Third Street, just north of Hell's Kitchen, the Marshall catered to a racially mixed crowd of artists and intellectuals. As Roi Ottley writes in *The Negro in New York*, the Marshall "became famous as the headquarters of Negro talent."[27] Ottley acknowledged the interracial nature of the club, explaining that whites went "slumming" at the Marshall, but that most who did worked as actors in blackface and patronized the club to "secure firsthand imitations."[28] Du Bois may have had no problem with the committee's initial mission to stamp out prostitution, but policing interracial sociability set off alarms for him. Concerned about the growing racial segregation of New York City (and the possibility that southern-style de jure segregation might establish itself in the North), Du Bois protested the committee's attempts to close the Marshall, arguing that it was "about the only place where a colored man downtown can be decently accommodated."[29] In Du Bois's view, when the committee attacked the Marshall, it engaged not in sexual policing but in the inscribing of racial segregation onto the geographical map of New York City. Closing down the Marshall would have made it difficult for African American men to do business in midtown, pushing them even further to the margins of the city's economic and political life.

Du Bois's protest put the Committee of Fourteen on notice that policing interracial sociability could alienate the allies it had cultivated in the African American community and create a backlash against their broader agenda of ridding the city of prostitution. As later articles in the *New York Age* suggest, the paper, and the community as a whole, did not support the repression of interracial sociability and sexuality. Instead, the paper executed a complicated balancing act in which it condemned interracial sexuality at the same time that it opposed any law that would prohibit these relationships. In an article titled "Marriage of Whites and Blacks," the paper criticized antimiscegenation laws for restricting the legal rights of African Americans and challenged the very legitimacy of "race" as defined in America. "We do not need to favor the marriage of blacks and whites as a personal matter," the paper declared, "but we do need to stand by the principle that blacks and whites shall be free to marry if they so desire, without legal or sentimental restriction, as other races are free to do. It may be best and wisest for people to marry within their race lines, but what are the race lines of the Negro people and what legal statute can run a truthful division between the white and black lines?"[30] Appearing as it did amidst numerous articles about the alarming northward spread of segregation, this essay illustrates the complicated alliances that African American leaders sustained with each other and with northern white reformers as they tried to protect the limited freedoms of northern African Americans from white leaders' attempts to turn cities like New York into cities like Birmingham. After all, President Wilson segregated the nation's capital in 1912, and African Americans understandably panicked when they thought that legal segregation would continue its march into northern cities.

These complicated political analyses and alliances made the Committee of Fourteen's repression of prostitution among African Americans difficult. The diversity of political opinions among African Americans about strategies of "racial uplift" and their growing political power in the city made it impossible for the committee to run roughshod over the needs and desires of the community. More cautious in its dealings with the African American community after its encounter with Du Bois, the committee largely ignored black prostitution in the city until the 1920s, when Harlem became a center of vice for all races. As Kevin Mumford has argued, this lack of attention led to the concentration of vice in black neighborhoods. But the committee's decision to ignore black prostitution resulted not simply from racism but from an intricate series of negotiations that began in an argument over black-owned clubs and spiraled outward to include discussions about racial segregation, the civil rights of African Americans in a northern city during the era of segregation, and the differing strategies the African American middle class embraced as the most likely to improve the position of their community. Rather than bargaining from a position of weakness, as Mumford's argument implies, African American leaders had the impact they did precisely because they possessed enough political power to force the committee to rethink its policies around interracial sociability. But, of course, these complicated political negotiations also limited the sources on African American prostitution available to modern historians.

Despite the fact that historians have little evidence about African American prostitution in New York, there are clear reasons why African American women appeared so often in New York's reformatories. In part, their over-representation reflects the sampling bias of arrests and commitments for prostitution. The limited investigations that the Committee of Fifteen and the Committee of Fourteen conducted into black prostitution indicate that black women were most likely to be involved in casual, rather than orga-nized, prostitution. Unlike the data for the 1920s, there was no evidence that black women worked in brothels in this period. Instead, they worked the streets and tenements in their neighborhoods, which made them more visible to police and more vulnerable to arrest. Moreover, without the "pro-tection" bought by madams, they made easy targets.

The courts also sent more black women to Bedford because other, less restrictive institutions that housed "fallen women" refused to take them. Women newly engaged in prostitution and wayward minors might be sent to a variety of privately run denominational facilities for Protestants (Waverly House, St. Mary's, and Wayside Home), Catholics (House of the Good Shep-herd), or Jews (Cedar Knolls). However, these agencies all refused to take black women.[31] While individual white social workers in these organiza-tions may have felt sympathy for African American women, the trend in New York corrections at the turn of the century was toward segregation. When rioting broke out at Bedford reformatory, the board of governors attributed it to overcrowding and interracial lesbian relationships and seg-regated the facility. As historian Estelle Freedman has argued, white correc-tional authorities in this period saw African American women as the aggres-sors in interracial lesbian relationships.[32] As a state institution, Bedford had to take African American women, but the private denominational homes did not. They may have viewed their refusal to accommodate African Ameri-can women as a way to protect white women from what they saw as African American lesbian sexual predators.

Individuals in the black community attempted to provide alternatives, organizing shelters for delinquent girls, but neither the Empire House nor the Sojourner Truth House would take girls convicted of prostitution. Like many similar white institutions, these homes chose not to waste their re-sources on prostitutes, whom they doubted could be redeemed. Young women who got pregnant out of wedlock may have violated the bourgeois tenets of the politics of respectability, but in the eyes of middle-class Afri-can American reformers, they were still salvageable. More importantly, with capacities of sixteen and fifty beds, respectively, these "homes" simply did not have the space to help more than a tiny percentage of the women and girls who passed through the system.[33] In the face of these appallingly inadequate facilities for black women, the courts had the choice of giving women unsupervised probation or sentencing them to Bedford.[34] Since most white Americans at this time viewed black women as inherently less moral than their white counterparts, it seems unlikely that the magistrates would send black women out into the community when they could as easily incarcerate them. Although black women may have prostituted more than white women because of the discrimination they faced in other kinds of employment, it is unlikely that they were as overrepresented in the trade as these statistics suggest.[35]

What is most interesting about black prostitution in this period, though, is that as the brothels gave way to less organized practices, white prostitution began to look more and more like black prostitution. If at the turn of the century black prostitutes worked mostly out of tenements and bars, by 1910 most of their white sisters had followed suit. While this resulted largely from racially neutral factors like the disintegration of the brothels, it does seem that the discrimination against black women in brothels may actually have provided them with more social and economic freedom. Independent prostitution offered more profits than brothel prostitution, and black women may have benefited earlier from the financial benefits that came from these changes. However, vice societies' failure to pay attention to African American prostitution in this period makes it very difficult to assess the conditions and characteristics of African American participation in the sex trade.

The Lessons Learned in the Brothels

Throughout most of the nineteenth century, brothels dominated the practice of prostitution in New York City. As historian Timothy Gilfoyle has argued, brothels were embedded in a larger world of commercial entertainment. According to Gilfoyle, brothels thrived in the entertainment districts scattered across the city and maintained symbiotic relationships with theaters and other establishments that either tolerated or openly encouraged prostitution. Theaters, for example, honored traditions such as reserving the third tier for prostitutes and their clients; some even went so far as to build catwalks between their third floors and the brothels next door.[36] As the factory system spread, however, landlords found it increasingly profitable to rent to industry rather than to brothel owners. Shifting land-use patterns and the changing economic base of the city led to the decline of entertainment districts. As these areas waned, the brothels themselves began to falter.[37] Taking Gilfoyle's discussion as a starting point, the question must be raised, how did women respond to these changes? I argue that as the brothels declined, women used their experiences in them to restructure prostitution in New York City.

Existing as they did in a web of entertainment venues, brothels of the nineteenth century shaped the sex trade in a variety of important ways. The high concentration of brothels in entertainment districts tended to limit prostitution to specific geographical areas, leaving others relatively free of commercial sex. As discrete spaces in themselves, usually apartments or buildings, brothels physically contained prostitution and established the basic rules by which it would be practiced. These patterns of geography and space shifted rapidly between 1907 and 1917 as prostitution became both more casual and more diffuse.

Evaluating the significance of the decline of brothel prostitution rests quite literally on the perspective or, more specifically, the eye of the beholder. Middle-class reformers applauded the disappearance of brothels and red-light districts because they believed this erased a visible stain of sin from both their city and its government. They saw the elimination of the brothels as a moral victory, one that indicated the superior moral convictions of the citizenry. It also cleared the way for middle-class white women to enjoy the benefits of city living. Middle-class matrons on their way to shop on New York's miracle mile no longer passed entertainment districts populated by "disorderly" women. Vice crusades literally reclaimed public space in the city for white middle-class women, whose own respectability could be tainted if they visited areas in the city where prostitutes plied their trade.

At the same time, the brothels' disappearance ensured that prostitution would become more visible to working-class New Yorkers. Prostitution did not go away simply because the brothels ceased to exist. Instead, prostitution scattered, spreading quickly through small-scale working-class commercial and residential spaces. Seen from a working-class perspective, prostitution became even more visible in early twentieth-century New York precisely because it disappeared from the view of the middle class. Abandoning the brothels, prostitutes enmeshed themselves tightly into the fabric of working-class life. Now they became an integral part of the community, visible to residents and business people, to adults and children, in essence to all of their neighbors.

In addition to these shifts in the visibility of prostitution, the new business practices in which prostitutes engaged originated in their earlier experiences in the brothels. Women saw both benefits and drawbacks to brothel prostitution. From their perspective, brothels financially exploited prostitutes but also provided protection from violence and police harassment. Financially, women could make good money in brothels, but they rarely were able to keep most of what they made. Most brothels required women to turn over cash in exchange for a paper or metal chit. At the end of the week, madams totaled the number of chits and calculated women's earnings.[38] This system kept women entirely within a credit economy, a practice that was not uncommon for American workers at the turn of the century, and performed the same function in brothels, ensuring women's dependence on the madam and furthering their economic exploitation.[39]

In addition, madams took half of the money from every trick and overcharged women for essentials like food, rent, clothing, and medical expenses. As one investigator described, "two dollars house. All night price is $20. Girls pay $15 for board and half of what they earn besides. . . . Must purchase clothes of Madame . . . [and] are always in debt."[40] Or, as the Immigration Commission's report stated, women were charged "exorbitant rates" and "readily kept in debt."[41] Trapped in an exploitative credit system, prostitutes had little access to cash. This, in turn, made it difficult for them to save money and limited their ability to move up the career ladder to become madams.[42] While brothel prostitution offered excellent pay and a model for independent female entrepreneurship, it was also structured to remove financial resources from the hands of prostitutes. It was a rare prostitute who accumulated the capital to set up and run a house of her own.[43]

However, brothels also had their benefits. Most important, they provided a sheltered space in which prostitutes could ply their trade. As discrete and private spaces, brothels protected prostitutes from both johns and police in a variety of ways. One investigator for the Committee of Fourteen commented that the women he met had only "been 'on the town' a short time" and as a result were not "bold enough for street work."[44] Brothels concentrated prostitution in one building, shielding women from the exposure of streetwalking, which often drew the attention of police. In addition, brothels usually provided security in the form of bouncers who would eject disorderly clients. Finally, brothels paid bribes to the police to stave off raids. As one investigator described, "this place has strong police protection. One girl asked our investigator to call. He replied 'Thursday.' She said 'No, on Friday, we are to be raided Thursday night.'"[45] And, as in this case, when police protection failed, as it sometimes did during election campaigns or political scandals, madams "went bail" for the women and worked hard to keep them out of jail.[46]

Brothels proved to be a balance between coercion and exploitation, on the one hand, and relative safety and profits, on the other. In essence, brothels provided important patterns, both positive and negative, for women to emulate. The examples of independent female entrepreneurship must be weighed against more unpleasant experiences, such as financial exploitation and coercion. When the brothels declined, the women who staffed them took the lessons they learned in them when shaping new forms of prostitution in the city. Women consistently attempted to replicate the aspects of brothel prostitution they liked—such as its relative safety—while reducing those traits they disliked—such as financial exploitation.

Had the brothels not faltered, prostitutes might never have gained the opportunity to have a voice in the structure of prostitution. In the early twentieth century, a variety of pressures smothered brothels, making them far less viable institutions than they had been at their height in the nineteenth century. As Timothy Gilfoyle persuasively argues, changing land values and land-use patterns dissuaded many landlords from renting to brothels. But this alone would not have given prostitutes an opportunity to restructure the way they practiced their trade. Other similarly exploitative systems might have filled the void left by the brothels' demise. However, simultaneous with New York's rental market shift to make room for light industry, the state legislature also passed a law regarding liquor sales that inadvertently created a new social, economic, and physical space for prostitution. Raines Law hotels took the brothels' place as the primary site of sexual exchange in the city. These new "hotels" gave women an excellent bargaining position and allowed them a significant say in how prostitution was practiced.

Prostitutes and Prostitution in the Raines Law Hotels

In 1896, the New York State legislature passed a temperance law that proved crucial in scattering prostitution throughout New York City's working-class neighborhoods. Originally intended to discourage drinking on the Sabbath, the Raines Law required an annual fee for saloon licenses, forbade any establishment except hotels to sell liquor on Sundays, and required that all hotels have at least ten beds.[47] The unintended consequences of the Raines Law proved worse than the original problem. In response to its passage, most saloon keepers, rather than close on Sundays, partitioned their back rooms, put in ten beds, and began renting them out by the trick to prostitutes and their customers.

The Raines Law not only failed to discourage drinking on the Christian Sabbath, it also had a profound impact on a number of aspects of New York City's working-class commercial and sexual culture. First, the hotels' loose structure gave prostitutes the ability to abandon the brothels and become independent proprietors. Selling sex out of these saloons, prostitutes kept an unprecedented amount of their wages and began to establish themselves as active participants in the new and decentralized economy of pleasure, vice, and entertainment. In addition, the alliances between prostitutes and proprietors fundamentally changed the conditions under which women sold, and men bought, sex. Functioning primarily in neighborhood bars and gathering places, they shattered the well-organized "sex industry," haphazardly replacing it with a more local and small-scale economy. Because they drew from the neighborhood, Raines Law hotels reflected the racial segregation of the city's housing stock, and African Americans and whites rarely mixed. Only in neighborhoods like Hell's Kitchen, where working-class African Americans and whites lived side by side, did the hotels cater to an interracial clientele. Finally, located primarily in tenement basement bars and saloons, the new "hotels" permeated working-class residential neighborhoods and housing stock. This led to a rapid expansion in the practice of prostitution throughout working-class commercial, social, and living spaces.[48]

Raines Law hotels sprang up all over the city after the passage of the new excise law, and their presence had a profound impact on prostitution in the city. Like saloon owners, prostitutes quickly realized the implications of the law. Using their experience in brothel prostitution, they struck bargains with owners over the terms and conditions by which they would use these new social and entertainment spaces. In 1900, these "hotels" already made up a significant proportion of the places in which prostitution was practiced, and by 1907, they dominated the trade.[49] When the congressional commission into "white slavery" held its hearings on conditions in New York City in 1910, the policemen interviewed stated that Raines Law hotels were "about the only thing that is running today."[50]

Ironically, the brothels themselves contributed to the success of the Raines Law hotels by maintaining networks of casual prostitutes who helped madams cope with periodic surges in demand. At the turn of the century, many brothels used casual or independent prostitutes to deal with the overflow that occurred on days of heavy demand, a practice madams called "sitting company." As one investigator described, "there are 5 girls who sit in company Saturday and Sunday nights, thus helping out on the busy nights."[51] Girls who sat company invariably had other jobs and used prostitution to supplement their wages. In one brothel, for example, the girls who sat company were "usually employed in stores and offices where their wages will not support them." Another investigator commented that the girls were "otherwise employed in department stores." "They do not reside in the house," he continued, "but come in these engaged evenings, and in police protected houses such as this are safe."[52]

Thus, the brothels themselves, because they experienced periodic and predictable overflows of patrons, supported more casual forms of prostitution. Although the system certainly worked in the madams' best interest, this reliance on a workforce outside of their control eventually helped establish a market for prostitutes who worked independently within the brothel system. As the pressure on the brothels increased, and as they became less profitable for their owners, more and more women moved into other forms of prostitution that gave them more freedom.

Given the opportunity to set some of the terms of how they would work, prostitutes wanted to preserve the relative safety of brothels at the same time that they tried to do away with financial exploitation. The inexperience of most saloon owners in managing prostitutes and their concentration on other kinds of businesses gave prostitutes an excellent bargaining position. Most proprietors initially sold alcohol and, as a result of the passage of the Raines Law, became involved in prostitution as a profitable sideline activity. They negotiated with prostitutes as one small proprietor to another, crafting equitable arrangements for the splitting of profits.

The agreements prostitutes reached with proprietors tended to follow similar patters and significantly increased the prostitutes' revenues. Prostitutes working out of Raines Law hotels kept all of the money they made from their tricks. In addition, they usually received a cut of the proprietor's take on bed rents. In one typical description, the investigator reported that "the prostitutes consist of girls having the privilege of regular soliciting places, and streetwalkers. There are no residents. They only use the rooms. . . . The woman . . . get[s] a percentage of the $2. paid for the room. They also receive a percentage for the amount of drinks which the man is induced to buy."[53] This description explains why some bar owners eagerly allowed prostitutes into their establishments. Instead of viewing prostitutes simply as independent entrepreneurs, many proprietors realized that prostitutes could function as active partners in increasing liquor sales. Getting men to buy drinks became one of the prostitutes' important duties, and most owners rewarded this by sharing some of the profits. As one investigator reported of the Churchill Hotel near Times Square, "rates $1 and up . . . girls get commission on drinks."[54]

These arrangements made sense for bar owners who, after all, began by selling liquor and then expanded to providing space for prostitution because of the opportunity presented by the Raines Law. Their cooperation made prostitution from the hotels even more profitable for prostitutes, which decreased the desirability of brothel prostitution even further. Understandably, prostitutes working out of Raines Law hotels reaped impressive profits. One investigator reported of the San Souci that "the women in this place consider $30. a fair night's work and say that they average from five to ten men every evening."[55] At a time when working women's salaries in New York State averaged a little over six dollars week, prostitutes in the hotels made far more money than they ever could in any kind of legitimate employment.[56] They also kept far more than any brothel prostitute would see of her earnings. This represented a profound shift in their status. Prostitutes in the new hotels exchanged their position as a dependent workforce excluded from the cash economy for partnerships with other independent proprietors that benefited both parties.

In addition to profitability, Raines Law hotels offered the same kind of protection to prostitutes that brothels did. As sheltered and busy spaces, Raines Law hotels afforded some protection from violent johns and police harassment. Prostitutes often chose the hotels because they were afraid, at least initially, to work without any protection. A decade or two earlier, these women might have sought out brothels; now they found shelter and profits within these newly available commercial spaces. In a hotel on East Twenty-Third Street, an investigator stated that the four women working there "rarely go out on the street, but solicit in back room," and later he added that the "rear room of saloon [is an] open soliciting place." Referring to another hotel that protected streetwalkers from police harassment, an outraged neighbor wrote, "I have seen women permitted to take refuge in the hotel when chased by plain-clothes men."[57] Undoubtedly, many of these women had arrangements with the hotels' proprietors. George Kneeland, in his study of conditions in New York in 1912, argued that many women working the Raines Law hotels solicited on the street and then brought their patrons first to the bars and then later to the rooms.[58] It is also possible that the hotels protected even those who did not have formal arrangements. After all, it made good business sense to shelter fleeing prostitutes who might later decide to rent rooms.

Prostitutes and Raines Law hotel proprietors made bail arrangements that further reduced prostitutes' risks. One investigator summed up the standard agreement concisely when he commented that the "proprietor goes bail for the girls."[59] Thus, regardless of raids, prostitutes had an ally outside of the criminal justice system who would provide bail if they were arrested. In the congressional investigation into "white slavery" in 1910, a police officer testified that in addition to furnishing bond, proprietors "who had influence with the courts, have not merely furnished bail, but have gone further and used their influence perhaps to have light sentence imposed at times on girls whose money went to them in part."[60] Finally, most proprietors took a lesson from madams and paid off the police.[61]

The shifting nature of prostitution in the Raines Law hotels did not protect prostitutes from all exploitation, and there is evidence that some women relied on pimps. Pimps had been a part of the brothel system, though sources are contradictory about how widespread pimping was, either in brothel prostitution or during the Raines Law hotel period. Contemporary authors like George Kneeland and Maude Miner describe widespread pimping in their analysis of prostitution in New York at the turn of the century.[62] Miner worked for years as the first female probation officer assigned to the Women's Court, where she counseled women and intervened on their behalf with magistrates over sentencing recommendations. Although she had extensive experience in the court system, she also embraced an analysis of prostitution that makes it difficult to evaluate her statements about the pervasiveness of pimping. In her 1916 publication *The Slavery of Prostitution*, Miner argued that prostitution resulted from depraved male desires to exploit innocent women.[63] In one case, she even excoriated a father whose strictness, she argued, drove his daughter first from his home and then into prostitution. In Miner's view, prostitution resulted from men's greed, lust, and cruelty, and her analysis of prostitution in general, and of pimping in particular, must be seen in this context.

Evidence from undercover investigators' field reports calls into question the high levels of pimping alleged by the published sources. Pimps rarely, if ever, make an appearance in the field reports of the Committee of Fifteen or the Committee of Fourteen in this period. Evidence in the Lillian Wald Papers, which contain both undercover investigations and interviews with prostitutes, suggests that many women "supported men," but the authors of these studies also consistently describe the women in Raines Law hotels as "independent" workers.[64] The interviews with prostitutes themselves make no reference to pimping, though they provide a wealth of other data, such as why the women entered the trade and where and how they practiced it.

Finally, the thirty-two years of field reports written by the Committee of Fourteen investigators indicate that pimping had a low profile in the period between 1900 and 1917. This conclusion comes in part from contrasting the reports from this period with those of the war years and the 1920s and 1930s, when pimps played an increasingly important role in the managing of the trade. If pimping was as widespread in the years between 1900 and 1917 as it was in the years following, why do the earlier reports (often written by the same investigators) contain so few references to it?[65] Why the sudden, startling, and often dismaying surge of reports that contained descriptions of pimping in the 1920s? The evidence on pimping is contradictory and difficult to interpret. Obviously, it existed, but the degree to which it dominated the trade or the lives of the women remains unclear. While pimping may have existed before the war, it was neither as extensive nor as exploitative as what would follow.[66]

Even if some women supported pimps, prostitutes working from Raines Law hotels displayed an assertiveness and self-confidence that could be startling. At times expressing pride in their work and their identities as prostitutes, they sound more like savvy business people than downtrodden social outcasts. One woman testifying in court found the prosecutor's questions particularly annoying. When he asked, "Why did he give you money?" she replied with some irritation, "I told you I was a prostitute, [he gave me money] because I went with him and he paid me for my work that I done."[67] This woman had embraced her identity as a prostitute and expected others to understand that and to respect it. In another case, conversation between two women in a bar reflected the pride that at least one of the women felt in her identity as a prostitute. According to a witness, one woman, when called a whore by another, retorted, "I am a whore, a regular whore, I am proud of it." The first woman answered sheepishly, "I am a whore myself, but only a half-assed whore."[68] The artist John Sloan captured the essence of this professional pride in his lithograph "Sixth Avenue and Thirtieth Street" (Figure 3.1). According to the art historian Robert Snyder, the image portrays a prostitute walking proudly down the street in a busy working-class neighborhood.[69] Dressed fashionably and pulling on a glove, she walks with her head held high and a steady gaze. She displays a proud, almost haughty demeanor. Other women on the street turn to look at her as she walks past, but their gazes do not reflect hostility. Two girls on the left-hand side of the frame glance at her furtively as they talk, perhaps speculating on her profession.

As independent agents for their own and others' businesses, prostitutes worked very hard with saloon owners to make these establishments flourish. Both tried to draw and keep customers, and in so doing, they transformed local bars into more extensive commercial spaces that provided a wide range of services. As part of an expanding, local, working-class economy of pleasure and entertainment, Raines Law hotels catered mostly to local men and had a stake in keeping their regular customers happy. Just how important that could be became obvious in a court transcript from the trial of a Raines Law hotel proprietor in Brooklyn. In one of the few surviving descriptions of the atmosphere of these establishments, the investigator chronicled what

FIGURE 3.1. *John Sloan, "Sixth Avenue and Thirtieth Street," lithograph, 1908.*
(National Museum of American Art, Smithsonian Institution)

he witnessed while sitting in the bar of the hotel. The testimony shows the remarkable extent to which prostitution permeated working-class bar sociability and the ways in which prostitutes and the proprietor collaborated to give local men pleasure and entertainment at a profit. As the investigator reported:

> Deponent observed automatic piano playing in adjoining room, to the music of which two men and two women were dancing in a manner suggestive of sexual intercourse. . . . Deponent said to the said Jim Proprietor, while the dance was going "That is some dance." The said Jim Proprietor replied "Yes." Deponent also saw an intoxicated man accompanied by a woman on said premises moving to a stairway which led to upper floors. The said Jim Proprietor called out "Hey, Sam, get a room ready." In a short time the unknown woman returned to the room where the deponent sat, her hair disheveled, and said to the said Jim Proprietor "I had a hell of a time with him, no more drunken men for me." . . . The unknown man then said to the said Jim Proprietor who was present "Hey, Jim, how about it, I haven't got the price of a room." The said Jim Proprietor said "Give her a standup —— in the corner," indicating a part of the said enclosure.

This testimony evokes the casual, neighborhood feel of these hotels. Prostitutes danced and joked with their clients, and they used the time to sexually arouse the men. This stands in sharp contrast to working-class brothel practices in which madams severely limited contact between prostitutes and johns, usually allotting them five to ten minutes for sexual intercourse.[70] In this bar, sexual intercourse did not appear to take much more time than that, but the prostitutes had extended social contact with the johns before they went to their rooms.

This scene also indicates the extent to which proprietors made business decisions that, while cutting into their profit margin, helped the neighborhood patrons and prostitutes. In this case, the proprietor waived his room rents and allowed a customer to have a "standup." Obviously, the proprietor made enough money from the drinks he sold and from other patrons renting rooms that he could afford to allow a steady customer a break now and then. Choosing to forgo the bed rent, this proprietor made his customer feel more like a friend, increasing the possibility that he would continue to patronize this bar and spend his money there. In addition, waiving the bed rent pleased the prostitute because it ensured that she could make her fee, even if it meant standing up in the hallway to earn it. Ultimately, Jim's decision made economic sense, because for him prostitution brought in more money through drink sales than it did through bed rents. However, the "standup" was not simply about economics. It also revealed the ways in which prostitutes and proprietors relied on each other. It was their alliances and perhaps their friendships that made these bars the kind of social space they were. The prostitute who serviced the drunken man expressed this best when she came down and complained to Jim about how much she disliked her last trick. Disheveled, tired, and probably annoyed, she treated Jim like a sympathetic confidant who would listen to a friend fed up with the more upsetting aspects of her job.

The investigator's testimony about events later on in the same evening reinforces the picture of these "hotels" as places where prostitutes and proprietors joined to make money and keep patrons happy. Continuing his story, the investigator stated:

> About this time deponent observed an unknown man who appeared to be a deaf and dumb mute seated at a table with an unknown woman; the said unknown mute was making motions with his hands to the said unknown woman, whereupon Joseph F. Christie said to the said Jim Proprietor "the deaf and dumb mute is having a tough time over there making her understand him." The said Jim Proprietor then called out in a loud voice to an unknown woman "Florence, go over there and help May get him." . . . About this time deponent observed an unknown woman seated at a table who called out in a loud voice "Here is the way you say F——," at the same time indicating the deaf and dumb language with her fingers. Shortly thereafter deponent heard the said Joseph F. Christie say to the said Jim Proprietor "Where did the dummie and the woman go?" and heard the said Jim Proprietor say to the said Joseph Christie "Oh, she got him, they went upstairs; that damn fool is a married man and lives around the corner." [71]

Jim and the prostitutes working out of his bar knew their regular clients well and worked together to meet their needs and turn a profit. Jim knew the deaf man and his family. A frequent patron of the bar, the deaf man obviously had come there for sex before. One of the prostitutes had picked up sufficient American Sign Language slang to communicate the basic information necessary for a prostitute to do her business.[72] Perhaps she had had him as a client in the past, or perhaps she simply learned ASL from previous contacts with him in the neighborhood. Most important, she and Jim cooperated with each other and with the other prostitute to "get him" as a client for the bar.

As this anecdote indicates, Raines Law hotels provided a relatively safe and profitable space for prostitutes to conduct their business. In addition, they also functioned as strong institutions of sociability for neighborhood men. Drinking, dancing, and sex all came together under the same roof, and men could use the space to engage in heterosocial and heterosexual relationships and camaraderie. It is this aspect of the hotels that helped change the place of prostitution in working-class neighborhoods. Ultimately, Raines Law hotels led the way for prostitution's inclusion in working-class sociability, commercial relations, and neighborhoods.

Prostitutes and Working-Class Life

The Raines Law hotels rapidly transformed the practice of prostitution in the city as well as the places and manner in which prostitution functioned in working-class communities. Offering an opportunity for independence for prostitutes and more profits for saloon owners, these hotels created a small-scale market in prostitution that diffused throughout the neighborhoods of the city. As a result, prostitution shifted both in location and in character, leaving the elaborate entertainment districts of the nineteenth-century city and entering the bars, saloons, dance halls, candy stores, cigar stores, and soda shops of New York's working-class neighborhoods. Always used in a multiplicity of ways, New York City's tenements became the primary sites of sexual commerce, and prostitution became more, and not less, visible to the working class.[73]

Raines Law hotels opened up opportunities for other establishments to cater to prostitutes and their clients. As women increasingly chose to work in more casual, less supervised, and less coercive or exploitative conditions, prostitution diffused rapidly through the social and commercial space of working-class New York neighborhoods. Candy stores and cigar stores, for example, became important places where prostitutes made contact with men. Providing essential social space for working-class neighborhoods, these stores also proved to be ideal meeting places for prostitutes and their johns. The owners of these establishments, hoping for profits, readily consented to this trade.

As early as 1901, cigar stores in tenements functioned as sites for small-scale prostitution. The New York Society for the Prevention of Cruelty to Children complained that Rose Stella ran a disorderly resort "carried under the guise of a cigar store." Arguing that the daughter of this woman "was exposed to the bad influences of these surroundings," they cooperated "in efforts to bring the offender to justice, and rescue the child from her degrading environment."[74] In another incident, an investigator reported that a particular store had "many girls in the back. The woman who attends to the store told me to call some other time, the girls have customers at present."[75]

As part of a series of reports on disorderly tenements, the evidence of prostitution in these stores shows how they were integrated into other respectable neighborhood institutions. Even more than Raines Law hotels, these stores catered to a very local clientele. Few outsiders even knew how diversified these businesses had become. The annual report of the Committee of Fourteen for 1913 reflected the integration of prostitution into the commercial and housing stock of working-class neighborhoods.[76] Beneath a photograph of an ordinary-looking building containing a cigar and stationery store as well as a tailor shop, the caption identifies the building as "a tenement occupied by disorderly women" and cites the date of convictions of prostitutes who presumably had operated out of it (Figure 3.2).

Some soda fountains and candy stores also allowed casual prostitution, usually along similar lines to the agreements between prostitutes and Raines Law hotel proprietors. In one store, for example, they "sometimes charge 25 cents for soda and gradually make it known what their business is. $2 is the rate for the steady girls. . . . The girls who are steady here use the back room for immoral purposes."[77] Another description indicated similarities to Raines Law hotels, stating that "$2 the rate for [a] girl, and girls get a percentage on candy, etc., sold."[78] Just as prostitutes in bars often got a cut of the alcohol they sold, women working out of candy stores sometimes shared the profits of sales with proprietors when they increased business or helped boys and men spend their money. As in Raines Law hotels, prostitution in candy and cigar stores functioned within commercial frameworks.

The ultimate integration of prostitution into working-class communities occurred when women prostituted in the city's tenements. Prostitution had always existed in the housing stock of poor New Yorkers, but it became even more prevalent after the demise of the brothel in the early years of the twentieth century. The city acknowledged the growing problem in 1901 when it introduced laws prohibiting solicitation and prostitution in the tenements.[79] Until that time, the laws governing prostitution had involved streetwalking or the keeping of a disorderly house. The new laws did little to suppress the trade, and the Committee of Fourteen consistently complained that the Tenement House Commission failed to enforce the law, allowing prostitution to flourish in housing spaces in poor and immigrant neighborhoods. Prostitution in the tenements forced working-class New Yorkers to confront the activity on a daily basis. John Sloan's 1909 painting "Three A.M." represents the way many prostitutes' lives looked as seen through the windows of crowded tenements, a view common in working-class neighborhoods (Figure 3.3). The painting shows two women in a small tenement kitchen, smoking, cooking, and drinking tea as they chat in the early hours of

FIGURE 3.2. *"A Tenement Occupied by Disorderly Women,"*
photograph in Committee of Fourteen, Annual Report, 1913.

FIGURE 3.3. *John Sloan, "Three A.M.," oil on canvas, 1909.*
(Philadelphia Museum of Art: Gift of Mrs. Cyrus McCormick, 1946)

the morning. According to art historians Rebecca Zurier and Robert Snyder, "Sloan based this painting on a household he observed through his studio window while working late at night." The close quarters of working-class housing, with tenements pressed up against each other and with windows and fire escapes opening onto buildings only a few feet away, made the visibility of these scenes inevitable and ensured that working-class neighbors had intimate knowledge of each other's domestic arrangements.[80] This proximity and the community's response to it served to highlight the differences between working-class and middle-class attitudes about prostitution.

Examples of tenement prostitution suggest the multiple uses to which these buildings could be put. Investigators reported mixtures of business, vice, and family apartments. One investigator for the Committee of Fifteen described "2 story, butcher store; 2 families upstairs; no children; 2 girls at door soliciting," and "4 story and store, saloon; 22 families, 26 children. Prostitutes in lower hall soliciting man. In back room of saloon white and colored men getting policy slip from party writing same."[81] The Committee of Fourteen decried the spread of prostitution into the tenements in its annual reports from 1912, 1913, and 1914. In 1914, it wrote that "the greatest existing evils at the present time are prostitution in tenement houses and apartments."[82] In the same report, it noted that tenement prostitution arrests had doubled from the previous year.[83] Court records provide similar evidence. Not only do many cases involve prostitution in the tenements, but they also explain some of the reasons for this development, namely the profits for small landlords. In one disorderly house case, a witness reported that the defendant "said that she could make all the money she could, and she wouldn't rent no room to no decent people."[84] Similarly, in *Jews without Money*, Michael Gold's autobiographical account of his childhood on the Lower East Side, he described an argument between his mother and their landlord. When Gold's mother asked the landlord to evict the prostitutes in their building, he refused: "'Yes,' he said, stroking his bushy beard, 'those girls are whores. But they pay three times the rent you do, and they pay promptly. So if you want to move out, please do so. A black year on it, but a landlord must live.'"[85]

Many of the women who worked out of these crowded tenements seemed unconcerned about being identified as prostitutes by their neighbors. Women soliciting in tenements did so from the side doors and main entrances of tenements, from their windows, and in the streets in front. Michael Gold wrote that "on sunshiny days the whores sat on chairs along the sidewalks. They sprawled indolently, their legs taking up half the pavements. . . . The girls winked and jeered, made lascivious gestures at passing males. . . . They called their wares like pushcart peddlers."[86] In a disorderly house case, a witness complained that the prostitutes "make their bargains . . . right under our window . . . and my wife got out of bed, and opened the window, and told them to get out or she would throw water over them."[87] Investigators for the Committee of Fifteen and later the Committee of Fourteen found similar conditions. In one report, an investigator passed a house and "heard a buzzing noise from the window." He looked up and saw two women who "whistled for me and beckoned with their fingurs [*sic*] to come up."[88] Hanging out their window, motioning to men passing by,

FIGURE 3.4. *"Woman (Alleged Prostitute) Talking to Two Men on the Street,"*
photograph in Committee of Fourteen, Annual Report, 1913.

these women could hardly be called discreet prostitutes. A photograph published by the Committee of Fourteen in its annual report for 1913 reflects the
visibility of prostitution in working-class neighborhoods (Figure 3.4). In it,
two ordinary-looking men chat with an attractive woman on the street. Concerned that the reader might misinterpret this interaction as innocent, the
author carefully notes that "the man's hat is off not to be polite, but because
the day is hot."[89] For the middle-class and elite readership of the committee's reports, a gentleman removing his hat denoted respect for the woman,
a totally inappropriate action if the woman was a prostitute. It is possible
that the day was hot, and it is also possible that the man knew the woman

was a prostitute but still gave her the courtesy of removing his hat when he spoke to her. The prostitute in the photograph looks over his shoulder and smiles happily for the camera.

The relative visibility and openness of this sort of prostitution does not mean that these women were indifferent to their neighborhoods or to the people with whom they lived and worked. In fact, prostitutes often functioned as integral parts of the community, relying, as other women did, on networks of friendship to sustain them. One investigator, for example, reported with some distaste that "the disord. [sic] women have a new scheme to hide themselves from the police. . . . As soon as they move in a house they get acquainted with their neighbors and generally every tenant has children. Finally they take in a child to play with. If a stranger comes in and they don't want to be known as disorder. women they have the child on the arm and the stranger thinks that she is a good woman. . . . if one of their friends comes they give the child back to the parents."[90] This strategy implied a high level of acceptance among the neighboring families and integration into support networks. Not only did these families not report prostitutes to police, they actively participated in protecting them. In addition, they did not seem to worry about the detrimental effects that prostitution might have on their children. Lending their children to prostitutes for the afternoon, these neighboring women enjoyed a welcome relief from some of their domestic responsibilities.

Some prostitutes seemed to crave these relationships and worked hard at being good neighbors. Gold described the prostitutes in his neighborhood as "crazy about children, . . . [they] petted us and gave us nickels." "They thought it a privilege to visit my mother," he wrote, "and to drink tea in a decent home."[91] Emma Goldman also describes prostitutes as excellent neighbors, desperate for positive attention. After she moved into a furnished room house that she only then discovered was occupied mostly by prostitutes, she reported that "they competed with one another in being kind to me, in giving me their sewing to do and helping in little ways."[92]

Most working-class neighbors felt ambivalent about prostitution. On the one hand, they disliked the disruptive effects of prostitution, but on the other, they also exhibited far more compassion for prostitutes than middle-class people did. Analyzing letters to the mayor, Rachel Bernstein has argued that working-class criticism of prostitutes tended to be very practical. Neighbors complained about the noise or the general disorderliness and drunkenness that accompanied prostitution.[93] In court records, a women testified that she had "been annoyed continually by men calling, and saying, 'Is the girls upstairs?'"[94] Bernstein found that working-class women complained about the loss of money when a husband or son squandered his wages (and thus family income). However, she argues that these women did not blame the prostitutes but the men. Prostitutes provided a temptation to men, but the men themselves were responsible for succumbing and spending their wages.

Working-class attitudes about prostitution also came from their understanding of what caused the practice, and here they differed significantly from the middle class. Middle-class reformers in this period proffered a number of competing analyses of prostitution, but in general they believed that it had a corrosive effect on innocent children and represented the disintegration of family and morality. Robert W. de Forest provides a typical example of this attitude in an article he wrote for the journal *Charities and the Commons* in 1903. He argued that the city should clean up the tenements because "the working man on the East Side, whose family must live in the tenements, and whose children are subjected to surroundings and temptations which he cannot avoid by his own action, as can the resident of Fifth Avenue, cannot take care of himself, and justly claims protection from this contamination."[95]

Working-class patriarchs might not agree with de Forest's description of their weakness, but they also had a different analysis of prostitution and its causes. In contrast to middle-class arguments that prostitution resulted from "moral" failings in the woman, working-class neighbors tended to see prostitution as a sign of a profound economic crisis within the family. Although prostitution resulting from desertion or widowhood might be seen as a symptom of family disintegration, it also served to support families in the face of economic disaster. To working-class people who witnessed prostitution and its causes in their own neighborhoods and, at times, among friends and family, prostitution reflected a desperate attempt to keep families together, not an "immoral" lifestyle that tore them apart. Many neighbors sympathized with women who prostituted to hold a family together and, if possible, lift it out of financial crisis. The spectacular wages that a prostitute could earn made the profession particularly attractive to women who had heavy family responsibilities. One investigator ran into just such a situation on Mott Street when a visibly pregnant woman solicited him and brought him to her apartment. The woman explained that her husband had gone out of the city to look for work and did not support her and her children, one of whom was asleep on the bed. According to the investigator, "she asked me for ten cents and said: 'Come in, I will give you a fuck for the luck of ten cents as you are a nice fellow.' . . . she threw herself on the bed beside the young boy and exposed her person to me for the purpose of prostitution."[96]

Working-class people expressed their more tolerant attitudes toward prostitution when they dealt with daughters committed to the reformatory for prostitution-related offenses. Although some families felt the shame of a prostitution conviction keenly, shunned their daughters, and lied about their whereabouts, others continued to support their daughters, writing letters that expressed their love and concern. One German American father addressed a letter to his daughter "Dear Little Trudy" and stated that "I was glad to get your letters as it would seem to me you have at last seen your mistake and if you stick to the right your past can do you no harm as we will all be glad to help you as I have always known it wasn't your nature to be bad. Keep up your courage Trudy. . . . You do not have to ask for our forgiveness as you have already one [sic] that. Be brave little girl and I will write often."[97] Obviously, this man disapproved of prostitution or he would not have described her actions as a "mistake." However, he also wanted her to know that she was not ruined by it and that he and the rest of her family still loved her and believed in her. She could overcome her mistake, and the family would support her while in the reformatory and welcome her back when she had served her term.

Husbands and fiancés sometimes tolerated prostitution when it allowed the family to gain important resources to sustain it. According to Bedford reformatory's report, white inmate Martha Hauer solicited men on the streets to help establish her fiancé in his trade. "She intended to save enough from her prostitution to buy them a home and start her husband in business for himself," the social worker reported. "She kept putting off getting married although 'Harry' had often urged her to take him to Brooklyn to meet her people and let him support her." While this young man clearly benefited from his fiancée's prostitution, he also urged her stop. He did not seem to have a strong moral objection to prostitution, although her subsequent commitment undoubtedly delayed their wedding.[98]

Working-class neighbors, although they did not approve of prostitution, often viewed prostitutes themselves with pity. Betty Smith describes this kind of compassion in her autobiographical novel *A Tree Grows in Brooklyn*. Walking one evening with her father, ten-year-old Francie watches as a woman solicits her father. Even at this young age, Francie knew a prostitute when she saw one and asked her father, "Was that a bad lady, Papa?" He gently replied "no," and explained that "There are very few bad people. There are just a lot of people that are unlucky."[99] Bad luck and financial instability, then, more than "immorality," caused prostitution in the working-class worldview. Michael Gold's mother also viewed prostitutes with pity, as he writes: "My mother disapproved of their life, and told them so with her usual frankness. But she was too kindhearted to keep them out."[100]

This financial analysis of prostitution prevented working-class families from seeing it as a threat to their children. Like their middle-class counterparts, working-class families had no desire to see their daughters grow up to be prostitutes. The overwhelming number of parents who brought girls before the children's court for incorrigibility indicates that working-class parents did not tolerate what they saw as sexual misbehavior.[101] However, many working-class families did not shun prostitutes, and as we have seen, some even allowed prostitutes to "borrow" their children, because they believed that prostitution resulted from a financial crisis and not from a contagious moral failing. While prostitutes may not have set the best example for young children, their mere presence did not directly threaten children's healthy moral development.

Some working-class neighbors believed that prostitutes actually protected children. As one man argued in court, "I think that such houses ought to be in existence, on account of [a] person's daughters walking in the streets wouldn't be able to walk the streets, if there weren't such places."[102] Middle-class men often made this argument about prostitution, using it to justify the continued existence of red-light districts that concentrated prostitution in certain (usually working-class) areas of the city. The men who usually made this argument did so precisely because they believed that the existence of districts protected their wives and children from witnessing prostitution. What makes this particular incident significant is that it came from a neighbor testifying about a disorderly house in his tenement. His children probably witnessed prostitution every day, but he still believed that prostitution protected his daughters because it functioned as a sexual safety valve for neighborhood men, who might otherwise prey on respectable womenfolk. In essence, he rejected the idea that prostitutes would set a bad example for daughters, instead arguing that prostitution protected them from assault.

Tenement prostitution exemplified the extensive diffusion of prostitution into working-class residential housing. Tenement prostitutes solicited openly and often used their earnings to support family members. Integrated into the communities in which they lived, these women sometimes worked as casual prostitutes, using prostitution to supplement other income. Their presence reflected the real differences between working-class and middle-class attitudes about prostitution. While working-class neighbors may not have approved of prostitution, they also understood why women resorted to it and the very real crises that pushed some women into this work. Neighbors saw prostitution as an attempt to save the family, and not a threat to it, and as a result responded with far more tolerance and acceptance than their middle-class counterparts exhibited.

Hidden Commerce: Prostitution in the Furnished Room Districts

Not all women wanted their activities known, however, and furnished room houses in residential neighborhoods provided the necessary anonymity for clandestine prostitution. The patterns of the women working out of these establishments diverged significantly from those of women who worked openly in neighborhood bars, candy stores, or tenements. Instead of making the most of their financial opportunities by openly soliciting as independent prostitutes, these women pursued a secretive path that allowed them to appear to adhere to working-class expectations of respectable women's behavior. Much like the treating girls discussed in the previous chapter, these women walked a fine line between profiting from sex and maintaining a tenuous but important sense of respectability. Taking advantage of the new legitimacy of women's employment, their visibility in public, and their new opportunities to live unsupervised in the city, furnished room prostitutes hid their activities from their neighbors and families in an attempt to benefit from prostitution without paying the price in reputation.

Scattered throughout working-class neighborhoods and comprising the majority of rental housing in some areas, furnished rooms provided accommodation for single men and women who lived and worked independent of their families. As in other cities, New York's economy relied on these workers, and the city needed a place to house them. Living independent of family reduced, though it did not eliminate, the close supervision of the social and sexual lives of young people.

Furnished room houses, although they often tolerated prostitution, did not evoke the same associations with vice that saloons and Raines Law hotels did. Far closer to rooming houses than to the infamous houses of assignation, furnished room houses facilitated the diffusion of prostitution into working-class living space without the concomitant loss of reputation for the women involved. Prostitution in these houses could be quite casual, and most of the female inhabitants pursued prostitution as a profitable side activity rather than a full-time job. In places like these, the diffusion of prostitution began to have its most profound social and sexual effects. If Raines Law hotels increased prostitution in neighborhood social and housing space, the furnished room houses made it possible for women to practice prostitution not just casually but secretly, while passing as respectable women in their neighborhoods.

Furnished rooms provided enormous profits for their owners at little risk, and landlords rarely concerned themselves with their tenants' business. When asked in court "Did you have any talk with Annie Brown?" an irritated landlady retorted, "What should I talk? I got fifty-two tenants, I should talk with every tenant?"[103] Like Michael Gold's landlord in *Jews without Money*, they tolerated prostitution in exchange for high rent. Landlords could make at least twice as much money renting to prostitutes as renting to families or single people. In a house on St. Mark's Place, one report said, "exorbitant rents are the only revenue of the landlady. Rooms rent from $6 to $15 per week."[104] The crucial factor in running such houses was allowing the young women to have "privileges," that is, the right to bring young men to their apartments.[105]

Landladies and young women often negotiated over just what would be tolerated in the rooming houses. In one encounter, a female undercover investigator asked directly, "Does that include privileges for receiving company?" The landlady answered reassuringly, and the following conversation ensued: "'Certainly—I suppose you're making a business of it?' 'What do you mean?' 'Receiving men callers and living on that.' 'Certainly we are.' 'I'm glad you told me this frankly. It's always better, for in some places you might get turned out.'"[106] In this case, the landlady was glad to know how the tenants planned to use their rooms. This information would help her anticipate problems with other tenants and possibly with the police. Perhaps more important, though, it meant she could comfortably justify charging her new tenants higher rents. Investigators asked another landlady similar questions, and she happily agreed to rent to girls who intended to "receive gentlemen callers," but warned her prospective tenants not to "let the other tenants know too much about you."[107]

Even without the landladies' warnings, most prostitutes working out of furnished rooms tried to keep their activities discreet. One investigator described the rather elaborate and secretive business arrangements of a group of prostitutes on Delancey Street. "[B]oth men and girls solicit on streets and men also in saloon and in eating houses," he reported. "The women go out with shawls on their heads as though going on errands and do not go far." He continued by specifying the arrangements made for receiving callers. "Individuals or parties rent the rooms empty and furnish them," he explained. "They are not rented with privileges but it is no one's affair what the lodgers do. $2 is the price charged men visitors for a short stay." The prostitutes living in this house clearly intended to blend in with the women in their neighborhood. By going out with shawls on their heads, they looked more like busy housewives out shopping than like prostitutes.[108]

As a result, prostitution in the furnished rooms blurred the visual line between "respectable women" and prostitutes, adding to the confusion over women's identity and sexual activities and ultimately destroying the idea that anyone could identify a prostitute by sight. Court testimony in disorderly house cases illuminates this confusion, reflecting the ways in which both furnished room prostitutes and treating girls threw older sureties into confusion. One man asserted that you could tell a prostitute from a good woman. When pressed by the prosecution for a description of the woman in question, he said, "Well, she was dressed what I would call loud."[109] In another case, the witness had a vivid memory, stating that "The appearance of the women was of a light, fantastic nature. The women were gotten up cheaply, for show, large hats and big feathers, and painted cheeks."[110] In other cases, men vehemently denied that you could still identify prostitutes by their style. "I don't know that prostitutes dress in that particular fashion," one witness said to the judge. "You can't tell them that way, by dress."[111] Another man simply stated, "I cannot tell a prostitute by her looks."[112]

Many of these women dressed like working-class women because that was what they were. They held jobs and used sex to augment wages or to make ends meet during times of unemployment. Living in rooming houses gave them the opportunity to make extra money from prostitution without actually being identified by friends, family, and future spouses as prostitutes. These young women usually worked in groups of two or three, pooling resources and sharing profits, safety, and company. As one investigator reported, "girls here seem new. They go on the streets in neighborhood without hats and are quite timid." He met one pair who "were working at shirt waists. One invited him to go with them to a hotel, the other said their rooms were best."[113] These young women appear to have both been employed in other work, namely making shirtwaists, and were relatively savvy about the business of prostitution. Although the investigator assessed them as timid and new to the game, they understood enough of prostitution to debate the merits of going to a hotel or returning with him to their rooms. That they showed any doubt at all about the safety of prostituting from their rooms indicates that they wanted to safeguard their reputations by keeping this illicit activity a secret.[114]

Clandestine prostitution saved many women's reputations, but some prostitutes kept a low profile because they felt genuine concern for the people in their neighborhoods. Although they obviously did not maintain the same community ties as women who prostituted openly from tenements, they still valued their communities and attempted to protect them from what could be viewed as "moral" harm. A white woman incarcerated at

Bedford explained why she lived with "prostitutes and drug users." According to her social worker, she "would not live with decent people while she was prostituting because she was afraid she might contaminate them."[115] Another woman became outraged in conversation with a man when he callously brushed off her concerns over the visibility of their transactions. As the investigator who witnessed the incident reported,

> of the men said to her, well ain't you going to take him to your room you've got the keys, she said I told you once I ain't going to take anybody to my room[.] the man said what are you afraid of anyways, she said there is always somebody sitting on the stoop at this hour (about 10 o'clock) a bunch of women and children, and I don't want them to see me bring anybody up, the man said thats nothing I'd screw my own sister if I got the chance, as soon as he said that the woman got mad and said go on get the H—— out of here I got no use for a man that'll say that, why you wouldn't even respect your own mother.[116]

Clearly, this woman did not want to damage her reputation by being seen taking a man into her room. However, her specific reference to women and children and her rage at his complete lack of concern for familial and community well-being suggest that she was also worried about the effect visible prostitution might have on her neighbors. The references to mothers and sisters in their conversation evoked the two explicitly desexualized roles for women in working-class American culture. Rather than cultivating a mercenary attitude, this prostitute chastised a potential client for his own disregard for women and children, or more specifically, mothers and sisters. This attitude reflects a profound ambivalence about prostitution and its place in working-class cultural and residential life. Unlike the tenement prostitutes who clearly did not shrink from soliciting clients from front stoops and doorways, furnished room prostitutes often wanted to hide their behavior and reduce the harmful effects they thought it might have. This demonstrates both their fear of exposure and a real investment in working-class sexual values, which, though more sympathetic than those of the middle class, never endorsed prostitution as a respectable occupation for women.

This ambivalence fundamentally characterizes the choices of the clandestine prostitute. Unlike the treating girls who began to appear in the late 1890s, clandestine prostitutes went against the sexual values of their communities when they accepted cash for their services. As a result, they did not expand working-class conceptions of acceptable sexual behavior for women. Rather than exploring other kinds of sexual and economic exchange, they bowed to community sexual values that, while expressing sympathy for individual prostitutes, still condemned women who commercialized sexual relations that working-class people believed should have been limited to the noncommercial realm. These women's desire to keep their activities a secret upheld working-class sexual values by acknowledging the condemnation of prostitution as a way of life and a sexual choice for women. Nonetheless, the presence of clandestine prostitutes in working-class communities subverted notions of the easy identification of women who crossed these lines. Working secretly and often casually, they presented their working-class neighbors with a confusing picture. Neighbors might guess that they prostituted, but few knew for sure. While this might expand the category of "immoral women" to encompass most women living independently, it also helped to undermine working-class sexual codes by making it genuinely difficult for neighbors to distinguish between prostitutes and nonprostitutes.

This confusion was furthered by the fact that many neighbors knew, or at least suspected, that some of the women in their building or on their block periodically prostituted. As one investigator reported, "in conversation with bartenders, waiters and others I learned that 'they all got their own rooms around here. Go to any of those rooming houses on Livingston Street, and if you happen to know a girl's name, you'll get in.' It is the consensus of opinion that 'Plenty of them (girls) are trotting around.'"[117] Although this may reflect the general opinion that most girls living apart from family were inclined to "trot around," the quotation also reveals very specific information and practices. Although the waiters and bartenders asserted that most of the girls prostituted, they did not identify them as prostitutes and made it clear that women had some acquaintance with men before they would offer their sexual services. Were these young women charity girls, prostitutes, or merely women living independent of family, sexually chaste but open to slander from loose-talking men in nearby saloons? Some of these girls probably did prostitute casually, but they did so only with people they knew, and as a result, remained more incorporated into neighborhood networks of friendship and company than into the larger marketplace of commercial sex.

Furnished room prostitution was one avenue that women who needed extra money could take and still maintain their sexual reputations. Through this survival strategy, women participated in the transformation of sexual practices that resulted from their ability to live independent of family. This kind of casual and clandestine prostitution contributed to the incorporation of sexual activity and commercial exchange into heterosexual interactions among working-class people. Stirring already muddy moral waters, these young women engaged in behavior far different than that of treating girls, but ultimately to much the same effect. Although clandestine prostitutes did not have the same explicit desire to open up women's sexual possibilities, their secretive activities made it more and more difficult for working-class people to distinguish between surface reputations and real commitment to a value system that condemned commercial sexuality. Taking advantage of the new social organization of the city and its opportunities for anonymity and independent living, these women made decisions that balanced issues of economics against issues of reputation and respectability. Even more than treating girls, clandestine prostitutes walked a fine line between profiting from their sexuality and maintaining their respectability. If forced to make a choice, however, most of them probably would have ultimately favored their reputations over the money they could make.

In the years before World War I, many prostitutes followed another path, taking full advantage of a revolution in the public presence of women as well as their growing importance in commercial activities. Rather than hiding their behavior in the hope that they could remain in the moral mainstream, these women chose to sell sex openly in their neighborhoods and in that way entered the economic mainstream of small proprietors providing entertainment and services to local consumers. Although the war would change both forms of prostitution, for the time being, women had attractive options about how to exchange sex for cash if they chose to do so. The choices these women made had a profound impact on the commercial economy of working-class neighborhoods as well as on working-class attitudes toward commercial and sexual values.

Chapter Four

A FIGHT ON THE HOME FRONT

THE REPRESSION OF PROSTITUTION

DURING WORLD WAR I

The extreme governmental measures invoked against prostitutes during World War I forced prostitution and treating to diverge radically. The Selective Service Act charged federal and local authorities with protecting the troops from moral and physical contagion, which led to a wide-scale repression of prostitution. Over the course of the war, the federal government, working through various state and local agencies, incarcerated 30,000 prostitutes.[1] This repression of prostitution did not lead to the desired reduction in venereal disease because the government shied away from incarcerating charity girls. It also failed because the government spent its resources on "reforming" men's morals rather than providing them with prophylaxis that would actually protect them from infection.[2] Aware of the fact that charity girls could also spread venereal disease, various local, state, and federal law enforcement agencies tried to discourage treating in the camps but usually stopped short of arresting charity girls. When officials did interfere with treating, they did so only with "girls," namely women under eighteen, whom they either returned to their families or sent to social service agencies dedicated to "reforming" wayward minors.[3] Their reluctance to restrain charity girls resulted from the fact that, like working-class women, the government defined treating as a private matter, even though it occurred in the same dance halls and theaters as prostitution and for similar motivations and profits. Thus, the war marked a turning point in the relationship between prostitution and treating. The incarceration of prostitutes for plying their trade in the cash economy encouraged the expansion of treating and its increasing social acceptability. During the war, treating took on a patriotic glow, as young girls combined their own hunger for urban amusements with their desire to boost the morale of the "boys in uniform."

However, the story of treating and prostitution during World War I does not simply mark the shifts in the relative safety of the two practices. The crisis of the war, and working-class and middle-class responses to it, profoundly changed the ways many Americans conceived of "appropriate" sexual behavior and expression. Constructing narratives about the evils of prostitution, the moral depravity of prostitutes themselves, and the innocence of the "boys" in uniform, middle-class vice reformers employed by the War Department sought to penalize prostitutes while maintaining the virtue of those men who bought their services. However, their vilification of prostitutes rarely spilled over to charity girls, whom reformers viewed as misguided yet well-meaning patriots. These stories, conflicted as they were, allowed the federal authorities to cast themselves as both saviors of male and female innocence and mediators in working-class sexual and patriotic expression. The power that these reformers garnered from their War Department positions allowed them to interfere to an unprecedented extent in the lives of working-class people. But their narratives also reflected the acceptance of treating as a behavior within the pale of American sexual values and activities. Furthermore, within working-class communities, and certainly among working-class girls, treating became so widely practiced that it began to merge with casual heterosocial interaction, consumption of entertainment, and courtship.

This chapter traces the wartime regulation and repression of prostitution and its impact on the structure of prostitution in New York City. Beginning with an analysis of the motives and ideologies of officials in the War Department, it then explores how bureaucrats' understandings of prostitutes as evil, soldiers as innocent, and themselves as saviors played out in the policies they designed to protect America's boys in uniform. Moving onto the local stage of New York City, it examines how these policies disrupted earlier patterns in the organization of prostitution and the ways in which women adapted to their deteriorating position. Wartime policies that characterized prostitutes as dangerous changed the place that prostitutes held in the entertainment economy of the city and set the stage for the exploitative and often violent environment that prevailed after the war.

The Regulation of Prostitution during the War

The entrance of the United States into the European war immediately raised concerns about venereal disease and its effect on the efficiency of the troops. Military authorities worried particularly about manpower strength. Reports on sick days lost to venereal disease during the episodic U.S. interventions in the Mexican Revolution in the early years of the twentieth century argued for a strong response. Yet federal officials remained torn over which strategy to employ. One possibility was that the U.S. government acquiesce to the seemingly inevitable association of armies and prostitutes and create a "regulated" system. The French had pioneered this solution, establishing brothels for the troops and inspecting prostitutes for infection on a weekly basis. French doctors working for the government identified those women found to carry venereal disease and removed them from the brothels for treatment.[4]

American military officers who believed the troops needed and would find heterosexual outlets favored this plan.[5] One doctor summed up this attitude when he commented on his time in the army during the Spanish-American War. He stated "that the enlisted man—through with his day's work—was not considered a good soldier unless he got drunk and spent his leisure hours with prostitutes."[6] Entrenched in the army's establishment, these men argued that the instincts required for good fighting went hand in hand with, and were reinforced by, a ruggedly masculine sexuality. Repressing men's sexuality would feminize the troops and decrease their capacity to fight. Those in favor of adopting the French system of regulation argued that, rather than ignore the problem, the government should provide its armies with safe prostitutes. That way, men could have sexual access to women without risking the venereal infections that had such a devastating effect on troop strength.[7]

On the other side of the debate, social purity activists, both inside and outside the military, argued that the government had a responsibility to protect the troops from the moral dangers of prostitution. Their position reflected an alternative understanding of manhood, sexuality, and disease. Rather than seeing men's sexual needs as inevitable or even desirable, they espoused the elimination of the sexual double standard. Men and women, they argued, should both abstain from any kind of sexual contact outside of marriage. This would make both women and men stronger and would restrict sexuality to the confines of marriage.[8] In their view, moral purity, once reserved largely for middle-class white women, should become the standard for all Americans. Using sex only for procreation within marriage, they argued, would purify America spiritually and morally. Social purity reformers' vision of America's new army highlighted their belief in the basic virtue, strength, and innocence of American manhood. They held that American troops needed to be protected from the influences of vice. Young men should be able to risk their lives, but not their souls, for the cause.

While social purity activists asserted the innate goodness of male soldiers, they possessed a conversely negative opinion of prostitutes, viewing them as immoral and weak and as vectors of disease. In addition, through a telling slippage of reasoning, these reformers held prostitutes responsible for spreading venereal disease to innocent women and children. That men played a crucial role in this sexual transaction did not figure in their logic.[9] In light of this gendered view of disease transmission, it made perfect sense for social purity activists to lobby the government to separate America's "noble" boys in uniform from prostitutes. Doing so would protect and preserve troop strength and morale and save their families and future children from the ravages of venereal disease.[10]

Social purity reformers had been investigating the connections between disease and the military since the turn of the century, and they were well positioned to press solutions on the War Department when the United States declared war on April 2, 1917. The army, like much of America, had a serious problem with venereal disease. In the early twentieth century, an estimated 30 percent of soldiers suffered from venereal disease. Furthermore, this number counted only new infections, not the overall rate of infection.[11] Perhaps more upsetting for military leaders, fully one-third of all lost manpower days came from soldiers under treatment for venereal disease. Immediately after the United States declared war, Secretary of War Newton Baker moved to address the issue of venereal disease and the troops. He created the Commission on Training Camp Activities (CTCA) to repress prostitution and liquor sales and to provide troops with wholesome entertainments that would take the place of prostitution and other forms of vice. Baker appointed Raymond Fosdick, an important New York Progressive-era vice reformer, to run the CTCA.[12] Fosdick had impressive social purity credentials and had conducted an important military investigation into vice conditions along the Mexican border in the early twentieth century. In Fosdick, purity reformers had a true champion, one who could guarantee that their understanding of the relationships among sexuality, disease, and civic virtue would become the ideological force that drove federal policy on prostitution.

Shortly after the creation of the CTCA, the U.S. Congress passed the Selective Service Act, and its language marked an acceptance of the vision of purity reformers and their beliefs about prostitutes and soldiers. Mobilizing the nation for war, the act also contained provisions that attempted to eliminate soldiers' contact with vice. Section 12 of the act prohibited the sale of liquor to soldiers and sailors in uniform. Section 13 concerned prostitution and troops' access to women of "ill repute." It gave the secretary of war broad powers "to do everything by him deemed necessary" to suppress "houses of ill fame, brothels, or bawdy houses within such distance as he may deem needful of any military camp, station, fort, post, cantonment, training, or mobilization place." Furthermore, anyone involved in prostitution "or who shall violate any order . . . otherwise punishable under the Articles of War,

[will] be deemed guilty of a misdemeanor and be punished by a fine of not more than $1000, or imprisonment for not more than twelve months or both."[13]

Government officials argued that they designed these acts to control the spread of venereal disease and prevent the loss of troop strength to sick days for "social hygiene reasons." The provisions regarding prostitution, however, concerned the protection of the morals of the troops more than they actually safeguarded soldiers' health. For example, the military discontinued its policy of distributing condoms to the troops—the most efficient means of preventing venereal disease—when a storm of protest erupted.[14] Thus, although the military had the means to prevent the transmission of venereal disease through the use of prophylactics, it relied instead on the "moral education" of the troops and the repression of prostitution. Eschewing more concrete solutions to disease prevention allowed social purity activists within the government to create a debate about venereal disease that focused on morality rather than on the disease itself. Setting the terms of debate in this way made it possible to use extreme governmental measures to attack prostitutes as the source of infection for soldiers and sailors.

The portrayal of the troops as vulnerable and innocent became a crucial part of the narrative that the directors of the government's wartime social hygiene campaign presented to the nation. By advancing this image of the troops as innocent and in need of protection, social purity activists cast America's fighting men in a remarkably passive role. Unable to act on their own behalf, soldiers needed to be sheltered from influences that would ruin them and interfere with their usefulness to the nation. Often relying on martial metaphors, this narrative placed America's reformers and civilians, and not the troops, in the masculine, paternal position of vanquishing the enemy on the field of battle. Presented as a nationwide effort, the battle for purity quickly took center stage on the home front.

In a pamphlet printed by the War Department and distributed to public and private agencies on the local level, Major Bascom Johnson pushed this masculine narrative to its logical extreme. "The Allies in France," he began, "have been battering their way forward from one line of defense to another. A similar campaign is being waged in America against commercialized prostitution near military camps. Its aim is to protect our military forces from prostitutes and other carriers of venereal diseases in order to keep them fit to fight." Transfixed by the promise of victory on the horizon, he reported that "the first objective of this campaign has been quickly reached—the enemy's first line of defense has been obliterated."[15] Within Johnson's vision, reformers occupied the masculine position of protectors, paternal figures waging a battle for the hearts and souls of America's troops against a vicious, canny, and entrenched enemy. Prostitutes appeared as enemies with their own geographical "lines of defense." By transgressing the chastity appropriate for their sex, prostitutes became a masculinized force, worthy adversaries for the social purity activists fighting one of the most important battles of the war. This narrative made reformers the heroes, the true men of the war, at the same time that it infantilized soldiers. Curiously passive, America's military personnel became children, sweet and virtuous, cognizant of their duty, but unable to protect themselves from an enemy that peddled disease and death in the guise of a "good time."

This narrative accomplished several important rhetorical aims. First, it invested what had been a prewar domestic reform movement with patriotic and political significance. The importance of the cause and the innocence of the victims required Americans to take drastic steps to root out vice in their communities. "Eternal vigilance," Johnson stated, "is just as much the price of municipal cleanliness as it is of liberty."[16] Johnson's wording, though intended to be stirring, was also ironic. From this perspective, the "morally clean city" required that the civil rights and civil liberties of some citizens be severely abridged. Sacrificing liberty at the shrine of municipal cleanliness, the federal government pursued a policy that cast moral crusaders as men, soldiers as children, and prostitutes as the enemy.

This argument also transformed a foreign war into a domestic one and made local efforts at disease prevention seem crucial to the success of the military. In advancing the vision of prostitutes as the enemy, social purity reformers invited interested citizens to join them in the home-front battle and become the real soldiers of the Great War. Americans, Johnson asserted, had to attack prostitution "in its second and third lines of defense, in communities near which large bodies of soldiers or sailors are located."[17] Moving the front from France to the streets and neighborhoods of America's cities empowered ordinary citizens to do battle with the forces of liquor and prostitution. The focus on vice emphasized the urgency of wartime efforts and gave people local and visible ways to support a distant war that many Americans had until recently opposed.

Federal officials pursued their objectives by drafting policies that classified prostitutes as internal enemies. Detention and internment became federal and state authorities' preferred policy for handling people who violated government regulations concerning the sale of sex near troop concentrations. Although reliant on local governments and private organizations for enforcement, federal officials set these policies themselves. The attorney general provided legal justification for the government's actions, commenting that

> the Surgeon General of the Army . . . has called my attention to the fact that . . . prostitutes, are, in the majority of cases, carriers of venereal disease. These persons, even though prosecuted and convicted, eventually regain their freedom. I am informed that many of them return to the practice of prostitution and, unless cured of their disease before release, infect a large number of soldiers and sailors before they are again caught violating the law. I feel that it is the duty of this department to do all within its power to minimize the dangerous effects arizing [*sic*] from this situation.

He continued by summarizing the efforts of the Office of the Surgeon General. As prostitution "is a prolific source of these diseases," he stated, "this campaign includes both the suppression of prostitution, and the medical examination, quarantine, and cure of prostitutes afflicted with such diseases." Such policies, he argued, were constitutional, and "the Department of Justice entertains no doubt upon the right to subject a person convicted of prostitution to a medical examination in order to ascertain whether or not she is afflicted with a communicable disease."[18]

The attorney general intended to make indefinite incarceration of prostitutes easy for local authorities. If local health or criminal statutes proved inadequate, the attorney general would institute provisions by which women convicted of prostitution could be involuntarily tested so that their venereal disease status could be taken into account during sentencing. When prostitutes were found to be infected with either syphilis or gonorrhea, they would be confined to an institution for treatment and kept there until a doctor certified them to be free of disease. This policy enabled local authorities to incarcerate women based on their health status rather than on any crime they committed, and it extended their detention for periods that far exceeded their actual sentence.[19] Although state and local authorities welcomed the support of federal policies and laws, the attorney general's instructions represented an unprecedented level of federal involvement in what had previously fallen exclusively under state and municipal control.

In fact, although law enforcement agencies and public health officials did subject prostitutes to special scrutiny, the treatment they received spilled over to other civilians. For example, individuals convicted of nonsexual crimes sometimes found themselves subject to the new regulations regarding venereal disease.[20] In a circular letter addressed to state health authorities, the surgeon general called their attention to the fact that many prisoners suffered from venereal diseases and that "these prisoners are still in the infectious stage when released." To prevent this, the surgeon general required state marshals working in penal institutions to inform public health officials of the infectiousness of particular prisoners at least five days before their release. "You will, therefore," he explained, "have in your possession such information as may be necessary to enable you to deal with the case according to the regulations of your State Health Department."[21] In other words, people found to carry sexually transmitted diseases, regardless of their crime or sentence, could be held indefinitely. Finally, the federal government offered to pay for the testing of prisoners, "provided the prisoner will in all probability remain in confinement a sufficient length of time to determine the result of the test and render her non-infectious prior to her release."[22] All of these precautions severely restricted the civil rights of prostitutes and other people caught up in the criminal justice system.

These rights were further abridged by medical science's limited understanding of venereal disease. Because doctors did not have an accurate test for gonorrhea or syphilis, the surgeon general instructed that "laboratory findings should not be taken as final, except in the case of positives," noting that "a positive reaction in the case of gonorrhea is hard to get." As a result, the surgeon general urged local health departments to be liberal rather than conservative in their diagnosis and to rely on sociological as well as medical information. "Treatment," he advised, "must be based upon the physical condition of the patient; i.e., history of promiscuity, vaginal discharge, and other clinical symptoms."[23] Admitting that "there is no outstanding treatment for either gonorrhea or syphilis," the surgeon general concluded that "the best plan is to . . . watch carefully the individual patient and her reactions."[24] The medical uncertainties of venereal disease detection and treatment further limited the freedom of suspected individuals, because federal authorities extended the period people could be incarcerated by encouraging health departments to pursue liberal diagnoses and conservative assessments of "cures."

Of course, the military did face a critical problem when it confronted the problem of venereal disease. As its propaganda indicated, the military lost the use of troops to venereal disease, which affected military efficiency. For example, Fosdick wrote to Major Snow in May of 1918, reporting that "I have been informed of a statement made by a Major in the regular army that out of a single regiment slated to sail last Monday from the port of New York, and stationed at Camp Merritt, 700 men were left behind for venereal disease."[25] According to one War Department poster, printed in bold type with a photograph of a U.S. battleship, Secretary Daniels reported that "during 1916 . . . there was in the Navy a daily average of 456 men disabled because of venereal diseases. Add to this the number of men necessary to care for them and we have enough men on the non-effective list to man a modern battleship" (Figure 4.1). Sexually transmitted diseases reached epidemic proportions in the early twentieth century, and without effective diagnosis or treatment, prevention became a crucial part of control for military authorities. This striking poster communicated both the real danger of losing troop strength to disease and the more symbolic danger of sacrificing masculine prowess to moral laxness.

The military had cause to be concerned about prostitutes, because many did have venereal disease. Contemporary estimates of infection among prostitutes vary widely during this period. Some reformatories, such as New York's Bedford, reported rates as high as 90 percent, but scientists were reluctant to apply these estimates across the board because of obvious sample bias. Penal institutions housed the prostitutes who were most likely to show active venereal infections.[26] In the more varied prostitute population of New York City, for example, public health officials found that "the total number whom we found to give evidence of gonorrhea or syphilis or both was . . . approximately fifty-eight percent."[27] Estimates on the neighborhood level could be even lower. The general secretary of the Committee of Fourteen acknowledged that "a similar raid in Brooklyn, involving whites as well as Negroes, showed a proportion of infection of about twenty percent."[28] While this is a staggeringly high number, it is considerably lower than most of the propaganda produced during the war led citizens to believe. One pamphlet claimed that 96 percent of all white prostitutes in red-light districts were infected.[29] It also asserted that 90 percent of all sexually acquired syphilitic infections in men derived from prostitutes, either professional or amateur.[30] Of course, depending on how health department officials defined "professional" or "amateur," this category could include a large proportion of sexually active working-class women. War Department propaganda often made explicit reference to the direct connection between prostitution and disease (Figure 4.2).

Although prostitutes had high rates of venereal infection, so did both the general population and soldiers and sailors. One survey of New York City hospitals found that 19.6 percent of all white patients admitted for routine procedures had syphilis. Other clinics in the city reported even higher numbers, 28.1 percent at the Post Graduate Hospital and 25.7 percent at Bellevue.[31] Furthermore, somewhere between 25 percent and 30 percent of soldiers tested positive for syphilis or gonorrhea at the time of their induc-

EFFICIENCY?

SECRETARY DANIELS reported:

"During 1916 (when the Navy was one-fourth its present size) there was in the Navy a daily average of 456 men disabled because of venereal diseases.

"Add to this the number of men necessary to care for them and we have enough men on the non-effective list to man a modern battleship."

She was Built to FIGHT

Keep Her Fit and Fully Manned

FIGURE 4.1. *"Keep Her Fit and Fully Manned," poster produced by the American Social Hygiene Association (New York: Marchbanks Press, 1918). (Box 78, Record Group 165, National Archives)*

Prostitution and Disease
Go Arm-in-Arm

FIGURE 4.2. *"Prostitution and Disease Go Arm-in-Arm," poster produced by the American Social Hygiene Association (New York: Marchbanks Press, 1918). (Box 78, Record Group 165, National Archives)*

tion into the military.[32] These statistics indicate that prostitutes posed a risk to some servicemen, but that between a quarter and a third of all soldiers entered the military already suffering from venereal disease. According to one confidential memo from the War Department, of the soldiers under care for venereal disease in U.S. Army hospitals, approximately 85 percent entered the army already infected, leaving only 15 percent who contracted the disease after enlistment.[33] The War Department calculated that in 1917 the army lost three-quarters of a million workdays because of the 178,204 men out sick.

Venereal disease may well have posed a significant threat to "efficiency" in the war effort, but the question remains whether the military pursued an effective course in repressing it. Rather than rely on dubious medical assessments, the federal government instructed local authorities to use other, more social criteria such as personal history and sexual behavior. The government's approach to the problem made a great deal of sense, given medical limitations and the ideological vision that drove policies. After all, there was little anyone could do about the difficulties in diagnosing and treating venereal disease. Medical science simply did not have the tools available yet to give accurate and reliable assessments of people's condition. Having abandoned condoms as the most effective form of prevention, there was little else the military could do. That the majority of victims of these polices were an unpopular criminal minority, namely prostitutes, made them that much easier to enforce.

Venereal Disease Control in New York City

New York's turn-of-the-century experiments in the study, control, and repression of prostitution provided an excellent model for the federal government as it sought to eliminate soldiers' access to prostitutes. New York City pioneered the repression of prostitution and vice in the early twentieth century by attacking it from different angles, including new methods of policing, changes in criminal and public health law, and intervention by social workers. Many of the actions that the federal government encouraged states and municipalities to undertake had already been underway in New York for some time.[34] For example, while New York City had eliminated brothels from the city by 1910, the removal of red-light districts did not become a national priority until the war.[35] While the War Department's Social Hygiene Division could boast that it had "assisted in the closure of 124 red light districts," "helped care for 30,000 delinquent women and girls," and "assisted in the enforcement of laws and ordinances relating to venereal diseases in communities surrounding naval and military camps," these gains appear almost backward in light of New York's early attempts to eradicate the "social evil."[36] Nor did New York State need the federal money allocated for the building of prison facilities to house delinquent women and girls. Unlike most western and southern states, New York had undergone turn-of-the-century prison reforms that gave it adequate prison facilities to cope with the influx of women arrested for prostitution-related offenses.

Finally, New York passed a series of laws before the war that attempted to eliminate fining and institute mandatory prison sentencing for prostitutes. Fining, many reformers argued, amounted to an unofficial licensing system, as prostitutes could easily pay their fines and continue their business. They were right in this assessment. Under most Raines Law hotel agreements, proprietors kept a fund on hand to bail out prostitutes and pay their fines. Most reformers believed that only time served in the reformatory, preferably one with a rehabilitation program, could dissuade women from prostitution. Thus, in 1913 New York State passed "an amendment of the Inferior Criminal Courts Act of New York City (a state law applicable only to N.Y. City)" that held that "no woman may be fined for a violation of the laws against prostitution." Instead, city magistrates substituted "probation, commitment to a reformatory institution or to the workhouse for from 5 days to not more than three years." In addition, the law required that "in the case of women previously convicted twice within a year or three times within any length of time, the commitment is to the Parole Commission for a period not to exceed three years."[37]

As a result of these early reforms, New York City entered the war with the most severe laws against prostitution in the nation. However, despite the progress New York State had made in the repression of vice, the city faced problems greater than other urban areas could even comprehend. Not only did the city actually have troop concentrations within its limits, such as the naval yard in Brooklyn and the army cantonments in the Bronx and Queens, but soldiers came to New York from all over the Northeast on their leave to see the big city before shipping out. Improvements in transportation—trolleys, subways, trains, and taxi cars—made it possible for young men to go to New York on weekend leave while stationed in camps on Long Island as well as in New Jersey, Connecticut, Pennsylvania, and upstate New York. A letter regarding the return of the fleet at the end of the war warned of a veritable invasion, stating that "on either December 27th or 28th Admiral Usher expected twenty-four destroyers with an average complement of 500 men, 9 dreadnoughts, complement 2000, as well as several destroyers, so that upwards of 30,000 men are expected to visit the city."[38] Few other cities had to cope with both such massive temporary influxes and huge permanent concentrations of troops. Fosdick himself called New York "perhaps the most single critical point in the United States" in the fight against venereal disease.[39]

The War Department quickly found an ally in the Committee of Fourteen, and in May of 1917, the CTCA formally asked the Committee of Fourteen to oversee the coordination of various federal, state, and local organizations dealing with the issue of vice for the entire state of New York.[40] The committee also agreed to send undercover investigators to camps as far south as Philadelphia and as far north as Bridgeport, Connecticut.[41] But even New York's preeminent vice society had difficulty forcing local agencies to comply with new federal and state laws. For example, some judges demanded higher standards of evidence than the new laws required. As the general secretary of the Committee of Fourteen explained with some irritation to the director of the New England Watch and Ward Society, "Under the New York law prostitution has been construed as the offer to commit sexual intercourse for hire, as well as the act itself. . . . Unfortunately, the judges, however, prefer in order to strengthen the evidence, that the woman be paid and expose herself."[42] Other judges disagreed with the committee's undercover investigative style and refused to believe evidence presented by investigators at trial. In one instance in 1917, a judge presiding over a pimping case refused to believe that the investigator had not actually engaged in sexual intercourse with the woman in question. Because the investigator conducted his interview with this woman while lying between her legs on a deserted dock, the judge's incredulity is understandable.[43] Finally, other city agencies, such as the Tenement House Department, refused to discontinue old practices of fining instead of mandatory sentencing to penal institutions.[44]

The organization of prostitution in New York City also hamstrung wartime efforts to control it. As the previous chapter explained, brothel prostitution had virtually disappeared from the city by 1910.[45] The scattered nature of prostitution made it difficult to address with the simplistic measures recommended by the War Department. After all, it was much easier to close a brothel than to track independent prostitutes as they moved about the city looking for patrons. Firmly entrenched in working-class business, entertainment, and residential life, New York's prostitutes were mobile and well-connected and could respond flexibly to the threat of new crackdowns on vice. The new laws prohibiting prostitution in the vicinity of the camps made enforcement easier, but not easy. New York City officials had to devise new ways to keep the prostitutes they did find off the streets and out of trouble for the duration of the war.

In 1918, the New York State legislature amended the health law, giving the state health department the right to examine men and women against their will if they were suspected of suffering from venereal disease. As the general secretary for the Committee of Fourteen described, "the proposed amendment would correct the only defect in the law as shown by practice." "Some way," he declared, "must be found by which suspected persons, not otherwise detained, may be kept under the control of the Health Department while their physical condition is being determined. Because a person has not been convicted of prostitution does not relieve him or her of being a venereal suspect. In the case of persons arrested and charged with prostitution, the difficulty might be met by having the trial postponed until after the report of the examination has been received."[46] This new law gave state and city health officials the right to cast their net widely when dealing with venereal disease. A similar law, however, had passed in 1911 and had been met with a storm of public protest and was declared unconstitutional. Measures that New York's citizens viewed as too extreme a violation of civil rights before the war could now be justified under the guise of military necessity.[47]

The new health law proved to be just what New York City law enforcement officers needed to suppress not only prostitution but many kinds of sexual activity, both commercial and noncommercial. In addition, out of all the legislation passed against prostitution during the war, this law had the harshest effect on prostitutes. Although it enabled the Board of Health to test anyone suspected of carrying venereal disease, it pursued different treatment programs for prostitutes and nonprostitutes. While the city trusted most nonprostitutes to continue treatment through clinics, prostitutes had to remain in the workhouse or reformatory until declared noncontagious. As a result, the city incarcerated prostitutes but not other carriers of venereal disease. Infected prostitutes, moreover, served sentences far longer than those appropriate for a misdemeanor—as prostitution was—a pattern supported by federal legislation and instructions. In New York, a state with sufficient prison facilities, public health measures became an informal internment program, and the hospitals and workhouses of the city, holding pens for women the military did not trust about the town during the war.

Wartime Regulation and the Structure of Prostitution

Wartime regulations profoundly restructured prostitution in New York City. In less than a year, the new laws and the glaring differences in the enforcement of provisions against liquor versus those against prostitution severed long-term alliances between prostitutes and bar owners. The destruction of the Raines Law hotels as a safe space for prostitutes left women with little protection from violence or coercion at the same time that punishments for involvement in prostitution rose substantially. The organization of prostitution changed dramatically as prostitutes turned to intermediaries for protection from johns and the police. Disrupting earlier relationships that helped prostitutes assert some control over their work, the war presaged the coercive, exploitative, and violent path that the trade would follow in the Prohibition era.

As I argued in the previous chapter, the decline of the brothels led prostitutes to develop relationships with bar owners that gave them unprecedented control over their wages and working conditions. The Raines Law brought small-scale entrepreneurs from both groups together in an extremely profitable alliance. It also scattered the practice of prostitution throughout working-class residential neighborhoods, making enforcement of antiprostitution ordinances difficult. With the brothels gone, repressing vice became a game of cat and mouse, a situation that forced New York's vice crusaders and police to develop new tactics of policing. The urgency of the war effort, the vilification of prostitutes as an internal enemy, and the laws this vilification helped to pass allowed police to justify extraordinary, and often extralegal, measures to make New York a clean city. Because prostitutes were hard to find and often operated independently, police needed new strategies to track and expose women suspected of illicit sex. Undercover investigations, fingerprinting, the use of informants, and the pursuit of raids without a warrant all allowed police to wage war on prostitution in the city. Though effective, some of these tactics further abridged prostitutes' remaining rights and significantly increased police corruption. Wartime police practices designed to make New York a safe city for soldiers also expanded police involvement in and regulation of the illegal economy.

During the war, New York City police went undercover to try to root out prostitution in and around the city. Their efforts significantly increased their success in apprehending and convicting prostitutes. According to the Committee of Fourteen, undercover cops suppressed street prostitution by arresting streetwalkers either after being "solicited directly by the women, or observ[ing] women soliciting other men." In the tenements, "they gain[ed] access to these women, either through solicitation by them on the street, [or] through the use of stool pigeons, anonymous complaints and otherwise."[48] Convictions for these kinds of arrests reached 80 percent.[49] Furthermore, a series of new regulations enacted during the years prior to the war functioned cumulatively to ensure higher conviction rates. The city instituted fingerprinting as a consistent police policy in 1910, which enabled magistrates to track women individually and made the identification of repeat offenders possible.[50] Before this, a woman could simply use a different name or move into a new precinct and establish a new identity for herself. Fingerprinting made it possible for magistrates to distinguish between women recently entered into the life and "hardened offenders." New laws took advantage of fingerprint technology to establish hierarchies of redeemability among prostitutes in sentencing guidelines. As the general secretary of the Committee of Fourteen explained,

> three years ago the use of fines as a penalty in these cases was abolished, and the women are now placed on probation, sent to a reformatory or rescue home, or may be committed to the Workhouse. Under a recent law,

women convicted twice within two years, or three times within a longer period must be committed to what is known as the Parole Commission, which . . . can hold them for two years . . . releasing the prostitute when in their judgment the proper time arrives, but keeping her under parole for the whole period.[51]

Supporting the general secretary's contention, the Bedford reformatory inmate records contain references to women caught for prostitution under other names and sentenced to the reformatory as recidivists.[52]

New York clearly benefited from early systems that, like fingerprinting, finally began to pay off. But in a very real way, the fervor of the war gave local and federal antivice agents the moral authority to take any measures they saw fit to eliminate prostitution from New York's streets and places of amusement. Tactics that the public and the courts had viewed as too extreme an assertion of coercive state power over individuals during peacetime appeared perfectly reasonable when implemented during the war on behalf of America's troops. Some judges continued to insist on a higher level of evidence and questioned the legal and moral propriety of undercover police investigations, but, on the whole, the judiciary allowed police to make use of whatever methods they deemed necessary to control vice.[53]

Abuses in the application of these new measures increased police corruption and profoundly limited the rights of prostitutes under the law. The use of stool pigeons allowed police to attack prostitutes without actually witnessing them break the law. As regular informants, stool pigeons had considerable loyalty to the police who paid them. Consequently, they possessed few moral qualms about infringing upon the legal rights of prostitutes or even innocent women or upon any abstract notions of civil rights. Northern-born African American Dotty Evans insisted that she had been a victim of such tactics when she was incarcerated at Bedford reformatory in 1917. She told her social worker that a man had followed her to her apartment when she came home from work one night. He propositioned her, and when she refused him, two detectives arrested her. According to Evans, "they winked at the man and told him to go away or they would arrest him too." Evans said she thought he "was a stool-pigeon and that the detectives were suspicious of her because she had been coming home late at night." While many women at Bedford referred to their arrests as "frame-ups," few had husbands like Evans's, who hired a lawyer to defend her.[54] The use of stool pigeons in vice work vastly increased both the number of arrests and the corruption of the police department. The Seabury Investigation, conducted in the 1920s, uncovered hundreds of incidents in which police used perjured testimony of stool pigeons to convict the women in question. Testifying for the Seabury Investigation, one stool pigeon revealed that under the direction of the police he fabricated evidence and framed innocent women.[55] The freedom that judges gave police led to extensive corruption and, at times, real miscarriages of justice.

Finally, as the general secretary of the Committee of Fourteen pointed out, police often raided private residences suspected of prostitution without a warrant, "largely upon the hope of obtaining the necessary evidence after entrance to the house has been gained." Commenting on the patently illegal nature of this procedure, he stated that "this is a rather dangerous proceeding and would not be tolerated, except as the police administration, as happens in New York today, has the confidence of the community."[56] In other words, were it not for the war, the "confidence" New Yorkers placed in their police force, and the unpopularity of the defendants, the community would not allow raids that violated due process. Wartime propaganda about prostitutes as internal enemies allowed police to engage in activities that, at other times, might have aroused considerable public protest.

These new enforcement policies all made prostitution more dangerous. At the same time, differences in the implementation of Selective Service Act provisions about liquor and prostitution disrupted business arrangements between prostitutes and Raines Law hotel proprietors, which, in turn, altered the structure and practice of prostitution. Theoretically, the limitations that the Selective Service Act placed on both the sale of liquor and the sale of sex should have strengthened these connections, as both bar owners and prostitutes faced renewed pressure together. In practice, however, police and vice officials never enforced the laws governing the sale of liquor to soldiers with the same zeal. By failing to enforce liquor regulations at the same time as they stepped up efforts to control prostitution, federal and local officials drove a wedge between former allies. Furthermore, the disruption of these relationships, which had so benefited prostitutes in the past, occurred exactly when prostitutes most needed the protection and support of their old allies.

From the beginning, New York judges resisted the implementation of the laws forbidding liquor near the camps. In April of 1917, New York State passed a law supporting the Selective Service Act's ban on the sale of liquor near troop concentrations.[57] Two Brooklyn judges quickly found the act establishing dry zones around "special points of danger" unconstitutional, because they viewed it as an unreasonable restriction on commerce. This effectively hamstrung the effort to control liquor sales to soldiers and sailors in the city proper.[58] As Frederick Whitin, the general secretary of the Committee of Fourteen, wrote to a supporter in December of 1917, "You probably know that the New York authorities are as yet loath to declare a dry territory around naval stations like the Brooklyn Navy Yard." [59] Furthermore, officials doubted that such zones would work, as earlier attempts at geographical restrictions on liquor sales had failed miserably. When the state of New Jersey ordered the closure of saloons around the docks, "the men and their friends . . . [were] able to get liquor by going to New York on the Hudson Tubes." As a result, Whitin stated dispiritedly, "the closing of the saloons has not been as effective as the efforts of the Army and Navy had hoped." [60]

Unable to impose dry zones around the camps, the authorities resorted to investigating individual establishments, taking note if they sold liquor to military personnel. Such establishments could then be prosecuted and shut down for violations of federal and state laws prohibiting any sale of liquor to men in uniform. Some places openly catered to military clientele and bent the rules to give soldiers a beer. As one investigator reported of the Manhattan Casino, there were "about 25 men in khaki uniform here, they were all sitting around with civilians, some of them were being served with liquor by some of the waiters that were taking chances, the others were ordering soft drinks but were switching glasses with their civilian friends." [61] As this remark indicates, not only did bar owners and waiters sometimes make exceptions for soldiers but the soldiers themselves actively pursued alcohol. The image of the innocent soldier in need of paternalistic protection from vice fades in light of their aggressive behavior. In fact, their desire for liquor and propensity to get obnoxiously drunk made military personnel unpopular neighbors in areas that abutted camps and cantonments. As the general secretary of the Committee of Fourteen pointed out, "the chief complaint by reputable citizens was that soldiers went freely into the saloons using them for lavatories and public comfort stations and that all too frequently when they came out they were intoxicated or semi-intoxicated; that in quite a number of instances had these drunken soldiers insulted the women on the streets and clashed with the males." [62] While these incidents may appear to the modern reader to be a normal part of life around military installations, they contrasted sharply with the image of its troops that the War Department promoted.

Soldiers went to great lengths to get around laws that denied them liquor, making it easy for most establishments to serve them and profit from military business without taking serious risks. In addition to relying on civilian friends or women they met to switch drinks, soldiers paid civilian men and boys to purchase liquor for them. [63] As one investigator described conditions in July of 1917 around South Ferry Station, at the southern tip of Manhattan, "liquor is not being sold to men in military uniform . . . but the soldiers and sailors will send in boys and men to get a 'flask' of whiskey or beer . . . which are consumed by the soldiers and sailors in the side streets." He also noted a shift in the surrounding petty economy to accommodate such men. "Some boys," he commented, "have 'beer cans' ready which they rent out to the soldiers."[64] Soldiers also cajoled civilians into switching clothing with them, so they could enter bars undetected. Indeed, a local business sprung up around providing soldiers with civilian clothes. A furnishing store in Brooklyn made profits at night catering to soldiers' needs for clothing and storage: "the soldiers, or sailors come in this store for the purpose to change their military uniforms; they leave their uniforms in a locker and put civilian clothes on, then they go out to New York, or remain in this vicinity."[65] Most soldiers and sailors pursued alcohol with such single-minded intensity that few establishments had to take risks in selling to them. Unlike prostitutes, whose mere presence indicated a broken law, soldiers and sailors could disguise themselves so that bar owners could honestly claim they believed they were refusing military personnel either liquor or service or both. One man summed the situation up succinctly when he told an investigator on December 8, 1917, that "No saloon keeper could be blamed for it, because he couldn't know who that civilian was."[66] Soldiers' desire for liquor, when combined with a recalcitrant judiciary concerned with preserving the economic rights of small businessmen, made it extremely difficult for law enforcement officials to make a dent in liquor sales.

The few cases that officials brought against bar owners were more about persecuting ethnic Germans than about violations of the liquor laws. Despite the large and well-established German population in the city, New York was not immune to the anti-German sentiment that swept the country during the war. According to the *New York Times*, in December of 1917, federal agents raided several clubs "in every instance owned by men of foreign birth, most of them of German origin." The owners of these clubs protested that they had "taken out American citizenship papers," that they did not sell liquor to soldiers, and that they should not be persecuted for their ethnicity and alleged sympathy to the enemy. In addition, the *Times* reported that in one club "the raiders found Negro men dancing with white women and white men dancing with Negro women."[67] Similar to their vilification of prostitutes, federal officials saw German club owners as loyal to the enemy and conspiring to weaken the U.S. military from within by plying innocent soldiers with alcohol and illicit sex. However, little of the evidence offered in court supported these claims. As the *Times* described an incident in Grab's Saloon, one soldier "was not a very willing witness, but in answer to repeated questions admitted that he was intoxicated on the night of the raid. . . . He said that he obtained the drinks through the 'substitution' system; that is, a civilian companion, would order beer and he would order a soft drink and when the drinks were served they would exchange glasses. . . . He said that neither of the Grabs ever personally had served him a drink."[68] Though they could not prove their case, federal officials still damaged the reputation and business of the German men involved. After the war, Grab sued the marshal who had raided his club for $200,000 to compensate for lost revenues.[69]

The difficulties associated with enforcing liquor laws combined with the ease of prosecuting prostitutes to destroy the alliance between Raines Law hotel proprietors and prostitutes. While selling liquor to soldiers was now technically illegal, few proprietors were ever punished for it. And, of course, they were perfectly entitled to sell liquor in general. Prostitution, however, was illegal, and tolerating it during the war became very risky. The very benefits that prostitutes had brought to bar owners before the war—encouraging men to buy liquor, drawing customers, and providing a new source of income in the form of bed rents—now put owners in danger of provoking the wrath of law enforcement. Furthermore, while a few judges blocked individual violations of due process, rules of evidence, or civil rights, none defended the rights of prostitutes to sell their bodies in the same way that the Brooklyn justices defended the rights of bar owners to sell liquor. The unpopularity of prostitutes, their image as spreaders of disease, and their lack of political and social power made them easy targets for law enforcement, forcing proprietors to choose between their past alliances and their future business. Overall, the war had a more profound impact on prostitutes and the organization of prostitution than it did on any other form of commercial entertainment in the city. As making alliances with prostitutes became too dangerous for most bar owners, prostitutes lost a crucial relationship that had enabled them to control the conditions under which they worked. Rather than pulling the two types of small proprietorships together, the disproportionate enforcement of prostitution violations relative to those concerning liquor divided former allies.

Even when prostitutes remained in Raines Law hotels, the war transformed their relatively egalitarian and mutually beneficial arrangements with bar proprietors. These increasingly became coercive, foreshadowing the relationships between pimp and prostitute after the war. One investigator reported an incident in which the owner required one woman working out of his bar to sleep with a patron. In this case, the owner acted more like a pimp than a proprietor providing space and a degree of safety to another business person. As the investigator described it:

Tom Cummins came out from the inside room and said that the bitch in the corner wouldn't screw him. This he said to Johnny Burns the owner. The latter said wait a minute I'll go in and give her hell. He did and returned in about five minutes saying "it's alright." . . . He told me that he knew all of the girls and had even "screwed" all of them many times as he put it. He had that much hold on them that they did as he said. If the girls weren't nice and obliging to the men he came in and talked to them and gave them "Hell" again as he put it.[70]

Coercing the women working out of his bar to sleep with his friends, this man exemplified the deterioration of the relationship between proprietors and prostitutes. Johnny Burns might have been a Raines Law hotel owner or just a bar owner, but his relationship to the prostitutes who frequented his place was radically different than that in earlier Raines Law hotels. Women working out of his bar apparently could not refuse sex with customers and yet continued to do business there. Their sexual acquiescence to him heralded their sexual submission more generally. In addition, the tone of the interaction and Burns's description of giving women "hell" would become typical of the structure of prostitution in the postwar period. Coercion, threats, and violence became a regular part of prostitutes' relations with the men who helped them ply their trade.[71]

Some women resisted the incursion of increasingly violent men into what had been a practice dominated by independent prostitutes. In one report, an investigator described a scene similar to the one that occurred at Burns's bar, but with a very different outcome. The investigator stated that "I picked out a blond waitress and went up with her on the upper floor. The hall was dark, she took me in a small room lighted a candle, then took her skirt off, when she was ready to lay down she asked me for money. I said that I was told by 'T' not to pay anything. She said: 'Nothing doing, Tony got nothing to tell me I wouldn't stay with no man living without money.' . . . Tony was still sitting there, soon I came in he asked me if I had a good time, I said that I didn't stay with her, because she wanted money of me. He said, that the waitress ain't his girl and he cannot force her."[72] Clearly, the waitress in Tony's bar still worked independently, and owner and prostitute maintained a relationship similar to those in the Raines Law hotels. Distinguishing herself from both treating girls and the newer prostitutes who allowed men to dictate their choices, she asserted her right to pick her customers and set her fee. For his part, Tony respected her choices. However, for all his supportiveness, his conclusion remained chilling. In stating that she was not his and he could not force her, he implied that, if she were his, he could. More than the prostitute working out of his bar, Tony reflected the future of prostitution, in which few women escaped the supervision of men.

Wartime regulation of entertainment further severed the ties between prostitutes and bar owners, throwing many prostitutes out to shift for themselves on the streets. During the war, police closed down cabarets suspected to be immoral and required that all others finish their business at midnight. One investigator found that prostitutes whom he had met while assessing conditions around Times Square in the winter of 1917 now worked the streets rather than finding clients in the cafés, cabarets, theaters, and bars. Stopping several as they passed by, "I asked them how they were getting along now that the cabarets had to close up at midnight and they said it was bad for them as far as the cabarets were concerned in that they couldn't stay all night as they used to. They said that they had to go out and get them (meaning men) on the street. Several of the girls had never tried the streets they said, but it was a matter of necessity now." Relying on his previous experience in this area, he commented, "I know that this was true that some of these had never been on the streets before, always depending on meeting men at the cabarets or else by appointment." He reported extensive streetwalking from Thirty-Second to Fiftieth Streets and on all the side streets in between.[73] Another investigator reported a conversation that took place on September 2, 1917, with a man who said that the streetwalkers in his neighborhood had "come to him and ask[ed] him to stake them to a quarter and a half a dollar, he said of course they all give it back to him but when a hooker has to go around borrowing quarters and halves so that they can get a bite its enough proof that they are not getting any too much dough, he said they are all starving around here."[74]

The loss of the Raines Law hotels as spaces from which to ply their trade dealt a severe blow to the independent prostitutes who had flourished in New York City before the war. Forced out of the hotels because of the danger they now brought, and faced with new forms of enforcement and skyrocketing arrest and conviction rates, prostitutes responded in a variety of ways to ameliorate their immediate conditions. The very factors that led them to change their practices, however, also restricted their options for maintaining themselves without the help of other people. There is some evidence that "call flats" began to emerge late in the war. Managed almost entirely by women, call flats were small-scale secretive brothels that relied on telephones to coordinate their business without drawing the attention of police. In a letter to the War Department, one man said that he knew "of a private apartment so private that there is a pass word. The lady in charge receives sailors in uniform. The apartment is used for immoral purposes and the lady has a private stock of drinks of all kinds charging far more than the regular price."[75] Call flats would become the dominant site of prostitution in the 1920s. However, extensive police activity, federal and state policies, and wartime propaganda made reestablishing the brothels on a large scale difficult. In addition, few women possessed the necessary capital. As a result, prostitutes had to rely on their own, relatively limited resources to continue to ply their trade.

Having lost a crucial sheltered location for prostituting, women had to move to other spaces. There is no consistent evidence that streetwalking increased during the war. At certain times, such as when the fleet came in, or in certain places, such as theater or dance hall districts, the number of women on the street soliciting was higher than during the prewar period. Describing street conditions around Times Square on the evening of November 17, 1917, an investigator remarked that "observations this evening showed conditions were appalling. Roughly I should say there were many thousand soldiers and sailors and officers in the city last night (Saturday). . . . They were to be seen singly or (and mostly) in couples trios and quartettes walking about the streets either soliciting girls or being solicited by the girls and women."[76] Overall, however, streetwalking held steady and may have declined in areas of the city not dedicated directly to entertainment. After all, the conditions that expelled women from Raines Law hotels made them even more vulnerable on the streets. Prostitutes also lost ground in theaters and other traditional entertainment spaces. Stricter police regulation of cabarets and theaters precluded prostitutes establishing relationships with the proprietors of these establishments. The scarcity of legitimate business partners who earned money in a variety of ways forced prostitutes to turn to people who focused their economic activities largely or exclusively on prostitution. This inevitably led to a decline in the revenues prostitutes kept and in their autonomy.

Pimps became one solution for women grappling with the new dangers. If any john might be a police officer or a stool pigeon, prostitutes needed shields between them and their potential clients. The increase in pimping allowed many women to continue to prostitute, but often at the cost of losing control over their wages and working conditions. Pimps and other go-betweens could warn women about police, steer clients toward them, and bail them out of jail. These arrangements, however, clearly stripped away the autonomy many prostitutes had developed under the Raines Law hotel system. For example, in November of 1917, one investigator "observed a pimp upbraiding a rather well dressed prostitute. The woman was about 35 and the pimp about 25 yrs of age."[77] This prostitute apparently had turned over control of her work to a man ten years her junior. Although using pimps often began as a positive step that prostitutes took to deal with increased police harassment and harsher sentencing, it also decreased prostitutes' autonomy and opened the door for others to profit from, coerce, and exploit them. By the middle of the war, the days of independent prostitution were waning.

Prostitutes responded to the new sanctions by carefully choosing which men they would service, and ironically, most women chose military men as their sexual partners. A national report written by the War Department's Section on Women and Girls on five hundred sexually delinquent women found that 47 percent listed soldiers and sailors as their primary partners. (Sexually delinquent women would have included both prostitutes and women engaged in noncommercial sexual activities.)[78] Later in the war, the Section on Women and Girls released a second report that provided specific information on New York City. It found that 62 percent of sexually delinquent women named soldiers and sailors as their primary sexual partners.[79] In part, these numbers reflect the desires of soldiers and sailors themselves. Despite the War Department's attempts to protect the innocence of the boys in uniform, military men pursued women with the same single-minded intensity that they pursued liquor. One investigator reported that "many soldiers and officers too were out picking up [women]." As he walked down Broadway, he observed "many sailors with prostitutes some of whom I knew."[80] In this example, the investigator identified soldiers as aggressors rather than the passive and innocent victims depicted by the War Department. Most descriptions of conditions during the war indicate that soldiers and sailors actively pursued prostitutes, sex, and alcohol with little regard for community conventions. However, there is also clear evidence that prostitutes solicited soldiers. An investigator reporting on Times Square on November 17, 1917, commented that "it was a common thing to see a prostitute either alone or in the company with another pass a soldier or two and deliberately seize his hand. It worked in every instance that I observed."[81] Soldiers and prostitutes sought out each other's company, despite vigorous attempts on the part of law enforcement to keep them apart.

Prostitutes had both practical and patriotic reasons for preferring military men to civilians. First of all, prostitutes preferred soldiers because they were safer. Although New York City vice cops could don plain clothes and pose as civilians, they could not legally masquerade as soldiers and sailors.[82] As the Committee of Fourteen's general secretary explained with regret, "I [brought up] the question of having the investigators wear sailors' clothes, but was told by the Police Department that such clothes would be considered a disguise and would be unlawful."[83] With the stakes for arrest so high, prostitutes quickly learned to trust men in uniform more than civilians. At Shotwell's Dancing Academy, an investigator tried to pick up a young woman standing on the balcony with a couple of sailors. When he inquired "what chances there was of me taking her out tonight, she said she is dated up, she is going to the Ritz for supper, I told her I'd take her out tomorrow night, she said are you in the service, I said no, I aint a gob, she said then you wont take me out, I am afraid of men in civilian clothes, you may be a bull [a police officer], She said I wont take any chance with a civilian."[84] This stated preference for soldiers was really quite ironic. After all, legislatures passed the laws on prostitution and public health specifically to deny soldiers access to prostitutes. However, the ways in which police enforced the laws made prostitutes more rather than less likely to seek out soldiers. During the war, civilians had difficulty getting prostitutes' attention, because many prostitutes developed an aversion to civilians.

Many women went with soldiers because they assumed soldiers had more money to spend. Although they earned modest salaries, soldiers and sailors had few opportunities to spend their wages and usually collected them before they went on leave. They planned to spend a good deal, and most prostitutes knew this. One investigator summed up this attitude in a report dated March 10, 1918, by stating that "the women don't care much for civilians because they can get more out of the 'boys.'"[85] Increased safety combined with economic motives to make soldiers more attractive clients than civilians. Many reformers viewed this approach as mercenary and denounced prostitutes' role in spending soldiers' money as a particularly vicious form of exploitation. Just before they left to sacrifice their lives for their country, reformers protested, soldiers were relieved by unscrupulous prostitutes of both their money and their innocence. One man reported at a conference that "he had unearthed a well defined plot on the part of outsiders to lay plans to reap the harvest, it being estimated that the men on shore leave would have a total of about $6,000,000. in their possession. He alleged that hundreds of prostitutes were traveling to New York and that arrangements had been made to accommodate them and their customers."[86] This description, however, completely obscured soldiers' willing involvement in these exchanges and their active pursuit of pleasure. In addition, such claims only considered the profits prostitutes made from soldiers, not the ways in which soldiers benefited from prostitutes' company.

While prostitution was obviously about earning money, this did not preclude prostitutes from showing sailors and soldiers a good time. Prostitutes often functioned as tour guides to the world of entertainment, taking men to different cabarets or introducing them to different kinds of food or drink. Exploring the city became a rite of passage for soldiers stationed near New York. Prostitutes profited from this role but also took it seriously as part of their effort to boost morale. The war increased the urgency of showing johns a good time, because so many young men visited the city for the first time and would soon ship out. Ultimately, it is difficult to assess prostitutes' motivations for choosing the clientele they did, but they were probably mixed. There were obvious safety-related and economic factors, but these may have masked more personal and patriotic reasons for providing soldiers with sexual and entertainment services. Prostitutes may have combined economics with emotions when they deliberately chose soldiers. Certainly there are reports of prostitutes shifting to locations that gave them access to soldiers and sailors. However, the surviving historical evidence on their activities does not provide adequate explanations for their behavior.

Prostitutes' attempts to avoid venereal infection also lent themselves to multivalent, or perhaps ambivalent, readings. The War Department, social purity reformers, and many medical doctors argued vigorously that prostitutes could not prevent venereal infections. In a pamphlet written for the American Social Hygiene Association, Dr. William F. Snow stated:

> Medical prophylaxis is more difficult in application to women and is further complicated by the classes of women to be protected. The prostitute plying her trade under the cheapest, most sordid conditions of the vice district has little time or inclination to cooperate in any prophylaxis program; the clandestine prostitute endeavors to avoid discovery and is difficult to reach with any advice; the inmates of the so-called higher class houses can ill afford to offend their patrons by refusing those men who are probably infected or by adopting protective procedures best calculated to protect others.[87]

By this estimation, not only would prostitutes not know how to prevent infection, but the very characteristics of their trade made doing so impossible.

However, prostitutes did know about venereal disease, and their discussions of it prove that a vibrant culture surrounding prostitution kept some of them informed of methods to prevent disease. Although young women sent to Bedford reformatory as wayward minors knew little about how to avoid disease, women who admitted to prostitution discussed their strategies openly with prison officials. Francie Stone's social worker wrote of the extensive precautions the young white prostitute took: "she has been in the habit of examining the men before she has intercourse with them. . . . When asked as to the dangers of prostitution, she says, 'disease' and states that she has a syringe bag and bichloride tablets. She will always take douches after getting through. She is now taking medicine in pills."[88] Women attributed their knowledge of disease prevention to other prostitutes who had advised them on the topic. Sally Marshall, a young white prostitute who admitted to plying her trade to sailors in Brooklyn for several months in the summer of 1917, learned about washing and douching from other prostitutes. According to her social worker, "She had been instructed by other girls not to go with a man 'if discharge was running from him.'"[89]

While prostitutes before the war undoubtedly had some understanding of disease prevention, evidence from 1917 and 1918 indicates that elevated wartime concerns began to change behaviors. Before the war, many prostitutes considered it an insult if a john insisted on using a condom for sex, because it meant that he felt the woman was unclean.[90] Some prostitutes still acquiesced to using them, especially if the client admitted he had venereal disease and expressed a desire to protect her. During the war, some prostitutes began to seek out ways to prevent the spread of disease. For example, one prostitute reported that her john, a lieutenant, "used a condom and came off before he got in."[91] In that case, it was unclear who initiated condom use, but the prostitute did not object to it, as many would have before the war. Other women resorted to "perversion," by which they meant oral sex, because they thought it reduced infection risks for the men whom they serviced. Police caught Sally Marshall prostituting with sailors "while using a perverted method of intercourse on the beach at Coney Island."[92] Marshall did not explain why she performed oral sex, but other prostitutes made the connection between disease and perversion clear. At a bar in Brooklyn, an investigator discovered to his dismay that a prostitute he had been conversing with "was a pervert of the most abandoned type. She told me not to mind that all the girls from s&h's were that way and that in the long run it was much safer as a man in that way took no chance of becoming diseased." The taxi driver who took the investigator home confirmed this, explaining "that all the girls from the above place were perverts."[93] These women clearly thought out their practice and used oral sex as a way to protect their clients, and themselves, from disease.

Some prostitutes understood the risks of disease as well as the government's motivations for both policing prostitution and incarcerating women for the duration of the war. An African American laundress who supplemented her earnings with casual prostitution explained all of this to an undercover investigator. As he wrote in his report, she said that "the police are very strict, are picking the girls up off the street, she also told me that they have their blood tested and if they find anything wrong with them are sending them away to the workhouse till after the war, said theres [sic] been so much sickness in the camp from these women that the government has got to do it, told me Camp Merritt is filled with disease." Thus, the war gave prostitutes considerable incentive to remain disease-free and to keep soldiers healthy as well, and some of them keenly understood the connections between these issues. Avoiding transmission of disease through douching, treatment for existing infection, oral sex, or the use of condoms was better for themselves and their clients. Reflecting both business acumen and an attempt to reduce risk for those they serviced, some prostitutes made a concerted effort to prevent the spread of disease, indicating that they had begun to think about the issue in new ways. Wartime propaganda about disease and military efficiency may have precipitated this shift.[94] While the choices prostitutes made did not fall into the same patriotic category as buying war bonds or volunteering at an army hospital, we should not discount this indirect evidence about prostitutes' preferences for soldiers and for practices that reduced the risk of disease as simply a cold calculation of economic benefits. Prostitutes possessed complicated motivations that may well have included a genuine desire to entertain soldiers while keeping them fit and healthy. Disagreeing with War Department propaganda about abstinence, some prostitutes felt that showing soldiers a good time and attempting to contain the spread of venereal disease represented valid ways to support soldiers, if not the larger war effort.

Wartime conditions and War Department policies had a profound impact on the lives of ordinary prostitutes. While there are no reliable statistics on the number of women incarcerated for prostitution in New York City, the Bedford reformatory inmate case files show a surge of prostitution commitments in May, June, and July of 1917, indicating an initial offensive against prostitution at the beginning of the war. New law enforcement and judicial practices had the capacity to catch more women and retain them in custody for longer periods of time. Furthermore, those women arrested for prostitution and found to be diseased served longer sentences for similar offenses, sometimes staying at Bedford and other facilities for the duration of the war.

In addition to changing the basic nature of prostitution as an economic practice, wartime repression also had a disastrous effect on the lives of individual prostitutes. Records from the Committee of Fourteen, for example, indicate an increase in the involvement of the Society for the Prevention of Cruelty to Children in the lives of prostitutes and their offspring. A prostitute's involvement with soldiers could lead to the removal of her children from her custody. In one case, for example, the general secretary wrote to the superintendent of the children's society stating that a twelve-year-old girl should be removed form her mother's care, "it being alleged, with a good deal of positiveness, that Mrs. Eid has immoral relations with the soldiers."[95] The committee recommended that other children be removed simply because their mothers sold liquor to soldiers out of their apartments.[96] Although association with soldiers may have protected women from arrest, it also complicated other aspects of their lives.

The unprecedented repression of prostitution during the war, the resources brought to bear on it, the new techniques, and, most important, the new harsh punishments profoundly changed the nature of prostitution in New York City. All aspects of their personal and professional lives simply became more difficult for prostitutes. Furthermore, the disruption of earlier alliances between prostitutes and Raines Law hotel proprietors disadvantaged prostitutes and made them turn to other people to help them escape persecution. These solutions, however, had ominous implications for prostitutes' control over their lives, profits, and working conditions.

Wartime measures also made prostitution significantly more dangerous than treating. Instead of facing fines and short jail terms, women convicted of prostitution could be sentenced to long prison terms, and if found to have venereal disease, could be incarcerated indefinitely. Charity girls, on the other hand, escaped punishment even as reformers struggled to discourage treating with the boys in uniform. The war thus changed the relationship between prostitution and treating, making the latter practice not just more morally palatable but significantly safer as well.

Chapter Five

DOING OUR PART FOR THE
BOYS IN UNIFORM
SEXUALITY, TREATING, COURTSHIP,
AND PATRIOTISM

In 1917, the New York City mayor's Women's Committee on National Defense issued a report describing their work with the young women who flocked to the encampments of soldiers in the city. The committee argued that "when these young men are . . . invested with the glamour of military uniforms, they are bound to cause trouble to the younger and more excitable members of the feminine population in the district." Patriotism or, in this case, the glamour of the uniform enticed young girls to visit the soldiers. Wishing to stress the importance of their intervention between young girls and soldiers, the mayor's committee stated that their workers frequently "found disorderly conduct, found girls accosting soldiers and sailors and vice versa, found open and disgustingly familiar necking on the part of young people who admitted that they had known each other for only a few hours or minutes."[1] Staffed by middle-class matrons, the mayor's committee reflected one side of a growing debate over the meaning of young women's sexual involvement with soldiers during World War I. Middle-class women deplored this behavior, calling it a misguided expression of patriotic sentiments. Soldiers, on the other hand, actively promoted the link between sexuality and duty to country, giving many girls' sexual adventures a patina of patriotism. Furthermore, the arguments that associated patriotism with sexuality encouraged some young women to see sex as a valid way of expressing patriotic sentiments or at least supporting soldiers and their sacrifices.

This chapter focuses on how the war changed the character and popularity of treating and the ways in which different groups discussed the value and the meaning of these changes. My argument revolves around the connections, implicit and explicit, between sexuality, patriotism, and the war effort. Three different groups—treating girls, soldiers, and middle-class female War Department officials—all contributed to the debate over the working-class girl's sexuality and its relationship to patriotism. Although these groups disagreed over whether or not treating with soldiers was good or bad, their debates about patriotism and sexuality led to treating's increased popularity. More than any other factor, the war—its conditions and rhetoric—paved the way for the incorporation of treating into the mainstream of American sexual norms.

As treating became more popular and visible, it influenced courtship practices among New York's working class. Wars often accelerate the pace of courtship, and this war proved no exception. Young people engaged in sexual intercourse earlier than they might have before the war, and some married more quickly as well. More important, working-class courtship moved firmly into the realm of commercial amusements, because treating and the wartime economy made such a shift seem both easier and more desirable. By the early 1920s, most working-class courtship took place in commercial amusements rather than the neighborhood and family gatherings that had brought together the previous generation. Finally, the war began to blend treating and courtship, a process that would eventually result in the dating culture of the 1920s. As courtship turned into dating, it began to absorb treating's characteristics, with men paying for dates, and women reciprocating with a range of sexual favors. Courtship in the 1920s would be a more commercialized affair, both in its location and in its logic.

Beginning with a description of the conditions in New York during the war, this chapter discusses how the war itself changed patterns in the practice and popularity of treating. It then turns to the rhetorical strategies of soldiers and War Department officials, which, though radically different in aim, associated sexuality with patriotism. While soldiers argued that a soldier's sacrifice for his country demanded a similar sexual sacrifice from young women, women in the War Department's Section on Women and Girls attempted to steer "khaki-mad girls" into more acceptable forms of war service. When they attempted to influence girls' behavior, however, protective workers met with significant resistance, and both soldiers and young women routinely slipped through their patrols and ignored their advice. In many ways, young women and young men "won" this debate, as it was their interpretation of treating as a form of patriotism and their activities that allowed for treating's absorption into courtship, profoundly shaping the ways women and men would interact in the decades that followed.

Wartime Changes in the Practice of Treating

As the primary embarkation and return destination for soldiers and sailors, New York City routinely faced huge influxes of military personnel. The city itself hosted extensive troop concentrations, especially in the outer bo-

FIGURE 5.1. *Reginald Marsh, "Marines in Central Park," tempera, 1934.*
(Courtesy of The Honorable and Mrs. William Benton)

roughs of Brooklyn, Queens, and the Bronx. Furthermore, soldiers and sailors from all over the Northeast came to visit the city on their leave.[2] While Reginald Marsh painted "Marines in Central Park" in 1934, his depiction of marines and young women in New York's Central Park captures the excitement that parks and camps held for young military personnel and the young women who came to visit them during World War I (Figure 5.1). The high troop concentrations allowed for a free and easy sociability between hundreds of young men and women and constituted a veritable nightmare for those attempting to keep them apart. As the director of the Committee on Working-Girls' Amusements summarized on September 19, 1917, in "the vicinity of Van Cortlandt and Pelham Bay Parks, where troops are encamped . . . the conditions are appalling and . . . the camps at both these Parks are swarming with young girls after the soldiers."[3] In describing another camp, a War Department official commented that "conditions near this camp were wild, some thousands of people being in the neighborhood. Hundreds of young girls, many of them ranging in age from 10 to 16 roamed through the park, laughing, joking and acting familiarly with soldiers."[4] In many ways, the descriptions of the encampments echo those for commercial amusements like Coney Island in the prewar period. It is certainly true that young women viewed the camps this way, flocking to them for excitement and for the chance to be "treated" to entertainment. These reports also highlight the crucial changes that treating underwent during the war. While the first identified young girls' fascination with men in uniform, the second focused on the youth of the girls involved. Characterizing the conditions as "appalling" and "wild," the observers captured the excitement of the camps and the attraction they held for young women. The reports also called attention to the drop in the age of charity girls, their obvious preference for soldiers and sailors, and their willingness to engage in sexual activities in highly visible, often public places. These changes stemmed from young girls' romanticization of soldiers and of wartime more generally. Their brand of patriotism, aimed at helping the morale of individual soldiers, led in turn to the increasing acceptability of the practice of treating. Conversely, patriotism also allowed young women to frame their desire for male company, sexual activity, and commercial amusements in an acceptable way.

Even though many things about treating changed during the war, its basic outlines remained the same. Most obviously, charity girls preserved both the economics and the language of treating throughout the war. Their soldiers took them to ice-cream parlors, dance halls, and bars, paying their way and occasionally buying things for them.[5] For example, one young African American woman from Bedford reformatory argued she was not a prostitute, explaining that she "has had sexual intercourse often with four or five men who have given her presents and taken her out to the theatre and dances."[6] Like this young woman, other charity girls also maintained their use of the language of gifting. For example, several black and white inmates at Bedford during the war insisted that they only received "presents."[7] Treating also retained its working-class character. Investigative reports from the Committee of Fourteen and War Department records both found that the majority of young women socializing with military personnel in the camps held jobs in either factories or domestic service.[8] Finally, as before the war, some charity girls declined to have intercourse with their male friends. After conversations with soldiers at the Grand Central Palace, one investigator reported that some young women resorted to oral sex, while "others masturbated the fellows in the hallway."[9] What a soldier could expect still depended a great deal on what a young woman wanted to give him. However, as we shall see, soldiers' and sailors' overt appeals to patriotism, and their sense of sexual entitlement, began to destabilize the treating exchange in men's favor.

Despite these obvious continuities, the war brought real changes in the practice of treating that eventually helped make it more widespread. The most startling difference was the sharp drop in the age of young girls who engaged in the practice. Before the war, the age of most treating girls fell between 17 and 25. One document produced by the War Department's Section on Women and Girls, "Summary of 3000 Case Records Compared by State," found an average age of 18.6 but argued that "the marked central tendency of the group is young."[10] In their reports, War Department officials in New York City frequently identified girls as young as 12 flirting and "spooning" with soldiers. On September 25, 1917, one protective worker reported that "two soldiers and two young girls about the age of 16 each were back here. The soldiers buttoning up their trousers and the girls with their dresses up fixing something. It was evident that they had just finished having sexual relations."[11] Inmates from Bedford reformatory also reflect this drop in age. Arrested by the police for running away from home to consort with sailors at Coney Island, Sarah Goldfarb told her social worker that "it is all right to go with fellows if they are the right kind; 'girls of 13 or 14 do.'"[12] In a board meeting for the Committee of Fourteen, Maude Miner, director of the New York Probation and Protective Association, told the committee that "The girl question is the greatest that has ever been, only she is so much younger— sometimes even only 9 or 10."[13] As the war progressed, younger and younger girls made the trip to the camps to socialize and treat with soldiers.

Another change lay in young women's obvious preference for men in uniform, to the exclusion of any other suitors. As one investigator reported, "I rarely have seen so many young girls in pairs on the streets, but never a look did they give me, nor were the plain clothes police . . . able to get any advances from them. It was most noticeable that their attention was entirely for the soldiers and sailors."[14] On September 2, 1917, another investigator reported that men he met complained that "these girls will have nothing to do with the civilians, they are all after the uniform. . . . an ordinary fellow used to have a chance with them before the soldiers got here but now it is nothing but the soldiers, they told me they are mostly a lot of young girls, anywheres from 13 yrs. up."[15] Miner confirmed this pattern, describing how girls "neglect the men in plain clothes and go for the men in uniform."[16] Treating girls before the war had periodically pursued men they felt would have more money, such as older men, or for African American women, white men, but they seemed to have few other consistent patterns in their choices. During the war, many young women deliberately pursued military men to the exclusion of all others.

Perhaps the most important change brought about by wartime conditions was the increased visibility of sexual activity (at times including sexual intercourse) between charity girls and soldiers. Treating girls and soldiers routinely engaged in sex play in plain view of passersby. One investigator observed that on the evening of September 25, 1917, "many soldiers sitting of [sic] the benches with the girls the latter in about half of the cases were on the laps of the soldiers" and "hugging and kissing was being indulged in by every couple but one that I saw." The same investigator also reported seeing "a soldier in the act of sexual intercourse with a girl right on B'way. . . . The couple was standing up the grass being wet."[17] Some girls caught having intercourse with military personnel and sent to Bedford had also engaged in sex outdoors. One social worker reported of her white charge, "informant believes she almost always had intercourse out of doors."[18] As these examples indicate, treating girls and soldiers used public parks, benches, and even the side of the road to have sex. Unlike prostitutes, who avoided having sex in the open, treating girls willingly had sex in public. While this difference illustrates prostitutes' understandable fears of being caught, it also demonstrates treating girls' willingness to flaunt public conventions. Before the war, young people sometimes resorted to the hallways of tenements, public bathrooms, and occasionally parks, but they usually tried to hide their sexual activities.[19] The war dramatically increased the number of couples having sex in places visible to the public. Part of this new visibility derived from the new connections drawn between young women's sexuality and their patriotism. The emergence of treating before the war had begun to validate sexual barter specifically and sexual permissiveness more generally. When combined with the new aura of wartime romanticism and sacrifice, young people felt that their behavior could stand the test of public scrutiny.

These three changes, the drop in the age of treating girls, their preference for soldiers, and the visibility of their sexual relations, all coincided during the brief engagement of the United States in World War I. These factors all point to the increasing acceptability of treating and the association of that acceptance with girls' attitudes toward soldiers and sailors. Young women's testimony supports these connections. One girl, identified in the report as thirteen or fourteen years old, told an investigator that she slept with a particular man because "she 'only wanted to make him happy before he went away to be killed.'"[20] While she did not refer to patriotism explicitly, she clearly romanticized the plight of this soldier, and she saw giving him sexual access to her body as a way to make his final days at home enjoyable. In essence, she saw having sex as a way to act patriotically. This is not to argue that girls expressed an explicit support for this war. No one, for example, made direct references to Wilson's war message. Charity girls, however, clearly invested soldiers with a level of desirability and romance that few men enjoyed in either the pre- or postwar period.

Other young women's testimony supports the conclusion that the romanticization of soldiers and the immediacy of war influenced young women's decisions to treat. One stated that "She liked spending time with uniformed men 'because they were going off to war and she felt sorry for them. . . . they were always good to her and never used bad language.'"[21] When questioned by a War Department official in June of 1917, another woman explained her upcoming marriage to a soldier by stating that "he wants to marry me and I said alright, he is a nice sort of fellow," and the official reported that "she expects him to go to France shortly." She asserted, however, that this marriage would not keep her from going with other soldiers. "I could never stick to one man," she explained pragmatically, "as soon as he goes away dont [sic] you think I'll want something too."[22] Treating with soldiers proved too much fun for her to stop, even after she married. In many ways, this young woman's response is an extreme but accurate summation of charity girls' attitudes toward soldiers, the war, commerce, and sexuality. The war increased the motivation to treat, both for fun and for patriotism. Men's imminent departure made it that much more urgent that both they and the girls around them enjoy their last moments at home.[23]

Charity girls during the war blended their own desires with those of soldiers. Like the girls who treated before the war, they wanted access to entertainment and fun, and some wanted sex and intimacy with the men they met. Rather than changing the basic nature of the treating exchange, the war instead rendered it more acceptable and more widespread. The glamour of war and the romance of entertaining a soldier or sailor, perhaps for the last time, led young women to pursue treating at a younger age and in a more public way. Charity girls were not alone in these associations. Both soldiers and War Department officials made the connection between sexuality and patriotism even more explicit.

We Are Fighting for You Girls:
Soldiers, Masculinity, and Sexual Entitlement

Of course, soldiers and sailors had their own opinions about treating and their rights to sexual satisfaction. The way they argued their points with the girls, and with each other, revealed a great deal about their conceptions of masculinity and its relationship to military service. As young men who found themselves in a variety of new settings and social relationships, military personnel had a number of different masculine identities from which to choose at any given moment. While many expressed aggressive sexual entitlement, others envisioned themselves as the protectors of women. The War Department obviously encouraged the model of "protective masculinity" in its propaganda and posters, but some young men came to it on their own. All of these masculine identities revolved in some way around patriotism and women's sexuality. On the whole, soldiers expressed an astounding level of sexual entitlement. Most openly encouraged young women to view treating and sexual favors as a form of patriotism.

The romance of war and perhaps the age of the girls involved gave soldiers more bargaining power than most men had enjoyed before the war. In addition, soldiers, particularly in groups, clearly adhered to a masculinity that revolved around overt sexuality and frequently demanded sex from women. One man summed up the common attitude: "we are fighting for you girls, and you ought to do something for us."[24] This young man made the connection between war service, sexuality, and patriotism quite clear. Patriotic duty on a soldier's part mandated a reciprocal duty on the part of the young women he socialized with while at home or on leave. Young women should offer sex willingly because of the sacrifices the soldier made to defend young women, their homes, and their country. This attitude rested on a sense of reciprocal bodily sacrifice. If men would sacrifice their bodies in war for the nation, young women must also sacrifice their bodies for the pleasure and affirmation of the soldiers. In this model, both sacrifices reflected an active engagement with patriotism. This logic played on women's sense of agency, asking them to willingly give their bodies, as soldiers did, to support the war effort. Other military personnel argued that the young women who visited the camps came for sex and that young, virile men only provided girls with what they wanted. "Hell we do not hurt the girls," one soldier declared. "There is a lot of 'padding' going on but we wouldn't give it to the girls if they didn't come looking for it. No soldier will rape a girl. It only queers the whole bunch."[25] His assessment emphasized the willingness of girls to come to the camps to entertain soldiers and their desire to have sex while there. Both of these young men used the pronoun "we," indicating that their highly sexual masculinity was rooted in a group identity for soldiers. Soldiers who expressed "oversexed" identities and demanded sex probably did so to impress each other as much as they did to convince the girls they met.

The sexual competition among men in the military is expressed most clearly in a watercolor by Charles Demuth painted in 1917 titled "Dancing Sailors" (Figure 5.2).[26] In some ways, this image looks very much like a typical treating encounter during the war. Young men in uniform dance with girls at a public amusement and, after paying for these entertainments, will most likely negotiate some sexual payment in return. However, despite the

FIGURE 5.2. *Charles Demuth, "Dancing Sailors," watercolor on paper, 1917.*
(© The Cleveland Museum of Art, Mr. and Mrs. William H. Marlott Fund, 1980.9)

female figures in the image, the painting is also overtly homoerotic. As art historian Jonathan Weinberg argues, "the sailor on the left seems to stare past his clinging partner to exchange glances with the male to his left. The legs of the two adjacent male dancers appear to brush against each other as the couples dance on the floor. The central focus of the composition is not on the bodies of the women, which are mostly covered by their long loosely fitted dresses and the backs of their male partners, but on the muscular bodies of the sailors—particularly their buttocks."[27] While Weinberg emphasizes the homoerotics of the sailors' gaze and their overt interest in each other, the painting also depicts the men's evaluation of each other's success in finding a sexual partner. It expresses both sexual interest and sexual competition.

As in the Demuth watercolor, soldiers went out together and often expressed overt interest, even voyeurism, in evaluating each other's sexual escapades. Undercover investigators and protective workers both describe soldiers traveling the city in groups, particularly when in search of entertainment. Of course, young men in a new city would be likely to explore it with their friends, that is, fellow soldiers, but the all-male culture of the military also fostered competition between men in their heterosexual interactions. Feminist theorists and historians of sexuality and manhood have highlighted the homosocial aspects of fraternity-group sexual activities or those of other exclusively male groups.[28] Similarly, many young soldiers during this war often pursued sex in the way they did to impress each other.

Sexual conquest and excessive sexual appetites were clearly linked in many young men's vision of their identity as fighting men and of the appropriate behavior of soldiers on leave. This conception reflected an old association between fighting and sexuality common in both American and military culture. Proponents of these beliefs asserted that virile young men needed to find sexual outlets if they were to be effective fighters. And, in fact, some soldiers literally combined violent conquest and sexual conquest in their behavior. Even though the soldier quoted above stated that "no soldier would rape a girl," the documentary evidence shows that soldiers' sense of sexual entitlement often resulted in harassment and sometimes in rape.[29]

Military men frequently accosted women on the streets and proved extremely persistent in their efforts to obtain female attention. One investigator witnessed a group of sailors harassing a married woman outside a saloon in Brooklyn. When the woman's husband stepped in briefly to buy beer, the "woman was accosted by one of the many dozen sailors loitering about the corner. The first one was ignored by the woman, then another tried it and still another[,] the woman growing more uneasy all the while. Each time a sailor was refused recognition by the woman, he would step to the side while another tried, observing each next man's attempt. This kept up until the [husband] appeared again." The husband, though outraged by the treatment of his wife, decided that discretion was the better part of valor and beat a hasty retreat.[30] Women could not walk in areas near the camp without being propositioned repeatedly by men in uniform. One young woman, while out on an evening stroll in Van Cortlandt Park on August 2, 1917, "was accosted ten times by soldiers while walking North on the East side of B'way." In addition, "soldiers insulted her."[31] Both women and community members complained to various authorities, but the problem, particularly in New York City, and particularly when the fleet was in, became too large for anyone to control.

This kind of public harassment exemplified attitudes toward sexuality, masculinity, and women that at times spilled over into violence. One soldier boasted to an investigator in June of 1918 about "being out with the girl that works in Griffens . . . said he jammed her 3 times in the car, she started kick-ing[,] said he got her all wet and she feel sick." [32] A group of sailors raped Sarah Goldfarb when she ran away with another girl to Coney Island. The men offered to get them a room but demanded sex in return. As Sarah tear-fully explained to her social worker, "You never want to do such a thing[,] only I did not want to stay on the street all night. I didn't think they would do such a thing. You know some fellows have pity." Sarah said that this was her first sexual experience, and her social worker concurred, commenting, "her naive description of what happened would seem to indicate that she is truthful." [33] Just as the call to patriotism gave soldiers bargaining power, it seemed also to loosen their sense of just how far they could go to get what they wanted. The romanticization of soldiers and their plight thus proved to be a double-edged sword for charity girls. On the one hand, it increased the acceptability of intercourse and sexual barter. By the end of the war, treat-ing was firmly entrenched in working-class heterosocial and courtship prac-tices. On the other hand, it allowed men to demand what had previously been offered willingly or perhaps not offered at all. Although some girls still got away without being compelled to have intercourse with military men, others lost control over the treating negotiation. Confidence in their new right to sexual satisfaction made some soldiers and sailors more willing to force girls.

Investigators' descriptions reveal a level of public licentiousness that ob-viously affected the landscape and atmosphere around troop concentra-tions. One investigator observed in a report dated June 6, 1917, that "some of the sailors strolled about with their hands on their private parts. . . . a few had their trousers open and walked about that way." [34] Not only did these sailors openly display their genitals, but they also pursued sexual activities with no recognition of cultural or social boundaries. One investigator wit-nessed several male couples composed of sailors and civilians kissing on the street corner. Later on, another group of sailors stopped him and asked if he knew "where they could get a girl. One said anything will do[,] black or white. We don't draw the color line." "It seemed to me," he commented rather bemusedly, "that the sailors were sex mad." [35] These men appeared willing to cross any cultural line for sex, ignoring prescriptions against both homosexual and interracial sexual acts. [36] Their attitudes led the investigator to sympathize with the women in the area, and he observed philosophically that "this was perhaps the reason why girls, unaccompanied, could not be found in the neighborhood." [37]

A few soldiers chose to explore a different sort of masculinity, one that cast them as paternal or brotherly figures of young women about to stray from sexual virtue. According to one woman's case file from the Bedford Hills State Reformatory, she was rescued from one soldier, who had gotten her drunk, by another, "who had recently enlisted and was guarding the bridge near Coney Island." Paraphrasing the girl's testimony, the social worker reported that her defender "sent the man away and told Trudy that she was too intoxicated to go back to New York and that he would take care of her until she was able to return."[38] The two sat on the beach at Coney Island all night, waiting for Trudy to sober up. This encounter emphasized the conflict between two kinds of masculinity available to soldiers. While one young man was sexually aggressive and probably got his date drunk to take advantage of her, the other stepped in as her protector and sent the first young man away. Protecting young women from other men's advances demonstrated a young man's chivalry.

While young soldiers clearly had different forms of masculinity available to them, the vast majority relied more on an aggressive and highly sexual one. In part, this may have resulted from the fact that soldiers spent leave time in groups. If the young man stationed to guard the bridge had been with his friends, he might have been less likely to defend Trudy. However, it is also clear that both of these forms of masculinity revolved, in one way or another, around women's sexuality and men's access and rights to it. When the officials at the War Department formulated propaganda, they tried hard to cultivate protective masculinity, often in the face of the aggressive sexual activities of soldiers and sailors on leave.

The War Department and Conflicting Notions of Masculinity

The entrance of the United States into World War I immediately raised concerns about venereal disease among the troops. In an attempt to reduce the number of soldiers contracting venereal disease, War Department propaganda invoked protective masculinity that stressed young men's relationships to their mothers, sisters, and daughters at home. Furthermore, it promoted a vision of masculinity that attempted to disassociate aggressive sexuality from aggressiveness more generally. Officials wanted troops who would fight fiercely in battle but resist the temptation to have sex with prostitutes and charity girls. Violence and sexuality, they argued, could be separated in the identities of America's troops.

A set of exhibit posters produced by the YMCA evoked protective masculinity by associating all women with the women in a soldier's family (Figure 5.3).[39] One of them reads, "Take no liberties with any girl that you would not have another man or boy take with your sister," and it pictures a soldier and a young woman standing together at a railing, presumably at some enter-

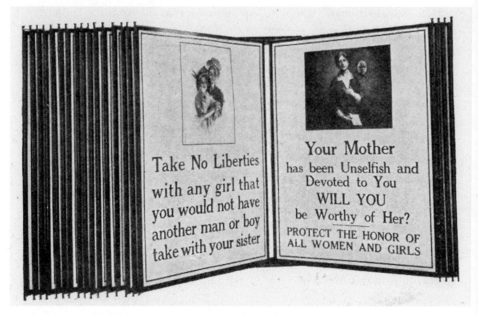

FIGURE 5.3. *"Take No Liberties" and "Your Mother Has Been Unselfish,"* exhibit posters from the Sex Education Bureau of the National War Work Council of the YMCA. From M. J. Exner, M.D., *"Social Hygiene and the War,"* Social Hygiene 5 (1919): 285.

tainment event. By asking the young man to act as though all young women were his sister, it urges him to uphold the chastity and virtue of all the young women he meets. As he takes responsibility for them, other men, he hopes and the poster implies, will take care of his sister while he fights abroad for his country. This appeal universalized the value of chastity for all women and asked the soldier himself to remain chaste as a way to ensure the chastity of women. The facing poster in the exhibit continued this theme of duty to, and protection of, the women in one's family. The text reads, "Your mother has been unselfish and devoted to you. Will you be worthy of her? Protect the honor of all women and girls." Stressing the soldier's duty to protect all women, it evokes the soldier's relationship to his mother and her sacrifice. To be a good man and a good soldier, a young man has to remember his debt to the women in his family and repay it by refraining from sex with young women he might meet.[40]

As these posters demonstrate, the War Department expressed concern about the virtue of young women and manipulated soldiers' relationships with the women in their families and, in particular, with their mothers to promote chastity. However, the main goal of these propaganda efforts was to preserve troop efficiency by reducing the number of men afflicted with vene-real disease. As a result, most of the slides shown to the troops appealed to the glamour of war and young men's desire to be soldiers and fight bravely for their country. A series of slides used in a lecture in the training camps em-phasizes that being sexually active with any woman, prostitute or not, could hurt a man's chance to participate in the war (Figure 5.4). "A real soldier is a game sport. He is not afraid of taking chances—of the right kind," the first slide states. Picturing a soldier with a young woman and then young men engaged in trench warfare, the second and third slides continue, "But if he falls for this kind of chance," a sexual encounter with a young woman, "he may sacrifice his chance in the big game." Better to remain chaste than risk an infection and miss out on the "big game" of war.

These slides also demonstrate the War Department officials' attempts to disassociate sex and violence in the minds of soldiers. In these images, the two issues are diametrically opposed. Giving into one (sexual intercourse) could deny young men the opportunity to experience the other (war). Other posters produced by the War Department are even more obvious in their attempts to disrupt these traditionally interconnected aspects of soldiers' male identity. In a poster issued by the surgeon general of the army, the text directly associates violence and masculinity with chastity (Figure 5.5). "You kept fit and defeated the Hun," it states. "Now set a high standard, a clean America! Stamp out venereal diseases." Having vanquished America's foes in war, young soldiers could now, by remaining chaste, attack the internal enemy of venereal disease. The poster's image emphasizes the strength and physical bravery of America's fighting men. Standing with legs spread, the young soldier in full battle gear dominates the landscape, towering over the Prussian war helmets scattered at his feet. Obviously both masculine and warlike, this is the image of a young man who set a new, high standard by refraining from sex while maintaining his violent male identity.

These posters contested older attitudes, both inside the military and out-side of it, that associated masculinity, sexuality, and violence. By redefin-ing masculinity as protective (rather than exploitative) of women's sexuality, the War Department sought to change behavior and extend men's protec-tive feelings about the women in their families to the women of America as a whole. At the same time, other posters supported this universally protec-tive masculinity by arguing that masculinity, chastity, and violence were not mutually exclusive categories. Instead, chastity and sexual restraint could be used in the service of violent masculinity. Meanwhile, officials in the War Department knew that they had to fight the battle against venereal disease

FIGURE 5.4. *"Not Afraid of Taking Chances," stereoscopic slides. From Assistant Surgeon General H. E. Kleinschmidt, USN, Navy Department on Training Camp Activities, "Educational Prophylaxis of Venereal Diseases,"* Social Hygiene 5 (1919): 31.

FIGURE 5.5. "You Kept Fit and Defeated the Hun," poster issued by the Surgeon
General of the Army. From Lt. Col. Seale Harris, Medical Corps, "G.H.Q. Bulletin
No. 54 on the Venereal Problem," Social Hygiene 5 (1919): 310.

on several fronts. Young women, as well as young men, had to be enlisted if this campaign were to succeed.

War Department Officials and Narratives about Treating

War Department officials put extensive resources into preventing venereal disease by controlling the activities of prostitutes. Incarcerating 30,000 women required a massive restructuring of both the criminal justice and penal systems of most states. However, officials quickly realized that prostitutes did not pose the only threat to soldiers' health. As the general secretary of New York's preeminent vice society commented, "as you know, the reports all show that in the great bulk of instances of illicit relations, the partner with the soldier is not a professional prostitute but what we call the 'charity' girl."[41] In seeking to eliminate this danger to the boys in uniform, women from the War Department asserted their own opinions about young women's sexual behavior. Although they differed from soldiers in their attitudes and approaches, they also clearly viewed treating in the camps as a form of patriotism and tried very hard to dissuade young women from engaging in it. The wild conditions in and around New York City's camps clearly constituted a threat both to soldiers' health and to girls' virtue, and the women's agencies of the War Department moved to contain the danger.

Two War Department posters exemplify officials' conflicting attitudes about the source of infection for soldiers as well as their concerns about prostitutes and treating girls. The first, like the posters discussed in the previous section, appealed to a young man's relationship with his family (Figure 5.6). "Remember the folks at home," it states ominously. "They are waiting for you to come back with an honorable record. Don't allow a whore to spoil the reunion." In this case, the prostitute threatens the soldier's relationship to his family. The second poster, however, was far more ambiguous about the source of danger (Figure 5.7). In it, a soldier and a sailor face each other and gaze at the image of a pretty, young white woman between them. The positioning of the figures implies that the men in the poster themselves are looking at a poster and trying to come to a decision. Although the woman looks pure and innocent, the text reads, "Friend or enemy? To the men of the Army and Navy." If the first poster represents the attitudes of officials in the War Department toward prostitutes, the second complicates the notion that prostitutes alone were responsible for venereal infections among the troops. Taken together, these two posters show the ambiguity that the activities of charity girls forced the War Department officials to explore.

Furthermore, the race of both the woman and the two men gazing at her typify the racial tone of the propaganda produced by the War Depart-

FIGURE 5.6. *"Don't Allow a Whore to Spoil the Reunion," poster issued by the War Department. From Assistant Surgeon General H. E. Kleinschmidt, USN, Navy Department on Training Camp Activities, "Educational Prophylaxis of Venereal Diseases,"* Social Hygiene 5 *(1919): 30.*

FIGURE 5.7. *"Friend or Enemy?," cover illustration of a* YMCA *booklet.*
From M. J. Exner, M.D., "Social Hygiene and the War," Social Hygiene *5 (1919): 284.*

ment. Despite the presence of both African American troops and African American women in neighborhoods near the camps of New York City, none of the propaganda directed at military personnel depicted African Americans.[42] Both the Bedford reformatory records and the investigations of the War Department and the Committee of Fourteen make it clear that African American women engaged in a variety of social and sexual activities with white and African American troops ranging from courtship through treating and prostitution. The War Department certainly gave in to the extreme racism of the South when it segregated the troops. It also insisted that all troops follow "local" customs of segregation even in many northern cities that had no such traditions and that, in fact, had laws prohibiting racial discrimination in entertainment and accommodation. According to Nancy Bristow in *Making Men Moral*, the War Department saw African American men and women as inherently sexually immoral and singled them out for increased surveillance.[43] But these assumptions, which affected the treatment of African American women around the camps in southern cities, did not extend to the propaganda that warned troops about venereal risks. Perhaps this is because, as Bristow argues, when imagining America and its troops, the War Department only saw a white nation and did not bother itself with those whose war service contradicted that fact. At any rate, African American women did not serve as a warning to white troops; all of the posters depicted white women as the threat to white soldiers. It was as if African Americans, either as soldiers or as camp followers, did not exist at all.

Although concerned about the spread of disease, women's agencies refused to place charity girls in the same category as prostitutes. Focusing on the girls' naïveté and their redeemability, War Department workers argued that girls should be educated rather than punished. The writers who designed the education and intervention programs called attention to young women's innocence and lack of judgment regarding men and their intentions. Katharine Bement Davis, director of the War Department's section "Work for Women," saw men as the aggressors in immoral relations. In an article for the journal *Social Hygiene*, Davis blamed young women's sexual impropriety on their naïveté. "Young girls," she stated, don't realize "that the uniform covers all the kinds of men there are in the world; men of high ideals, chivalrous instincts, who naturally treat every girl as they want every man to treat their mothers and sisters . . . or, in the worst instances, men who feel that their own physical appetites must be gratified, no matter who suffers." These young women, she asserted, often fell prey to men of bad intentions, and thus "many girls, through ignorance, through emotion, take steps which will lead to bitter regret."[44] Portrayed as innocent, charity girls emerge from the federal literature as passive and impressionable, swept up in the excitement of war.

Federal attitudes toward charity girls were complicated by the belief that sexual impropriety of any kind often led to prostitution. As Jane Rippin, director of the Section on Women and Girls, asserted, the typical charity girl went "from her own lover who has gone over seas, perhaps never to return, to other lovers in quick succession." Rippin's view of the slippery slope often equated treating with prostitution. "The 'charity girl' or 'patriotic prostitute,'" she argued, "is, as her name would indicate, a development of the war in the form of prostitution for patriotism's sake." The charity girl, Rippin insisted, "frequently expects to receive presents of rides, candy, suppers, etc., in return." Accurately describing the treating exchange, Rippin went on to concede that despite "the element of commercialism . . . [t]he 'charity girl' is not in the business of prostitution, although she may become a professional in time."[45] For both Davis and Rippin, charity girls occupied an intermediary category, one that could easily cross over into prostitution. In some ways, their views represented the success of charity girls themselves at asserting a separate moral and sexual identity. By the outbreak of the war, reformers saw them as a distinct group, governed by different rules than either chaste women or prostitutes. Like the girls themselves, these female reformers focused on motivations rather than on actual sexual acts or even profit. According to Rippin and Davis, the two most important officials in the War Department's efforts to control delinquent women and girls, patriotism, and not profit, drove young women to engage in sexual activities with soldiers. Davis wrote about charity girls as "young girls, thrilled with patriotism," for whom "the 'lure of the uniform' is everywhere recognized."[46] Rippin described charity girls as "khaki mad" and asserted that "it needs no special interest in problems connected with girls to discover the effect of these unusual times on the romantic girl between the ages of fifteen and twenty-five."[47]

Davis and Rippin clearly grasped treating's consumer orientation but misunderstood the shift in sexual norms that it represented. As Davis wrote, "these girls, who are used to choosing everything for themselves, from clothes to codes, know them to be good and put them on as they'd put on a new hat and walk out to help set the fashion."[48] While understanding the crucial material and consumer aspects of treating, Davis missed the new sexual norms young women introduced. Treating functioned as a way to gain access to entertainment, a public world often both economically and morally denied to young women, and to claim some ownership of their own sexuality within an admittedly limited set of constraints. This ownership commodified their bodies, but it also allowed young women, and not their parents, reformers, or most men, to decide how and when to use them. Seen in this light, treating represented both a shift in morality and a shift in more traditional gendered understandings of women's bodies. When Davis read treating solely as fashion, she trivialized its gendered and sexual implications. This position also allowed her to assume that convincing girls would be easy. Reformers would need only to convince young girls that sexual virtue was more fashionable than their own version of sexual morality. This model gave young girls the power to be consumers, but not the ability to create new products that suited their own needs and desires. Middle-class women would still dictate the new fashion.

War Department educational efforts exemplify this attitude by literally drawing a connection between girls' war service and fashion. One poster, designed to remake working-class girls' patriotism, warned of the dangers of "improper dress" (Figure 5.8). The poster featured two party gowns, one modest and the other risqué, and urged young women when attending parties with soldiers to refrain from wearing dresses that "may do harm by arousing emotions hard to control." The poster also contains coded class language, encouraging working-class girls to adopt the social attitudes and dress of their "betters." Explaining that the preferred dress is "modest, pretty, simple and inexpensive," and therefore within the reach of working-class girls, the poster then states that it has been "adopted by the Junior League in New York City." The class modeling that this kind of poster promoted was consistent with War Department officials' maternalism. They viewed themselves as mothers and believed that treating resulted from poor mothering. By blaming working-class parents, and in particular mothers, for young girls' sexual adventures, these middle-class women created a role for themselves in the lives of working-class girls. In essence, they could become the mothers of misguided girls and teach them proper morality and behavior.

Most War Department propaganda argued explicitly that sexual immorality among young women could be traced to the failures of their mothers. By far the most successful of these propaganda pieces was a widely shown forty-five-minute film titled *The End of the Road*.[49] Presented in the new and immensely popular medium of the motion picture, it told the story of two childhood friends, Mary and Vera, who migrated from a small town to the big city during the war.[50] On the surface, it was intended to convince young women not to give in to soldiers' demands for sex, but its underlying message validated middle-class women's position as the only appropriate moth-

FIGURE 5.8. *"Improper Dress," wall poster produced by the Section on Women's Work, Social Hygiene Division, War Department Commission on Training Camp Activities. From Katharine Bement Davis, "Social Hygiene and the War: Woman's Part in Social Hygiene,"* Social Hygiene *4 (1918): 526.*

ers of all girls and justified their intervention in the lives of working-class people.

The story in *End of the Road* turns out to be as much about the responsibilities of motherhood as it is about sexuality and gender. Vera's mother, clearly the villain, is a frivolous, grasping woman who ruins her daughter to further her own ambition. Rather than educating her daughter about sex and morality, she fills her head with ambitions of a wealthy marriage, clearly an inappropriate display of social climbing through sex. Mary's mother, on the other hand, teaches her daughter about sex and is her "friend." When the two girls leave for the city, their differing upbringings and sexual educations lead them down very different paths. Mary attends nursing school and eventually falls in love with a dashing older doctor. Urged on by her greedy mother, Vera, in contrast, goes to the city to find a rich young man. She works as a salesgirl in a department store, where she waits on and dates rich young men. Treating with them, Vera contracts venereal disease and is deserted by her lover. Mary rescues Vera from her desperate situation and, after taking her to an asylum for syphilitic women, convinces her to get treatment for her infection.

While *The End of the Road* highlights two middle-class young women, it also refers periodically to the more typical working-class girl who most concerned reformers. In one scene, Mary dissuades a young factory girl from going with a soldier for some fun in the bushes. Although the young girl avoids his embrace, she still develops syphilis from the one kiss they exchange. Distraught, she turns to Mary, who sends her to her mother in the country to recover. Mary functions both as a virtuous young woman and, in concert with her mother, a "protective worker" who saves young girls from themselves, insists that they have their venereal disease treated, and provides them with a wholesome environment from which they can embark into the world wiser and more responsible. Through the character of Mary, the film provides a model for young girls and validation for the maternal role of protective workers. Like Mary, these women would understand the dangers of ignorance and lust, serve their country, maintain the purity of the troops, and save young women from desperate ends.

As in the case of Rippin's and Davis's writings for *Social Hygiene*, the treating girl emerges as a sadly misguided but still salvageable and ultimately innocent character. None of the young women who falter in their virtue actually do so because of innate evil. The cause of Vera's downfall rests squarely on her mother's shoulders, while nervous exhaustion in the factories of the city led to the indiscretion of Mary's working-class charge. Both girls lacked guidance in their sexual and moral choices. Surely, the film seems to say, if someone could only oversee their activities, these girls would not have fallen. In these War Department narratives, venereal disease among non-prostitutes is the fault of mothers who fail to educate their girls properly.

Patrolling the Camps: Protective Workers and the Treating Girls of New York City

War Department officials prepared pamphlets, films, and lectures for young women, all aimed at convincing them to stay away from soldiers and remain sexually pure. The War Department's Section on Women and Girls also employed middle-class volunteers "of mature years to patrol the streets together and [endeavor] by their presence to prevent unfortunate conditions from being permitted to continue."[51] When protective workers visited the camps, they discovered chaotic conditions, resentful soldiers, and resistant young women. Still, they clung to their belief that treating girls were passive, naive, and impressionable. The reports they wrote reflected this contradiction and their attempts to reconcile their beliefs with the sauciness and the generally unrepentant behavior of the girls they met. Instead of giving girls "the straight talk," as national officials suggested, protective workers in New York City avoided discussing sex and relied more on threats and promises to convince the girls they dealt with.

Protective workers questioned girls about their religious training, their parents, and their home environment, but when deciding what to do with a girl, they tended to rely more on their own judgments of her character than on the information she provided. Cheerful and deferential attitudes made good impressions and weighed heavily in their assessments of girls and their "recoverability." Workers read resistance as sign of moral failing, and hostility indicated that girls had perhaps "crossed" into prostitution and left the liminal social category of the treating girl. These interactions emphasized just how much workers relied on their own understandings of charity girls as passive and innocent and of prostitutes as active and deliberately immoral.[52]

The importance of narratives of charity girls' innocence and passivity became obvious when officers dealt with the issue of disease. Despite the emphasis on disease in lectures, posters, pamphlets, and films like *The End of the Road*, none of the accounts of field workers ever mentioned protective officers using disease as a way to dissuade girls from sexual liaisons with the soldiers. One young woman turned the tables on a protective officer in the summer of 1917 when she asked about birth control. After accepting an offer of a lemon soda in a nearby shop, the young woman asked "if those rubber things the men used were safe and also if a man could ever tell whether she had had intercourse before." The officer avoided a factual answer and instead "waxed moralizing and only after[ward] I saw that she was a young girl who had been taking chances with men she knew."[53] This encounter demonstrates protective workers' investment in the innocence of young girls and their reluctance to discuss disease. When confronted with a young woman who asked about birth control, this officer relied more on her judgment of the young woman's polite and "naive" manner than on the obvious fact of experience she had had with soldiers and birth control.

Instead of discussing issues in which the girls expressed interest, protective workers turned to settlement work as the catch-all solution to young women's sexual activities. Settlement house activities served a dual purpose, both for the root causes of treating and as an incentive to get young girls to cooperate. Since protective officers attributed treating and "patriotic prostitution" to a failure of mothering and a lack of appropriate supervision, club work provided the perfect solution. In a settlement house, girls could congregate and enjoy various organized entertainments under the watchful eye of a settlement worker. Settlement house workers could take the place of the absent or inadequate mother and teach young girls about sexual and domestic responsibility. Finally, settlement work did provide girls with some free amusements that they could not get elsewhere. With few places to go for free entertainment, girls often leapt at the chance to participate in settlement activities. One protective officer commented with some satisfaction that the young girls she met "would like very much, they said, 'to join some girls club.' . . . A club where they could 'meet some nice people.'"[54] Such opportunities filled a real need for the girls and, as such, served as a powerful enticement away from the excitement of the camps.

Despite the incentives that protective workers offered their young charges, they often met with resistance. Most often, girls responded with flippancy to criticisms of their behavior and suggestions for improvements. Their lack of seriousness distressed protective officers, and it was often their attitudes more than their behavior that led officers to follow up on girls' cases. One woman met two Catholic girls on March 6, 1918, and in the course of her interrogation, asked them when they had last gone to confession and what they would say when next they did. According to her report, "the older of the two girls sobered up and said, 'Guess it will take me about a week to get ready' — then they both laughed. It wasn't an irreverent or ironical laugh — just the same inane, meaningless expression that characterized them in every thing."[55] To the protective worker, their laughter signified a failure to comprehend their circumstances, and an overall meaninglessness, emptiness, and lack of values that plagued their lives. This response, more than their actual behavior, caused this protective worker to despair over her young charges.

Of course, protective workers often met with more active resistance. Hostile and often assertive, young women challenged reformers' rights to intervene in their lives. And while reformers might prevail during the war, the trouble they had with young women and their soldier friends did not bode well for the success of their overall program to discourage sex between unmarried young people. Girls rejected the meddling of protective workers in a variety of ways. When accosted by protective workers, girls talked back, ran away, and sometimes simply ignored the women's entreaties. In the spring of 1918, when one protective worker tried to stop a young girl from phoning soldier friends at the camp, the girl shouted that she should "mind her own business."[56] Another set of girls rode the trolley cars up to Pelham Park on September 22, 1917, and resisted the protective officers' attempts to stop them: "they were highly indignant [and] said they had come to see somebody." Later the officer reported that "we noticed them still on the grounds; kept an eye on them, and met them as they started to the car—asked for interview. They were furious, accused us of following them, and refused to answer questions and boarded the car. Mrs. Cook followed, and . . . we finally secured following information. . . . all working at Lace Factory as menders; all frightened, and demanded promise that parents would not be told."[57] Belligerent throughout the entire encounter, the young women protested interference to the very end.

The resistance that reformers met in the camps was prophetic. Although reformers argued vigorously about the dangers to girls of associating with soldiers, young girls and soldiers continued to socialize. While both soldiers and reformers argued that treating in the camps reflected young women's patriotism, it was the soldiers, and not reformers, who held sway with young women. The patterns that emerged during the war indicated a real change in the place treating held in the world of working-class youth. Wartime conditions and wartime debates about the relationship between patriotism and sexuality gave treating a new patina of legitimacy. The ways treating changed during the war made it a more acceptable and more popular practice, which, in turn, brought it from the margins into the mainstream of working-class sexual and cultural life.

Courting during Wartime

What reformers feared most was that treating during the war would change courtship, increasing both the incidence of premarital intercourse and its acceptability. Wartime conditions and the presence of treating girls at the camps and in entertainment spaces with soldiers does seem to have shifted courtship practices significantly, in both expected and unexpected ways. These changes were gradual, began before the war, and continued after it. In addition, U.S. involvement in the war lasted only eighteen months, making assessments of its impact on a process as complex as courtship difficult. That said, the war clearly accelerated shifts in the location of courtship and in the behaviors appropriate to it. As during other wars, young people sped up the pace of their courtships, engaging in premarital intercourse earlier and marrying more quickly. But these changes might have happened anyway; after all, courtship in wartime often increases in pace. Perhaps more important was the shift in the location of courtship, away from neighborhoods and family events to commercial spaces. As I have shown, courtship did take place in these establishments, but only to a limited degree. The presence of soldiers with money and a wartime economy that put more money in the pockets of working-class young men allowed young people to expand their consumption of popular entertainment. Instead of an occasional foray into a movie theater or a dance hall, courting couples moved much of their courtship into these spaces, which, in turn, influenced how they courted. Treating provided an excellent model for how to interact in commercial spaces, and as more young men and women entered these spaces together, they both witnessed treating and began to extend its logic into their courtship practices. By the early 1920s, many young people came to expect a similarly gendered exchange in courtship, with men paying for entertainments and young women reciprocating with sexual activity. The increased visibility and popularity of treating during the war had the effect of exposing many young people to these interactions, shaping their sense of how their own activities should proceed.

War Department officials deplored this development. It was, after all, exactly what they had warned would happen and had worked against when they tried to separate girls from soldiers. In an article for *Social Hygiene*, Katharine Bement Davis stated that girls "know what the government is expecting of the enlisted men, but they know what life is, and that there's a long way to go before you make over a generation, but *they're going to be in on the making*" (emphasis in the original). Despite her dismissals of charity girls as frivolous and misguided, Davis here articulates her fear that these young women knew exactly what they were doing. "Making over a generation" involved changing the way that generation understood sexual norms and sexual respectability. While she hoped to convince these girls to choose to make over their generation in her image, Davis acknowledged that girls held real power in the example they set to their friends, their siblings, and their community. While their motivations undoubtedly stemmed from their own desire not to be classed as immoral women, charity girls did make over their generation, promoting a distinction between premarital sex and prostitution that would have a profound effect on courtship practices and working-class ideas about morality.

As in other wars, the draft compressed courtships that might have normally gone on for a few years into a few months or a few days. In her memoir, New York's most famous madam described her experiences before she entered the prostitution business. Polly Adler experienced an accelerated courtship, because "we knew that Willie would be soon going overseas." When he had received his orders, he immediately approached Adler at her cousin Lena's house: "Lena gave me a poke and look which said plainly, 'Close the deal at once.' Willie seemed to be in a hurry too, for the minute Lena and Yossell closed the kitchen door, he grabbed me in his arms and kissed me hard on the lips." When she drew back in disgust, "he must have thought I was offended at his freshness, for he hastened to make clear that his attentions were honorable. . . . There was nothing to do but tell him I didn't love him and wouldn't marry him," she concluded.[58] Willie may have wanted to marry Polly because he sensed her ambivalence and worried she might find another beau while he fought for his country. He also may simply have been tying up loose ends in his life, or perhaps he wanted to have sexual intercourse with her before he went and knew she would not agree to it without a marriage proposal. Whatever his motivations, the war certainly spurred his proposal.[59] Marriage also brought important benefits to young women whose husbands served in the military that may help to explain the general rush to marriage. After marriage, a woman could receive part of her husband's pay and also would benefit from a pension if he died.[60] This calculation might have lain behind Polly's cousin Lena's desire to see Polly "close the deal" with Willie.[61]

Perhaps more important for this discussion is the fact that many young people included intercourse in their courtship earlier than they might have before the war. Investigators for the Committee of Fourteen found an upsurge in premarital intercourse. One man spoke with some soldiers on September 21, 1917, who told him that "there ought to be a lot of war brides around here after we go. I said why and he said 'so many of them have been screwed."[62] While this might simply have reflected an increase in premarital intercourse outside of courtship, this soldier, at least, associated sex and marriage. He assumed that courtship, and not treating, was the goal of many of these young women and that men might acquiesce to these demands.

The Section on Women and Girls also noticed an increase in illegitimate births and associated them with soldiers and sailors. In one report on sexually delinquent women, 68 percent of those women who had babies out of wedlock named soldiers or sailors the fathers of those children. This startling fact indicates that wartime did increase both men's demands for, and women's acquiescence in, intercourse. Some of these women may have been treating girls, some were probably prostitutes, but others were undoubtedly young women who courted quickly. Wartime and the arguments of soldiers about "patriotic sacrifices" may have led them to give in to sexual demands earlier in the courting process than they might have in peacetime.[63]

Committee of Fourteen field reports confirm that young men took advantage of young women, promising marriage as a way of encouraging early sexual activities. One investigator met a young woman named Anna who told him that she expected to marry her soldier boyfriend by that Friday: "she expects him to go to France shortly, said he promised to give her all his money [and] said she thinks he will not touch a woman on the other side." Anna had been treating with soldiers, but she apparently had settled on one and agreed to marry him as long as he met what she saw as his basic marital responsibilities, namely financial support and fidelity. Later that day, this investigator met the soldier Anna intended to marry, who admitted "he was only kidding her, didn't intend to get married to her at all."[64] Edith Balmford also reported this problem in her study of runaway girls living at the Waverly House. Frances, she reported, "had been seduced by a soldier, who later was killed in France." The fact that she did not manage to marry her suitor caused her problems in the family. As Balmford explained, "her older brother had taunted Frances about this and incited the mother to unkindness because of it."[65] While men had seduced and abandoned women before the war, the certainty that they would be in Europe, or possibly dead, before anyone could force them to keep their word allowed many men to manipulate courtship and make promises of marriage more lightly.

In addition to the increase in premarital intercourse during the war, the location of courtship also shifted, hinting at changes that would develop more fully in the 1920s. Wartime prosperity and the lure of commercial amusements combined to draw more courting couples into these spaces. While unmarried soldiers did not make much, they also had few expenses and saved their money for leave in cities like New York. Some reformers worried about unscrupulous prostitutes taking advantage of naive soldiers and sailors, but a letter written earlier from the general secretary of the Committee of Fourteen to the director of the CTCA emphasized the troops' aggressiveness and their desire to spend their money on leave in female company.[66]

Identifying a disturbing trend brought to his attention by a protective officer, Frederick Whitin told Raymond Fosdick that the officer reported "many cases of sailors on shore leave approaching women of all kinds and appearances on the trolley car and stating that they have so much money in their pockets and so many days of shore leave and asking if they can help them spend the time and money."[67]

The availability of large numbers of young men in commercial amusements with money to spend definitely encouraged more treating, but it also increased the number of young people exposed to the activity. As before the war, reports on theaters and other entertainment spaces emphasized the mix of young women who attended them. But the war brought more young people into these spaces, exposing more of them to treating and other sexual activities and negotiations. One investigator reported in November of 1917 that "by no means were all the soldiers seen in company of girls with prostitutes" when they visited theaters and cabarets.[68] Another commented that "most of these girls out here appeared to be girls from ordinary families and perhaps working girls who go out for such larks [and] some of them had the appearance and actions of immoral girls judging from the way they permitted the soldiers to handle them and mall [sic] them." Although the author does not define what he meant by "ordinary families," the subsequent mention of "working girls" may indicate that "ordinary" meant middle-class. This suggests that middle-class youth began to observe treating exchanges during the war, which would explain its later importance in structuring the logic of both working-class and middle-class dating practices. This same report also mentioned African American women in the cabarets, noting that "some of the younger ones are on the streets looking for men."[69] Apparently, regardless of class or race, girls visited the soldiers and accompanied them to popular amusements. There is no real way to know, however, whether these girls engaged in treating or courtship with the soldiers who "malled" them.

The drop in the age of charity girls around the camps also suggests the effect they may have had on courtship practices in the 1920s. While many of these young women clearly went to treat, others seem so young that it is difficult to imagine them going to the camps for sexual purposes. One investigator described a girl so young that her physical appearance disturbed the soldiers watching her. He reported that "When I got off at the light I could see what was making the soldiers uneasy. The little girl had [a] short dress. . . . One soldier said 'look at her teddy bears' meaning her breasts which did not protrude even through her sweater."[70] Maude Miner also estimated the age of some girls at nine or ten years old.[71] But should we assume, as she does, that girls this young went to the camps to have intercourse with the soldiers? A more likely explanation lies in working-class child care and chaperone practices. Rather than forgo visiting the camps, some adolescent girls may have brought their younger sisters with them. In her work on Hell's Kitchen published in 1914, Ruth True notes that families often sent "a younger sister ... to go along, much below the age when the first daughter started, because, 'she's company for May.'"[72] In one case, she describes what she saw as the corrosive effects of exposure to courtship in popular amusements. "'Patsy'" she wrote, "was the frequent companion of her sister of fifteen. This girl, who had an unusual, vivid, and forceful personality, was alternately sought out by the fellows of the block and censured with their disapproval. She ruled Patsy as an autocrat, petting and punishing her, allowing her to 'tag around' and constantly using her as a go-between. There will be no question of a 'fall' for Patsy. As she was being taught, so in time she will naturally develop."[73] If younger sisters accompanied their older siblings to the camps, then many youngsters who did not treat themselves witnessed treating and sexualized courtship at a young age during the war. Others may have participated on the fringes, accepting sodas or ice cream from the military boyfriend of an older sister. Both participating in and witnessing treating during the war exposed many young people to its logic and to the association of commercial amusements with sexuality.

Both inmate case files and oral histories indicate that courtship during the war made extensive use of commercial space. Francie Stone, a young native-born white woman, met her sailor husband "at the Olympian theatre being introduced by a girl friend." They courted in popular amusements, had intercourse before marriage, and then wed. Stone had had sex with other sailors but insisted that her husband "knew of her previous illicet [sic] intercourse" before their marriage. Their union immediately ran into trouble. As the social worker reported, "she says he was not true to her, gave money to other girls, so she did the same."[74] Here, courtship and marriage required a monogamy of payment, with Francie Stone justifying her own infidelity when she found (or said she found) that her husband had given money to other girls. Yetta Epstein also often attended commercial amusements as part of her courtship during the war. She explained: "A cousin of mine kept company with his sister. They had tickets to the theatre and they asked me if I wanted to go. So he came and took me out."[75] As courtship and treating overlapped in commercial amusement space, treating provided a model for how couples might structure their interactions. Courtship in commercial amusements also allowed for more freedom with far less familial supervision. These factors may have led to the increased rates of premarital intercourse in this generation. However, the war only quickened these changes, with some couples engaging in premarital sex and using commercial amusements before the war, and many more doing so during the Roaring Twenties as dating evolved into a coherent system among the working class.

Although young women often avidly participated in the expansion of premarital sex in courtship, wartime changes in treating itself and the leaching of treating practices into courtship could also create dangers for girls. Patriotism may have made treating more popular and acceptable to both young women and young men, but it also validated men's sexual demands. The association of treating with patriotism and many soldiers' sense of sexual entitlement gave young men far more negotiating power. While the explicit argument soldiers made about patriotic duties may have faded after the armistice, their new assertiveness did not. Furthermore, as we shall see in the next chapter, treating's popularity led to the resexualization of women in public entertainment venues. Although most men no longer associated women's presence in a bar or club with prostitution, they did believe that most women were sexually available and would be willing to exchange sex for a few drinks and dinner. And, of course, many women did. This association of women in public with their sexual availability helps to explain why treating was not entirely a positive development for women and why the sexual and social autonomy American women experienced in the second half of the twentieth century did not emerge between 1900 and 1960.

Chapter Six

NUDES FEEL PINCH!
PROSTITUTION, PROHIBITION, AND THE
EMERGENCE OF AMERICA'S SEX INDUSTRY

Prohibition's ban on alcohol profoundly changed New York's entertainment and criminal economies, a fact that had drastic repercussions for prostitution. Introducing a division between venues that sold soft drinks and operated within the law versus those that sold alcohol and did not, Prohibition led to a huge increase in commercial entertainments that catered to adults. Dance halls, movie theaters, and amusement parks stopped serving liquor and became places where families could take their children and where adolescents could court their sweethearts. Burlesque houses, taxi dance halls, and speakeasies increasingly functioned as refuges for an older crowd in search of more exciting adventures. Ironically, Prohibition's bifurcation of the entertainment economy into these two broad categories did not mean that all entertainment aimed at adults operated outside the law. Seeing the profits that could be generated by sexually oriented businesses, many entrepreneurs during Prohibition chose not to sell liquor and operated their establishments in the open.[1] This led to a much broader legal traffic in sexualized entertainment that feminist and contemporary sex workers now refer to as the "sex industry." Characterized by the sale of sexual entertainment, rather than of sexual intercourse, sex work today is a multibillion-dollar industry that includes legal work in lap dancing, peep shows, stripping, and pornography. Generating enormous profits, it dwarfs traditional prostitution.

In the 1920s, sex work involved taxi dancing, hostessing, nude modeling, and burlesque and introduced patterns of racial discrimination that continue in the sex industry to this day. Like other aspects of northern economies, the legal sex trade in the 1920s hired only white women, a fact that benefited them in a number of ways. While nude modeling and taxi dancing might not be entirely respectable, they paid very well in comparison to other work available to women and were legal, allowing white women to profit from their sexualized labor without risking arrest and incarceration.

In this way, the sex industry both revolutionized sex work, making it more about entertainment than about sexual services, and mimicked the racial stratification of the northern economy. While white women could use legal sex work to earn good wages and avoid entanglements with the police, racial discrimination in the "legitimate" economy forced many black women into prostitution. As a result, black women became even more disproportionately overrepresented in New York's jails and reformatories than they had been at the turn of the century. The other significant and lasting impact of the development of a legal sex industry was its effect on the market for prostitution. When combined with the changes in courtship that made noncommercial sex more available to men (discussed in the next chapter), legal sex work lessened the demand for prostitution, driving prostitution to the margins of American sexual culture.

While the emergence of the broader sex industry marginalized prostitution as a sexual and economic practice, Prohibition's legendary impact on organized crime also affected the structure and practice of the trade in New York City. As organized crime moved in to manage the enormously lucrative liquor trade, it encouraged the corruption of New York's criminal justice system. Graft among police and judges had always been a problem, and scandals had periodically shocked New Yorkers with stories of police and judges using bribes to regulate, rather than repress, vice. But the money that poured through New York's criminal economy in the 1920s produced corruption on a scale never seen before. These conditions in the criminal justice system increased the level of violence directed at prostitutes and led to harsher sentences for women who refused to pay the exorbitant bribes demanded by police, lawyers, and magistrates. Now too dangerous to practice without intermediaries, prostitution witnessed a rejuvenation of the brothel system. Madams like Polly Adler showcased their "girls" before New York's elites in the nightclubs on Broadway, where they quaffed champagne and sold sex to anyone with the money to pay for it. In some ways, this made prostitution even more visible and more profitable, but the reemergence of the brothel heralded a decline in prostitutes' independence. Gone were the days when Raines Law hotel proprietors bargained with prostitutes over bed rents and liquor sales. Instead, prostitutes split their profits with madams and other intermediaries, exchanging control over their work lives for a modicum of safety. However, madams like Adler had little time to enjoy their dominance. When Prohibition ended in 1932, organized crime saw prostitution as an excellent substitute for its lost liquor revenues and staged a violent takeover of the business. Madams soon found themselves working as middle managers in a highly organized industry they no longer controlled.

Paradoxically, the Depression also led to profound disorganization at the bottom of the trade as women flooded into the casual forms of prostitution. Some working-class women had always combined prostitution with other marginal forms of employment, but the economic disaster of the Depression increased the number of women forced to rely on this strategy. With male breadwinners unemployed and work in the "legitimate" economy scarce, women resorted to prostitution to feed their families and pay their rent. Ignorant of the dangers of the trade and the strategies professional prostitutes used to avoid them, the women who moved into casual prostitution in the 1930s worked mostly as streetwalkers and bore the brunt of arrest and incarceration. This was particularly true for black women, who faced discrimination in both the sex industry and in the broader economy of New York City. As is the case today, by the late 1930s, the majority of black women in the sex trade walked the streets, suffered the most at the hands of the police, and profited the least from their labor.[2]

The Racial Dynamics of Taxi Dancing

In 1930, the Rodgers and Hart musical *Simple Simon* opened on Broadway. It included a slow, sleepy lament titled "Ten Cents a Dance" that described the mechanics of taxi dancing as well as the exhaustion and disillusionment of a women employed in the trade. "I'm one of those lady teachers / A beautiful hostess, you know," the character sang,

> One of the kind the Palace features
> At exactly a dime a throw. . . .
> Seven to midnight I hear drums,
> Loudly the saxophone blows,
> Trumpets are tearing my eardrums.
> Customers crush my toes.
> Sometimes I think I've found my hero.
> But it's a queer romance.
> All that you need is a ticket;
> Come on, big boy, ten cents a dance![3]

That a Broadway musical would refer to taxi dancing indicates how widespread and well known the profession had become. Taxi dancers worked for dance halls that charged "ten cents a dance" to a wide range of patrons. Perhaps the most visible of the new forms of sex work, taxi dancing operated in the open as part of a broader commercial entertainment industry that had been expanding since the last decade of the nineteenth century. It represented the new segmentation of that industry into "family" and "adult" venues as well as the emergence of the new field of sex work. Like other forms of sex work developed in the 1920s, taxi dancing paid high wages, required social contact with male patrons, and restricted its workforce to white women.[4]

Taxi dancing was paradigmatic of sexualized entertainment and sex work. Paul Cressey, a University of Chicago sociologist who studied the phenomenon in the 1920s, defined the taxi dance hall as "a commercial public dance institution attracting only male patrons, which seeks to provide them an opportunity for social dancing." The halls, Cressey explained, employed "women dance partners, who are paid on a commission basis through the ticket-a-dance plan, and who are expected to dance with any patron who may select them for as few or as many dances as he is willing to purchase."[5] The term "taxi dancing" derived from another modern occupation, taxi driver. Like the taxi driver, the taxi dancer was for public hire and received payment "in proportion to the time spent and the services rendered."[6] In these halls, men bought tickets to dance with women, and women collected these tickets and received 50 percent of the revenues generated.[7]

The taxi dance halls, or "closed halls" (as reformers called them), of the 1920s evolved out of the turn-of-the-century dance craze.[8] As early as 1913, dance halls began employing both women and men to teach dance steps to customers.[9] Because most halls had more male patrons than female, halls began to provide "instructresses" or "dance hostesses" whose job increasingly involved dancing with unattached men. Female investigators who explored the halls found dancing skills were not a primary requirement for the job. One woman reported that she "was hired as an instructress in spite of the fact that I said I was a poor dancer."[10] Very popular among male patrons, the employment of dance instructresses helped when overcrowding in the industry created intense competition between clubs during World War I. According to Maria Ward Lambin, who conducted investigations of New York's dance halls in the 1920s, the large commercial dance palaces like Roseland and St. Nicholas's Dancing Carnival served "soft drinks," had dance floors that could "accommodate from five hundred to two or three thousand patrons," and employed two orchestras, often "on a par with that of the first-class hotels." One investigator working for Lambin seemed particularly impressed by a hall that could accommodate three thousand patrons, which she described as "Beautifully decorated, lighted, ventilated, and kept. The atmosphere sensuous, not sensual."[11] Smaller, older clubs had difficulty competing with these huge dance palaces, which were better equipped, more attractive, and more centrally located. The struggle to make ends meet became so vicious in cities like New York and Chicago that less successful venues reorganized as taxi dance halls to stave off bankruptcy.[12] By the 1920s, cities across the country had "closed" dance halls that only admitted men and charged ten cents a dance.

Taxi dancing paid significantly better than other women's skilled and unskilled work. As Virginia Maynard wrote in an autobiographical exposé for the *Sunday Mirror Magazine*, she left her job as a cafeteria waitress because "I understood the income from those dives wasn't too bad," and "it sounded better than fighting off cheap cafeteria customers." "The next thing I knew," she said, "I was whirling around a sanded dance floor with any guy who had the price of the ticket."[13] In Maynard's narrative, the sexual harassment of women in waitressing made the more explicitly sexualized labor in the halls seem like a reasonable career option. If women had to endure "fighting off" patrons, at least in taxi dancing they got paid better for it. Reformers also admitted that the good pay drove girls into work as taxi dancers. A report written in 1924 by Lambin for New York's Advisory Dance Hall Committee commented on the high wages women could make in the trade. As she explained, "the twenty-five dollars a week which they can earn by dancing compares very favorably with the fifteen or sixteen dollars which they would be able to earn in the untrained occupations for which they are fitted."[14]

Reformers also disapproved of the architecture and physical condition of the taxi dance halls, often equating physical disorder with "moral" disorder. Compared with the beautiful, spacious, and well-lit dance palaces that lined Broadway, taxi dance halls were cramped, dirty, and decorated in poor taste. One of Lambin's investigators described a closed hall as "well lighted but no ventilation and atmosphere was vile, only tolerably clean. Rather gaudy murals decorated the walls."[15] Another criticized a hall for operating out of "a very cheap, sordid looking building."[16] The painter Reginald Marsh captured the seedy, "sordid" aesthetics of taxi dance halls in a sketch published in the *New Yorker* in 1932. The sketch depicts a taxi dance hall at the height of an evening's dancing. One man stops at the entrance to read the signs stating the prices, while the facing advertisement boasts "75 girls always in attendance" (Figure 6.1). Several men walk up the narrow stairs, one has stopped to pay his admission, and another checks his coat at the cloakroom. In the hall itself, the floor is roped off. Some dance hostesses sit slumped over on a bench, as if exhausted from their work, while another urges an elderly man to dance (Figure 6.2). Couples crowd the small floor, and though a sign overhead reads "no objectionable dancing allowed," the dancers move close together (Figure 6.3). The two men pictured in the center of the frame have spread their legs wide to accommodate the legs of their dance hostess part-

6.1. *"Taxi Dance Hall Exterior and Stairs"*

6.2. *"Foyer of Dance Hall"*

6.3. *"Dance Floor"*

ners. A fat man, presumably a manager, glowers at the couples but does not intervene.

White-owned taxi dance halls never hired black women to work as dancers, and New York supported few black dance halls. In a gossip column in the tabloid paper *Broadway Brevities*, reporter Ben Gould commented on the exclusion of black women from taxi dancing. Referring to a "high yellah," or light-skinned, black woman who worked as a taxi dancer, he implied that she passed for white to maintain her job in one of Broadway's all-white dance halls.[17] Only Harlem's black Alhambra Ballroom hired black women to dance with patrons. However, the Alhambra was a general dance hall, open to both men and women. It had more in common with the brightly lit "dance palaces" that working-class white boys and girls attended than the taxi dance halls that studded the side streets near Second and Third Avenues.[18] Like the reputable white establishments that sometimes faced an overflow of male patrons, the Alhambra hired "about 50 hostesses" to handle the chronic sex imbalance. It also catered almost exclusively to African Americans. The white investigator who visited in 1928 found only two other white men in a crowd he estimated at one hundred and fifty patrons. "I danced with a mulatto girl named Ella Greene," he wrote, "and I asked her if she stepped out for a wild time and she said 'I don't do anything like that, white boy.'"[19]

Fearing the financial draw of taxi dancing for young white women and the possible sexual repercussions of such employment, reformers criticized the halls for commercializing dance and thus, by extension, the girls who worked there. Reformers consistently used the word "soliciting," normally reserved for prostitutes' attempts to entice customers, to describe dancers' competition for patrons. One investigator commented that "the girls solicit dances," while another described how "It sounds much like a market place as each one tries to sell herself for the next dance."[20] John Kennedy, author of a *Collier's Weekly* exposé on "the dance hall evil," came to a similar conclusion. "Dancing was once a diversion," he argued. "Now it is a trade. It is a social trade, for in its recent and most widespread development it has enrolled thousands of girls who sell the social favor of their time and company—not any particular artistic skill."[21] Reginald Marsh captured hostesses "soliciting" in his painting "Ten Cents a Dance" completed in 1933 (Figure 6.4). In it, an attractive and heavily made up woman in a low-cut dress leans forward over the railing that separates the hostesses from the male patrons. Waiting for a dance partner, she smiles vivaciously at the viewer, while another hostess perches on the railing with her back turned but her face in profile. Her tight dress serves as its own invitation to patrons with a full booklet

FIGURE 6.4. *Reginald Marsh, "Ten Cents a Dance," tempera on panel, 1933.*
(Whitney Museum of American Art, New York; © 2005 Estate of Reginald Marsh /
Art Students League, New York / Artists Rights Society [ARS], New York)

of tickets. Marsh's painting expresses exactly what reformers feared most about taxi dancing, namely that it closely resembled both the behaviors and aesthetics of prostitution. According to reformers, women's "solicitation" of men in commercial amusements "hardened" young girls, making them susceptible to selling more than dance.

Reformers also found the practice of not allowing taxi dance hostesses to refuse partners a little too close to the "promiscuity" of prostitution. Although prostitutes occasionally did refuse men they disliked, most reformers assumed that prostitutes served all men with the money to pay for their services. This false stereotype fueled reformers' concerns about the "moral" dangers of working in taxi dancing. Kennedy spent much of his article describing a man "old enough to be her father" who monopolized a dance hall girl's evening. "He clutched a strip of tickets like a tape measure in a knotty fist stuck hotly into the small of Helen's back. Helen had to like him: the tickets said so."[22] In his analysis, taxi dancing forced the hostesses to socialize with and even "like" inappropriate or unattractive partners. Virginia Murray leveled a similar complaint but made explicit her concerns about the connections between selling dance and the temptation to sell sex. Hostesses, she argued, were "compelled to dance and associate with the patrons indiscriminately who offer all sorts of proposals generally considered conducive to sexual delinquency."[23]

Despite a rhetoric that associated taxi dancing with prostitution, reformers rarely found any actual prostitution in the halls.[24] In her 1924 report, Lambin and her investigators found no prostitution in the taxi dance halls, nor did they find much "improper dancing" (that is, dancing that involved close bodily contact or that simulated intercourse). Only one of the six taxi dance halls described in the appendix of the report tolerated such dancing, and even there, the investigator noted that "considerable of the dancing is unobjectionable," but that "some of it is very sensual and boisterous and a little of it overtly vulgar." In spite of these tame reports, Lambin recommended that all taxi dance halls be abolished.[25] Kennedy, author of the *Collier's Weekly* article "Devil's Dance Dens," quoted a New York City police matron who came to the same conclusion. "I'd close the closed halls in all cases," she remarked. "They're bad. We have a hundred women but we can't regulate them. We haven't the numbers; we haven't the power. . . . They're hothouses of vice."[26] Much to the dismay of police matrons and other interested parties, however, the halls were legal, and their profitability ensured that they would stay open.

Reformers' criticism of taxi dance halls stemmed more from their racial composition than any overtly sexual behavior on the part of instructresses or their clients. Most white dance palaces in New York did not admit black men, but four out of the ten closed halls visited by Lambin's investigators catered almost exclusively to "Orientals" who danced with the "white girls" employed by the halls. Other than noting the racial composition of these halls, Lambin only commented that the young white women working there appeared "to be hardworking and honest."[27] Mrs. Henry Moscowitz, chair of the New York City Recreation Committee, was far less restrained in an interview with the *New York Times* on the closed dance hall problem. Labeling the Asian clientele of the clubs "socially undesirable Orientals," Moscowitz announced a new campaign to clean up the halls and eliminate race mixing.[28] For Moscowitz, interracial mixing, and not dancing, proved to be the real problem. Because they promoted contacts between white women and Asian men, taxi dance halls threatened an unspoken but implicit racial hierarchy that placed white working-class women above and supposedly out of the reach of nonwhite men. Less restrained coverage in other New York papers deliberately stoked the white community's racial fears. In an article with the inflammatory title "Taxi Dancing Girls Slaves of Lust, Must Choose Insults or Poverty," the *Evening Graphic* described how "Young girls are forced to endure the foul advances of degenerate roués, yellow men and human beasts of the lowest social order openly and with the full consent of the law." "The yellow men slink in and out," the paper concluded, "and the tired, world-weary girls dance on at a nickel profit to the dance and the chance to arrange for dates later in the evening."[29] Both reformers and newspapers equated the public interest with the maintenance of a rigid racial hierarchy. Viewing white women as inherently innocent, these authors assumed that white women would never voluntarily associate with Asian men. In their reports and articles, they conflated social mixing with interracial sexuality and taxi dancing with prostitution across the color line. To them and to much of the white public, social and commercial interactions between white women and men of color were inherently sexual, immoral, and dangerous.

Despite this shrill invective, the white women working in taxi dance halls often preferred Asian men as clients because there was more money to be made from them. One white Committee of Fourteen investigator reported a conversation with a manager who told him, "The girls must dance with everybody alike, but they give preference to those men who frequent this place often. You see those Japs or Chinks, whatever you call them, they buy tickets in bunches. The girls know that and they prefer to dance with them and be on friendly terms."[30] Another reported that "a white man has very poor standing here, the instructresses ignore them and prefer the Chinese or Japs who spend quite some money on tickets, drinks and besides tip the girls."[31]

In his report on Chicago's taxi dance halls, Paul Cressey also noted that white hostesses preferred Asian men because they gave the women more presents. Sympathetic to the problems that young Asian men faced in America, Cressey focused primarily on their exploitation at the hands of unscrupulous dance hall girls who, he argued, viewed them as appropriate targets for manipulation and extortion. While he described Filipino men as innocent victims of American racism, Cressey had little positive to say about the young white women who danced with them. "Under such circumstances," Cressey wrote, "many Orientals are willing to pay exorbitantly for even casual contacts with taxi dancers. The girls, however, often regard them as 'fish,' as persons to be exploited." As a result, "Orientals, and especially Filipino young men, prove to be such lucrative sources of income that many young women, under the spur of opportunism, lay aside whatever racial prejudices they might have and give themselves to a thorough and systematic exploitation of them."[32]

New York's white dancers also treated and cheated Asian men, demanding far more from them in gifts and expenses paid than any white man would tolerate. Restrictions on Asian women's immigration and the racism of northern cities ensured that Asian men made up a captive population for the halls and their more mercenary dancers. One white male investigator observed dancers deliberately cheating Japanese men in treating exchanges. Commenting that these women "prefer to associate with another race," he identified them in his notes as "charity" and followed them to a "nearby Ice cream parlor," where the young women received "boxes of candies" and "hot chocolate or portions of ice cream" and "then permitted the Japanese to kiss them." When the couples left the parlor, the girls deserted their male companions, getting on the "cars or elevated trains in order to disappear quick as possible." Some of the men tried to insist on their sexual rights, and as the investigator noted, "appeared to be excited because they were fooled and left standing alone after being promised." It was possible, he speculated, that some of the girls did "have sexual intercourse with those Japanese, but I didn't see any of those girls in here go further than to the corner with them."[33] While individual charity girls might try to avoid providing the sexual favors their companions expected, most young women who reneged in a treating exchange did so furtively, and few women were bold enough to simply leave men standing at the elevated station. A group of women all engaging in the same violation of treating's basic rules implied a premeditated and communally accepted resolution to cheat. While World War I may have skewed the treating exchange in men's favor when both partners were white, Asian men represented a group some white women could exploit with relative ease. New York's racial hierarchy empowered these same white taxi dancers to approach treating with Asian men as an opportunity to swindle them. Undoubtedly, if any altercation ensued, the majority of white passersby, as well as white authority figures, would defend the innocence of white women over the claims of nonwhite men to their sexual services.

Periodic raids on clubs patronized by Asian men highlighted the vulnerability of Asian men who dared to dance with white women. Although the police and reformers both commented on the difficulty of making cases against taxi dance halls more generally, they often raided clubs that catered to Asians.[34] In one club, police arrested both the white dancers and the Asian managers and patrons. The court soon released the women because they were over twenty-one, but the *New York Times* commented that "the presence of several stern looking male parents in the court room indicated that for some of the girls there might be a family sequel to the story of their dancing with Filipinos and Japanese in a manner to justify a raid." According to the *Times*, punishment for the women would be private, patriarchal (or at least meted out by "male parents"), and based on their violation of racial taboos rather than New York law. In contrast to the private punishment of the girls, Asian men's punishment for violating racial taboos was public and meted out by the state. The court refused to free the Filipino men arrested in the same raid, holding them over for trial for operating a dance hall without a license, a charge rarely used against white managers.[35] In another case, the courts again freed all women over the age of twenty-one but fined an Asian man "after Detectives David Kavanagh and Thomas Dowd had testified he was annoying two white girls when the raiders entered the dance hall."[36] Regardless of the character of the event itself or the behavior of the white women involved, Asian men bore the brunt of the punishment for activities that would undoubtedly have passed unnoticed in the white-patronized clubs that police complained they had such trouble regulating.

Taxi dancing between white women and Asian men mostly involved economic judgments on the white women's part, but occasionally it resulted in the romantic relationships that the white public most feared. A Committee of Fourteen investigator danced with a young woman named Kitty Rafferty, who informed him that "four or five of the girls here are married to Orientals."[37] Similarly, Italian Rebecca Marziano, married a Filipino man she met "at a Filipino dance hall in Philadelphia." While Marziano and other white dance hall girls may have begun dancing with Asian men because of the money they made in ticket sales and treating exchanges, some fell in love, turning a relationship based on profit into a much more radical crossing of the racial divide. Marziano's marriage suffered from the family and community pressures that opposed such matches. According to her Women's Prison Association case file, "the family was upset by the marriage. The couple separated about six months ago because of her mother's interference."[38] Young white women engaging in interracial relationships faced ostracism from their families and communities, while their Asian partners faced reprisals from the state and from white men who found social contact between white women and Asian men threatening to America's racial hierarchy. In a decade when American nativism was on the rise, interracial marriages came at a high social cost for both parties. However, the possibility for such a union problematizes the assessment that taxi dance halls were solely places where white dancers played on the social and sexual vulnerability of their Asian patrons.

As taxi dancing grew more popular in the mid to late 1920s, white dancers began to use erotic dancing as a way of satisfying their Asian patrons without having to engage in more intimate forms of sexual activity. The earliest account of erotic dancing in a taxi dance hall came from a report written in 1924 by a white investigator for the Committee of Fourteen. He attended a hall where the "Chinese and Orientals dance with these girls imitating sexual intercourse by rubbing their bodies together." He insisted that the women preferred Asian men, describing how "when Chinese, Japs, Filipinos and others of that kind started to come in, they left all white men, that were there already and danced with them. . . . During intermission, these Orientals were buying these girls cigarettes and candy and sodas." [39] By 1928, investigators began to report both white and Asian men reaching orgasm on the dance floor in taxi dance halls. At the Rainbow Gardens on East 125th Street in 1928, an investigator wrote, "several of the girls danced indecently, rubbing their bodies against the men in a most suggestive manner." This produced "an effect and result at times similar to that of sexual intercourse," and one young man told the investigator that he was "'all messed up' and motioned to his trousers." When asked exactly what he meant by "messed up," he explained that "she was shaking it up and I had danced eight dances and had no more tickets but I said to her 'You've almost got it off, give me a dance and finish the job; she did and I'm messed up. She could shake her _____.' " [40]

Dancers used promises of sexual satisfaction as a way to induce patrons to dance with them. Of course, this was just what reformers had feared when they complained of the demoralizing effects of young dance hall workers "soliciting" partners. [41] One investigator reported that a woman "touched my private parts as she sat down alongside me and promised to satisfy me before five lights were over." [42] More direct, another woman promised her partner she would "starch your underwear." When this turn of phrase puzzled the investigator, she explained concisely, "I'll make you come." [43] The young women working in these clubs knew that men danced with them for sexual release and maintained a practical attitude about it. One investigator reported that after dancing with men, some of the girls examined their dresses carefully. His dancing partner explained that "Some of the guys they stain your dress while dancing and we have to rush into the washroom to clean the dress and change and we lose time by it." Rather than emphasizing the sexual activity itself, she complained about the time she lost rinsing semen from her dress. When the investigator asked her whose fault this was, she replied philosophically, "We don't blame nobody. It's natural. We are here for that."[44] Another stated, "None of the boys who come up here are out for dancing; they just want to be relieved."[45]

While the sexual satisfaction of men on the floor might have been viewed by the dancers as "natural," it was also extremely cheap when compared with Prohibition-era prices for prostitution. One of Maria Lambin's undercover investigators reported that "very few patrons spend more than their first dollar" in the halls, while another estimated the prices at "two to three dollars."[46] While a few dollars might seem like a lot to pay for dancing, it was a bargain when compared with what prostitutes routinely demanded in the 1920s. Most white prostitutes charged between ten and twenty dollars. Black prostitutes might more likely ask for between three and six dollars.[47] In addition to being a good deal, taxi dancing carried no risk of sexually transmitted diseases. Wartime education about disease had raised awareness about the damage it caused, which, in turn, made taxi dancing a safer option. Finally, taxi dancing had the benefit of being legal. While police rarely arrested men for soliciting prostitutes, preferring instead to have them testify against the women, entanglements with the police could still be embarrassing.

Because of the advantages it provided for both men and women, taxi dancing grew in popularity in the 1920s and 1930s and quickly became an important part of New York's legal sex industry. Periodically, racial scares about Asian men and white women drove different police administrations to try to clean up the halls, but they met with little luck. In 1930, for example, "higher police officials" attacked one hall in which they alleged that "Filipinos danced 'with white girls—many of them very young.'" However, when police matrons investigated, "No young girls were in evidence, and the youngest appearing told the policewoman in charge of the tour that she was working to help her husband support their two children. To a guarded suggestion that some of the male habitués must come around often to see girls they liked, she said they never did."[48] Because taxi dancing remained legal, crusades against it relied more on regulating the behavior in the halls than on trying to eliminate them. Police had used the ban on liquor in dance halls as an excuse to raid them before Prohibition, but as one *New York Times* article commented, "since prohibition has automatically nullified the liquor-selling section of the statue, there is nothing left on which to base prosecution of iniquitous resorts except the clause that makes habitual immorality punishable. This is hard to prove. Both the police and the social workers state that it is useless to try to convict on the evidence they can get."[49] Taxi dance halls provided important sexual services for men and work for white women, who benefited from the legality and safety of the halls as well as the high wages they received. After all, police could hardly arrest women because men ejaculated on their skirts, and women could not contract venereal diseases by dancing.

By the early 1930s, the devastation of the Depression had obviously affected the trade, driving down wages and profits and forcing managers to expand into even more explicit sexual services. In an article published in the *Journal of Social Hygiene*, Virginia Murray warned that "the Depression has hurt the dance hall business as to volume [and] the earnings of the hostesses have decreased." This, she argued, made "the insistent immoral proposals of the patrons become the more alluring."[50] While managers consistently claimed that their establishments merely provided "clean wholesome recreation at small costs," the complaints made to police about the halls indicate that economic pressures drove them to provide more than just "erotic dancing."[51] Newspaper articles from the early 1930s hint that women and men engaged in sexual activity in booths provided by the management. Male patrons could pay six dollars an hour to "sit out dances with girls" they selected. Although management denied that any improper conduct occurred, the *New York Times* reported that "patrons and girls" referred to the booths as the "love nest."[52] Although it is impossible to know just what happened in these booths in the 1930s, in many modern strip clubs patrons pay for a similar privilege and receive either fellatio or manual masturbation from the women.[53]

In 1931, the city responded to these unspecified, but well-known and obviously sexual, uses of the dance halls, by instituting new rules that "female entertainers at cabarets shall not be permitted to mingle and sit with patrons."[54] However, police apparently failed to enforce the rules, and when they attempted to do so in 1934, they precipitated a disagreement between managers and dancers that resulted in a strike. The *New York Times* reported that in response to the enforcement of the four-year-old rule and the subsequent drop in business, managers "cut the price of dances from 10 to 5 cents."[55] According to the *Times*, "Mrs. Lillian Berger, a former graduate nurse who is leading the strikers, said the reduction in the price of dance tickets had cut the commissions of hostesses from a former average of $25 and $30 to $10 and $15." Carrying picket signs "among the crowds in front of the ballroom," striking dancers explained their protest to potential patrons and succeeded in convincing men not to enter the halls. One sailor attempted to enter, "but he turned away after a striker spoke to him." "Well, anyway, we have the navy with us," she remarked. As the strike shows, by the 1930s, taxi dancers saw themselves as respectable women doing respectable work who could appeal to their patrons when they found their livelihood threatened. The popularity of taxi dancing made certain kinds of sexualized labor acceptable as well as profitable. White women in New York and other big cities relied on taxi dancing and other forms of sex work to support themselves and their families when other work proved scarce or did not provide sufficient income. Their ability to resort to this legal work kept them out of prostitution, an option not open to New York's women of color. Furthermore, the sexual services they provided both cost less than prostitution and involved fewer risks. When combined with the other forms of sex work in the burgeoning sex industry, taxi dancing contributed significantly to the marginalization of prostitution in American culture.

Tell That to the Judge: Deteriorating Conditions in Prostitution in the 1920s and 1930s

While taxi dancing threatened prostitution's market share, the effects of Prohibition on policing and organized crime led to a real decline in the conditions under which professional prostitutes plied their trade. Laws passed in wartime to reduce disease remained on the books, ensuring that women who had venereal infections would serve long prison terms if found guilty of prostitution offenses.[56] The money associated with illegal liquor sales spilled over into New York's criminal justice system, where officials seemed determined that at least some of the ill-gotten gains of the Roaring Twenties would line their pockets and bank accounts. Prohibition led to unprecedented levels of corruption in the criminal justice system, which dragged more women into the courts, where police, magistrates, lawyers, and bail bondsmen all conspired to fix cases. Prostitution convictions no longer resulted in small fines or short stints at the workhouse. Instead, women charged with prostitution-related offenses often found their bank accounts empty after run-ins with the authorities. The violence of organized crime also spilled over into prostitution. Police increasingly used violence in apprehending and arresting women suspected of prostitution, while some customers resorted to beating women who demanded that they be paid for their services. All of these factors forced women to turn to intermediaries, usually madams and pimps, to help them reduce the dangers of the trade.

In 1929, a corruption scandal of monumental proportions stunned New Yorkers and tarnished the reputation of the city's criminal justice system for years to come. As the Seabury Investigation of 1930 uncovered, graft reached epic proportions during the 1920s and involved not just the police but bail bondsmen, defense lawyers, prosecuting attorneys, and judges in the women's court. Traditionally, New York's police had accepted bribes from individual prostitutes or from madams on a monthly basis. This practice limited arrests, regularized payments to police, and functioned much like other kinds of city-run licensing. Under the new system in the 1920s, officers arrested women (usually by framing them) and asked to see their bankbooks. The police then passed these women's account information on to bail bondsmen, who thereby learned exactly how much a woman could pay for an acquittal. Bail bondsmen then demanded that amount in bribes, splitting the proceeds with the police, the lawyers for the defense and prosecution, and the judge. If a woman could not or would not pay, judges convicted them on the basis of perjured police testimony.[57] Women paid far more under this system than they had under earlier forms of corruption.[58] One woman testified that, after her arrest, a bail bondsman claimed he needed "$500 to take her case," telling her that "most of it was for the officers." He insisted that she show him her bankbook and demanded "a blank order on her bank." She later found that "the order she had signed in blank was made out in the sum of $1,080—the full balance on her account—and cashed." Although found innocent after paying her bribe, she had to hire another lawyer to "recover her bank book."[59]

The Seabury Investigation found that police routinely framed women with no previous record of prostitution, a fact that outraged the public when the scandal broke in 1930.[60] One stool pigeon, Mapocha Acuna, revealed that he had kept extensive records on his involvement with the police, including files on eighty-two cases in which he had personally witnessed the unjustifiable arrest of a woman on prostitution charges.[61] Bedford reformatory social workers also recorded several cases in which women insisted they were innocent. Maggie Shannahan, a married Irish woman, reported to her social worker that she had protested the arrest, telling the police that "You cant [sic] take us, you have nothing on us." The detective retorted, "the place has a bad name—you can tell that to the judge." When she did just that, the judge replied, "We have to take their word." Shannahan may have been lying to her social workers, but the evidence in her file supported her claim that she had never prostituted. Married and employed, Shannahan tested negative for venereal disease and had no previous arrests or convictions. While incarcerated at Bedford, she lost custody of her child to the New York Society for the Prevention of Cruelty to Children.[62] Public outrage over cases like this forced Governor Roosevelt to pardon and release six women still serving time in 1930.[63] While New Yorkers found the framing of innocent women the most outrageous aspect of the scandal, framing prostitutes for crimes they had not committed was also illegal. As New York's most infamous madam, Polly Adler, wryly commented in her memoirs, "perhaps if they [police] had confined themselves to shaking down people like me, who were violating the law, public indignation would not have risen to such a pitch, but their persecution of innocent women could never be condoned, and it was the testimony of these pitiful victims of police frames—the dramatic 'human evidence'—which not only proved their individual undoing, but resulted in the abolition of the vice squad."[64]

Police corruption also increased individual officers' sense of their personal power. Their identity as men who enforced the law but did not necessarily have to follow it made violence far more common in prostitution arrests. The physical punishment meted out by police to women suspected of prostitution in the 1920s stands in stark contrast to the much lower levels of violence found in the records from earlier in the twentieth century.[65] The police routinely used violence to gain access to apartments where they thought prostitutes worked.[66] In one case, an investigator accompanied officers on a raid in 1921 where "they had to brake [sic] the door in order to get in that apartment. By that time that prostitute got out through fire escape in an adjoining apartment where a respectable family was living and pleaded that [they] let her hide in bed. They allowed her to do that, but Glazer got in there and pulled her out from there and placed her under arrest."[67] The Seabury Investigation also recorded extensive police violence against prostitutes. In his published report, Samuel Seabury used the story of one woman to exemplify endemic police violence. Mrs. Potocki, who supported two young daughters on her earnings as a charwoman, made the mistake of allowing two undercover police officers into her apartment. One officer rose and "struck her first on one side of the jaw and then on the other." He demanded a five-hundred-dollar bribe, attempted to rape her, and "beat her severely." When her friend came to her aid, the other officer "struck her on the jaw with such terrific force that the blood spurted from her mouth," and then he took her "by the hair and dash[ed] her against the wall."[68]

Police violence either coincided with or encouraged violence on the part of johns. Sources after the war revealed johns using threats, violence, and drugs to get what they wanted. One man decided that he did not want to pay for sex, even though he knew the woman he met was a prostitute. In a conversation with an investigator beforehand, he stated that rather than pay her, "he'd give her s——." When the man returned from upstairs, he informed the investigator that he "got his and didn't give her a cent, if she didn't give up, he would have punched the S—— out of her."[69] Another woman told an investigator that she had been detained by men who raped and assaulted her. After getting her drunk, the men took her "in a taxi cab to Pennsylvania Hotel and kept there in a room a day and a half." She finally escaped with the help of two other women. As she reported, "her clothes were torn in pieces," and "two women came to her rescue and got their share."[70] These incidents reveal a frightening level of violence that some men now thought was their right to mete out to prostitutes.

Although the Seabury Investigation shocked New Yorkers in 1930 and 1931, it did not curb either police corruption or police violence over the long run. For a year or so after the scandal, police did little to restrain prostitution, leading the Committee of Fourteen to complain about their timidity and the resulting increase in vice.[71] Madams like Adler also noticed the change and rejoiced. As she commented in her autobiography, "Whatever else it may have accomplished, ironically enough, the Seabury investigation turned New York into a wide-open town. While the guardians of the law were busy answering questions, the law-breakers had a holiday."[72] However, the holiday did not last long. Social workers from the Women's Prison Association found renewed police corruption as early as 1932. In one case, an Italian woman met two men on the way to Coney Island with a friend. When they got "fresh with her and [she] said she would not go to the Island with them . . . they placed her under arrest." Violetta DeVicio told her social worker that "she was not afraid of being arrested but in court she found that their word was taken against hers."[73] If DeVicio's claim is accurate, judges as early as 1932 resumed the practice of taking unsupported police testimony as sufficient evidence for a conviction.[74] It also shows that undercover police officers sometimes made sexual demands on women either before or after their arrest. *Broadway Brevities* published a satirical cartoon of this practice in 1933. The cartoon depicted a police officer explaining to a judge that his partner would be in to testify as soon as he finished "pumping" a woman for evidence (Figure 6.5). In 1934, the *New York Daily News* was reporting bail bondsmen in the magistrate's courts charging illegal fees and "taking liberties with girls arrested in vice cases, on a pretense of examining them for birthmarks."[75] By the late 1930s, police themselves admitted that they had arrested women on false pretenses. In 1938, police arrested Eula Mae Johnson, a young African American woman from the South, merely for talking to a prostitute. As Johnson's social worker noted, "the detective who arrested them admitted that he knew nothing about her but assumed that she must be bad too since she was associating with the Freeman girl."[76] Johnson's race probably affected the outcome of her trial. Both police and judges proved more willing to accept "guilt by association" as evidence in cases against black defendants.

By the mid-1930s, the entire system of the women's courts and the general philosophy of punishing women for prostitution had come under attack.[77] Women from groups as mainstream as New York's League of Women Voters

"We ain't got no information yet, but Joe's still in there, pumping the other one!"

FIGURE 6.5. *"Sting of the Law," cartoon from* Broadway Brevities, *Oct. 12, 1933.*

and the Women's City Club suggested that prostitution be decriminalized, that prostitutes be treated rather than incarcerated, and that customers be punished.[78] These criticisms had been part of a middle-class feminist analysis of prostitution since the early 1920s, but they also resulted from middle-class women's concerns about the corrosive effects of the Great Depression on women's economic choices.[79] As economic conditions grew worse, more and more women resorted to casual prostitution to get by, a fact reflected in prison records and widely discussed in the numerous newspaper articles that covered prostitution in the 1930s.[80] Middle-class social workers and lawyers who worked directly with the women's court spearheaded these efforts, but they met with little success. However, their criticism of the system did make police defensive both about their tactics and about their mission in repressing vice. When responding to complaints about the new practice of wiretapping, Police Commissioner Valentine admitted that "It is true we will never be able to stop it [prostitution], but we have a job to do and a definite responsibility. We have laws to enforce even though those laws are not popular. We are not prudes and we are not snoopers, but we must have evidence."[81]

While New York's police hierarchy claimed that they found prostitution enforcement distasteful, they argued that they could not ignore it because lawlessness would ensue. Whatever they said in public, however, officials were also responding to the new interest the FBI took in prostitution in the mid-1930s. Allegedly reacting to a rise in "white slavery" cases, J. Edgar Hoover's G-men used the Mann Act (which made the transportation of women across state lines for immoral purposes a federal offense) to initiate a series of spectacular raids in cities thought to be soft on prostitution. Seemingly determined to humiliate local police departments, the FBI neither informed them of the raids nor allowed their participation. As the *New York Herald* reported of the FBI's activities in Atlantic City and Philadelphia, "the raids went off like clockwork, the FBI depending entirely upon its own personnel and not bothering to notify local police." When Atlantic City police finally found out about the raids and offered assistance, Mr. Hoover "politely but firmly informed [them] . . . 'we're getting along all right.'"[82] Given the national government's willingness to involve itself in prostitution cases, New York police risked losing control over law enforcement in the city if they ignored prostitution. Only vigorous repression of prostitution would keep Hoover out of New York and preserve New York's shaky reputation as a clean city with an honest police force.

As Good as the Bank of England: The Return of Madams, Pimps, and the Brothel System

Corruption in the courts and police violence drove prostitutes into the arms of intermediaries, and as a result, professional prostitution became more tightly organized under madams, pimps, and, by the 1930s, organized crime. Relying on madams and pimps had obvious drawbacks. Both groups exploited prostitutes financially and, at times, physically. But to remain in the field, prostitutes needed to adapt. By the late 1920s, few professional prostitutes worked outside of a reemergent brothel system. At the same time, black women and men made impressive strides in claiming some of organized prostitution for themselves. While the majority of black women who prostituted in the 1920s did so casually, some moved into call prostitution and prostitution management.

The most common institution of prostitution in the 1920s was the "call flat," a variation on the old brothel of the nineteenth century. The name derived from madams' reliance on telephones to organize their business. Madams advertised their flats on cards that listed only phone numbers, often distributing these cards in face-to-face interactions in speakeasies or on the street.[83] At the same time, madams used the phone to manage their labor force, keeping a list of prostitutes they could call on to meet customer needs. One madam kept a book of red Moroccan leather for her business in which she wrote the names, numbers, and descriptions of over a hundred women she used. A typical entry read "Louise Smith, blond, well built and speedy."[84] These tactics reduced problems with police because they allowed madams to screen customers more effectively and limited the number of prostitutes in the apartment at any given time. In their daily routines and agreements, call flats took their logic from the brothel system of the late nineteenth century.[85] For example, madams managed all aspects of the business and took the traditional 50 percent of all money made on tricks. As one prostitute explained to an investigator, working for the highly successful madams Jennie the Factory and Sadie the Chink was a "fifty-fifty proposition."[86] But there were also some differences. Prostitutes rarely lived in the flats, which allowed them more independence and improved their financial situation. No longer a captive population, they avoided the price gouging so common to brothels and could enjoy a social and family life outside of their work. In addition, although call flats did have concentrations in the Village, Times Square, and Harlem, they were widely distributed throughout New York's housing stock, and they did not openly advertise. Finally, call flats in the 1920s operated on a far smaller scale than their turn-of-the-century counterparts. Whereas earlier brothels might feature eight to fifteen girls, call flats in the 1920s and 1930s rarely employed more than four or five women.[87] The small scale made these flats harder to detect, which was never a goal in the wide-open world of early twentieth-century brothels but became a necessity in the more dangerous 1920s.

Working under a madam had its benefits. As in nineteenth-century brothels, madams in call houses organized work and took care of contacts between prostitutes and the outside world. The infamous madam Polly Adler, for example, opened her house with a list of men who might be interested: "I called some of the men I'd had before, and they brought their friends with them. Also I made some new contacts on my own, and my enterprise was off to a prosperous start."[88] Madams also established relationships with speakeasies that gave them the right to sit and solicit business for their call flat. Madam Lucille Rodgers used Joe's Romanian Garden Restaurant in Brooklyn as well as several local burlesque houses to make "the acquaintance of patrons who are good spenders."[89] Polly Adler described speakeasies as "a display window for the girls."[90] Speakeasies benefited from this relationship because it pleased the customers, brought in trade, and helped with liquor sales.[91] Madams also provided protection for prostitutes. They paid off the police and took care of the women working for them when raids could not be avoided. One of the white women who worked for Sadie the Chink and Jennie the Factory told an investigator that her bosses were "as good as the Bank of England." When pressed to explain this comment she replied, "In case of a raid. They take care of the girls."[92]

Madams also tried to protect prostitutes from pimps, whom they viewed as exploitative and immoral. Modern readers might see pimping as competition for madams, but in the 1920s and 1930s, pimps often managed women who worked in brothels and did not interfere directly in brothel management. In this context, competition does not explain the criticism madams leveled at pimps.[93] In her autobiography, Polly Adler offered several reasons why her readers should see madams and pimps differently. She stressed the fact that she did not take "new girls" who had never been in the trade. In contrast, "a pimp seeks out a girl and seduces her into the life." Adler also complained that a pimp did "everything in his power to keep her a prostitute, for if she quit the racket, it would reduce his income. And, instead of helping her to save her money, he takes every cent she's got and beats her into making more." Realizing that her readers might see this explanation as self-serving, Adler concluded, "I do not mean to imply that I was a fairy godmother to whores, or that any madam is. But I made an equitable business arrangement with the girls which gave them their fair share. I provided the capital, set up the business and ran the greatest risks so far as the law was concerned."[94] According to Adler, pimps were parasites who ruined women, while madams made mutually profitable business arrangements with established prostitutes. Other madams shared Adler's attitude about pimps, and one went so far as to beat a prostitute when she brought her pimp to a club and flaunted her relationship with him. The madam (Alice) told the reporter from the *New York Daily News* that she "beat up Betty merely by way of a maternal chastisement." "I try to be a mother to all my girls," she explained.[95]

Madams' criticisms of pimping among "their girls" reflected their understanding of the trade but also the more general disdain Americans expressed toward men who failed as providers. One neighbor wrote to Bedford reformatory about a southern African American inmate it had recently paroled: "I think it is a shame that little Effie Sears that was parole [*sic*] . . .

is every night selling her body to support a man that will not work."[96] For both white and black Americans, men's "refusing to work" and relying on women's earnings brought disgrace because it represented a profound reversal of men's usual role as breadwinners and as protectors of women and their sexual virtue. In contrast, madams (and women more generally) did not have the same commitment to the virtue of other adult women. While Polly Adler's comments reflected her sense that no one (either male or female) should bring a woman into prostitution, once a woman had arrived at that destination, there was little shame in employing her. Thus, pimps, because they "broke in girls" and because they violated important understandings of appropriate male behavior, could be excoriated by madams who crossed no such gender lines. Indeed, in the case of Alice and her errant prostitute Betty, Alice viewed her actions as an appropriate part of her gender role, that of a "mother" disciplining a "daughter."

Despite the general hostility toward the practice, pimping expanded after the war, gaining ground rapidly in the 1920s and 1930s. Women turned to pimps for the same reasons that they turned to madams—for protection— even if, as Polly Adler and other madams argued, pimps demanded far too high a price. A pimp who worked with a prostitute outside the brothel system often made contact with men for her, or as one social worker summarized, "sent men to her room."[97] When women worked the streets, pimps watched their activities and evaluated prospective clients. For example, one prostitute brought an undercover investigator to an ice-cream parlor. As he explained in his notes, she made "all rendezvous and appointments with men" in the parlor "in order to have pimps look [them] over before she starts out with them."[98] Pimps "looked over" clients, vetoing those who they thought might be with the vice squad. When they failed to prevent an arrest, pimps also handled the legal difficulties, raising money for bail and hiring lawyers. They also congregated outside the Women's House of Detention, shouting information about cases from the sidewalk to the women locked up on the second and third floors. One independent prostitute "spoke with scorn of the pimps who stand outside the Hse. of Det., all dressed up, waiting for the girls to come out, in the 'most beautiful suits.'"[99] In a rare letter between a pimp and prostitute seized by Bedford reformatory, Mitzie Hillman's pimp wrote that he tried to pawn a diamond ring for her bail. I "was so broken-hearted when I heard of you being arrested that night," he declared, assuring her "I will be over to hear your case to-morrow morning at eleven o'clock sharp." He promised "to get even" with "that no good mother f—— what is done all the squealing on you and the rest." He also offered sympathy, telling her "it sure is breaking my heart to see you go back, after being out for a short while."[100] Another pimp even managed to visit his prostitute at notoriously strict Bedford by "convincing the chaperone that he was her brother."[101]

Working with a pimp also had its downside, and Polly Adler and other madams were not far off in their criticisms. The Bedford Hills State Reformatory and Women's Prison Association case files support the contention that pimps introduced many women into the trade, usually by establishing sexual relationships with them and then gradually drawing them, or forcing them, into prostitution. While these girls did not entirely fit the "seduced and abandoned" stereotype of nineteenth-century reform women's literature, they did prove vulnerable to emotional, affectionate, and sexual appeals by men they found charismatic. Young Hungarian Gretl Meyer's family committed her to Bedford in 1926 to disrupt her relationship with a man they suspected of pimping. According to her social worker, Gretl knew he had pimped in the past and said that "It made her 'embarrassed.' He used to be a 'man hustler'—'had girls.'" However, to Gretl, his charms outweighed his past sins. As the social worker wrote, "She is sure she loves him very much and wants to go to him. At the same time she wonders whether he might not make her 'work for him'—maybe take her far away so that she could never get back to her parents."[102] Pimps also relied on violence to keep women financially productive. One investigator for the Committee of Fourteen reported a conversation with a prostitute who was "afraid to talk, claiming that [if] she squeal[ed] on him, he [would] shoot her."[103] While the case of Alice and Betty reported in the *New York Daily News* shows that madams used violence to keep prostitutes in line, the historical record suggests that pimps relied on it far more regularly.

While white madams and pimps made headlines in the 1920s, black men and women increased their participation in all aspects of prostitution during the decade. Most of this growth saw them concentrated at the bottom of the trade, but they also made gains in brothel prostitution as both prostitutes and managers. Before the war, some black men may have pimped, and some black women may have served as madams, but there is little evidence of these activities in the historical record. What evidence does exist about black prostitution at the turn of the century shows that black women either walked the streets or worked out of tenements in neighborhoods, traditionally the most casual forms of prostitution.[104] The 1920s marked a period of expansion of black women's involvement in brothels as both prostitutes and madams and of black men's participation as prostitutes, pimps, and what investigators called "male madams."[105] For example, one white investigator reported a black male manager ("madam") running an interracial call flat in Harlem.[106] Black men's involvement in pimping also grew significantly in this period. In the Bedford reformatory case files for the 1920s, white women with pimps outnumbered black women nine to one. In the 1930s, pimps had gained ground with black prostitutes, and black women made up seven of the thirteen women with pimps noted in the Women's Prison Association case files.[107]

The growing prominence of African Americans in the upper levels of prostitution and prostitution management in New York City stemmed from a number of factors. First, the black population itself doubled every ten years from 1900 through 1940 through a combination of migration from the South and immigration from the West Indies. Extensive discrimination in employment in the legal economy forced some black women and men in this rapidly growing community to turn to the underground economy to support their families. They worked in gambling, liquor sales, and, of course, prostitution. Even when they could find jobs in the legal economy, the high wages in prostitution (even in work as dangerous as streetwalking) drew some blacks, just as it did whites. Black women, for example, dominated the quasi-legal category of domestic in a house of prostitution. Despite being a devout Baptist and a member of Adam Clayton Powell's Abyssinian Baptist Church, one northern-born black woman stated "quite definitely that she knew the type of person for whom she was going to work but the salary was so much better than any she could earn on another housework job and the work was extremely light." When she was arrested in 1938 during a raid, the black madam who employed her immediately bailed her out of jail, negotiated for the charges to be dropped, "and paid her full wages of $12 due her for one week, although she had not worked there that long."[108] Most black women in domestic service earned less than a dollar a day, a fact that made the twelve-dollar weekly wages this woman received extremely appealing.[109] Opportunities for this sort of work undoubtedly increased as Harlem became one of several places where vice (both black and white) flourished in the city.

White fascination with black culture (and sexuality) may have helped blacks gain a foothold in the more lucrative aspects of prostitution. Far more profitable than catering to local black men, the interracial trade offered higher wages in prostitution and prostitution management but also required more organization. While some white men contented themselves with picking up black women streetwalking in Harlem, others wanted a more comfortable experience, and black men and women opened call flats that catered to this trade.[110] These flats showed the same sophisticated organization as most white call flats in this period: they provided drinks for clients and socializing between johns and prostitutes, and they maintained elaborate lists of white and black prostitutes in case the clients were dissatisfied with the current selection of women.[111] Even as some blacks moved into management positions in vice, however, developments in prostitution in the 1930s limited their success. The few men and women who boldly stepped into the high-end trade were swamped by the tide of desperate black women who had never considered themselves prostitutes, and who turned to it as a last resort when jobs disappeared and families faced eviction and starvation.

Nobody Could Tell What You Would Do if You Were Hungry: Prostitution during the Great Depression

If the 1920s marked a shift in power from prostitutes to madams, the 1930s witnessed a similar and equally devastating shift away from independent madams to male organized-crime leaders like Lucky Luciano and Dutch Schultz. By the late 1930s, most women in professional prostitution, madams and prostitutes, black and white, worked under organized-crime syndicates who siphoned off profits and used violence to enforce their will. To "mobsters," prostitution represented a profitable venture when the demise of Prohibition ended their illegal liquor trade. However, the economic distress of the Great Depression continually acted as a solvent on this solidifying, male-dominated hierarchy as unemployment drove more and more women into the most casual and least organized forms of the sex trade. What emerged was a two-tiered system, highly organized at the top and chaotic, poorly paid, and extremely dangerous at the bottom. Under the control of organized crime, women working at the top of the hierarchy suffered from financial exploitation and, at times, from physical abuse, but they avoided entanglements with the law. The women who poured into sex work at the bottom fled the rising tide of unemployment, eviction, and hunger. Working in the most exposed forms of prostitution, namely streetwalking and tenement prostitution, these women, who were disproportionately black, faced violence, low pay, and periodic arrest and incarceration.

Organized crime began to encroach on prostitution management as early as the 1920s, when the mob began to use brothels as a place to socialize and conduct business. As Polly Adler said about gangsters using her various call flats in the 1920s, "quite often on their spending sprees they made my place a hangout."[112] Even as patrons, mobsters had a negative impact on working conditions and on women's control of the trade. In one incident, a madam initially supported her prostitute's right to refuse a client but changed her mind when she discovered that he was with "a bunch of gunmen." As the prostitute explained to an undercover investigator, "the outcome was I had to go in with him. . . . After he got thru with me he gave me $15 which all remained in my possession. Sadie said she don't want anything from me."[113]

The madam's failure to take her traditional 50 percent may have been a way of apologizing to the prostitute for backing down. Madams had little recourse against either the interference in management or the violence that often ensued.[114] Polly Adler reported that one incident with a "gangster" kept her "in bed a week with a swollen face, a raw throat, and a back that looked like hash from the whipping." But it was the loss of control that disturbed her the most. As she explained, "what made me feel sicker than anything was the knowledge that there was no way in which I could retaliate."[115] Since madams ran illegal businesses, they could not appeal to the police when faced with mob bullying.

Lost liquor revenues from the demise of Prohibition provided the economic impetus for gangsters to take over a business that many in organized crime had previously seen as distasteful and beneath them. As Adler described, "A big-time gangster regards a 'prostitution man'—that is, a man who makes his money through procuring, even indirectly—as the lowest thing there is. He will not even be seen talking to such a man for fear the taint will spread to his name."[116] But organized crime had expanded extensively under Prohibition, and it needed new sources of income. Prostitution proved the easiest and most profitable replacement after the demise of the liquor trade. Ostensibly organized under the leadership of Lucky Luciano, the prostitution "syndicate" in New York operated a "great chain of houses" throughout the city that "gobbl[ed] up those who had operated independently before the merger of 1933."[117] According to news reports from Luciano's trial in 1936, he gained control through violence. "Houses that would not join were wrecked and their inmates beaten," the *New York American* wrote in its coverage of the trial, "while minor vice racketeers were threatened with death."[118] Madams testified that they gave over 10 percent of their earnings to the syndicate in exchange for the guarantee that no prostitute or madam would ever spend time in jail.[119] In June of 1936, the state convicted Luciano and sent him to prison.[120] Some people, both inside and outside the trade, believed that Luciano had been framed. The defense repeatedly complained that the prosecution promised the madams who testified immunity from prosecution under New York's compulsory prostitution laws, statutes that carried a possible sentence of twenty years. Such women, they argued, simply could not be trusted to tell the truth. Polly Adler (who had not testified against Luciano) argued that he had been framed, but her own description of the 1930s confirmed the takeover by organized crime. She herself reluctantly came under the protection of Dutch Schultz in the mid-1930s.[121] While they rarely saw eye to eye on business matters, she admitted that she could not continue to operate without mob protection.[122] Regardless of Luciano's guilt or innocence, by the mid-1930s, organized crime had taken over prostitution, and madams had become middle managers in a trade they had run in the city for over a hundred years.

The second major change in prostitution resulted from the economic devastation of the Depression. Thousands of women poured into casual prostitution, driving down wages and eroding working conditions. The Committee of Fourteen commented in 1932 that the newcomers flooding the trade had forced prices to drop by fifty cents between 1930 and 1931.[123] The Depression affected wages all over the sex industry, not just in prostitution. In May of 1932, *Broadway Brevities* echoed the committee's analysis in an article titled "Nudes Feel Pinch! Cootch Gals, Stag Ponies and Strippers Take It on the Chin When Flesh Price Drops." The reporter noted that "Old Boy Depression has smashed the nude-woman-racket a paralyzing blow. Never before has it been so easy to secure beautiful baby dolls to entertain . . . at such low costs."[124] The cartoon accompanying this article joked about the falling price for sex and women's willingness to offer deals. Titled "What a Bargain," it depicts a fat woman bending over in a shop window to organize a display of canned vegetables. Next to her enormous bottom, a sign reads, "Special Today: Any can in the window 10¢" (Figure 6.6).

Professionals who worked in the courts, in the repression of vice, and in providing services to the poor all noted a dramatic increase in prostitution during the Depression. In 1932, Virginia Murray, director of New York's Traveler's Aid Society, remarked that social workers "have some reasonable ground . . . for thinking that there has been an increase in flagrant commercialized prostitution over the last few years." She also noted a surge in the number of women stating that they entered prostitution because "they were unable to get work and were without resources of any kind."[125] These reports continued into the early 1940s.[126] Social workers during the Depression shifted their analysis away from condemning the "immorality" of the women involved and argued instead that economics forced women into prostitution. These purely economic explanations of prostitution among middle-class professionals sometimes conflicted with working-class women's own understandings of their misfortune. Ethel McBride, a white woman from rural Virginia, told her social worker in 1933 that "she firmly believed that God was punishing her by seeing that she did not get employment." Exasperated, the social worker "suggested that perhaps God had nothing to do with this but that it was a faulty economic structure which caused many people to be unemployed." At this, McBride began to cry, insisting through her tears that "unless I can believe that God has power to punish me, what have I left to believe in?"[127]

Guy: *"I gotta get in on that."*

FIGURE 6.6. *"What a Bargain," cartoon accompanying an article by Peter Good, "Nudes Feel Pinch!: Cootch Gals, Stag Ponies and Strippers Take It on the Chin When Flesh Price Drops,"* Broadway Brevities, *May 16, 1932.*

Newspapers echoed the concerns of reformers, and by 1932, they regularly published reports about unemployment and low wages driving women into prostitution. In a 1934 article for the *New York World Telegram,* reporter Gretta Palmer commented that "the women who are brought to the trial here are the saddest victims of the depression. They are poor little derelicts, shabbily clad, who would hardly turn to this most wretched form of livelihood if there were any other open to them."[128] Two years later, in the midst of the Luciano trial, the *New York Post* commented on the paltry wages offered in women's employment and asked its readers, "Could Luciano's madams have a better recruiting agent than these salary schedules?"[129]

Increasingly, both black and white women arrested for prostitution cited economic need as their primary reason for engaging in prostitution. Their stories reveal the desperation of women with unemployed or absent husbands, hungry children, and dependent parents. Black West Indian Larissa Peabody explained her plight to social workers at the Women's Prison Association. According to her social worker, Peabody provided the only income for "her sick mother and infant child." Unemployed and unable to afford the fee many agencies demanded to place women in domestic positions, Peabody chose to abandon her infant rather than watch it starve. "Feeling that she did not want the baby to suffer from want of food," her social worker wrote, "she decided to wrap the baby and leave it on the most prosperous door step she saw. She had the child wrapped and was going down the street with tears in her eyes when she met a girl whom she had known when in school." After she explained her plight, the woman offered to let her work out of her small call flat in Harlem and told her to take the baby home.[130] White women faced similar dilemmas. Summarizing the testimony of a white prostitute in the Luciano case, a reporter for the *New York Evening Journal* wrote, "Mary went on to say that she had two children and then her husband died and she had two babies and no man to support them or her."[131] In addition to lack of male support and responsibility for dependent relatives, women specifically mentioned hunger, unemployment, and imminent eviction as the main reasons they prostituted.[132] When asked by a social worker if she would return to prostitution, one African American woman admitted she might, "because nobody could tell what you would do if you were hungry."[133]

Some women hid the source of their income from their families out of shame or fear of relatives' judgment. Larissa Peabody, for example, "told her mother . . . that she was living in a position in the Bronx" and visited her mother and baby only on her "day off."[134] Other women practiced prostitution at home in full view of husbands and children. One investigator came face to face with this reality in early 1932 when he met a white woman who offered to prostitute with him in her apartment. He accompanied her upstairs and noticed "a man sitting at a table and three children roaming around." When he asked her who they were, she explained, "That's my husband and my three children. Don't mind them. I'll close the door. You don't have to worry." Appalled, the investigator asked, "How come you do a thing like that in the presence of your family?" She explained, "My husband is sick and out of work. . . . I have to do that on account of the depression. Every dollar helps."[135] Some women also argued that prostituting was more honorable than their other alternatives. When Dolores Hamilton's social worker asked her "how she happened to pick [prostitution] instead of something else," she explained that "stealing was dishonest."[136] In another case, one African American family even chose prostitution over applying for welfare. The woman's common-law husband explained to her social worker that "they had never had any help from any charity bureau."[137] In this case, pride in the family's independence was a factor in deciding to prostitute rather than accept charity. Their choice reflected the attitudes of many working-class African Americans who valued financial independence and self-reliance over the bourgeois respectability advocated by the African American middle class.[138] It may also be that they accurately assessed their chances of receiving charity through New York's relief agencies. Both before and during the Depression, New York's public and private relief agencies routinely discriminated against African American applicants for aid.[139]

While women of all races resorted to prostitution to make ends meet, the statistics indicate that black women did so more often than white. In the records of the Women's Prison Association, women who prostituted out of economic need were relatively evenly split between black and white women. Of the thirty-three cases where women reported economic need as their primary motivation, sixteen were black. When evaluating the meaning of these numbers, however, it is crucial to take into account the demographics of New York City. In 1930, blacks made up just over 4.7 percent of the population, and they tallied only 6 percent by 1940.[140] Seen in that light, the data suggest that black women's economic opportunities deteriorated so significantly during the Depression that they resorted to prostitution in numbers far greater than their proportion in the population.

Of course, black women had always been overrepresented among those women arrested and incarcerated for prostitution, but these trends grew more extreme every decade, highlighting the ways that racism limited their options in the legitimate economy, in the sex industry, and even within the hierarchy of prostitution itself. Katharine Bement Davis reported in 1910 that black women made up 13 percent of the prostitutes in Bedford reformatory, even though at that time blacks only composed 2 percent of the population of the city.[141] By 1924, when Willoughby Cyrus Waterman analyzed arrest statistics in New York City, he found that black women (African American and West Indian) accounted for 46 percent of the prostitution arrests. He argued that this stemmed from police practices rather than from an overrepresentation of black women in prostitution as a whole. "The arresting officers," he explained, "in an endeavor to increase their total of arrests, were centering their attention upon those persons who were especially defenseless and were ignoring more clever violators of the law."[142] By this, he meant that police went after streetwalkers, traditionally the most visible, most casual workers in the trade. Women just entering prostitution often started in streetwalking, as did women who prostituted casually to meet immediate economic needs. Because of racial discrimination in the sex industry, black women, especially those with little experience, most often went into streetwalking and suffered the consequences.

In 1939, Marguerite Marsh identified similar patterns in her analysis of the women's court proceedings. She reported that the percentage of black women had increased to 54 percent of all arrests because of their relegation to street prostitution.[143] Critiquing police practices, she argued that "young, attractive, clever women once arrested avoid repetition of the acts which are likely to result in arrest, unless under pressure of great need."[144] Only inexperienced women worked in streetwalking, which explained the high incidence of arrests among these groups. New York, it seems, had far fewer professional black prostitutes than white ones. Discrimination in the labor market, however, drove more black women into casual prostitution, which accounted for their higher arrest rates when compared with those of whites. Marsh also noted that racism in the courts contributed to black women's overrepresentation in New York's jails and reformatories. She found that once in court, black women fared far worse than whites: "Only four out of twelve magistrates whose decisions were studied had acquitted relatively the same percentage of the white and Negro cases coming before them."[145] New York's judges compounded the already severe problems of racism in New York's economy and policing by incarcerating black women for crimes that only resulted in parole or suspended sentences when the perpetrator was white.

Racism in the legitimate economy forced black women into sex work, and racism kept them out of the legal side of the trade. While white women may have remained a numerical majority in sex work, they occupied the most desirable positions—those that either remained legal or sheltered them from arrest. Black women, on the other hand, bore the brunt of the punishments the state handed down for prostitution. An imaginative researcher, Marsh had a novel solution for this problem. Noting that most of the arresting officers were white, she argued that in Harlem "an adequate police plan to keep certain streets free of white men, particularly in the late night and early morning hours, would do much to remove for many of the young Negro women the present temptation to engage in prostitution as an easy way to make money."[146] Needless to say, this analysis, which cut against the prevailing hierarchies of race, gender, and class that allowed white men access to any streets and any women they desired, did not appeal to New York's city government and was never implemented.

The 1920s and 1930s marked a period of time in New York when the legal side of the sex industry expanded and prostitution became increasingly marginalized, both socially and racially. Alfred Kinsey noted this trend when he remarked in his 1948 *Sexual Behavior in the Human Male* that "the present-day male is making such contacts [with prostitutes] only two-thirds, or even half, as often as the older generation." Kinsey attributed this shift to the "definite increase in the amount of intercourse with girls who are not prostitutes."[147] As we will see in the next chapter, Kinsey's arguments about increasing premarital sex rates are convincing. But it is also clear that the sex industry itself helped to sideline prostitution as an important sexual outlet for American men. Providing legal sexual services proved very popular both among white women and among the male patrons of various races who found sexualized entertainment less dangerous, more entertaining, and often cheaper than resorting to prostitutes. While many American men today have been to a strip club, if only for a bachelor party, few have actually paid a prostitute for sex. America's sexual practices have changed, and prostitution, which during the nineteenth and early twentieth centuries made up a significant proportion of American men's premarital and extramarital sexual contacts, has dwindled accordingly.

In Cole Porter's *Kiss Me Kate*, first produced on Broadway in 1948, the song "Always True to You in My Fashion" captures one direction treating took in the 1920s and 1930s. Kate justifies her liaisons with other men to her beau by explaining that, while they mean nothing to her emotionally, she uses them to pay for things she wants. Leaving the sexual dimensions of the exchange unspoken but implied, she explains that when

> Mister Harris plutocrat,
> Wants to give my cheek a pat,
> If the Harris pat
> Means a Paris hat
> Bébé, Oo-la-la!
> But I'm always true to you, darlin', in my fashion,
> Yes I'm always true to you darlin', in my way.[1]

Emerging from World War I more popular than ever, treating split into two very different sorts of activities practiced by very different sorts of women. Because the dangers the war introduced into prostitution only intensified under Prohibition, older women began to use treating to meet concrete expenses in addition to the more traditional exchange of sexual favors for entertainment. Paris hats may have been rare, but practical items like shoes, stockings, and room rents became more common. For older women, treating became a way to meet material needs without taking the risks of casual prostitution. By the 1930s, the economic model treating provided pervaded the interactions of women and men in commercial amusements. Associated largely with prostitution at the turn of the century, by the 1930s and 1940s, women's presence in commercial space did not signal sex for sale so much as sex for barter. But this reshaping of heterosexual relations did not always benefit women or allow them to use commercial spaces freely. Women in public commercial space remained "available" to men's advances, sexual objects to be consumed. Treating had shifted the moral meaning of their presence and how they might be paid for their time but did not disrupt the sexualized nature of their place in the public.[2]

The other side of treating, practiced by young girls, disappeared into the emerging system of dating that replaced older patterns of courtship in the 1920s. In dating, a young man and a young woman went out together to the movies, the theater, or perhaps the skating rink or an amusement park. This shift from family- and community-sponsored events to commercial entertainment made the issue of money suddenly very important in the negotiations between young couples. Dating in commercial amusements raised the question of who should pay for these entertainments and with what. Treating provided a model of how to manage these relations by suggesting that boys could pay in cash, and girls could reciprocate with sexual intimacy in the form of kissing, fondling, and, at times, intercourse. Treating's economic logic became embedded in dating, and it continues to lurk under the surface of the practice to this day.[3] Furthermore, when sexual exchange came to be expected as a part of any given date, sexual activity among young people increased. Because young people usually dated several partners before they settled into a serious relationship, the very casualness of dating encouraged more relaxed attitudes toward sexual intercourse. Much to the consternation of parents, an epidemic of "petting" swept the nation. Petting involved noncoital sex, encompassing everything from kissing and fondling to mutual masturbation and oral sex. Petting's association with dating encouraged adolescents to experiment with sexual activity sooner in their relationships than earlier generations had done.[4] Dating's absorption of treating's logic meant that sexual activity, though not always intercourse, became an important part of how young women and young men interacted. This slowly began to shift American sexual behavior, so that by World War II, nearly 50 percent of American women engaged in premarital intercourse, and a small but growing number did so with men whom they did not marry.[5] Rates for premarital intercourse would continue to increase throughout the century. This development marked a real shift in the value of chastity for Americans of all social classes. By World War II, many "good girls" who dated also engaged in premarital intercourse, though it would still take the debates sparked by feminists in the 1960s for America to acknowledge this fact.

The commercial setting of dating also meant that families lost control over courtship. While both middle-class and working-class parents allowed courtship to shift out of the family and into the commercial realm, many still had grave concerns about the kinds of families that would emerge from this new system. Because they often lived in multiethnic and multiracial neighborhoods, working-class parents dealt in a much more concrete way than middle-class parents with what they saw as inappropriate matches. Some white middle-class families undoubtedly objected to interfaith or interracial relationships, but the class, ethnic, and racial segregation of New York's neighborhoods and schools made it unlikely that their children would have the opportunity to form such attachments. Working-class parents, on the other hand, faced the daily reality of ethnic, religious, and racial mixing. Even as they acquiesced to the general shift in courtship patterns away from home and family, working-class parents saw it as their duty to patrol the boundaries of religion and race. Thus, while dating successfully replaced older forms of courtship, it did not represent a complete triumph for the independence of children in marital choice.

Stockings, Shoes, and Room Rents: The Materialism of Treating among Older Women in the 1920s and 1930s

Older women who used treating after the war often did so out of financial need and to avoid resorting to casual prostitution. Unlike the girls before the war, the majority of women who treated throughout the 1920s were in their twenties and thirties and reported marriage, divorce, widowhood, or desertion as part of their life experiences. Their status as older women, often supporting children or other family members, contrasted sharply with that of the adolescent girls who flocked to the ice-cream parlors near the camps and associated treating with patriotism. On January 19, 1917, one investigator wrote up a typical experience with a woman he identified in his notes as "charity." In the course of their conversation, he found out that she had been married and supported a young daughter by working as a milliner. When he asked her what she expected in return for sex, she said, "I have responsibilities; that is why I am working. You understand me, I don't want money for going with you. I am not a regular." Employing popular slang for a prostitute ("regular"), she distanced herself from women who would take money from a man. "I have to like a man," she explained. "Of course if I go out with you and we have a party (sexual intercourse) and you want to give me a present, it would be all right, but I don't go for the money or I surely would not work."[6] Despite the fact that many women had to resort to casual prostitution to stretch their meager wages and cover family responsibilities, this woman, and many like her, saw evidence of work as proof of her status as a nonprostitute.[7] New York's laws on vagrancy supported this way of marking identity, because judges often used employment status as a way of determining the likelihood that a woman might be prostituting.[8]

The older women who engaged in charity during the 1920s used it to meet material needs. In the twenty-five incidents in the Committee of Fourteen Records in which women specified what they would expect in exchange for sex, thirteen identified some kind of concrete compensation for their company and sexual services. Of these, nine asked for clothing, and another five sought monetary gifts in the form of specific bills paid, or in one case, a charge account at Best's Department Store.[9] In over half of the instances, then, women asked for either clothing or some kind of monetary remuneration. In the other cases, four asked for candy and two for entertainment, or they explained that they were interested in company and sex, with some unspecified exchanges occurring later when they had "gotten to know" the man.[10] This breakdown contrasts sharply with the approach of treating girls before and during the war, who rarely asked for more than an evening on the town.[11]

Men noticed the new materialism and the rising cost of "charity." The headwaiter at the Little Hofbrau Haus told one investigator not to bother with the charity girls he met there. "Instead of wasting time on them," he advised, "why don't you go to a real whore. It will cost you cheaper in the end."[12] The headwaiter had a point: women who treated to make ends meet evaluated their possibilities very carefully. One investigator reported that a woman in Shea's Gilsey House on Coney Island "said that this other woman told her that Sheas was a better place to pick up men than in Gormans, said there are a lot of cheap guys in Gormans, they won't let you order anything more than a beer, but the men you pick up in Sheas, you can get more money out of them."[13]

Women engaged in this more explicitly material form of treating because the dangers of prostitution introduced by the war only intensified in the 1920s. In a surprisingly candid discussion in 1927, two women explained to an investigator exactly what they expected in return for sex and why. As the investigator reported, "both women informed me that they had been married, were living apart from their husbands, but expressed a desire to meet some nice men who would treat them right." When he asked them what they meant by "treat them right," they told him, "Well, you know, take us out to dinner and to a show occasionally—some regular fellow we could depend on, that would pay us about $25 a week." One of the two explained that "as far as going out and picking men up on the street for the mere sake of money, I would not consider it, the dangers are too great for both my health and other ways."[14] While these women might have been either prostitutes or charity, their assessment of the dangers of prostitution reflected the realities of life in the trade in the 1920s.

Like the milliner mentioned above, women who were identified as charity in the 1920s carefully distinguished between their activity and that of prostitutes. An Irish American maid who worked for the Paramount Hotel told an investigator who pressed her about price, "I am not that kind. It is a matter of pleasure with me. Of course, if you want to give anything that's up to you." [15] Even popular culture of the 1920s and 1930s reflected an acceptance of the new material turn treating had taken. In a series titled "The Forgotten Woman: The Diary of a Girl Out of Work," run by the *Broadway Brevities* newspaper in the depths of the Depression, the plucky heroine routinely quit jobs when men pressed her for sex. When she worked as a taxi dancer, for example, she explained, "I will not be pawed!" and then hit a customer when he persisted. "Sorry I broke his glasses, though," she commented insincerely. "Hope he recovers." However, the forgotten woman also picked up men and took them to her room for the evening. After one such adventure, she asked for financial help the next morning: "'Darling, I hate to mention it but my rent's due and could you lend me a few dollars.' Did he do it? He did not! He slapped me in the face and called me an awful name." [16] This character did not see herself as a prostitute and took offense at the "awful name." The series suggests that asking for help with rent in exchange for sexual favors during the Depression had moved out of the category of prostitution. Instead, such behaviors now occupied an intermediate space of quasi-respectability that good women could occupy when their need was great.

Like the "forgotten woman," some women during the Depression relied on treating for material support, even as they resisted slipping into what they saw as "genuine" prostitution. One woman stated that she had no room to take the investigator to, explaining, "If I were in the profession, which I am not, I would make provision for that. But as I am looking for employment and must absolutely get something or I don't know what I'll do, as my room rent is due tomorrow and I only have as you see here, eight cents." [17] The records of the Women's Prison Association reflect the intense economic pressures and family responsibilities that drove women to walk the fine line between a treat and casual prostitution. One white Catholic, Elizabeth Manning, had separated from her husband, and by 1936, his child support payments had dwindled to nothing. Although she had been arrested for prostitution, her file stated, "it is Mrs. Scheff's [Manning's social worker] impression, however, that Mrs. M. had not actually been prostituting, but that the likelihood was that she had one or two men friends." [18] What is so interesting about this exchange is the fact that even her social worker, a woman who worked daily with prostitutes, acknowledged the difference between prostitution and this very material form of charity. The Great Depression swelled the ranks of casual prostitutes, but some women, aware of the very real dangers posed by coerced prostitution, arrest, or incarceration, used treating to fill the enormous gap that had opened up between what they could earn and their expenses.

Treating during the Depression was not without its dangers. There is some evidence that men became more insistent about their rights to women's bodies and sexuality. In *Hard Times*, Studs Terkel interviewed a petty criminal who cast the treating exchange in a particularly chilling light. "If she had two drinks with him," he stated, "and she didn't lay her frame down, she was in a serious matter. She could have one, and explain that she made a mistake by marrying some sucker, that she was trying to fulfill her marriage commitment. But in the thirties, if you had a second drink and she didn't make the commitment where she's going to lay her frame down for you, the entire matter was resolved quickly to the point and could end in mayhem. She was in a serious matter."[19] According to this interviewee, treating in the 1930s could be deadly serious, partly because women faced such disastrous economic choices, and partly because some men asserted they had rights to sex when they paid a woman's way. The social and sexual space that treating opened up over the course of its thirty years as a linguistic and identity category did not always benefit women. While women could enter public commercial spaces and not be taken for prostitutes, they still owed something for the drinks and entertainment they consumed.

Treating's Disappearing Path: The Incorporation of Treating into Dating in the 1920s and 1930s

The other side of treating in the 1920s and 1930s involved its incorporation into the emerging practice of dating. In her history of courtship in the twentieth century, *From Front Porch to Back Seat*, Beth Bailey described the emergence of the dating system among college students in the 1910s and 1920s. According to Bailey, among the white middle class, dating involved a young man asking a young woman to attend a commercial amusement where he paid for their evening. This took dating out of the female and family realm of the front parlor, where parents supervised and visiting cost nothing, and into the cabarets and movie theaters of the new entertainment economy. As Bailey explains, "an invitation to go out on a date was an invitation into man's world—not simply because dating took place in the public sphere (commonly defined as belonging to men), though that was part of it, but because dating moved courtship into the world of the economy. Money—men's money—was at the center of the dating system."[20] Dating removed family supervision, replacing it with peer oversight, and inserted money into the already complicated negotiations between young women and men. Dating also represented an attenuation of the courtship practice. Unlike courtship that was supposed to lead to marriage, any individual date might or might not develop into a more serious relationship. Dating introduced an element of social promiscuity into the activities that led to marriages. While courting signified serious intentions toward marriage, dating worked more like shopping, wherein the different parties could try each other out, test compatibility, and compare and contrast the current partner with other potential mates.

Historians locate the beginnings of middle-class dating in the 1910s, but the time line and origins of dating among the working class have remained unclear. Explicitly examining the practices of the white middle class, Bailey does not explore working-class sources. John Modell casts a broader net, addressing the urban white middle and working classes as well as their African American counterparts in his book *Into One's Own*. Modell argues that although working-class youth clearly had the freedom from parental supervision to develop a dating system, they did not, because they lacked the financial resources to do so. Identifying high school as a crucial site in the development of dating, he asserts that working-class youth did not possess "the effective, school-based, same-age peer group that oversaw behavior within the dating system."[21] In addition, Modell asserts that middle-class youth visited commercial amusements as couples, while working-class whites went in larger, mixed-sex or homosocial groups, which, he posits, meant that the working class failed to develop or participate in dating in the 1920s.[22] Urban black youth, Modell adds, regardless of their class status, followed the white working class. On the whole, they "socialized commonly in large mixed-age settings of various sorts."[23]

Despite Modell's contentions, there is evidence that working-class youth had developed a system they called "dating" by the 1920s. Although none of the women who came in contact with Bedford reformatory or the Women's Prison Association mentioned dating, the women in Carney Landis's survey of sexual behavior, conducted from 1935 through 1937, made extensive use of the term. Coming from the working and lower-middle classes and various white ethnic backgrounds, these women's responses to the Landis survey indicate that by 1935 the word "date" had become a common linguistic term in American working-class youth culture.[24] Furthermore, several of the older married women referred to experiences they had had in the 1920s as dating. Though their use of the word "dating" may have been retrospective (that is, they may have applied a term popular in the 1930s to behavior that occurred in the 1920s), their descriptions suggest that a dating system was in place among New York's working class as early as the 1920s.

Women in the Landis study stated that as adolescents they longed to participate in what they called "dating." Their explanations emphasize that their interest centered on participation in the system itself, and not on the attentions of, or desires for, any particular young man. Describing her first date at age sixteen in the early 1920s, one Russian Jewish woman stated that being on a date made her feel "very much flattered, [I] felt important" but that "the boy left no definite impression."[25] An Irish American woman, commenting on her memories of dating in the 1920s, recalled, "[I] went through a period when I would have given anything to have a date, including my virtue."[26] While most women did not contemplate trading their virtue for a date, these responses indicate that by the 1920s these women saw dating as a coherent system and one in which they wanted to be involved. One native-born Protestant woman admitted that on her first date "[I] didn't like the boy. Thought it was nice to have a date though."[27] To these women, as to many of the white middle-class women Bailey described, the date, and not the boy, was the important thing. As one woman explained, "[I] felt I had to have a boyfriend because other girls did."[28] Dates brought status to young women as well as the fun of a night on the town. Their use of the term "date" may have been anachronistic for what they did in the 1920s, but they certainly understood that they participated in a system, one that allowed them more freedom to meet and socialize with boys they did not intend to marry. Conversely, the dating system also involved intense social pressure to conform to this new form of heterosocial and heterosexual interaction. While these women expressed satisfaction over their ability to find a date, their discussions also revealed an underlying anxiety about the costs of not participating. As dating did among the white middle class, this system conferred status through participation and did not necessarily involve liking a particular boy, or boys in general, much less wanting to marry the partner they "dated." Women who opted out of dating might find themselves socially ostracized or labeled "queer."

Working-class dating, like that of the middle class, took place in commercial entertainments. In a series of articles published in the *New York Times* in 1924, reformers expressed concern about the time and money young working people spent in commercial amusements. According to one article, young people in New York spent over five million dollars a year in halls that had an admission fee of ten cents.[29] The head of New York's Commercial Recreation Committee commented that "it is part of the general unrest which is sweeping over all society; it is the 'out-urge.' Young people are unwilling to stay at home. They must be entertained. The working boy and girl are like the rest. They are seeking fun and companionship; for many of them the dance hall is their only place of amusement." Another article estimated that "14 per cent of the total male and 10 percent of the total female population between the ages of 17 and 40 attend the dance halls once a week."[30] While these reformers did not identify the race of the young people involved, studies of black girls conducted in the 1920s show that black youth attended dance halls extensively.[31] Dance halls had become ubiquitous in the lives of young people in New York, and the children of all races and social classes flocked to them.

Of course, dance halls had been popular in New York for over a decade, but before the war, working-class youngsters attended them in same-sex groups and not in heterosocial groups or as courting couples. The experiences of Russian Jewish immigrant Chava Brier provide an excellent example of this pattern. Brier came to New York in 1913 at the age of fourteen. She remembered going out with a group of five girls from work, explaining to her interviewer that "I had a lot of friends, boyfriends I didn't care for, you know, only we were five girls [and] we used to see shows, you know, we lived nice, you know, very decent."[32] Even Italian girls could sometimes go out, as long as they did so only with other girls. Lucrezia Grogone remembered pooling resources with other girls: "we used to have a good time, the girls in the shop, we used to put [in] a quarter each week and we used [the money]... [to] go on a picnic, or go any place, for dinner or to a show."[33] Ruth True also observed that younger Irish and Italian girls in her Hell's Kitchen neighborhood usually went to dance halls with other girls but that courting couples avoided them. As they grew older, True explained, "the young girl usually settles down to keeping steady company some time before her early marriage, and goes less to the dance halls." Summarizing the case of sixteen-year-old Josie, who spent three nights a week in the halls, she reported that Josie said, "When I'm eighteen or nineteen I won't care about it any more. I'll have a 'friend' then and won't want to go anywheres."[34]

But working-class couples in the 1920s often went to dance halls and clearly made use of them for dating purposes. Lithuanian Jew Deborah Waxman moved to New York in 1922, where she immediately plunged into the exciting world of commercial entertainments. "There was plenty . . . to do and at that time everything was so cheap," she reminisced with obvious delight, "so we went to theaters, we took subway rides, there was a double-decker trolley car where we used to take rides, we went boat riding, there was so many things, nowadays you, well you can't afford it." Asked by her interviewer if she went with girlfriends on these adventures, she replied that she went "with my fellow."[35] The women in the Landis survey concurred, mentioning dance halls and movie theaters as their most common destination for "dates," though they also referred to school and to ethnic society dances, golfing, and skating.[36] Whereas couples before might have combined commercial and family activities, by the 1920s, most sociability, and particularly dating, went on in the dance halls, movie theaters, and skating rinks of New York's public for-profit entertainment venues.

Just because working-class youth attended commercial amusements on dates, however, does not mean that they defined dating in the same way as their middle-class counterparts. Evidence from the Landis survey indicates that when working-class youth dated, they often did so as part of larger social groups. One Irish Catholic woman remembered double dating with her older brother in the early 1920s: "my brother went with his girl and the 4 of us went to movies."[37] Dating in this context meant going to the movies with a sibling who also brought a date. Another described group activities: "[I] always had boyfriends—always went in groups," she wrote. "The first boy[,] the one who got fresh. Quite fond of him and thrilled."[38] Rather than attending commercial amusements only in couples, as the middle class did, working-class youth folded dating into social situations with larger mixed-sex groups. Attending commercial amusements in homosocial groups did not end in the 1920s, but it began to give way to heterosocial groups, which often, but not always, included dating pairs. Larger groups allowed peers to observe each other's activities carefully. As a result, peer supervision of dating in the working class was far more direct than that of the middle class, where couples usually went out alone and young people relied solely on gossip to keep the partners in line.

By the 1920s, working-class youth also began to use commercial amusements as a place to meet people they might want to date, something respectable girls assiduously avoided before the war.[39] Jewish immigrant Chava Brier explained this caution, stating that the men one met in such locations "might be bums, who knows what they were?"[40] Bums might make fine dance partners, but they did not represent a good choice in marriage. The anonymity of the commercial amusements made them fun places to play, a fact that many charity girls took advantage of, but before the war, most young women realized that the men they met through family and community ties could be trusted more than strangers they met while out dancing.

The presence of charity girls may also have restrained the behavior of other girls. Men in the halls might assume that they could take liberties with women they met there because some women allowed such liberties in exchange for their entry fees. For respectable girls interested only in dancing, meeting men in the halls might lead to confusion over their status and dangerous misunderstandings. By the 1920s, these concerns had begun to evaporate. Referring to the dance halls on Broadway, a *New York Times* article reported, "some boys and girls go to them together, but frequently they go alone, in the hope of picking up a partner when they get there." [41] Girls from all ethnic and racial backgrounds began to use the halls as a place to meet men they might date. Swedish immigrant Ingrid Larson met her fiancé when he "played in an orchestra in the dance hall where she was accustomed to going every night." According to her social worker at Bedford, this wayward minor and her fiancé had been having intercourse for several years and "expected to marry." The fiancé visited her regularly at Bedford, and "investigation showed him to be industrious and honest." [42] An immigrant from Spain who moved to New York with her family at age twenty-one reported that she "never went out with anyone. Just met them at dances." [43]

Some young women's experiences revealed the same sort of dangers of trusting men they met in commercial amusements that made many prewar young women so cautious. Ruth Reed's *Negro Illegitimacy in New York City* and Anne Bingham's more general study, *Determinants of Sex Delinquency in Adolescent Girls*, both told the stories of young women who ran afoul of men in dance halls. According to Reed, one young African American migrant from Virginia met a man at a dance hall who "told her at the time of their meeting that he was looking for a wife. He had promised marriage within a few days." After she became pregnant, however, he admitted that "he was already married," and "he refused to be of any assistance to her." [44] Meeting men at dance halls had its dangers, and the expansion of courtship practices into entertainment space disadvantaged naive young women who took men at their word.

As these young women's experiences illuminate, the lack of parental supervision often led to more sexual activity in dating. With young people both meeting and dating their future mates in commercial space, older relations had less to say about behavior during courtship. In this context, peer supervision often translated into peer pressure to engage in various kinds of sex play. One Scotch-Irish woman remarked that she initially "felt it was wrong to kiss a boy. . . . In high school I noticed the other girls who did let boys kiss them had more fun than I so I experimented." She did not really enjoy her foray into petting, however. As she explained, the "first boy that kissed me put his hand down my neck. That upset me." Some young men took advantage of peer expectations to pressure girls into petting. As one native-born white woman described her early dates at age sixteen in the mid-1920s, "One boy used to take me to Paradise Roof once a week. . . . He held me awfully tight—I liked him. [He] held me tight in and asked me why I didn't do what other girls do." [45] Another woman reported that she had not intended to pet but felt compelled to when she and her date went to a friend's cottage with another couple. As she explained, "Nothing like that had ever entered my head—the other couple went to bed together and nothing for us to do but the same."[46] Girls learned from other girls, as well as from the boys, that petting was an important part of dating, and since the venues in which they dated lacked supervision, there was little that families, or at times the girls themselves, could do to put the brakes on sexual experimentation.

But the driving force behind sexual expression in dating among the working class came not from a lack of supervision or from a desire to explore sexuality, but from the exchange model that treating provided. Moving courtship into commercial venues required that someone pay for the evening's entertainment, and working-class girls in the 1920s still struggled over their access to cash. Less likely to receive allowances than either their fathers or their brothers, working-class girls entered the realm of dating at an economic disadvantage. Treating provided an example among working-class youth for how such relations could be negotiated. One fifteen-year-old African American girl made this logic very clear in her comments in Enid Severy Smith's 1935 publication on unwed mothers in New York City. "I did not have much fun unless somebody took me out to parties and dances," she said, "and when you go out with a 'boy friend' he expects you to be nice to him, and sort of pay for the treat; at least that is the custom so I am told. He was kind in taking me places, and it cost him money, and I did not see any great harm in being nice to him, and in doing as he asked. He told me everything was all right, and that everybody did these things."[47] Her explanation vividly highlights the way that treating had folded into dating by the 1930s. Literally using the word "treat" to describe the entertainment she received, she referenced the older practice of treating. But her other linguistic choices set her activities within the context of dating. Her use of the term "boy friend" and the longevity of their association made her activities more like dating. Rather than meet a man she did not know at a commercial amusement and convince him to pay for her evening with sexual intercourse, she relied on a boy she knew who took her out, paid, and expected intercourse in return for his investment. Casual as dating could be when compared with more serious courtship, it still required more sustained relationships than the older treating exchange. Clearly engaged in dating, she also understood the economic demands embedded in the practice, demands that derived from treating.

While her boyfriend exaggerated when he told her that "everybody" had sexual intercourse, he did not really lie. By the mid-1920s, many working-class couples who dated understood that intercourse could be part of the exchange, especially if they had dated for a while. One American-born white woman described losing her virginity at age seventeen in the late 1920s in just such terms. "Had been dating several months," she explained. "Had met him on a vacation. He had invited me to visit his home, just an ordinary date. Came gradually. . . . Felt under obligation . . . my vacation [at] no expense." When she got pregnant, she "went to my family doctor, who recommended a friend" who performed an abortion.[48] Unlike many of the women in the Landis survey who reported love as their motivation for engaging in sexual intercourse, this woman articulated the pressure of accumulated spending on the part of her date. She emphasized the economic nature of dating, the importance of sexual exchange, and its debt to treating. And like many women interviewed by Landis, she did not marry this man, a failure that located her activities within the realm of dating rather than courtship.

For most young women, intercourse came later in dating. But unlike the women who brought seduction under promise of marriage cases at the turn of the century, women in the 1920s did not always wait for an open promise, instead going on their own feelings of commitment, an admittedly risky shift in practice. One Polish Jewish immigrant explained why she had sex with a man she did not marry, stating that she "felt we were going to be married. Didn't occur to me we wouldn't."[49] Another American-born Russian Jewish woman said that she was "under the impression that we were engaged" when she consented to intercourse. She then elaborated, writing in the Landis survey, "I was much in love, had know each other for 3 [or] 4 months, had been petting. He urged me on so, felt I would eventually marry him—considered experimenting necessary to see if we were suited—we were—but broke it off for other reasons."[50] A Scotch-Irish young woman explained her choices in terms of her mother's advice, which she apparently ignored. "Mother had said, 'remember being engaged isn't being married,'" she wrote on her survey, but "as soon as I really fell in love there was much caressing—at first mostly the breast," which eventually led to sexual intercourse.[51] As dating blurred the line between casual sociability and formal courtship, young women began to engage in intercourse without explicit promises. None of these women married their first lovers, even though at the time they thought they would. Their experience highlights the effects dating had on how young women envisioned courtship and what behavior might be appropriate in it. Feelings of love and the emerging societal attitude that love and sex went together began to override reticence to engage in sexual intercourse. These shifts also eroded more formal courtship practices, allowing women to "assume" engagement, even if no promises had been made.

Petting and dating went together, and for the working class, they did so because of the economic logic that treating introduced and dating absorbed. This explains the surge in premarital intercourse that Kinsey reported, the widespread acceptance of petting in the generation that came of age immediately after World War I, and the clear class differences he found in the rate at which young people engaged in these activities. Of the women born before 1900 (and thus engaging in courtship in the 1910s and early 1920s), 31.1 percent engaged in premarital intercourse with their fiancés, and 15 percent engaged in premarital intercourse with men who were not their fiancés. For women born between 1900 and 1909 (engaging in courtship in the 1920s and early 1930s), the numbers jumped to 40 percent for premarital intercourse with their fiancés and 27.2 percent with other men. A 12.2 percent increase in a decade, these numbers show that by the 1920s, more than a quarter of the young women Kinsey surveyed had premarital intercourse with men they did not marry.[52] Perhaps more significant for a cultural understanding of both treating and dating is Kinsey's discovery of an even greater growth in the number of young people who engaged in petting. As with premarital sex, Kinsey found that the most significant shift in petting occurred between the generation that came of age before World War I and the generation that matured during and after it. Before the war, 29 percent of girls and 41 percent of boys petted before the age of sixteen. After the war, those numbers jumped to 43 percent of girls and 51 percent of boys. In addition, Kinsey found a marked reduction in the age at which petting began and an extraordinary increase in the number of young people who petted until they achieved orgasm.[53] As with his data in all other areas of shifts in sexual practices, Kinsey found that working-class girls led this revolution.

Despite the increase in premarital intercourse, America's illegitimate birthrate did not rise significantly in this period.[54] In part, this was because young people had a more sophisticated understanding of contraceptives. In the Coser interviews, 75 percent of Jewish women and 45 percent of Italian women used birth control during their marriages; both groups listed condoms as their most common form of birth control.[55] This does not mean that all of these women knew about birth control before they married, but rather it suggests that information about it was widely available in the community. Clinics in the 1920s and 1930s reported that the number of couples using some kind of family planning had almost doubled since the turn of the century, with the highest increase coming in condom use.[56] Reviewing Kinsey's data on birth control practices for New York City, Modell found that couples cut reliance on withdrawal (a notoriously ineffective form of birth control) by half and began to use condoms instead.[57] Wartime exposure to, and education about, condoms and disease prevention undoubtedly accounted for some of the increase in their use. In addition, the *Crane* decision handed down by the New York State court in 1918 ruled that condoms could be sold for disease prevention, exempting condoms from the Comstock Law of 1873, which forbade the distribution of birth control and birth control information.[58] While it did not affect the rest of the nation, in New York in the early 1920s, men could buy condoms in a wide variety of places. As the manufacturer of Trojans commented, condoms were "gypped around on street corners, [peddlers] would approach you on the street or in your office; barbers would approach you, you could get them in delicatessen stores, candy stores, tailor shops—every place, every conceivable places where a man might go to make a purchase, they would be offered to you."[59] The widespread availability and use of condoms helped to keep the premarital pregnancy rates stable, even as more people engaged in premarital sex.

Abortion also kept this rate low. The inmate case files for both Bedford reformatory and the Women's Prison Association mention abortion far more than any other kind of birth control. Furthermore, the women interviewed by Coser also refer to abortion as a common and widely available practice. Only 19 percent of Jewish women and 16 percent of Italian women in the Coser study acknowledged having abortions themselves, but 54 percent of Jewish women and 45 percent of Italian women knew of someone who had had the procedure. While most of these abortions occurred in the context of marriage, many unmarried women would have heard these stories as well and might have known how to obtain an abortion, or at least whom to ask.[60]

The number of abortions increased in the 1930s as couples who put off marriage because of economic circumstances had to deal with the consequences of their prolonged engagements. Women's Prison Association records reflect this trend, showing that men began to play a role in obtaining abortions for their girlfriends and fiancées in the 1930s. Southern African American Missy Engs became pregnant in 1938 by a man she dated. Unfortunately, he had tuberculosis, and instead of marrying, "he gave her $10. which she spent on medicines in an attempt to get rid of the child."[61] Courting couples who postponed marriage because of economic circumstances made these family planning decisions together, and the case files indicate a sharp increase in men's participation in financing abortions. In fact, they were so widely available that at least one young Italian Catholic woman hid her pregnancy from her family, her friends, and her fiancé because she wanted to keep the baby. As the social workers noted in her file, "she did not tell anyone about her pregnancy until she was four or five months pregnant, so that they could not have forced her to do away with the child."[62] Abortions may have been illegal and dangerous, but couples relied on them as a form of birth control both within and outside of marriage. As the Depression lengthened courtships, more unmarried couples used abortion to manage the pregnancies that sometimes resulted from premarital intercourse in the context of committed relationships that, for financial reasons, could not yet become marriages.

The logic of economic exchange that defined treating also pervaded middle-class dating practices as well. Beth Bailey comments on the "centrality of money" in dating, which, she argues, "had serious implications for courtship." "Not only did money shift control and initiative to men by making them the 'hosts,'" Bailey writes, "it led contemporaries to see dating as a system of exchange best understood through economic analogies or as an economic system pure and simple."[63] Bailey rightly sees this economic model as conferring power on men in the dating system: "what men were buying in the dating system was not just female companionship, not just entertainment—but power. Money purchased obligation; money purchased inequality; money purchased control."[64] The question Bailey fails to ask in her analysis of the dynamics of middle-class dating, however, is where did this economic model come from in the first place? There was no reason that middle-class girls could not pay their own way. Unlike working-class girls, who remained the least likely in their families to have access to spending money, middle-class girls received allowances, usually equal to those of their brothers. As dating developed among the middle class, couples easily could have worked out a system where they split the bill, what many by midcentury referred to as "going Dutch." Quite simply, middle-class girls in the 1920s and 1930s had the resources to pay for their own entertainments, but under the dating system, they never did.

Even more puzzling, perhaps, is the fact that middle-class courtship before the development of dating did not require that the young man spend money. In fact, because it took place in the girl's family home where her parents could keep an eye on the proceedings, middle-class courtship actually required the girl's family to provide refreshments and an appropriately genteel parlor in which to meet.[65] Middle-class courtship sometimes did involve the exchange of "love tokens," but the etiquette books all stressed that these should be of little value.[66] What, then, accounts for the shift in middle-class courtship from young men's spending no money to their providing the funds for the entire evening? It is possible that the "love token" system evolved from books and flowers to entertainment expenses, or that the idea that young men pay simply emerged as courtship shifted from the parlor to the dance hall. But it seems much more likely that the economic logic embedded in both working-class and middle-class courtship emerged from the same source. Treating provided the model for the economic and sexual exchange that became a hallmark of dating for young people of both classes.

Middle-class youth in the 1910s and 1920s certainly had the opportunity to witness treating in the dance halls and movie theaters of New York City. The Committee of Fourteen's investigative reports mention the presence of "college men" in different bars and dance halls in the city, where they socialized with working-class women—prostitutes and charity girls alike.[67] The war accelerated this kind of cross-class mixing, as both enlisted men and officers flocked to New York's entertainment spaces. By the 1920s, researchers also noted the influx of middle-class youth into previously working-class venues: "into these halls come many types seeking many ends," one sociologist wrote, "there are those fascinated by the promise of a thrill, college boys whose purpose is to 'sow wild oats,' high school girls and boys in search of sophistication. . . . Here they mingle freely with others in an emotionally charged atmosphere."[68] Exposed to the treating exchange, it seems likely that middle-class youth adopted some of its parameters as they developed their own version of the dating system. Certainly, middle-class young men in the 1920s assumed that when they spent money on their dates, they could expect something in return. As Beth Bailey writes of middle-class dating in the 1920s, "Men paid for everything, but often with the implication that women 'owed' sexual favors in return."[69]

For young people in the 1920s, treating provided a model that structured dating patterns. Young men paid for dates, and young women reciprocated with sexual activity. But treating did more than provide the foundations for a sexual exchange system in dating. It was also responsible for much of the increase in sexual activity that occurred in the decade. While young people obviously took advantage of less supervision to experiment with sex, dating required that some sex play occur when a boy spent money on a girl. Furthermore, because dating was more casual, the scope of sexual experimentation widened considerably as both boys and girls began to engage in petting and, at times, sexual intercourse with people they did not intend to marry. By the 1930s, more than a quarter of all women interviewed by Kinsey had engaged in sexual intercourse with someone they did not marry, and that number would continue to rise throughout the twentieth century.

When Family Still Mattered: Religion, Race, Class, and the Regulation of Dating in the 1920s and 1930s

When the largely white middle-class readers of *Parents' Magazine* opened their October 1931 issue, they found an article by Floyd Dell titled "Why They Pet" that addressed growing parental anxiety about dating and petting among adolescents. As the fictional mother in this story remarked, "I could understand it . . . if it were a question of being in love with somebody. But

Phyllis is too young to be in love. . . . And besides, she admits that she isn't really in love with any of the boys she pets with." Petting and dating upset parents because it seemed so indiscriminate. It involved sexual activity but appeared to only have a tenuous relationship to marriage. According to Dell, however, the new ideal of companionate marriage required that young people be sexually compatible. In his vision, petting was both necessary and natural. Dell compared petting to an infant drinking milk "without having any theories to the effect that he is providing himself with calories and vitamins. . . . his instincts know what it is about." In fact, Dell argued, young people who restrained their sexual impulses endangered their health and their sanity. "Healthy adolescent petters don't need to know why they pet," he declared. "But perhaps their parents do."[70] Arguing that *not* petting during dating actually threatened the formation of happy, healthy families, Dell shifted the burden of parental supervision of courtship from preventing too much sexual expression to encouraging it, because sexual compatibility had now become the cornerstone of healthy middle-class marriages.

"Why They Pet" acknowledged the working-class origins of sex play in courtship, arguing in its brief history of courtship that "poor people on the farms and in the cities . . . worked together and played together, they got acquainted with each other, they petted (so you see the custom is really not new at all), and they married for love instead of for property reasons."[71] If white middle-class parents found the working-class origins of petting less than reassuring, Dell promised them that race and class would prevent their daughters from sliding down the slippery slope from petting to premarital intercourse. As he explained, only "young people brought up in the strict Latin or Oriental tradition of sex-segregation" would allow "these youthful freedoms . . . [to] lead to such results. Or they may do so if there has been a lack of love at home, or other conditions, economic, social or emotional, which have already demoralized the children's instincts."[72] Because America's white middle-class youth came from superior Protestant homes with plenty of love and financial support, petting could only strengthen their marriages. Biology required that young people practice at having sex and intimacy, but that very same biology, embedded in the superiority of the white race, Dell assured his readers, would protect middle-class youngsters from the possible excesses that such practice brought about in the inferior races.

Not surprisingly, working-class parents also expressed concerns about dating and petting, though for them the issues of race and religion were a daily reality, and not, as they were in Dell's article, abstract concerns. Like middle-class parents, working-class parents acquiesced to the shift in space and supervision that dating represented with little rancor or resistance. With the notable exception of Italians, working-class New Yorkers of all ethnicities allowed their children to date. In part, this was because the entertainment spaces in which dating took place had been popular with both parents and children since the turn of the century. By the 1920s, parents had their own extensive experiences in these spaces and did not see them as a threat to either their authority or their values. It was also a reflection of the Americanization (and for African Americans, urbanization) of New York's working class. The immigrant generation viewed many of the new characteristics of dating as American innovations, and by the 1920s, it had embraced them. Working-class parents only intervened in dating when children crossed the religious or racial boundaries that still mattered in New York's multiethnic, multiracial working class. Instead of supervising courtship directly, parents now patrolled the perimeters of appropriate choices. For white working-class families, this meant policing the boundaries of religion and race. For blacks either in or aspiring to the middle class, this required policing the boundaries of class. In this way, dating did not inspire a debate between parents and children over appropriate courtship behavior so much as it forced parents to take a stand very late in the courtship process when they felt their children had made inappropriate choices. While parents acquiesced to dating as a system, they still wanted to control this aspect of courtship, namely the race, religion, and class of the families their children would create.

Data from the Coser study indicate that both Italians and Jews opposed interfaith marriages for their children. One Italian woman strongly disapproved of her son's choice of a Protestant woman as wife. She would not allow the couple into the house and treated the children from this union with less affection than she gave her other grandchildren.[73] However, unlike their immigrant parents, who insisted that Italians marry Italians, second-generation Italians allowed for interethnic relationships as long as the partner was Catholic. In the Coser interviews, second-generation Italian women spoke with approval of their children's Irish, Polish, or German Catholic partners. When asked whether they would mind if their children chose marriage partners who were not Italians, one woman responded, "No. I don't mind, like Irish, German," while another commented, "No, no. I wasn't how do you say, how do you call it—prejudiced when you want them to marry their own kind."[74] Jewish women interviewed by Coser were even more adamant that their children marry within the faith. Since membership in the Jewish community is based on the mother's line, these families defended not just their community's religious purity but in many ways the survival of the Jews as a people. One woman explained what she wanted from her daughters' marriages: "A nice Jewish boy, that's what I wanted, the rest is, was up to them." "They fell in love with their husbands," she added with approval.[75] In other areas of dating, however, Jewish parents allowed their children a great deal of freedom. One woman described the rules she had for her children. "I all the time checked my children when they, uh, when they went out, and if they came later than 2 o'clock at night, they have to call me up and tell me where they are. The girl and the boy the same thing. They didn't come home before 2 o'clock, they had to call me and tell me what happened."[76] Providing little supervision over dating itself, she still insisted on Jewish marriages.

Some Jewish families reacted with violence or attempted to call on the authority of the state when their children chose non-Jewish mates. Seventeen-year-old Cecile Horowitz's orthodox Jewish parents became incensed when Cecile began dating an Italian boy in the neighborhood. Rather than see her marry outside of her faith, Cecile's mother directed her brothers to beat her, and when this did not work, had her committed for insanity. After her evaluation, Cecile's doctor declared her sane and released her from Central Islip State Hospital, telling the Women's Prison Association caseworkers that Cecile was at "present living with an Italian boy that she wants to marry but that she is not promiscuous in her sex relations." Since social workers and other middle-class professionals at the time described any premarital intercourse as "promiscuous," her doctor meant that Cecile and her fiancé had not consummated their relationship. Cecile finally married her beau when her desperate parents tried to have her committed as a wayward minor.[77] The fact that she had not actually had intercourse with her fiancé did not seem to matter to her parents; it was the relationship itself that they opposed.

White parents of all ethnicities resisted interracial matches. Zara Pinsky's parents brought a wayward minor charge against her when she began keeping company with their African American boarder. He "sent her music and the girl encouraged his attentions, although the mother protested." When Zara got pregnant, she insisted the child was his and that they should marry, but "her mother and father won't let her 'as he is colored.'" While Pinsky's parents may have seen an illegitimate, interracial grandchild as a disaster, they still opposed her marrying the father of her child. Illegitimacy was still better than interracial marriage. After the birth of her child, the mother and child went to live with her lover, who declared that "he would rather shed blood than separate from Zara."[78]

Lillian Adelman's parents also sought state intervention by having her committed as a wayward minor when she moved to Harlem to live with an African American man who "wanted to marry her." As social workers mediating the conflict wrote, the mother admitted that Lillian "acts in a rational manner but the mother simply cannot believe that she is in her right mind to have acted as she has. The girl tells her mother quite frankly that she is in love with this colored man, that he wanted to marry her." Lillian's mother found her behavior baffling, particularly because, as the social worker explained, "before this difficulty came up L. frequently went with very nice young Jewish men. Most of them were college students, but she always stated that she did not care for them." Lillian's mother simply could not understand why Lillian would throw away her chance at a good middle-class Jewish match. Casting about for possible explanations for Lillian's behavior, her mother seized upon a white stereotype of African American sexuality, namely the idea that African American men and women were "oversexed." The social worker noted that "her mother cannot understand the attraction towards the colored man and thinks perhaps L. is highly sexed and is getting satisfaction on this basis." In this analysis, exposure to African Americans' "hypersexuality" brought about a similar response in an otherwise normal Jewish girl.[79] Once stirred, the logic seemed to go, Lillian could no longer be sexually satisfied by good Jewish boys. Although working-class and an immigrant to America, Mrs. Adelman echoed the racism of many middle-class white Americans. This shows not only how quickly immigrants learned about America's racial hierarchy but also how quickly they learned that assimilation required adopting American attitudes about race. Understanding race differences and upholding them in family formation became an important way that immigrants could signal their assimilation to American culture. The Adelman parents' opposition to an interracial and interfaith marriage ran so deep that their own marriage foundered. When Lillian ran away to Harlem to live with her fiancé, her father became "so upset over the situation that he too has left home. He blames his wife, stating that she over indulged L. and was not strict enough with her."[80]

Black families may also have opposed interracial marriages for their children, but unfortunately the record does not reflect their attitudes on this issue. However, studies on unwed motherhood and social work case files do show black parents' willingness to interfere when they saw their children going astray. Despite assumptions by sociologists in the 1920s and 1930s that black families and the black community more broadly accepted illegitimate pregnancy, evidence from case files indicates that black families did not approach illegitimacy any differently than working-class white families did and that many black parents viewed illegitimacy as shameful.[81] Like some white families, some black families did accept pregnancies out of wedlock. But others, particularly those of middle-class status or with middle-class ambitions, viewed unwed motherhood as a family disaster. Because female chastity played such an important role in the politics of respectability so influential among middle-class black families, out-of-wedlock births threatened not just the family's reputation but its claims to respectability and middle-class status.[82] In addition, many middle-class black families vehemently opposed cross-class marriages for their daughters and disrupted dating relationships that they saw as inappropriate.

In her 1926 study, *Negro Illegitimacy in New York City*, Ruth Reed did not find a casual attitude toward premarital pregnancy among black girls and their families in New York City. Describing the willingness of some families to help daughters with illegitimate children, Reed carefully pointed out that "this does not mean there was on the part of these families any lack of shame at the fact of an illegitimate birth in the family."[83] Her informants often expressed embarrassment about their pregnancies and a desire to hide the fact of their child's illegitimacy from family and friends. One southern African American family sent their daughter to New York with her sister in pursuit of the young man responsible. The sister "hoped to bring about a marriage or, failing that, to escape the disgrace of having the girl's condition discovered by friends at home."[84] Some West Indian families also found illegitimate pregnancy shameful. One young woman "was ashamed to write her mother in Jamaica but a letter was finally dispatched by the agency. The mother wrote refusing to have anything to do with her daughter since her disgrace. She spoke of the sacrifices she had made to give the girl cultural advantages and said that the girl had 'thrown herself away.'"[85]

By 1935, however, Enid Severy Smith's *A Study of Twenty-Five Adolescent Unmarried Mothers in New York City* would argue that blacks and whites had different cultural values about premarital sex and pregnancy. Smith stated in her introduction that African American unmarried mothers "suffered little from social disapproval and their status was, in most circumstances, as favorable as that of the married women who were similarly situated economically."[86] According to her calculations, "7 out of the 10 colored girls studied made a distinction between the attitude of colored and white people in regard to unmarried motherhood, and consequently these 7 colored girls did not consider motherhood out of wedlock disgraceful."[87]

However, the black women whose stories she quoted often made a more subtle distinction between their individual family's beliefs and the values of the wider black community. One twelve-year-old unwed mother commented that "my companions did not feel it made such difference if a girl had a baby—lots of them that went to school had babies, and it was rather common. Of course my people felt different from the rest of the colored people; my father could never get over it."[88] Although Smith does not identify the class status of this informant, class may have played a factor in the conflict between what she reported as common in her community and her own family's reaction. Other girls did not comment on their family's reaction but expressed their own fears about the stigma of illegitimacy. Thirteen-year-old Jane explained that she wanted to get married because "my baby should have a father. I want her to have a nice home."[89] In this case, the girl seemed concerned about economic issues and the difficulty single mothers faced in providing "a nice home" for their children. Fourteen-year-old Etta focused more on the issue of respectability and the stigma of illegitimacy. "You see I don't mind having a baby particularly," she said, "but it's the trouble of explaining things to the child that worries me. . . . Should I tell my boy when he gets bigger that he does not have any father, or shall I tell him that his father died, or deserted?"[90] Smith's own data thus reflected a careful distinction that her informants made between "the community" and their families when it came to sexual values. While she ignored this in her analysis of their cases, her sources provide evidence that black families did not always take premarital pregnancy in stride.

Either cultural values in the black community had changed very rapidly in the ten years between Reed's work and Smith's work or else Smith and other sociologists believed so strongly in these cultural differences that they found, or encouraged, these responses in their informants. Although neither author discusses the class background of their subjects, these discrepancies may also reflect class differences in the black community. While working-class blacks may have accepted premarital pregnancy, many in the middle class objected to the violation of female chastity, and thus bourgeois respectability, that these births represented.

Data from the Bedford reformatory and the Women's Prison Association case files suggest that many black families, both American and West Indian, found premarital pregnancy shameful. One woman's stepbrother wrote to Bedford in 1923 declaring his family's unwillingness to involve itself in her case. According to the social worker, "he feels that the best thing for her is 'to let the law take its course' as she has never been any good and has caused the family much embarrassment."[91] A West Indian girl who became pregnant by a boarder living in the family home fled to the Florence Crittendon Home when her father put her out on the street in a rage. Her mother told the social worker that the father of the baby "is a married man and she wants to have him arrested. She did not wish to take Helen back home as she was afraid that her father might injure her in her present condition."[92] Black families, it seems, proved little different than white families in their reactions to unwed pregnancy. While some black and white families accepted daughters and their children back into the home with little fuss, others reacted with shame, outrage, and, at times, violence. Historian Regina Kunzel has shown how middle-class African American academics and professionals in the 1930s argued that unwed motherhood was a class issue. Respectable African Americans, these intellectuals insisted, did not tolerate unwed pregnancy. It is clear from the historical record that these arguments, instead of simply being a way for the African American intelligentsia to explain the embarrassing behavior of "low-class" blacks, actually reflected the family politics of the black middle class and the strivers who sought its membership.[93]

Like whites, African American and West Indian families did not always want their daughters to marry the men they dated.[94] In these cases, social class motivated black parents' interventions in courtship and marriage decisions. In one incident, a young woman became pregnant by an unskilled laborer she had dated. When he found out about the pregnancy, he proposed that they marry. Her mother, however, believed "that the man was far beneath her daughter" and opposed the match. In another case, a young woman dated a man that her mother declared was "the last person on earth who she would permit her daughter to marry." According to Reed, the couple had a baby out of wedlock, and "when the baby was ten months old, the girl married the father of her child. The mother refused to allow them to enter her home."[95] The Women's Prison Association recorded a case in which the daughter of an African American minister got pregnant while dating her childhood sweetheart. The family allowed a marriage "in order that the child might be legitimized." But after the birth, the girl's father "took steps and had the marriage annulled. He did not feel that Paul was the type of fellow whom he wished her to be married to," because Paul was of "humble parentage."[96] A keen understanding of social class and social hierarchy pervaded these decisions. Illegitimacy threatened claims of middle-class status, as did inappropriate matches. Middle-class black families, or those who aspired to middle-class status, opposed matches they thought "beneath" their daughters, occasionally even severing family ties to show their displeasure.

Among all of New York's diverse social groups, only Italians consistently resisted the development of dating and continued to exercise significant control over courtship itself. Black, Jewish, native-born white, and other immigrant families might oppose certain marriages because of race or social class, but they rarely controlled who their children went out with or what they did on their dates. In the midst of the transition between family-oriented courtship and the more peer-centered dating, Italians and Italian

Americans watched their girls very carefully, intervening in both courting practices and marital choice. Even into the second and third generation, Italian conceptions of honor rested heavily on the bodies and reputations of young girls, and Italians as a group resisted Americanization in family formation and relations.

Italians vehemently opposed social freedoms for their daughters into the 1920s and 1930s. Marianna Contadini married in 1929 but still courted like Italian women who came to the United States nearly two decades before. As she explained to her interviewer, "I could hardly even look outside. . . . Over here, my father wouldn't let me. . . . I never went out with my husband, no other boys." When "I started to keep company with my husband," she explained, "my sister always came along with us." [97] Another Italian woman concurred, explaining, "my family was a good family. They watch us." [98] As Contadini's experience indicates, Italian Americans did allow their girls to take advantage of commercial amusements but continued to chaperone them long after other groups had dispensed with this kind of family supervision. An American-born twenty-year-old woman of Sicilian parentage wrote in her survey for Landis that her father believed "it would be just too bad if we have a boyfriend. Thinks men should come to house and ask parents to marry us. . . . We were told that a girl that plays with a boy is a bum, and no good. [We were] not allowed to wear make-up or bobbed hair." [99] Italians resisted the very premise of dating itself. Like this woman's father, they believed not only that Italian girls should court under the watchful eye of their parents, who would have a veto over their choices, but that they should not go out with different men. Born in New York, this woman was twenty years old at the time of her interview in 1935, indicating that Italian opposition to dating and more liberal courtship practices lasted well into the 1930s. The casualness and "promiscuity" of dating that appealed to young Americans offended Italian assumptions about the implications of casual mixing for a woman's reputation. As I showed in the first chapter, most Italians did not believe that young women who considered several young men as mates could possibly maintain their reputations.

At times, Italians' strictness actually caused the problems that they feared might result from unsupervised dating. In her 1923 study of sex delinquency in New York, Anne Bingham found that Italian girls ran away from home more than girls of other groups precisely because of the restrictions placed on them by their families. As she explained, "in such a cosmopolitan city as New York, however, where there is mingling of races, Italian girls are apt to compare their home rules with less strict ones imposed on their companions and may become very discontented and resentful." Even as these girls resented their treatment, however, they "did not attempt to conceal their pride in the fact that as a people Italians strive to keep their daughters virtuous."[100] Families who restricted their daughters activities continued to make disparaging comparisons between Italy and America when they did so. In 1935, one Italian mother had her daughter declared a wayward minor for staying out late and going out with men. As the social worker described, "Mrs. G[eorgio] complained a great deal about the difficulty of bringing up girls in New York City. She said that in Italy it is different but here she does not know what to do with them." Restrictions on her free time caused Mrs. Georgio's daughter, Isabella, to "run away from home four times, the first in 1933 and the last March 21 1938."[101]

Serafina Falcone's 1936 involvement with the Women's Prison Association exemplifies the continued resistance to dating among second-generation Italians. The social worker stated that "the old-world standards of courtship, love and marriage are deeply ingrained in both Mr. and Mrs. F, and it is very doubtful if they will ever be able to accept a more Americanized point of view." At around age fifteen, Serafina began to "protest against the limited freedom allowed her by her parents, and demanded that she be permitted to attend dances and movies." A neighbor saw this conflict in ethnic and religious terms, insisting that "when she was 14 she began having trouble with her parents because she chose Jewish friends. Her Italian family felt that she should not do this." This could have been a reaction to cross-faith friendships, but it also reflected that, unlike most Italians, second-generation Jews usually accepted dating. On one of her unauthorized trips to a dance hall, Serafina met a young Italian man named Arthur. Forbidden to date, Arthur and Serafina ran away together and began living in a furnished roomed, at which point Serafina's mother told her social worker "that S. had disgraced the family and that under no circumstances would she permit her return to the home, unless she were married to Arthur." Humiliated by her behavior, Serafina's family refused to greet her on the street. "This hurts her very much," the social worker noted, "she hopes that in time they will again recognize her."[102]

Arthur had his own problems. A product of the same cultural system as Serafina, he felt ambivalent about taking as a bride a young woman with sexual experience, even if he initiated that experience himself. As a social worker summarized, Arthur felt "that her reputation among his friends is that she has been very free and promiscuous with men and that his family has always objected to her for this reason." In this case, concerns about family opinion mingled with those of his peer group, suggesting that Arthur had internalized dating's peer orientation as well as his family's attitudes about reputation and sexuality. Arthur eventually overcame his doubts and married Serafina. In this saga, Serafina first got into trouble not for sexual activity but because of her desire to date. When thwarted repeatedly by her family, she ran away to be with her fiancé. The sexual double standard embraced by Italians allowed her own boyfriend to doubt his desire to marry her. Since she was no longer pure or possessing a good reputation in the community, he agonized over whether he should keep his promise of marriage. Although Serafina's story had a happy ending, it easily could have led to her becoming an outcast from both her family and her community.[103] Still clinging to their "Italian" or "Old World" ways in the 1930s, many Italian and Italian American families resisted the promiscuity, lack of supervision, and publicly oriented nature of the dating system, preserving the purity of their community through rigid control over their daughters' sociability and sexuality.

While ethnicity, race, religion, and class shaped families' responses to marital choice in the 1920s and 1930s, most families in New York acquiesced to the new system of dating. For the working class, courtship developed into a form of dating in which dating pairs attended commercial amusements embedded within larger social groupings. Middle-class youth also saw dating as a peer-supervised activity that went on in commercial amusements, though they resorted to less direct methods of supervision like gossip. Both forms of the practice drew heavily on a system of sexual barter that first emerged in treating at the turn of the century. Boys paid for dates, and girls returned their investments by engaging in kissing, petting, and, at times, intercourse. By the 1940s, the specific language of treating had disappeared entirely, replaced by a less specific set of economic and sexual assumptions embedded in the practice of dating. When asked who paid for dates in the 1940s, elderly working-class New Yorkers interviewed for this project all responded that boys did.[104] For example, when answering the question of who paid, Sandy Kern, a Jewish woman, stated emphatically, "the boy always, always, always; there was no Dutch treat."[105] None of my respondents had ever heard of "treating" or "charity," indicating that these terms had passed out of use by the time they began to date. However, when I described the practice to them, several identified it as dating. An Italian, Mike Trombetta, responded to the definition of treating by asking, "Oh, you mean dating?"[106] Sandy Kern uncovered the logic of treating that still remained in dating in the early 1940s: "I knew that that was something you had to go through, to go on a date. . . . You had to let him kiss you goodnight, hold you. . . . I think they felt they earned that. . . . I think the whole, the whole date, you know, the theater, the dinner, if there was no dinner we'd go for ice cream . . . it would all work up to when he felt he had earned the right to maul you."[107] Unrecognizable as a distinctive practice by the 1940s, treating still lurked in the economic and sexual logic of dating.

But this incorporation has had negative consequences that continue to resonate today. Summarizing the findings of several researchers on sexual violence among adolescents in the 1980s and 1990s, historian Joan Brumberg noted that 32 percent of girls thought it was okay for a boy to demand sex if the couple had been dating for some time, "and 40 percent of the boys believed that forced sex was acceptable if the 'guy' spent a lot of money on the date."[108] These numbers reflect both the lingering importance of economic and sexual exchange in dating and a serious misunderstanding between young women and young men that at times leads to violence among dating couples. In the studies Brumberg cites, young women emphasized the quality and longevity of the relationship, while young men saw paying for dates as an economic investment in sexual favors. Clearly, the disappearance of treating as a linguistic and identity category has done both women and men a disservice. When treating existed as an acknowledged category, women and men shared a common language, however imprecise, in which they could negotiate the terms of their interaction and bargain over entertainment and sex. After it became incorporated into dating, it lost its linguistic specificity, and young women and young men approached these interactions with very different assumptions. If this recent research is any indication, girls' bodies bear the burden of the disappearance of treating into the less specific and more universal practice of dating.

Conclusion

A NEW TYPE OF GIRL IN AN OLD TYPE OF DELINQUENCY
WOMEN, SEXUALITY, AND VENEREAL DISEASE DURING WORLD WAR II

In the summer of 2001, Maureen Dowd wrote in the *New York Times* that the days of going Dutch are over. "It doesn't matter if the woman is making as much money as the man, or more," Dowd explained. "She expects him to pay, both to prove her desirability and as a way of signaling romance." According to Dowd, the practice of "going Dutch" arose with feminism and the idea that women and men should approach dating as equals. But many in the generation that came of age in the 1990s apparently felt a need to return to an older model whereby men paid. In part, this was because women had other ways of determining the gender politics of their dating partners. As one woman Dowd interviewed explained, "There are plenty of ways for me to find out if he's going to see me as an equal without disturbing the dating ritual. . . . Disturbing the dating ritual leads to chaos. Everybody knows that." Dating's rituals of payment had become a way of signaling romantic interest, separating the date from other forms of heterosocial interaction. The coauthor of a study on college dating emphasized both the economic and romantic confusions that arose when expectations had not been clearly spelled out. "One Yale girl described the ridiculous situations that can come up because of all the confusion over who pays for what and when it is a date," she reported. "She found herself arguing on the sidewalk with a guy over who should pay for a Slurpee. A guy will ask a girl to the movies and she will think they are just hanging out. Then he offers to pay, changing the whole outing into a date."[1] Even as Americans move into a new century, the economic aspects that treating lent to dating remain embedded in the practice. Who pays and for what are still important in modern American heterosexual interactions.

Treating represented a brief intermediary category of sexual barter that, though fleeting, had a profound effect on the cultural understandings of women's presence in public space, on courtship practices, and on prostitution. Lasting only a few decades, treating behavior was not new and did not prevail for long. As historian Christine Stansell has shown, the Bowery Gals of antebellum New York ventured onto the streets and into the concert halls of working-class Manhattan and may have exchanged sexual favors for entertainment when they did so.[2] But these young women did not name what they did, and it was the linguistic and identity markers of treating that gave it its lasting impact and, paradoxically, also limited its effects. Emerging as an explicitly named category in the 1890s, treating challenged the long-held association between women in public and prostitution. Invading spaces like the theater that in the nineteenth century had reserved their third tier for prostitutes, charity girls opened up public entertainments for women by vigorously declaring that not all women in public spaces were prostitutes. A wide variety of women followed charity girls into the movie theaters and dance halls of urban America, transforming these spaces into a playground for respectable working-class girls, and by the 1920s, for respectable middle-class girls as well. However, this shift in American understandings of who could make use of these spaces did not eliminate the sexualization of women's presence in public. Treating expanded the possible interpretations of women's public appearances, but it did not challenge the basic assumption that women in public were sexually available and interested in men's advances.

Treating also had a profound effect on courtship and its twentieth-century incarnation, dating. Emerging as treating waned, dating incorporated the logic of sexual barter into its practices and underlying assumptions. As contemporary studies of American teens have shown, many young people still believe that when boys pay for dates they have earned a reciprocal payment in kissing, fondling, and, at times, intercourse.[3] The disappearance of treating as a specific language and identity did young people a disservice, because it silenced discussions that had, under treating, spelled out the expectations of both parties. What had been spoken of before was now hushed, and what had been negotiated was now assumed but often contested. Late twentieth-century concerns about "date rape" derive from many sources, but dating's absorption of treating and the misunderstandings that follow from it have certainly played some role in this problem.

Treating's profound impact on sexual expectations in courtship also led to a sharp decline in the importance of prostitution in American culture. As sex researchers have found, American men resorted to prostitutes with less and less frequency following World War I.[4] Sex with charity girls and, increasingly, with dates and fiancées profoundly affected the demand for prostitution. When combined with the growing sex industry, increases in premarital intercourse have driven prostitution to the margins of American sexual culture. Although it has ceased to be a significant part of the sexual lives of most Americans, prostitution remains an important symbol in popular culture, and prostitutes themselves continue to be scapegoated as threats to the public health and to the physical and moral well-being of the American family.[5] This disjuncture between the actual incidence of prostitution and its symbolic value could be seen clearly during World War II when War Department officials continued to blame prostitutes for spreading venereal disease, even though their own research showed that these infections overwhelmingly came from contacts with nonprostitutes.[6]

Experiences during World War II also explain why treating's revolution had more of an impact on sexual behavior than on the public's willingness to admit that sexual behavior and values had changed. Even when it emerged as a named activity, treating addressed practical problems and not broader ideological frameworks of gender and sexual inequality. After all, treating was about fun. In their pursuit of entertainment and excitement, charity girls disrupted the association between prostitution and sexual promiscuity in the minds of many Americans. By the 1920s and 1930s, few people believed that all women who had intercourse outside of marriage were whores. Radical as this shift was, however, charity girls did not lead an articulated assault against America's sexual double standard. Even though treating had a profound effect on behavior, it challenged but did not overturn the idea that chastity formed the foundation of women's social worth. As a result, during World War II, Americans continued to condemn premarital intercourse in public discourse, even as it became the norm in private behavior. In many ways, the symbol of prostitution allowed for this slippage by maintaining the fiction that prostitutes, and not mainstream America's daughters, provided the lion's share of the sexual services for America's troops. Casting prostitutes as villains allowed Americans to ignore the profound behavioral changes already underway in courtship and to put off any real challenge to a sexual double standard that assumed male sexual promiscuity to be normal but condemned intercourse before marriage for women. It was not until the late 1960s, when the baby boom generation combined behavioral changes with an analysis of the gender politics of the sexual double standard, that Americans finally began to engage in a meaningful conversation about the difference between private behavior and the public's acceptance of chastity for women as an ideal.

Despite the panicked reactions of contemporaries who warned of sexual anarchy, the United States' mobilization for World War II did not usher in significant changes in American sexual behavior or values. Instead, the war accentuated the gradual changes that the dating revolution of the 1920s and 1930s brought about. Reacting to the problem of venereal disease and its impact on military readiness, federal officials first assumed, as they had during World War I, that prostitutes constituted the greatest threat to soldiers' health. However, research soon proved that nonprostitutes overwhelmingly outnumbered prostitutes in soldiers' sexual contacts. This startling fact forced policy makers to refine their strategy. While continuing to repress prostitution, government agencies began to condemn what contemporaries referred to as "pickups" or "victory girls," that is, women who had intercourse with soldiers and sailors out of a sense of patriotism, or excitement, or simply as part of the new dating culture. Abandoning the World War I era's attempts to hold men and women to a single moral standard, officials acquiesced to the notion that engaging in sexual intercourse was natural and necessary for soldiers and began to educate them about disease prevention. During World War II, the War Department also launched a propaganda campaign that, while it acknowledged the sexual activities of nonprostitutes, did so by expanding the category of "bad" women. In these posters, prostitutes and pickups alike tempted the troops, spread venereal diseases, and, by extension, provided aid and comfort to the enemy.

Most of the strategies used to combat venereal disease during World War II closely resembled those implemented during World War I. As historian Alan Brandt summarized succinctly, the government followed "an essentially conventional approach to venereal disease control: a combination of education, repression of prostitution, medical treatment of the infected, and rigorous case finding and contact tracing."[7] Of these measures, only contact tracing was new, introduced by Surgeon General Thomas Parran in 1936.[8] Under pressure from Parran to prepare for the problems of venereal disease in war, Congress passed the May Act in July of 1941, which again authorized the federal government to establish "moral" zones around troop concentrations, forbidding prostitution and liquor sales in designated areas. Although the act was only invoked twice during the war (in Tennessee and North Carolina), the federal pressure it represented encouraged local governments to severely repress prostitution in their jurisdictions.[9]

The federal government recommended that local communities forcibly isolate "recalcitrant infected persons with communicable syphilis or gonorrhea."[10] As in World War I, this resulted in the arrest and detention of thousands of women for prostitution-related offenses.[11] Treatment for venereal disease had improved significantly between the wars, but this did not affect the sentences prostitutes received. Therapy regimens that had taken six months during the 1910s and early 1920s had been shortened to two weeks even before the widespread use of antibiotics in 1944.[12] However, local governments incarcerated prostitutes for far longer than it took to cure them. In New York, the city's welfare commissioners recommended getting rid of suspended sentences and short commitments for prostitution-related offenses, because these punishments released women too quickly. They suggested instead that the city rely on supervised probation and "commitment to institutions that have programs of rehabilitation."[13] Sentences could be very long for a crime that New York State still defined as a misdemeanor. One judge sent a woman to a reformatory for two years after she had been cured of venereal disease. Apparently, he saw the reformatory as the only place that might convince her to give up prostitution. As he noted, "after the first disillusioning experience she regarded herself as a bad girl and that nothing mattered."[14]

The addition of contact tracing to the panoply of strategies used to control venereal disease undoubtedly helped track down those with infections, but it also violated their civil rights. In New York, public health laws authorized the police to arrest women who had been identified by soldiers as possible sources of venereal infection without any other evidence. New York's police commissioner, Lewis Valentine, explained the procedure: "In the event the subject is located but there is insufficient evidence for an arrest under Section 887 of the Code of Criminal Procedure [prostitution], the Health Department is immediately notified by telephone and they in turn invoke Section 343 of the Public Health Law of the State of New York, which gives the Health Department and health officers the authority to seize and detain for treatment any person suspected of having a venereal disease." This meant that women could be arrested without police having to provide any evidence against them. New York would also test a woman who had been acquitted of prostitution charges. "If she is found venereally infected," Valentine explained, "she is forced in. We call it a 'force in.' She has been acquitted of the criminal charge, but she is forced in under the Public Health Law."[15] While these tactics helped New York control its venereal disease problem, they also wreaked havoc on the lives of prostitutes.

Even short-term detentions could create hardships for prostitutes and their families. One wife of a soldier prostituted to support her mother and small children, because her husband's request for a dependency allowance had been denied. Identified by another soldier as the source of his gonorrhea, she spent two weeks in a clinic undergoing treatment. According to her interviewer, Mary did not blame the soldier, "because she might have infected many others and is glad to receive treatment." However, "during the time that Mary was confined to the clinic, a period of almost two weeks, she received no earnings to contribute toward the support of the family. When the family was visited, their rent was in arrears over two weeks, and they had been having great difficulty in providing sufficient food for the children."[16] Even when prostitutes avoided the typical reformatory commitments of six to eighteen months, the economic conditions that drove them into the trade worsened if they had to undergo in-patient treatment. While many non-prostitutes received out-patient care, health departments routinely detained prostitutes for their treatment.[17] Ironically, in this case, the military itself forced this woman into prostitution by drafting her husband and then refusing to honor his request for support of his dependents.[18]

Public Health officials hypothesized early in the war that "80 percent of military infections were traceable to commercial prostitutes."[19] When combined with reports from social purity organizations that warned of huge increases in prostitution (including one report that claimed prostitution had risen a startling 64 percent between 1941 and 1942), these estimates panicked officials responsible for dealing with disease among the troops.[20] However, research conducted in the early 1940s showed that venereal disease rates among prostitutes were actually much lower than people assumed. A vigorous treatment campaign spearheaded by the surgeon general in the late 1930s and prostitutes' growing understanding of prevention caused their infection rates to drop significantly in the interwar period. In New York, mandatory testing of women arrested for prostitution indicated that about 34 percent suffered from venereal diseases. While that number is high, it was considerably lower than the estimates during World War I, which ranged from 58 to 90 percent, depending on the study.[21] In addition, contact tracing during World War II revealed that prostitutes did not constitute the main vector of disease. One report on juvenile delinquency asserted that in New York "promiscuous teen-age girls" outnumbered prostitutes "four to one as sources of venereal infections."[22] By 1944, the vast majority of cases of venereal disease in New York City came from sex with what officials referred to interchangeably as "pickups," "victory girls," or "khaki-wackies." A study analyzing individual contact reports for the army found that, among white troops, 32 percent of infections came from "friends," 62 percent from pickups, and only 6 percent from prostitutes. Among blacks, 44 percent derived from contacts with friends, 42 percent from pickups, and 14 percent from prostitutes.[23] While dropping rates of venereal disease among prostitutes may have accounted for some of these changes, the prostitution-related transmission rates are startlingly low. These numbers demonstrate both the increase in premarital intercourse that dating brought about and, conversely, the marginalization of prostitution in American sexual culture.

Friends and pickups posed significantly more danger to troops than prostitutes did, because by the 1940s, men were much more likely to have intercourse with them than with professional prostitutes. These findings forced officials to conclude that repressing prostitution would not solve the problem of disease among the troops. They also needed to confront the issue of "pickups" and their appeal for soldiers.

The category of "pickup" was a slippery one, but government officials associated it with patriotism and youthful hysteria, and not with the greed and depravity they attributed to prostitutes. "Pickup" itself was a new term, as were its synonyms, "victory girl" and "khaki-wackie." But the definition and hallmark behaviors of pickups were familiar from World War I. One report written by the Social Protection Division stated that "the 'pick-up' girl is defined as the young amateur, in her teens, who is frequently crowding out her stepsister, the professional prostitute, as a public menace." Like their assessments of the "khaki-mad" girls of World War I, officials saw pickups as misguided girls who used sex to express patriotism. "This new type is less interested in money than in excitement," the report continued. "She frequently has 'uniform hysteria.' The lure of the uniform impels her to go where soldiers and sailors congregate."[24] Another pamphlet argued that "Life in an army cantonment area for any girl or woman is likely to be complicated by many pressures not the least of which is that crystallized in the current popular song 'You Can't Say No to a Soldier.'"[25] During World War II, even popular culture supported young women's inclination to view sex with soldiers as a form of patriotic service.

However, during that war, officials faced the problem of "khaki-wackies" on a scale unthinkable during World War I. In part, this was simply because the war lasted longer, required a more significant reorganization of the economy, and resulted in a greater disruption of people's lives. The military mobilized over twelve million men and women into the armed services, and large numbers of adults and teens moved about the country seeking work in the defense industry. All cities hosting either troop concentrations or defense industries struggled with problems in housing, socializing, and policing. New York City faced particularly severe difficulties with female migrants coming to the city to meet soldiers. For example, patrols of Times Square netted 431 runaway girls in 1942, 587 in 1943, and 568 in the first half of 1944.[26] This geographical mobility attenuated families, making supervision of adolescents even more difficult. As one educational consultant for the American Social Hygiene Association described, "The problems and conditions affecting teenage youth, on the national scale, include: juvenile delinquency, truancy, migrant youngsters, inadequate housing, too much spending money, sexual promiscuity among all socio-economic groups, a lack of parental interest and supervision."[27]

Both the levels of "sexual delinquency" and the social classes involved frightened commentators. One report on juvenile delinquency noted with alarm that sex delinquency (which only existed as a category for girls) rose 104 percent between 1941 and 1942.[28] Rates of illegitimate pregnancy provided a more concrete measure of increases in sexual intercourse before marriage. According to a survey conducted by the Federal Children's Bureau, homes for unwed mothers "experienced about a 10 percent increase in admissions."[29] By this very concrete measure, rates for premarital sex had jumped significantly. But the social class of these girls also upset reformers. An American Social Hygiene report on juvenile delinquency explained with concern that "This 'pick-up girl' is frequently from a good family. Policewomen the country over agree that while many of them might get into trouble 'anyway, anywhere,' many others represent a new type of girl in an old type of delinquency."[30] By World War II, middle-class girls had joined their working-class counterparts in embracing sexual intercourse as a natural, if dangerous, part of dating activities.[31]

Although these reports implied that the war created these problems, in fact, they were simply extensions, or exaggerations, of the trends in dating that had already significantly increased the rate of premarital intercourse. Mrs. T. Grafton Abbot, a worker for the American Social Hygiene Association, admitted as much when she commented that "The war alone cannot be blamed for all the above-mentioned problems and conditions. But it has increased the opportunities for many youth to become independent of their families."[32] In this formulation, youth attitudes about sex had changed, and only strict parental supervision could keep them from acting on their new values. According to the distressed Grafton, during the war, young people felt "that this type of behavior is not wrong."[33] The war may have accentuated these inclinations, but the fact remains that rates of premarital intercourse had steadily increased throughout the twentieth century. By the 1930s, a majority of young men and over 40 percent of young women had intercourse before marriage.[34] Dating and petting, more than the war, brought about the increases in premarital intercourse that distressed the officials in the Social Protection Division. Although a long-standing trend, this revolution in sexual behavior took on broader political significance because of wartime concerns about venereal disease and military readiness.

Rather than exhort young women and soldiers to remain chaste, as War Department workers had done during World War I, federal officials resorted to very practical solutions, like setting up chemical prophylaxis stations and making condoms widely available to military personnel. Some commissaries sold packages of three condoms for ten cents, while others handed them out for free. Although this decision met with outraged protest from social purity activists who wanted an abstinence-only campaign, the military continued to make practical prevention a part of its strategy. Overall, the government distributed fifty million condoms a month to troops during the war.[35] Congress also reversed long-standing policies that had punished military personnel for contracting venereal diseases. Since 1912, the army had withheld pay from men under treatment for diseases or injuries not incurred in the line of duty, a practice Congress had made law in 1926. However, the surgeon general argued that this policy actually helped spread disease by encouraging men to hide their infections, and in September of 1944, Congress abolished it.[36]

Both of these shifts in policies reaffirmed the sexual double standard by accepting a vision of male sexuality that saw men's desire for heterosexual intercourse as natural and necessary rather than subject to self-restraint. Perhaps the War Department was simply bowing to the inevitable, something it had refused to do in the previous war. One military study found that 80 percent of unmarried troops and 50 percent of married troops had intercourse outside of marriage during the war.[37] A medical officer acknowledged this ruefully, commenting that "the sex act cannot be made unpopular."[38] By the 1940s, the American public agreed with him about the inevitability of men's sexual promiscuity. In one survey of three thousand registered voters taken in 1942, Gallup pollsters found that 55 percent acknowledged that troops would visit prostitutes and believed that the government should require "all prostitutes to take a regular weekly medical examination and quarantine those who are diseased." One man asserted that "We don't want to deprive the boys and in this way the boys will be protected." Like the military's policy of handing out condoms to the troops, these attitudes reflected American beliefs that soldiers and sailors both needed and were entitled to sex with prostitutes. Others saw male sexuality as a danger to the community, a natural force that would spill over onto "good" women if not given proper outlet. "If the women are clean," one woman responded, "they should be allowed to stay. Otherwise there would be too many rape cases."[39] In her vision, prostitution provided an important safety valve protecting the community from the explosive sexuality of America's soldiers. Although social purity reformers during World War I promoted sexual chastity for both men and women, by World War II, the sexual double standard had reemerged as the dominant paradigm of sexuality. For men, sex was inevitable. Rather than fight this paradigm, both the public and the government believed that responsible officials needed to make sex safer for the troops.

This retreat from chastity made the educational campaigns during World War II more difficult, a fact reflected in the ambivalent portrayal of soldiers in the era's propaganda. While posters in the 1940s did encourage soldiers to refuse temptation, visually they emphasized the difficulty soldiers had in making choices about sexual interactions. Several posters literally depicted men with their heads turned one way and their bodies another. In one image, a soldier's body faces forward, but he looks back over his shoulder at a beautiful woman labeled "Prostitution," who is tempting him with "Two girls I know want to meet you in the worst way." The two girls, "Syphilis" and "Gonorrhea," stand seductively on the stairs behind her, their faces drawn as death masks (Figure C.1). The ambivalence of his posture is striking and very similar to another poster in which a soldier turns in response to a young woman's call of "Helloooo soldier" (Figure C.2) In this poster, Hirohito and Hitler express delight as the man looks her over. Choosing not to have intercourse probably was difficult for many young men, but emphasizing soldiers' bodily indecision was an odd strategy in a educational campaign about avoiding venereal disease. These portrayals of soldiers lacked the triumphant postures of the men in World War I posters like "You Kept Fit and Defeated the Hun" (Figure 5.5), which depicts a proud soldier standing atop a pile of Prussian war helmets with a wide stance, a huge grin, and an American eagle perched on his shoulder. If posters during World War I made saying no to prostitutes look easy and manly, during World War II it looked hard.

In addition to portraying soldiers as conflicted over their sexual urges, the propaganda of World War II also abandoned the protective masculinity promoted during World War I. The poster "Welcome Home" (Figure C.3) shows a soldier returning to his family but does not specifically mention mothers, sisters, or brides. Instead, it simply says, "For the welcome home on that furlough you'll want a clean past. . . . Avoid V.D." Vague references here to cleanliness replace the familial reminders of World War I posters like "Take No Liberties," which warns that the girl a soldier seduced might be someone else's sister (Figure 5.3). "Welcome Home," also lacks the guilt-inducing appeals to remain loyal to one's self-sacrificing mother. While the woman with her arm around the soldier is probably meant to be his mother, the image has neither the visual nor the textual drama of "Your Mother Has Been Unselfish" (Figure 5.3), which asks, "Will you be worthy of her? Protect the honor of all women and girls." Protective masculinity had apparently

FIGURE C.1. *"Two Girls I Know Want to Meet You," wall poster produced by the War Department, Office of the Surgeon General, Preventative Medicine Service, Venereal Disease Division. (Record Group 112, Still Picture Records, Special Media Archives Services Division, National Archives; ARC Identifier: 531492)*

FIGURE C.2. *"Ja! Ve Should Giff Medals,"* wall poster produced by the War Department, *Office of the Surgeon General, Preventative Medicine Service, Venereal Disease Division.* *(Record Group 112, National Archives; ARC Identifier: 531492)*

FIGURE C.3. *"Welcome Home,"* wall poster produced by the War Department, Office of the Surgeon General, Preventative Medicine Service, Venereal Disease Division. *(Record Group 112, National Archives; ARC Identifier: 531492)*

fallen by the wayside between the wars, leaving soldiers to make their decisions about sexual behavior without the overriding guilt that characterized propaganda during World War I. Soldiers needed to avoid venereal disease because it affected their ability to fight, not because they owed a debt to their mothers or because they had an investment in the sexual purity of America's girls.

In fact, the only real similarity in messages between World War I and World War II propaganda was the blame assigned to prostitutes for spreading venereal disease. One poster instructs viewers to "smash the prostitution racket" because "prostitution spreads venereal disease" (Figure C.4). Other posters continued the World War I association of prostitutes with the enemy. One pictures an attractive (though vaguely sinister-looking) woman identified as "pick-up," "street walker," and "prostitute," holding a martini glass labeled "venereal disease." Titled "Axis Agents," the poster warns that her proffered drink is "a toast to Hitler and Hirohito" (Figure C.5). A third pictures Hitler, Hirohito, and an shapely woman in a red dress with a skull for a face marching in lockstep. "V.D." the poster reads, "worst of the three" (Figure C.6). As in World War I, these posters argued that prostitutes spread venereal disease to innocent soldiers and, as such, represented a fifth column of the enemy army within the United States. But, of course, during this war, officials had data showing that prostitutes represented only a tiny fraction of the women spreading venereal disease among the troops. The lingering importance of prostitution in these posters highlights the value of prostitutes as scapegoats. With prostitutes to blame, Americans did not need to acknowledge the profound changes in sexual practice that had swept the nation in the years between the wars.

The War Department did acknowledge the danger of pickups in its propaganda, but it did so by expanding the category of "bad women" who aided the enemy. "Axis Agents" blurs the line between sleeping with soldiers for patriotic reasons and prostitution by labeling the woman holding the glass both a "pick-up" and a "prostitute." "Helloooo Soldier" goes even further and eliminates the category of prostitute from its text altogether. It identifies the woman hailing the soldier as a "pickup" and informs the viewer that "over 40% of the pickups are diseased," while Hitler and Hirohito look on from the window of "Hotel Shoddy" and applaud the woman's efforts on their behalf. Another poster depicts three attractive women, one of whom winks at the viewer while the text advises, "Loaded? Don't take chances with pickups. Loose women may also be loaded with diseases" (Figure C.7).[40] These posters reflected the realities of the military's contact tracing, which proved that nonprostitutes posed more of threat to the troops. But rather than shift

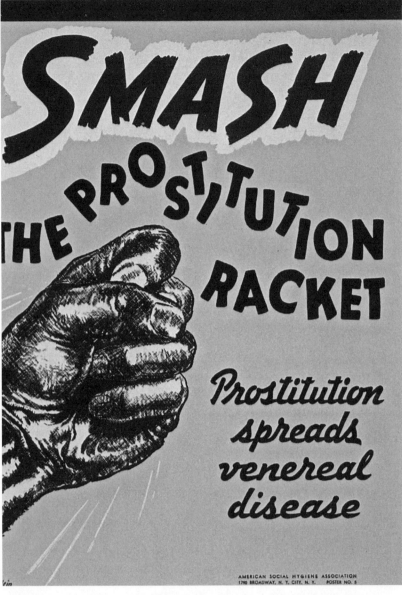

FIGURE C.4. *"Smash the Prostitution Racket," wall poster produced by the War Department, Office of the Surgeon General, Preventative Medicine Service, Venereal Disease Division. (Record Group 112, National Archives; ARC Identifier: 531492)*

FIGURE C.5. *"Axis Agents," wall poster produced by the War Department, Office of the Surgeon General, Preventative Medicine Service, Venereal Disease Division. (Record Group 112, National Archives; ARC Identifier: 531492)*

FIGURE C.6. *"V.D. Worst of the Three," wall poster produced by the War Department, Office of the Surgeon General, Preventative Medicine Service, Venereal Disease Division. (Record Group 112, National Archives; ARC Identifier: 531492)*

FIGURE C.7. *"Loaded? Don't Take Chances with Pickups,"* wall poster produced by the *War Department, Office of the Surgeon General, Preventative Medicine Service, Venereal Disease Division. (Record Group 112, National Archives; ARC Identifier: 531492)*

the emphasis away from prostitution, the posters include all women who have sex with soldiers under the mantle of "bad women." When seen in light of the lack of reference to sisters, mothers, and brides so prevalent in World War I propaganda, this new approach to disease naturalized male sexual desires and cast all women in the role of potential seducers, disease carriers, and friends of the enemy.

While by no means a new vision of sexuality, America's return to the sexual double standard came at grave cost to women during and after the war, highlighting the real limitations of the revolution in behavior that treating promoted.[41] As surveys by sex researchers show, American sexual behavior had changed significantly in the first half of the twentieth century, even as Americans continued to tell themselves and each other that "good girls" waited until marriage to engage in intercourse. One solution to the problem of teen sex was earlier marriages, and in the 1950s, the average marriage age dropped precipitously. But even earlier marriages did not decrease the rate of premarital sex, which reached 50 percent for women, even among the white middle class.[42] The stigma associated with these activities remained strong and was borne entirely by women. Feelings of isolation and shame continued to plague those women whose sexual behavior mirrored that of their peers but did not conform to public prescriptions that insisted on premarital chastity for women. Reactionary in both its gender and sexual politics, the 1950s provides a particularly flagrant example of a time when people's behavior did not match their professed moral values. Even as treating spurred a dramatic shift in sexual behavior, it did not accomplish an accompanying shift in public discourse surrounding sexual ideals. Throughout the 1950s and early 1960s, women would continue to be caught between the new sexual practices and the older attitudes that denounced them. It was not until the feminist and gay liberation movements of the late 1960s that Americans finally began to bring their sexual ideology in line with the shifts in sexual behavior that had begun nearly a century before.

NOTES

ABBREVIATIONS

Bedford	Bedford Hills State Reformatory Inmate Case Files, Series 14610-77B, New York State Archives, Albany
C14	Committee of Fourteen Papers, Astor, Lenox and Tilden Collection, Rare Books and Manuscripts, New York Public Library, New York City
C15	Committee of Fifteen Papers, Astor, Lenox and Tilden Collection, Rare Books and Manuscripts, New York Public Library, New York City
Coser Data Set	World of Our Mothers Study of Jewish and Italian Immigrant Women, 1980–1983 Data Set, Henry A. Murray Research Center, Radcliffe Institute for Advanced Study, Harvard University
Covello Papers	Leonard Covello Papers, Balsh Institute for Ethnic Studies, Philadelphia, Pennsylvania
CSS Papers	Community Service Society Papers, Rare Books and Manuscripts Library, Columbia University, New York City
IR	Investigative Reports
Landis Papers	Carney Landis Papers, Kinsey Institute for Sex Research, Bloomington, Indiana
NYCILHP	New York City Immigrant Labor History Project, Tamiment Library and Archives, New York University, New York City
RG 90, NA	Records of the Public Health Service, 1912–68, National Archives, College Park, Maryland
RG 165, NA	Records of the War Department, General and Special Staffs, National Archives, College Park, Maryland
RG 215, NA	Records of the Office of Community War Services, National Archives, College Park, Maryland
TTP	Trial Transcript Project, John Jay College of Criminal Justice, New York City
Wald Papers	Lillian Wald Papers, Rare Books and Manuscripts Library, Columbia University, New York City
WPA	Women's Prison Association Records, Astor, Lenox and Tilden Collection, Rare Books and Manuscripts, New York Public Library, New York City

INTRODUCTION

1. "IR — 1913–14," Box 28, C14. Where I thought it was important to do so, I have identified in text or in notes the dates of reports or letters from the Committee of Fourteen files. Unfortunately, the reports and correspondence collected in these files often lack such details.

2. For increases in premarital sex rates, see D. Smith, "Dating of the American Sexual

Revolution," 426. For estimates on the rate of sexual intercourse between affianced couples versus those without such agreements, see Terman, *Psychological Factors in Marital Happiness*, 320–22.

3. Peiss, *Cheap Amusements*, 88–125.

4. For an analysis of the demography of New York City at the turn of the century, see Reimers and Binder, *All the Nations under Heaven*.

5. Although historians have assumed that these changes in American sexual values occurred first in cities, recent work by Sharon Ullman has shown that the "sexual revolution" of the twentieth century also occurred in small cities and towns in tandem with developments in cities like New York, Chicago, and Los Angeles. She argues that films, which found widespread distribution across the country, provided Americans with a multiplicity of models for understanding the shifts in sexual norms already underway in these communities. See Ullman, *Sex Seen*. I have focused on New York City because of the amazing source base available on sexual issues, but I agree with Ullman that these changes, spurred largely by developments in a national commercial popular culture, occurred around the country simultaneously.

6. D. Smith, "Dating of the American Sexual Revolution," 422–26.

7. For examples of modern dating involving assumptions about sexual and economic exchange, see Maureen Dowd, "The Manolo Moochers," *New York Times*, Aug. 29, 2001; and Brumberg, *Body Project*, 190.

8. Alfred Kinsey found that the generation of men who came of age before World War I were much more likely to visit prostitutes, and to do so more frequently, than men who came of age after World War I. Kinsey, Pomeroy, and Martin, *Sexual Behavior in the Human Male*, 603.

9. R. Alexander, *"Girl Problem,"* 88–91.

10. Brooks Higginbotham, *Righteous Discontent*, 185–230.

11. Wolcott, *Remaking Respectability*, 1–48.

12. Donovan, *Woman Who Waits*, 213.

13. For arguments about the meaning of the Cotton Club's policies and their relationship to white supremacy, see Clement, "From Sociability to Spectacle." Also see Lewis, *When Harlem Was in Vogue*; Huggins, *Voices from the Harlem Renaissance*; and Watson, *Harlem Renaissance*.

14. Taxi dancing developed in the 1920s as a form of dancing in which the man paid for dances with a female employee of a dance hall. The woman usually received half of the proceeds of these dances and also encouraged men to spend money on liquor. Although the dancers did not have intercourse with their patrons, they often brought men to orgasm on the dance floor. Cressey, *Taxi-Dance Hall*, 3.

15. Mumford, *Interzones*, 19–49; Dumenil, *Modern Temper*.

16. For discussions of the class and race divisions of contemporary sex work, see Delacoste and Alexander, *Sex Work*.

17. Peiss, *Cheap Amusements*, 88–125; Meyerowitz, *Women Adrift*.

18. Kunzel, *Fallen Women*; Lunbeck, *Psychiatric Persuasion*; R. Alexander, *"Girl Problem"*; Odem, *Delinquent Daughters*.

19. Ewen, *Immigrant Women*; Glenn, *Daughters of the Shtetl*; Gabaccia, *From the Other Side*.

20. Brooks Higginbotham, *Righteous Discontent*, 185–230. For other discussions of African American women's sexuality in the twentieth century, see E. White, *Dark Continent of Our Bodies*; Hine, "Rape in the Inner Lives"; and Freedman, "'Uncontrolled Desires.'"

21. Wolcott, *Remaking Respectability*, 1–48.

22. Hobson, *Uneasy Virtue*; Connelly, *Response to Prostitution*; P. Cohen, *Murder of Helen Jewett*; Rosen, *Lost Sisterhood*.

23. Gilfoyle, *City of Eros*.

24. Stansell, *City of Women*.

25. Bailey, *From Front Porch*; Rothman, *Hands and Hearts*; Lystra, *Searching the Heart*.

26. Many different private agencies studied and attempted to police vice at the turn of the century. The Committee of Fifteen began this work in 1901 but quickly disbanded when scandal rocked its pursuits and its founder died. The Committee of Fourteen took up the cause and investigated vice in the city from 1905 through 1932. Other smaller groups, often run by settlement houses, also periodically formed to study vice in their specific neighborhoods. Thus, the Lillian Wald Papers contain evidence from interviews with prostitutes in the early 1910s, and the Community Service Society Papers hold similar records of investigations in the 1930s and 1940s.

27. Funded by Rockefeller and run by a board of very wealthy New Yorkers, the Committee of Fourteen really was more elite than "middle class" in it's composition. However, it's ideology and practice reflected debates emanating from a middle-class analysis of social problems, in particular both the social purity movement and broader Progressive-era activism around criminality and prison reform.

28. "IR—Brooklyn and Related Material, 1914–15," Box 29, C14.

CHAPTER ONE

1. B. Smith, *Tree Grows in Brooklyn*, 26.

2. There is little information available about the courtship practices of nineteenth-century Irish or German immigrants. What little there is suggests that for the Irish, at least, intercourse in courtship was frowned upon and that premarital sex rates remained relatively low. This may help explain the drop in premarital sex rates that America experienced in the nineteenth century. Colonial rates for premarital sex hovered around 30 percent but dropped significantly, to approximately 12–15 percent, in the nineteenth century. Historians have attributed this drop to the cult of chastity that developed in the middle class. But there is little evidence that the working class followed the middle class's lead in this development. It seems far more likely that the influx of Irish immigrants to cities like New York lowered rates of premarital sex for the working class and had an effect on working-class sexual values more generally. For a discussion of premarital sex rates in American history, see D. Smith, "Dating of the American Sexual Revolution," 426. For a discussion of immigrant Irish sexual values and practices, see Diner, *Erin's Daughters in America*, 114–16. Diner's assumptions about "sex delinquency" among the Irish are partially borne out by Katharine Bement Davis's analysis of the women incarcerated at Bedford Hills State Reformatory. She found that the Irish were half as likely to be incarcerated at Bedford as their numbers in the population would suggest. K. Davis, "Study of Prostitutes," 174–78. For more on Irish women in America, see Fitzgerald, *Habits of Compassion*.

3. Inmate 2474 (American-born Polish and German Protestant), Box 14, Bedford. As

part of my agreement for use of these files, I have referred to cases by their inmate case number. Where necessary, I have changed the names to ethnically appropriate pseudonyms.

4. Inmate 2483 (white Protestant), Box 14, Bedford.

5. Cott, "Eighteenth Century Family," 107–35.

6. D. Smith, "Dating of the American Sexual Revolution," 426.

7. Terman, *Psychological Factors in Marital Happiness*, 320–22.

8. D. Smith, "Dating of the American Sexual Revolution," 433.

9. R. Alexander, *"Girl Problem,"* 25.

10. I assume that Joe Daly was Irish (and therefore Catholic); he certainly possessed a stereotypical Irish name. Because the Bedford case files only provided information on the ethnicity of the inmates themselves, however, it is impossible to know for sure.

11. Inmate 2474 (American-born Polish and German Protestant), Box 14, Bedford.

12. Inmate 3760 (Russian Jew), Box 1, Bedford.

13. Inmate 2474.

14. Ibid.

15. Inmates 2482 (American-born German Protestant), Box 14, 2479 (American-born German Catholic) and 2502 (white Protestant), Box 13, 3720 (northern African American Protestant), 3723 (southern African American Catholic), and 3735 (American-born Russian Jew), Box 1, 3494 (northern African American Protestant) and 3477 (American-born German Protestant), Box 3, 4360 (Italian Catholic), Box 5, 4504 (Black Puerto Rican Catholic), Box 7, and 4062 (Swedish Protestant), Box 11, Bedford.

16. Inmate 2501 (American-born Austrian Catholic), Box 8, Bedford.

17. Inmate 2474. It is unlikely that these preventative measures would work, however, and many women came to Bedford already infected with syphilis or gonorrhea or both.

18. For example, see Inmate 2496 (southern African American Protestant), Box 14, Bedford.

19. Inmate 2492 (white Protestant), Box 14, Bedford.

20. Inmate 2501.

21. *People of the State of New York against Daniel Lynx*, Case 1702, TTP.

22. Larson, " 'Women Understand,' " 383.

23. Ibid., 387–88.

24. Ibid., 387.

25. Comprised of several thousand felony trials in New York City between 1886 and 1929, the Trial Transcript Project still contains only a fraction of the felony trials in New York City. These records contained eleven examples of seduction under promise of marriage cases. Not all of these transcripts were complete, however, and only a few of them recorded the jury's verdict. For a discussion of the evolving value of chastity in seduction cases, see ibid., 381–89.

26. Their class status is unsurprising. Although Ellen Rothman argues that white middle-class youth had more freedom in their courtships than previously believed, she also found that few middle-class couples engaged in premarital intercourse. Furthermore, middle-class families would be unlikely to go to court over a breach of marital promise. Families might force marriages in the event of premarital pregnancy, but the importance

of maintaining the fiction of virginity (and thus respectability) kept these negotiations private. Rothman, *Hands and Hearts*, 119–43. Also see Lystra, *Searching the Heart*, 56–87.

27. Seven out of the eleven women were immigrants, and three more came from immigrant families, though they may have been born in the United States. Of the seven immigrants, six were Jewish (both Sephardic and Ashkenazic), and one was Greek.

28. True, *Neglected Girl*, 62, 73.

29. *People of the State of New York versus Samuel Rosen*, Case 2435, TTP.

30. Lvofsky's very willingness to bring such a case may have reflected her assimilation into American culture. ChaeRan Freeze argues that European Jews rarely pursued either seduction or rape cases because "neither the community nor the law was likely to punish the man who reneged on a promise of marriage." Taking such a case to the courts was an "onerous process" with "dismal prospects for success." Lvofsky may or may not have known the daunting odds in the Old Country, but she certainly knew that she could sue in the new. In this context, it seems particularly important that eight out of the eleven seduction cases involved Jewish women. If Freeze is correct in her assessment of the rarity of these cases in Europe, then young Jewish women like Lvofsky learned quickly that these cases might be successful in the United States. Resorting to court reflected an assimilation to American culture, one in which young women engaged a relatively neutral state to judge their disputes with men who they felt had wronged them. Freeze, *Jewish Marriage*, 38.

31. Case 2435, TTP.

32. *People of the State of New York versus Emanuel Millinger*, Case 2468, TTP.

33. Case 1702, TTP.

34. See, for example, *People of the State of New York versus John Bogden*, Case 1291, TTP.

35. Stansell, *City of Women*, 171–77.

36. *People of the State of New York versus Harry Rosenberg*, Case 343, TTP.

37. Case 1702, TTP.

38. Case 2435, TTP.

39. Julia worked as a domestic, and her mistress testified against John Bogden. Sadie Cohen lived with her own parents, and Sarah Hafif lived with her intended's parents. Cases 1291, 343, and 1812, TTP.

40. Case 1702, TTP.

41. *People of the State of New York versus John Nicholas*, Case 1970, TTP.

42. Ibid.

43. For another example, see *People of the State of New York versus Thomas Hawkins*, Case 2517, TTP.

44. Case 2435, TTP.

45. Case 1970, TTP.

46. Bernstein, "Boarding-House Keepers," 123–27.

47. True, *Neglected Girl*, 90–91.

48. Interview 25032, Coser Data Set. As part of my agreement for the use of these data, I have cited only the case numbers to identify the interviews and have changed the names to ethnically appropriate pseudonyms to protect the confidentiality of the women interviewed.

49. The vast majority of Italians immigrated to the United States from southern Italy,

usually from the countryside near Naples or from Sicily. They came from small villages in rural areas, though often near larger towns and cities like Palermo. Although 620,000 northern Italians immigrated to the United States in the years between 1892 and 1954, these numbers pale in comparison to the 3.3 million southern Italians who came during the same period. Coan, *Ellis Island Interviews*, 38, 61.

50. *"Domus"* is the word Robert Orsi uses to describe the Italian and Italian American understanding of family. It involved both a broad extended family and a gendered and generational authority within that family, with parents in charge and all young women subject to the authority of all men in the family. Orsi argues that the *domus* encompassed ideas of family, community, and at times, nation: "Indeed, the immigrants' memories of Italy were really memories of the domus. These people could not understand the proud italianita of Italian Harlem's middle-class immigrant professionals who had managed to find some identification with the Italian nation. The immigrants did not know an Italian nation—they only knew the domus in their paesi. So their memories and images of Italy were memories of strict family order and discipline, of family loyalty and mutual support." Orsi, *Madonna*, 78.

51. Covello, *Social Background*, 192–238.

52. As Coser, Anker, and Perrin explain in the introduction to *Women of Courage*, "A total of 100 Jewish and Italian women who moved to the United States before 1927 and were at least thirteen years of age when they immigrated were interviewed for the study" (9). These interviews took place between 1980 and 1985.

53. Covello, *Social Background*, 198.

54. Interview 25053, Coser Data Set.

55. Ruth True argued that when Italian girls chose their own mates, they rebelled against the authority of family and community. This, she believed, was a crucial part of Americanization for Italian girls. True, *Neglected Girl*, 112.

56. Interview 25039, Coser Data Set.

57. "Interview with Rosa Vartone," in Coan, *Ellis Island Interviews*, 51.

58. Covello, *Social Background*, 202–10.

59. Quoted in Orsi, *Madonna*, 85.

60. For examples of arranged marriages in the United States, see Series II, Tapes 10 and 11, Carlotta Vina, and Tapes 39 and 40, Lucrezia Grogone and Maria Vartone, NYCILHP. As part of my agreement for the use of these data, I have cited only the tape and series numbers to identify the interviews and have changed the names of the people involved to ethnically appropriate pseudonyms to protect their confidentiality. See also Interviews 25021, 25030, and 25053, Coser Data Set; and "Interview with Rose Vartone," in Coan, *Ellis Island Interviews*, 52.

61. Parentheses are from the original transcript. Interview 25055, Coser Data Set.

62. "Cultural Heritage—Social Heritage," File 10, Box 67, Covello Papers.

63. For example, one interviewee reported, "Oh, well, years ago nobody went out. The parties, they were in the house." Interview 25028, Coser Data Set.

64. Series II, Tapes 30 and 31, Graciella Filipelli, NYCILHP. Also see Interviews 25032 and 25009, Coser Data Set.

65. Interview 25032, Coser Data Set.

66. Covello documented that Italian families severely limited girls' ability to move

around unsupervised after they reached early adolescence. Covello, *Social Background*, 196–98.

67. Series II, Tapes 10 and 11, Carlotta Vina, NYCILHP.

68. Robert Orsi also documented this belief, commenting that it was part of Italians' intense investment both in female chastity and in managing the marriages of their children. Once a child brought someone home, the entire extended family would investigate whether this person would be a good mate and a good member of the *domus*, or family. Orsi, *Madonna*, 99–100.

69. Series II, Tape 2, Martina Tosca, NYCILHP. For other examples, see "Cultural Heritage—Family—Older Brother in Parent's Role," Folder 9, Box 67, Covello Papers.

70. Series II, Tapes 10 and 11, Carlotta Vina, NYCILHP. For other examples, see Series II, Tape 25, Paulina Mossini, NYCILHP.

71. Series II, Tape 16, Sylvia Peluso, NYCILHP.

72. On Italian Americans and honor, see Orsi, *Madonna*, 75–106, 129–49. For a more general discussion of honor, see K. Greenberg, *Honor and Slavery*.

73. "Cultural Heritage—Social Heritage," File 10, Box 67, Covello Papers. For another example of honor restricting a girl, see Series II, Tape 38, Carla Mastronari, NYCILHP.

74. "Cultural Heritage—Family Disorganization," Folder 8, Box 67, Covello Papers. For other examples of violence, see "Cultural Heritage—Family—Older Brother in Parent's Role," Folder 9, Box 67, Covello Papers.

75. Interview 25039, Coser Data Set. For other examples, see "Cultural Heritage—Family Control and Unity," Folder 7, Box 67, Covello Papers; and Interview 25053, Coser Data Set.

76. Interview 25053, Coser Data Set.

77. "Delinquency," Folder 16, Box 66, Covello Papers.

78. Series II, Tapes 43 and 44, Gloria Granato, NYCILHP.

79. Interview 25055, Coser Data Set.

80. "Cultural Heritage—Family Control and Unity," Folder 7, Box 67, Covello Papers.

81. Sholem Aleichem, *Tevye*, 39.

82. Ibid., 40.

83. Ibid., 45.

84. Ibid., 48.

85. Kramer and Masur, *Jewish Grandmothers*, 39.

86. Freeze, *Jewish Marriage*, 25–31.

87. Ibid., 20–21, 30–31.

88. Ibid., 22–35; Biale, *Eros and the Jews*, 149–75.

89. Glenn, *Daughters of the Shtetl*, 35–41.

90. Freeze, *Jewish Marriage*, 23. Founded in 1897, the Bund was an explicitly Jewish socialist organization that began organizing Jewish workers in the Russian Pale.

91. "Shadchens Find Business Bad," *New York Tribune*, Jan. 9, 1898, reprinted in Schoener, *Portal to America*, 118.

92. Eight of these women clearly married in Europe, and twenty-seven married in the United States. With the rest, it is impossible to tell from the interviews where they married. Coser Data Set.

93. I do not know how Coser recruited for her study, and it is likely that her recruit-

ment methods affected the pool she drew from. There certainly were some groups of Jews who cleaved to older patterns, such as the Hassidim who came from Poland and settled in Brooklyn. They proved much less willing to dispense with older practices and continue to this day to use matchmakers. Although Coser's sample included Jews who identified themselves as highly observant or orthodox, they were still far more interested in assimilating than the Hassidim.

94. Interview 15050, Coser Data Set.

95. Interviews 15029 and 15061, Coser Data Set.

96. Interview 15048, Coser Data Set. Also see Interviews 15084, 15040, 15012, and 15021, Coser Data Set; and Series I, Tape 25, Bea Tannenbaum, and Tape 35, Naomi Schlessinger, NYCILHP.

97. Interview 15012, Coser Data Set. Another woman's mother wanted her to marry a boarder in their building. "I said, 'You know, Momma, if I get married, if I marry him, and I have a family, I'll have children, the children will ask me, "How did you meet Poppa?" and I'll say, "on the way to the toilet"' (laugh). So . . . everyone had a good laugh, and that stopped it." Interview 15060, Coser Data Set.

98. Kramer and Masur, *Jewish Grandmothers*, 21.

99. Marie Ganz, *Rebels*, 58.

100. Interview 15040, Coser Data Set.

101. Interview 15051, Coser Data Set. The other reasons ranged from wanting to get married (Interviews 15065, 15085, and 15009), wanting to get out of a bad home or boarding situation (15040), and being very lonely in America (15067 and 15089).

102. Interview 15061, Coser Data Set.

103. Series I, Tape 51, Esther Frankel, NYCILHP.

104. True, *Neglected Girl*, 70–72.

105. Inmates 2516 (American-born Russian Jew), Box 14, 3714 (American-born Russian Jew), 3736 (American-born Austrian Jew), 3725 (Russian Jew), and 3735 (American-born Russian Jew), Box 1, 4529 (American-born Austrian Jew), Box 2, 4091 (American-born Russian Jew), Box 9, 4057 (Romanian Jew), Box 11, and 2509 (American-born Russian Jew), Box 13, Bedford.

106. Ganz, *Rebels*, 158–61.

107. Glenn, *Daughters of the Shtetl*, 42–49. Also see Bodnar, *Transplanted*, 57–83.

108. Kramer and Masur, *Jewish Grandmothers*, 26.

109. Interview 15029, Coser Data Set.

110. Interview 15084, Coser Data Set. Also see Interview 15060.

111. Howe and Libo, *How We Lived*, 128–29.

112. Glenn, *Daughters of the Shtetl*, 35–41.

113. Series I, Tape 59, Frieda Kaufman, NYCILHP. Gittel Pinsky met her husband at a political meeting in Europe. Series I, Tape 123, NYCILHP. Zelda Friedman met her husband through a group "of intellectual people to overthrow the Czar who was very, very bad." Interview 17003, Coser Data Set.

114. Coser, Anker, and Perrin argue that the marginalization and violence Jews fled from in Europe made them very anxious to assimilate as Americans and adopt American ways. They describe Jewish families as "outward looking" in contrast to Italians as "inward

looking" and resistant to Americanization. Coser, Anker, and Perrin, *Women of Courage*, 36–48.

115. Series I, Tape 25, Bea Tannenbaum, NYCILHP.

116. Glenn, *Daughters of the Shtetl*, 9–30; Freeze, *Jewish Marriage*, 32–35; Ewen, *Immigrant Women*, 37–47.

117. Interview 15029, Coser Data Set.

118. Series I, Tapes 116 and 117, Trudy Rothman, NYCILHP.

119. Series I, Tape 5, Chava Brier, NYCILHP.

120. Series I, Tapes 6 and 7, Lena Rubin, NYCILHP.

121. Interview 15004, Coser Data Set.

122. Interview 15023, Coser Data Set.

123. K. Davis, "Study of Prostitutes," 174–78, 190–92.

124. Chernin, *In My Mother's House*, 65.

125. Interview 15073, Coser Data Set. For Jewish attitudes about "freedom" in America, see "Interview with Jacob Lotsky" and "Interview with Sylvia Broter," in Coan, *Ellis Island Interviews*, 251, 260; and Interview 15061, Coser Data Set.

CHAPTER TWO

1. "IR—1914," Box 28, C14. For other examples of charity girls refusing to go to hotels, see "IR—Brooklyn, Inv. Reports and Related Info, 1913–14," Box 29, C14.

2. Peiss, *Cheap Amusements*, 88–125; Meyerowitz, *Women Adrift*, 101–7. Also see Peiss, "'Charity Girls.'"

3. Stansell, *City of Women*, 93.

4. Peiss, "'Charity Girls,'" 60–61.

5. Belle Israels, "The Way of the Girl," *Survey* July 3, 1909, 486.

6. Cary's choice to include the word in his catalog of sexual slang indicates its growing importance in American sexual culture. H. N. Cary, "Sexual Vocabulary," vol. 1 (unpublished manuscript, 1916), Kinsey Archives, Bloomington, Indiana.

7. Weiner, *From Working Girl to Working Mother*, 6. Economist Claudia Goldin estimates a slightly lower number, finding 35 percent of white single women between the ages of fifteen and twenty-nine years of age working outside the home in 1890. By 1920, she argues, 44 percent of white women worked outside the home. Goldin, *Understanding the Gender Gap*, 94.

8. Goldin, *Understanding the Gender Gap*, 94. Weiner's numbers are probably different because they include women of color and all single women, not just the group into which most single women fall, namely fifteen to twenty-nine years of age. Goldin looks only at white single women in this age group. African American women were a small part of the population in this period and were limited to the most poorly paid jobs. For example, many of them worked in domestic service, a field young immigrant women and native-born daughters of immigrant parents avoided when at all possible.

9. Gold, *Jews without Money*, 266. In a survey of social workers' opinions for the National Federation of Settlements titled *Young Working Girls: A Summary of Evidence from Two Thousand Social Workers*, the authors argued that the pay envelope gave girls independence from the family. They stated that the working girl's "opinion of herself as an inde-

pendent and all conquering being is reinforced by evident material accomplishment." The same survey concluded that "the fact that the girl has become a wage-earner automatically makes her a cooperating member of the family group." Woods and Kennedy, *Young Working Girls*, 34. Also see True, *Neglected Girl*, 47.

10. Decisions that families made when they were concerned about young women's virtue reflect their belief in the freedom that wage earning accorded family members. One family whose daughter eventually ended up in Bedford reformatory as a wayward girl attempted to curb her extracurricular activities by demanding that she quit her job. As the caseworker reported in her summary of the interviews conducted with the family, "Patient would not listen to the advice of her family but insisted on doing as she pleased. . . . The family finally decided that she would be less independent if she stayed at home with her mother and so they agreed to give her spending money, and piano lessons if she would remain at home from work and stop running out nights." Inmate 2516 (Russian Jew), Box 14, Bedford. Wage-earning daughters were crucial to a working-class family's survival, but they could also become discipline problems. Families concerned about both their girls' virtue and traditional patterns of authority sometimes had to choose between the extra income and their desire to control their wayward daughters.

11. Inmate 2505 (southern African American Protestant), Box 13, Bedford.

12. Inmate 2501 (American-born Austrian Catholic), Box 13, Bedford.

13. In addition, the mere presence of women on the street may have made it safer for other women to venture forth. As Elizabeth Kennedy and Madeline Davis note, the vast increase in women employed in wartime industries led to an understandable increase in women on the streets at any hour. This in turn made the streets of Buffalo, both during the day and at night, much safer for all women. Women took advantage of this new safety and visited many different parts of the city and many different types of establishments at all hours of the day and night. Kennedy and Davis, *Boots of Leather*, 374.

14. Goldin, *Understanding the Gender Gap*, 53. The remaining 14 percent, who retained some of their own wages, still turned over at least 50 percent.

15. Series II, Tape 38, Carla Mastrionari, NYCILHP. Also see Series I, Tape 108, Henrietta Farber, Tapes 116 and 117, Trudy Rothman, and Tape 134, Annette Silber, NYCILHP.

16. Series I, Tapes 116 and 117, Trudy Rothman, NYCILHP. The small number of women who lived alone were the exception to this rule. Across categories of nationality, ethnicity, race, occupation, and industry, two-thirds of these "women adrift" kept 100 percent of their wages. Those who did give some money to their families gave an average of 33 percent, a percentage of their wages far lower than that of young women who remained in their parents' households. Goldin, *Understanding the Gender Gap*, 94. For more on how much of their wages young women turned over, see Woods and Kennedy, *Young Working Girls*, 54–55; and Weiner, *From Working Girl to Working Mother*, 26.

17. Of course, these data are not a reliable sample, as this information was gleaned from literally hundreds of records, most of which contained no information about ethnicity.

18. Most charity girls at Bedford were held under the charge of "wayward minor," though a few were also accused of prostitution. Three-quarters of the white women who could be clearly identified as "charity" were either immigrants or the children of immigrants. Two-thirds of the African American women in Bedford whose records I surveyed

came from the South. The other third were born in the North or the West Indies. See Boxes 1–14, Bedford.

19. K. Davis, "Study of Prostitutes," 174–78.

20. Davis only comments on the percentages of Catholics, Jews, and Protestants relative to the population of New York. She found that the religion of women at Bedford largely followed their percentage in the population as a whole. Ibid., 190–92.

21. Inmate 2491 (American-born Irish Catholic), Box 14, Bedford.

22. Inmate 2480 (southern African American Protestant), Box 14, Bedford.

23. In the first twenty years of the century, New York actually became more racially segregated. In 1900, African Americans lived scattered throughout a series of very poor neighborhoods that also sheltered immigrants. Increasingly, though, both native New York African Americans and southern African Americans moved northward to Harlem. At the same time, white immigrants began to move out of Harlem in large numbers. See Ottley and Weatherby, *Negro in New York*; J. Johnson, *Black Manhattan*; and "Negroes of New York: 43 Studies of the History of Black People in the City of New York," Research Studies Complied by the Workers of the Writers' Program of the Works Progress Administration in New York City, 1936–41, Reel 5, Schomburg Center for Research on Black Culture, New York Public Library.

24. Again, the evidence from Bedford confirms this assessment. Most of the girls there were either from white immigrant stock or African American. Of the African American girls, the majority were born in the South or born of parents from the South, indicating that they were migrants rather than part of New York's small native African American population. See Boxes 1–14, Bedford.

25. For a more extended discussion of the demographics of treating, see Clement, "Trick or Treat," 80–96.

26. For a complete discussion of the transformation of vaudeville and of public amusements in general, see Nasaw, *Going Out*, 19–46.

27. Ibid., 104–19. Also see Peiss, *Cheap Amusements*, 88–162. For settlement workers' concern about this issue, see *Report of the Committee on Amusement Resources*, 5–6; "Circular from the Committee on Amusements and Vacation Resources of Working Girls," File: "Parks & Playgrounds," Box 28, Wald Papers; Addams, *Spirit of Youth*; and Woods and Kennedy, *Young Working Girls*. In addition, the field reports of investigators for the Committee of Fifteen and the Committee of Fourteen contain numerous references to the expansion of dancing into many different entertainment venues in the city.

28. Adler, *House Is Not a Home*, 21.

29. For fears that settlement workers expressed about the dangers of dance halls, see Jane Addams's classic *Spirit of Youth*. Another example of these fears comes in a letter written by a group of social workers to the director of the Committee of Fourteen requesting that the committee take "the initiative in a general movement against the music and dance halls. Not only are these the haunts and meeting places of the professional prostitutes, but it is there that many girls are started on the career. These resorts are a peculiar temptation to young girls in whose environments there are few opportunities for pleasure; they are taken there, ostensibly for the purpose of dancing or seeing a vaudeville performance, but really because the places are cheap and convenient for getting the girls tipsy. . . . It seems to me that one law which is essential is a statute prohibiting the sale of alcoholic liquors

at dance- and music-halls, for it is the drinking which makes the girls reckless and which, in many cases, is responsible for their downfall." A. V. Morgenstern to Dr. John Jay Peters, June 17, 1908, "General Correspondence—1908, March–June," Box 1, C14.

30. "Seek to Cut Cost of Modern Dancing," *New York Times*, Dec. 17, 1914, 13.

31. For examples of ethnic or politically sponsored dances, see Series I, Tape 59, Frieda Kaufman, and Tape 132, Malka Birnbaum, NYCILHP; and Ewen, *Immigrant Women*, 210.

32. Peiss, *Cheap Amusements*, 139–62.

33. A member of the Ashcan school of art that sought to depict life in the cities and among the poor, Sloan lived and worked in a tenement in a working-class section of New York City. His extensive collection of sketches and engravings depicts life in New York's working-class communities in a positive light. See Sloan, *New York Etchings*.

34. Ibid., figure 5.

35. New York Society for the Prevention of Cruelty to Children, *Thirty-Third Annual Report* (1907).

36. New York Society for the Prevention of Cruelty to Children, *Twenty-Ninth Annual Report* (1903). For other examples of evidence of the sexual content in working-class entertainments, see "IR—Theatre and Burlesque, 1918–20," Box 33, and "IR—Restricted—Manhattan, Named Streets and All Avenues, 1927–28," Box 37, C14.

37. Report dating from 1907, "Theatrical Investigation," Box 180, CSS Papers.

38. New York Society for the Prevention of Cruelty to Children, *Thirty-Third Annual Report*.

39. New York Society for the Prevention of Cruelty to Children, *Twenty-Eighth Annual Report* (1902).

40. "Theatrical Investigation," CSS Papers.

41. Norworth and Von Tilzer, "Take Me Out to the Ball Game," 258.

42. Woods and Kennedy, *Young Working Girls*, 8. For a historical discussion of this issue, see Odem, *Delinquent Daughters*.

43. Inmate 2501 (American-born Austrian Catholic), Box 13, Bedford.

44. Sussman, "Settlement Club," 24.

45. For other examples of girls using homosocial groups to discuss sexuality, sexual barter, and treating, see Inmates 2507 (northern African American Protestant), 2484 (white Protestant), 2497 (northern African American), and 2492 (white Protestant), Box 14, 2501 (American-born Austrian Catholic), Box 13, 3754 (white Protestant) and 3747 (American-born Welsh), Box 1, and 3737 (American-born Italian), Box 2, Bedford.

46. Kathy Peiss argues that girls treated in homosocial groups so that they could provide protection for each other. Peiss, *Cheap Amusements*, 113–14.

47. "IR—Department Stores II," Box 39, C14.

48. Ibid.

49. Working-class parents often shared this distinction between bad places and bad children. One young boy told an investigator that his father allowed him to go to the dance hall but insisted that he stay away from the side where prostitutes congregated. "One boy, a bright, clean looking chap, said to me: 'Father told me to stay away from the left side of the hall. I guess I know what he meant now,' and the speaker glanced toward the bar-room." "IR—1910–12," Box 28, C14.

50. Working-class girls risked significant repercussions if they lost their reputation

around their neighborhoods. Family members, especially fathers and brothers, often beat girls when rumors of sexual activity reached them. For examples, see Inmates 2501 (American-born Austrian Catholic), Box 13, 2516 (American-born Russian Jew), 2492 (American-born white Protestant), and 2474 (American-born Polish and German Protestant), Box 14, Bedford.

51. "IR—Department Stores II," Box 39, C14.

52. In many ways, these young women's definitions of prostitution were much closer to our own definitions than those of the middle class in this period. Many middle-class observers blurred the distinction between premarital or extramarital sexuality and prostitution. For examples of this blurring, see Fernald, Hayes, and Dawley, *Study of Women Delinquents*, 380.

53. *People of the State of New York versus Guiseppi Spano*, Case 1645, TTP. An almost identical conversation about "good" women took place between a prosecutor and a witness in *People of the State of New York versus Jack Miller*, Case 1743, TTP.

54. Inmate 2492 (American-born white Protestant), Box 14, Bedford. In another case, a social worker from Bedford reformatory wrote that an inmate "admits having been immoral but denies ever having taken any money." Another reported that the young woman "says she has never taken any money from them and she does not consider herself a prostitute." Inmate 2483 (American-born white Protestant), Box 14, Bedford.

55. Inmate 2486 (northern African American Catholic), Box 14, Bedford.

56. Inmate 2480 (southern African American Protestant), Box 14, Bedford.

57. Inmate 2501 (American-born Austrian Catholic), Box 8, Bedford.

58. Inmate 2484 (white Protestant), Box 14, Bedford. For other examples, see Inmates 2505 (southern African American), Box 13, and 2485 (American-born Irish Catholic), Box 14, Bedford.

59. Inmate 2497 (northern African American Protestant), Box 14, Bedford.

60. Inmate 2485 (American-born Irish Catholic), Box 14, Bedford.

61. As he wrote in his diary of this piece, "A bevy of boisterous girls with plenty of energy left after a hard day's work." Sloan, *New York Etchings*, figure 31. A simplified version of this subject was made for a cover of *The Masses*. See Snyder, "City in Transition," 45.

62. "IR—Strand Cafeteria" (1916), Box 28, C14.

63. "IR—1913–14," Box 28, C14.

64. "IR—Brooklyn-Investigative" (1914), Box 29, C14. An "aigrette" is a decoration for a hat, usually a plume or tuft of feathers.

65. Donovan, *Woman Who Waits*, 212–13.

66. Ibid., 212–19.

67. "Investigators' Reports—1916," Box 30, C14.

68. "Investigators' Reports—Restricted—Sa–Su," Box 36, C14.

69. "IR—Brooklyn-Investigative" (1928), Box 29, C14.

70. This quotation contains the only reference I found to the term "salamander." It obviously enjoyed only a brief popularity. "IR—Strand Cafeteria" (1916), Box 28, C14.

71. The undercover investigative reports from the Committee of Fourteen and the Committee of Fifteen periodically refer to the availability of condoms at drugstores. For example, see "IR—[untitled]" (1912), Box 29, and "IR—Special Inspections—1916–17," Box 31, C14. Andrea Tone argues convincingly that condoms were widely available, especially

in cities like New York. Tone, *Devices and Desires*, 92–115. Also see Gordon, *Woman's Body, Woman's Right*, 44–45, 63–64.

72. Inmate 2492 (white Protestant), Box 14, Bedford. In contrast, women who admitted to prostitution were far more likely to describe methods of preventing pregnancy and disease, even if these methods (by our standards) were often ineffective.

73. "IR—1916," Box 30, C14.

74. Brandt, *No Magic Bullet*, 40–41.

75. Inmate 2496 (southern-born African American), Box 14, C14. For other examples, see Inmates 2492 (white Protestant), Box 14, and 2469 (American-born Irish Catholic), Box 13, Bedford.

76. Prostitutes apparently thought oral sex was dirty and often refused to associate with other women who engaged in "perversion." For example, see "General Correspondence" (1908–12), Box 1, C14.

77. "IR—Brooklyn-Investigative" (1914), Box 29, C14.

78. "IR—1916," Box 30, C14.

79. "IR—Brooklyn/Queens-Investigators Reports, 1914," Box 29, C14.

80. Ibid.

81. Inmate 2492 (white Protestant), Box 14, Bedford.

82. "IR—1914," Box 28, C14.

83. Ibid.

84. "IR—[untitled]—1917" (night inspection reports), Box 31, C14. For other examples of hotels' association with prostitution, see "General Correspondence—1908," Box 1, C14.

85. "IR—1916," Box 30, C14.

86. "IR—1917," Box 31, C14. In another case, an investigator found two young women willing to have sex "if I would promise them a 'good time' and make them a 'little present' in the morning." "IR—Brooklyn/Queens-Investigators Reports, 1914," Box 29, C14.

87. "IR—1916," Box 30, C14.

88. "General Correspondence—1908," Box 1, C14. For other examples of men's assessments of women in places of public amusement, see "IR—Brooklyn-Investigative," Box 29, "IR—[untitled]—1917" (night inspection reports), Box 31, and "IR—[untitled]—1917," Box 32, C14.

89. "IR—1916," Box 30, C14.

90. Inmate 2475, Box 13, Bedford.

91. "IR—1913," Box 28, C14.

92. Like George Chauncey, I chose to use the term these men applied to themselves. In my sources, "fairies" were men who affected women's mannerisms (sometimes dressing in women's clothing) and had sex with other men. For an extended discussion of fairies, see Chauncey, *Gay New York*, 47–63.

93. "IR—St. and Cafeteria" (1912), Box 28, C14.

94. Series II, Tape 2, Martina Tosca, NYCILHP.

CHAPTER THREE

1. "Precinct 5—James Slip," Box 4, C15. The Committee of Fifteen was founded in 1901 by elite New Yorkers to attack vice in the city. After an embarrassing set of raids of gambling establishments, it began to focus more on prostitution. Between 1901 and 1905, when

it folded, the committee conducted a series of investigations into commercial sex. These investigative reports provide extraordinarily valuable information for historians of sexuality and vice. According to Rachel Bernstein, proposals like this one made a great deal of sense for women who wanted to support themselves and their families independent of men. In her dissertation comparing boardinghouse keepers and brothel keepers in New York City from 1880 to 1910, she found that only women who managed brothels (and not legitimate boardinghouses) could actually save enough money to buy property in the city. Her convincing assessment paints a bleak picture for women's legitimate business profits and successes. See Bernstein, "Boarding-House Keepers," 123.

2. Stansell, *City of Women*, 171–92.

3. Many people assume that streetwalking is the "lowest" form of prostitution and that, given a choice, most prostitutes would prefer more sheltered work. Hoigard and Finstad's work on prostitution in Norway casts doubt on this common attitude. In their interviews with streetwalkers, they found that many preferred work on the street to more "high-class" forms of prostitution because streetwalking simply involved sex and did not require that the prostitute socialize with her client. Many of the women they spoke with expressed contempt for their johns and had no desire to have more extended contact with them. Sex, in their view, was less intimate than conversation. Perhaps a better way to understand streetwalking is to think about it in terms of its accessibility for women. Streetwalking often marks women's entrance into prostitution because it is so visible and women can learn about it relatively easily. Thus, streetwalking fits in well with casual prostitution. Hoigard and Finstad, *Backstreets*. Some prostitutes in this period shared this attitude. Maude Miner quotes one woman as remarking, "After you've tried the streets, you ain't likely to be a slave in a parlor house again." Miner, *Slavery of Prostitution*, 16.

4. I base this assertion on Davis's data. She does not group the fathers' occupations by class, so I included in this category men in the professions and white collar occupations and business owners. K. Davis, "Study of Prostitutes," 178–88.

5. Ibid., 215–16. Davis did compile percentages on mothers' occupations and found that over 22 percent worked. Ibid., 218.

6. Ibid., 219.

7. Rosen, *Lost Sisterhood*, 139–42.

8. K. Davis, "Study of Prostitutes," 174–78.

9. I do not mean to imply that Russian Jews prostituted more than other Russian immigrants. In this period, Jews made up the vast majority of Russian immigrants.

10. K. Davis, "Study of Prostitutes," 176.

11. Dillingham, *Importing Women for Immoral Purposes*, 6–7.

12. Ibid., 7.

13. Ibid., 12.

14. *In the Matter of the Investigation as to the Existence in the County of New York of an Organized Traffic in Women for Immoral Purposes*, Case 3317, TTP. Anecdotal information from the Committee of Fourteen field reports supports these statistics and highlights the fascinating impact these women had on American sexual culture. Throughout this period and, in fact, well into the 1930s, New Yorkers referred to fellatio as "the French perversion." When I first found these references, I assumed that they were slurs, a way of distancing "Americans" from the distasteful and sinful practices of others. Most prostitutes refused

to perform fellatio, responding with loathing and outrage when men requested it. Prostitutes in brothels often took this distaste to extremes by ostracizing the women willing to perform the forbidden act. As one investigator reported, "the French girls in these houses resort to unnatural practices and as a result the other girls will not associate or eat with them. This is the general reputation of French girls, that they will resort to lower practices than any other class." While French prostitutes probably did not introduce oral sex into American sexual practices, they certainly popularized it. Men increasingly asked for the service, and as we will see in later chapters, by the 1920s, fellatio had become an accepted, if still controversial, part of American prostitution. Today, of course, oral sex is both more common and cheaper than intercourse because prostitutes view it as less intimate than intercourse and because they perceive it to have a lower risk for the transmission of HIV and other diseases. "IR—[untitled]—1905–10," Box 38, C14.

15. K. Davis, "Study of Prostitutes," 174. In her book, *Slavery of Prostitution*, Maude Miner does not mention black women at all, despite the fact that they must have made up at least 13 percent of the women she saw at Women's Court. After all, many women seen by that court did not even get to Bedford. Many were placed on probation, recidivists were sent to the workhouse, and newcomers to the trade often went to institutions within the city bent on reforming them in a less coercive environment.

16. U.S. Department of Commerce, *Statistical Abstracts, 1923*, 45.

17. R. Alexander, *"Girl Problem,"* 88–91.

18. Gordon, "Black and White Visions of Welfare."

19. Mumford, *Interzones*, 37–49.

20. In the early twentieth century, New York State passed legislation banning discrimination on the basis of "race, creed, or color" in public accommodations. African Americans in the city had to fight to have the law enforced, however, and they won several court cases regarding discrimination in public accommodation in the 1910s. See "Plans to Prevent Discrimination in Public Places in New York State," *New York Age*, Jan. 30, 1913; and "Must Admit Negroes to Dance Pavilions," *New York Age*, Feb. 16, 1918.

21. Evelyn Brooks Higginbotham first introduced this expression in her book on African American church women reformers organizing in the early twentieth century. See Brooks Higginbotham, *Righteous Discontent*, 185–230.

22. Wolcott, *Remaking Respectability*, 93–130.

23. "About Committee of Fourteen," *New York Age*, Nov. 2, 1911, 1. See also "To Raise the Moral Tone of Local Saloons," *New York Age*, Dec. 14, 1911, 1.

24. "Conduct at Public Entertainments" (editorial), *New York Age*, Feb. 29, 1912, 4.

25. David Elliot Tobias to Frederick Whitin, Oct. 8, 1918, "Tobias, David Elliot," Box 15, C14.

26. Ibid.

27. Ottley and Weatherby, *Negro in New York*, 156. James Weldon Johnson, who attended the club regularly, commented that it "attracted crowds of well dressed people" and that patrons had to book in advance if they wanted a table on the weekends. J. Johnson, *Black Manhattan*, 118–19.

28. Ottley and Weatherby, *Negro in New York*, 157.

29. W. E. B. Du Bois to Frederick Whitin, Sept. 23, 1911, "Du Bois, W. E. B.," Box 11, C14.

30. "Marriage of Whites and Blacks," *New York Age*, Dec. 19, 1912, 4. In another article,

the paper conducted an informal survey of opinion among its readership and found that "While the Negro citizens are not clamoring for amalgamation of the races, and are not interested in the subject as much as many whites appear to be, yet they take exceptions to the passage of any bill which has been designed to place the race in a humiliating position." "Bills against Intermarriage Being Introduced in Various Legislatures," *New York Age*, Jan. 23, 1913, 1.

31. From its opening in 1901 through 1914, when Davis stepped down as director, Bedford reformatory integrated black and white inmates. After Davis left, however, the new director insisted on segregating the facility, arguing that relationships between black and white inmates caused problems and disrupted the smooth functioning of the facility. R. Alexander, *"Girl Problem,"* 88–91.

32. Freedman, "Prison Lesbian," 397–400.

33. "The Empire Friendly Shelter for Girls," *New York Age*, Oct. 19, 1916, 1; "Girls' Home Completes Its First Year's Work," *New York Age*, Apr. 19, 1917, 1.

34. As Paul Tappan stated, "Negro girls are especially apt to be sent to Westfield [Bedford reformatory] if their home situation is considered bad and no other provisions can be made for them." Tappan, *Delinquent Girls in Court*, 82–83.

35. African American women may also have been forced to prostitute out of a lack of male support. In this period, African American women significantly outnumbered African American men in New York City. Ottley and Weatherby, *Negro in New York*, 183.

36. Gilfoyle, *City of Eros*, 111–12.

37. Ibid., 270–97.

38. Kneeland, *Commercialized Prostitution*, 10. One outraged patron compared the system to slavery in a letter to the Committee of Fifteen. He reported that "the boss an ugly dago wont trust the semi slaves of his with the money two minutes. Give me the money! I must give it to the boss. I implored her to wait, but I gave her the money. Did the boss give you half say I. No he gave me a check sez she. That was too much for me so I thought that all I could do to help that slave was to write to you. I believe in such places, but such semi-slavery I condemn." "Precinct 5—James Slip," Box 4, C15. Maude Miner also discusses these practices in *Slavery of Prostitution*, 14–24.

39. For a more extended discussion of this practice and it's implications, see Clement, "Trick or Treat," 18–36.

40. "IR—[untitled]—1905–10," Box 38, C14. Many sources confirm the exploitative nature of brothels, and, in fact, the pattern of giving half the price of a trick to the madam and also being overcharged for goods and services seems almost universal. For example, see Dillingham, *Importing Women for Immoral Purposes*, 25. The congressional investigation that created this report came out of a "white slavery" panic in the early twentieth century. This investigation and others like it concluded that no organized traffic in women existed. Because this was largely a middle-class phenomenon and because several scholars have analyzed it, I will not discuss it. For these discussions, see Mumford, *Interzones*; Grittner, "White Slavery"; and Bower, "Common Commercial Flesh of Women."

41. Dillingham, *Importing Women for Immoral Purposes*, 25.

42. Miner, *Slavery of Prostitution*, 14–17.

43. Clement, "Trick or Treat," 23–26.

44. "IR—[untitled]—1905–10," Box 38, C14.

45. Ibid.

46. Clement, "Trick or Treat," 31–33.

47. Committee of Fourteen, *Social Evil*, 37–39. Although temperance reformers supported the bill, it passed largely because it was intended to raise revenue for the state and the Republican party machine that ran it. In addition to the obvious problems that the law created, the city rarely attempted to enforce its provisions. The annual fee for a license was $1,200 for Manhattan and $975 for Brooklyn. The immense profitability of the statute made it extremely difficult to change once it was in place. Ibid., 37.

48. As the Committee of Fourteen states in *The Social Evil in New York City*: "From the passage of this law dates the immediate growth of one of the most insidious forms of the social evil—the 'Law' hotel. This growth was due to a heavy increase in the penalties for a violation and the expected increased enforcement of the law by state authorities beyond the reach of local influences. To illustrate, the license tax was raised from $200 to $800, and the penalty of the forfeiture of a bond was also added. To escape these drastic penalties for the selling of liquor on Sunday in saloons, saloon keepers created hotels with the required 10 bed rooms, kitchen and dining room. The immediate increase was over 10,000 bedrooms. There being no actual demand for such an increase in hotel accommodations, the proprietors in many instances used them for purposes of assignation or prostitution, to meet the additional expense incurred." Committee of Fourteen, *Social Evil*, 39.

49. When the Committee of Fifteen formed in 1901, it mentioned Raines Law hotels as an important site of investigation and repression. In 1905 its successor, the Committee of Fourteen, identified Raines Law hotels as its primary target for the suppression of vice in the city. The general secretary of the Committee of Fourteen dates the demise of the brothel to 1912, but my analysis of the records that the committee itself created indicates that very few, if any, brothels survived after 1910. "Response to Questionnaire from Mr. Joseph Mayer, American Social Hygiene Association, October 1918," "General Correspondence—1918-1," Box 4, C14. George Kneeland marks the end of the parlor houses (brothels) in 1907, though he attributes this less to the Raines Law hotels than to the spread of prostitution into the tenements. Apparently the police department initiated a series of raids of brothels in the Tenderloin and in other areas of the city in 1907. Already hard-pressed by rising rents and competition from Raines Law hotels, the brothels apparently never recovered. Kneeland, *Commercialized Prostitution*, 10, 37.

50. Case 3317, TTP.

51. "IR—[untitled]—1905–10 Mostly," Box 38, C14.

52. "IR—[untitled]—1905–10," Box 38, C14. Women who sat company provided a temporary workforce for the brothels. Despite their independence, they had monetary arrangements that were similar to the agreements between madams and the permanent residents of the brothel. They paid half of each trick to the madam and, in return, benefited from the relative safety of the brothel environment and the assurance that they would consistently receive clients. However, by sitting company, these women avoided paying brothel rents and prices for food, clothing, and medical care. Working out of the brothels limited their exposure, shielding them from the dangers that beset women working the streets alone.

53. Ibid. Both the Committee of Fourteen Papers and the Wald Papers contain numerous examples of these sorts of bargains.

54. Box 91, Wald Papers.

55. "IR—[untitled]—1905–10," Box 38, C14. Prostitutes themselves sometimes commented that they could not accept the paltry wages of other women's professions. A Manhattan police officer testified to the Immigration Commission that a prostitute told him, "I don't want to go into the dressmaking business and earn $8 or $9 a week when I can make that everyday on Broadway." "Appendix IV-B: Affidavits from Report of Commissioner of Police, New York," in Dillingham, *Importing Women for Immoral Purposes*, 45.

56. The Consumers' League of New York estimated that the average wage-earning woman in New York State made $6.54 per week. *Our Working Girls: How They Do It* (Consumers' League of New York, 1910), History of Women Collection, item 8608 (microfilm), Schlessinger Library, Radcliffe College, Cambridge, Mass. For other data on women's wages in this period, see Weiner, *From Working Girl to Working Mother*, 25. Similarly, the congressional investigation into the importation of women for immoral purposes estimated that prostitutes in the United States earned from two to four times as much in one day as a washerwoman could make in a week, and ten times as much as a woman could earn in most work in eastern Europe. Dillingham, *Importing Women for Immoral Purposes*, 9.

57. "General Correspondence—1908, July–December," Box 1, C14.

58. Kneeland, *Commercialized Prostitution*, 38–39.

59. Reel 106, Box 91, Wald Papers. The evidence for this practice is overwhelming in both the Wald Papers and the Committee of Fourteen Papers.

60. Case 3317, TTP. Also see Kneeland, *Commercialized Prostitution*, 38–39.

61. The German Hotel on Thirteenth Street paid for protection, and police warned the owners before every raid. The proprietor of the Gramercy, in contrast, refused to pay for protection and was "raided several times." Reel 106, Box 91, Wald Papers.

62. Kneeland, *Commercialized Prostitution*, 38–40.

63. Miner, *Slavery of Prostitution*, 10–12.

64. Reel 105, Box 91, Wald Papers.

65. The Committee of Fourteen had remarkably consistent personnel over the course of its tenure, including some investigators who worked for it for twenty or more years.

66. This conclusion is at odds with the work of Ruth Rosen, who argues that the destruction of the red-light districts in the vice crusades of the early twentieth century led to widespread pimping and more exploitation of prostitutes than under brothel prostitution. The difference may stem from the fact that this is a local study and Rosen's is a national one. As both Tim Gilfoyle and I have found, prostitution in New York City led, rather than followed, the country in both conditions in and organization of the trade and the strategies reformers used when they attempted to eradicate it. Rosen, *Lost Sisterhood*, 30–33.

67. Case 1743, TTP.

68. *People of the State of New York versus Alfred Daly*, Case 2145, TTP.

69. Snyder, "City in Transition," 48.

70. Here it is important to distinguish, as Gilfoyle does, between the class level of different brothels. Gilfoyle found that middle-class and elite brothels in the nineteenth century mimicked the architecture of middle-class homes, with tasteful parlors and shaded entryways. Men who patronized these establishments could sit and drink with the women before choosing a partner. Fifty-cent houses, on the other hand, usually had lines that extended out the door, down the street, and around the corner, often under the eye of the cop on the beat. These establishments limited men's access to women, and most of the

socializing went on between men. Gilfoyle, *City of Eros*, 164–65. A few very elite brothels probably continued through this period, though most of them reemerged in the 1920s. The extremely successful madam Polly Adler ran a high-price house in the late 1910s and early 1920s and describes similar arrangements in her autobiography, *A House Is Not a Home*. For other descriptions of the differences between high-class and low-class establishments, see Kneeland, *Commercialized Prostitution*, 3–23.

71. "IR—[untitled]—1915," Box 29, C14.

72. It is possible the gesture she used was not American Sign Language or even a recognizable regional or national slang. The record does not say. One woman's use of gesture that another did not know, but that the deaf and mute man understood, indicates knowledge of a more complicated version of sign language than most hearing and speaking people possess. It is likely that this man, if he was native-born, had had some education in American Sign Language, which was developed in the early nineteenth century with the beginning of state financed and administered institutions for educating deaf children. New York State established its first school for the deaf in New York City in 1817. For more on deaf education and American Sign Language, see Van Cleve, Vickrey, and Crouch, *Place of Their Own*, 45, 95–97, 107.

73. While the effects of the Raines Law hotels on the practices of prostitution are obvious, it is difficult to assess how long they held sway as institutions in their own right. The Committee of Fourteen argues in its published reports that it singlehandedly drove the Raines Law hotels out of business by 1912. However, the field reports by their investigators indicate that Raines Law hotels continued to dominate prostitution until the entry of the United States into World War I. In addition, Kneeland argued that most of the prostitution in the city in 1912, and in 1916 when he revisited the question, went on in Raines Law hotels. So while they may have declined in absolute numbers (the measure the Committee of Fourteen used in evaluating their successes), the hotels continued to be the most important location of prostitution. Kneeland, *Commercialized Prostitution*, 34–35, 52–58. The chief of police for New York City testified that the hotels ran openly in the city but that it was difficult to get evidence on them, and as a result, they stayed open. Ibid., 523–24.

74. New York Society for the Prevention of Cruelty to Children, *Thirty-Seventh Annual Report* (1911).

75. "Precinct 5—Batavia St.–Cherry St.," Box 4, C15.

76. Committee of Fourteen, *Annual Report, 1913* (New York: Douglas C. McMurtrie, 1914).

77. "IR—[untitled]—1905–10," Box 38, C14.

78. Ibid.

79. Worthington, "Women's Day Court," 405.

80. Snyder and Zurier suggest that this image depicted prostitutes, though apparently Sloan did not identify them specifically. Certainly, Sloan often portrayed prostitutes in his work, usually in a positive light. (See Figure 3.1). According to Zurier and Snyder, when the National Academy of Design exhibition rejected the work, a critic assumed the subjects were prostitutes and implied that the painting had been rejected on these grounds. As the critic commented with distaste, Sloan seemed drawn to these "characteristic bits of the underworld, and even the lower class of women in that world." Quoted in Snyder and Zurier, "Picturing the City," 177.

81. "Precinct 5—James St.–Water St.," Box 4, C15.

82. Committee of Fourteen, *Annual Report, 1914*, 18.

83. Ibid., 31. George Kneeland also commented on the diffusion of prostitution into tenements and the negative effects he felt this had on children growing up near them. See Kneeland, *Commercialized Prostitution*, 24–33.

84. *The People of the State of New York versus Elizabeth Merrill*, Case 90, TTP.

85. Gold, *Jews without Money*, 34–35. The New York Society for the Prevention of Cruelty to Children also complained about prostitution in the tenements, arguing that it had a negative influence of the moral development of children. See *Twenty-Sixth Annual Report* (1900), and *Twenty-Seventh Annual Report* (1901).

86. Gold, *Jews without Money*, 15.

87. *People of the State of New York versus John Kirkwood*, Case 1302, TTP.

88. "Precinct 5—James Slip," Box 4, C15. I have found many instances of young women soliciting from tenement-house windows. For example: "Two girls were looking out of the window on the 2d floor. I went upstairs, they would not let me in but they call men in." "Precinct 5—Batavia St.–Cherry St.," Box 4, C15. Interestingly, many nineteenth-century brothels placed women in windows to entice passersby. It was a relatively safe way for women to drum up trade, and it is not surprising that when prostitution diffused throughout the city, many prostitutes adopted this practice. In many ways, it made even more sense in this context. Women did not have to risk the streets. Soliciting from windows proved safer because women could assess the men who responded and decide whether or not to let them into the room. The physical divisions and barriers represented by the windows took the place of the cadets and bouncers that brothels employed.

89. Committee of Fourteen, *Annual Report, 1913*, 20.

90. "Precinct 11—104 Bowery–97 Elizabeth St.," Box 5, C15.

91. Gold, *Jews without Money*, 30–31.

92. Goldman, *Living My Life*, 104.

93. Bernstein, "Boarding-House Keepers," 140.

94. Case 90, TTP.

95. Robert W. de Forest, "New York Tenements Freed of Prostitution," *Charities and the Commons*, Aug. 29, 1903, 179.

96. Ten cents is a ridiculously low price; most prostitutes in this period, even those who catered to poor men, charged at least fifty cents. "Precinct 6—100 Mott–119 Mulberry," Box 4, C15. One woman provided an extreme example of the lengths some might go to make extra money. Living in a Henry Street "furnished room house," she met an investigator who reported that she "solicited me from the door to go up to her room telling me her husband would be out." Clearly a casual prostitute, this woman sold sex periodically to help with family finances. Just as obviously, she kept this profitable activity secret from her husband. "Precinct 7—19 Henry St.–19 Pike St.," Box 5, C15.

97. Inmate 2482 (American-born German Protestant), Box 13, Bedford.

98. Inmate 2502 (American-born white Protestant), Box 13, Bedford.

99. B. Smith, *Tree Grows in Brooklyn*, 171.

100. Gold, *Jews without Money*, 31.

101. For discussions of parents' concerns over their daughters' experimentation with sexuality, see Odem, *Delinquent Daughters*, 56–62, 138–39. Working-class families did pro-

test when prostitutes tried to involve their children in the practice. In one trial, a neighbor provided testimony about his wife's frustration about the women who prostituted outside of their building. He justified his testimony and his wife's repeated threats to "throw water over them" from her open window by explaining, "those very women stopped my son." In his view, the prostitutes crossed the line of neighborliness by attempting to entice his son. This would involve the son in prostitution directly and thus endanger him in a way that simply watching prostitutes bargain would not. Case 1302, TTP.

102. *People of the State of New York versus William White*, Case 1287, TTP.

103. *People of the State of New York versus Annie Brown*, Case 1651, TTP.

104. "IR—[untitled]—1905–10," Box 38, C14.

105. In another house, an investigator reported that the young women often split the money they made amongst themselves, but that "there is no other arrangement than rent with the landlord. This is an exorbitant rent for privileges." Ibid. In *People of the State of New York versus Elizabeth Merrill*, the landlady admitted renting rooms to girls with privileges because she made more money. Case 90, TTP.

106. "IR—1912," Box 28, C14.

107. As she commented practically, "Thousands of women receive men callers in New York—it's up to you." Ibid.

108. "IR—[untitled]—1905–10," Box 38, C14. Women in court cases often testified that they did not want their families to know about their activities. One woman refused to give her family's name, infuriating the prosecutor. In the face of his rage, she simply explained, "I don't want my people to know anything about this case." Case 1743, TTP.

109. Case 1302, TTP. When asked to elaborate, he obliged: "Well, she had on a red hat, with red trimmings, a long tan coat, black lapels, brown dress, princess gown."

110. *People of the State of New York versus Bruno Bretschneider*, Case 105, TTP.

111. *People of the State of New York versus James Connaughton*, Case 1412, TTP.

112. Case 105, TTP.

113. "IR—[untitled]—1905–10," Box 38, C14.

114. Women working in furnished rooms often banded together. In *People of the State of New York versus John Kirkwood*, the witness testified to a remarkable level of coordination and sociability among young women prostituting in the same rooming house. As he related to the court, the woman "heard a noise in the next room, and she whistled. . . . And the girl in the next room on one side whistled, in answer to this woman, and then a girl in the other room, on the other side, whistled, and the girl I was with asked the woman that last whistled, 'Are you alone?' And she said, 'No, I've got a John,' and she said, 'All right. I'll meet you on the corner, when you get through.'" Case 1302, TTP. In *People of the State of New York versus William White* (Case 1287, TTP), a client testified that the prostitute he was with had a conversation with the woman in the next room. "Is that you, Elizabeth," she allegedly said, "did you really get a man?" In another case, a prostitute testified that she and another woman solicited together often. Case 2145, TTP.

115. Inmate 2515 (American-born English Protestant), Box 13, Bedford. This woman admitted to being a "confirmed prostitute."

116. "Bklyn, Staten Island, Manhattan—Inv. Reports and Related Material, 1914–15," Box 29, C14.

117. "IR—Brooklyn-IR—Holograph—1913–14," Box 29, C14.

CHAPTER FOUR

1. A memo on the Interdepartmental Social Hygiene Board submitted to the Appropriations Committee of the House of Representatives, June 12, 1919, stated that the board "assisted in the closure of 124 red light districts," "helped care for 30,000 delinquent women and girls," and "assisted in the enforcement of laws and ordinances relating to venereal diseases in communities surrounding naval and military camps." "Prophylaxis Problems," Box 24, C14. Allan Brandt finds similar numbers. See Brandt, *No Magic Bullet*, 52–122.

2. Nancy Bristow argues that the reformers involved in the war effort used the war as an attempt to remake manhood in general, hoping that reformed soldiers would, in turn, teach their communities about citizenship. In the context of venereal disease, this meant instructing soldiers to refrain from intercourse outside of marriage. Military authorities did not hand out condoms, as they had during World War II, despite their widespread availability. Some camps also provided small-scale chemical prophylaxis for men returning from leave who admitted they had been with prostitutes. Bristow, *Making Men Moral*, 20–35.

3. See, for example, Boxes 24 and 25, C14.

4. For an analysis of the French system, see Corbin, *Women for Hire*. Brandt also discusses the French system and its impact on American troops in *No Magic Bullet*, 100–106.

5. The military also expressed concern over the level of homosexuality among the troops directly after the war. In the most obvious case, the navy conducted extensive investigations into homosexuality at the Naval Training Station in Newport, Rhode Island. Chauncey, "Christian Brotherhood or Sexual Perversion?"

6. Stone, *It's Sex O'clock*, 20.

7. Brandt, *No Magic Bullet*, 52–56.

8. Ibid., 52–61.

9. Despite obvious flaws in this logic, it remains a significant part of American responses to AIDS and prostitutes. Political cartoons from the 1980s identify prostitutes as the source of AIDS. See, for example, J. D. Crowe, "Death for Sale" (cartoon from the *San Diego Tribune*, 1987), reproduced in Gilman "Iconography of Disease," 106. Policy makers have also argued that prostitutes spread AIDS to the American family. For example, Judge Morton Perry of Dade County, Florida, stated that "these days a man who visits a prostitute can become a victim of AIDS, and not just him but his family, his wife, his lover, his unborn children." Madeleine Blais, "Lethal Weapon," *Miami Herald*, Aug. 16, 1987. When Salt Lake City considered a mandatory testing ordinance over the protests of the state Department of Health, a county official commented that a man would "go home to his wife, his wife gets pregnant and the infant gets infected. People die." "Tougher Penalties for HIV Positive Prostitutes Supported," *San Francisco Sentinel*, July 19, 1990.

10. Brandt, *No Magic Bullet*, 60–67.

11. Estimates for the number of men in the general population infected with venereal disease in this period are extremely high. In 1901, a New York County Medical Society survey of local doctors found that as many as 80 percent of men in New York City had been infected at some time with gonorrhea and another 5–18 percent had contracted syphilis. Brandt, *No Magic Bullet*, 12.

12. Ibid., 13, 53–60.

13. Sections from the Army Bill (H.R. 3545) approved by the president May 18, 1917, Document 19961, Box 39, Entry 393, RG 165, NA.

14. Brandt, *No Magic Bullet*, 98–99.

15. Major Bascom Johnson, Sanitary Corps, USNA, Director of Law Enforcement, War Department, Commission on Training Camp Activities, "Next Steps: A Program of Activities against Prostitution and Venereal Diseases for Communities Which Have Closed Their 'Red Light' Districts" (Washington, D.C.: Commission on Training Camp Activities, 1918), 1, Entry 376, Box 24, NM-84, RG 165, NA.

16. Ibid., 4.

17. Ibid., 5.

18. Attorney General of the United States, "Memorandum on the Legal Aspects of the Proposed System of Medical Examination of Women Convicted under Section 13, Selective Service Act," April 3, 1918, "Penal Information-408," Box 223, RG 90, NA.

19. Attorney General of the United States, "Circular Numbers 812 and 813," "Detention Homes—408.1," Box 223, RG 90, NA.

20. For an example of a woman who had been convicted of crimes other than prostitution being held indefinitely, see Inmate 3714 (American-born Russian Jew), Box 1, Bedford.

21. Surgeon General to all State Health Authorities, "Unnumbered Circular Letter," May 17, 1918, "Detention Homes—408.1," Box 223, RG 90, NA.

22. Surgeon General to United States Marshals, "Circular 855," July 10, 1918, RG 90, NA.

23. Surgeon General, "Unnumbered Circular Letter."

24. Ibid. See also Box 163, CSS Papers.

25. Raymond Fosdick to Major Snow, May 2, 1918, Document 26258, Entry 376, Box 54, NM-84, RG 165, NA.

26. Malzberg, "Venereal Disease among Prostitutes," 541.

27. Ibid., 544.

28. Frederick Whitin to Rev. Robert Bachman Jr., Aug. 23, 1918, "General Correspondence—1918-4," Box 4, C14.

29. American Social Hygiene Association, "Standards and Statistics of Prostitution, Gonorrhea, and Syphilis" (undated), Box 163, CSS Papers.

30. Ibid.

31. Ibid.

32. Frederick Whitin to Mrs. Robert Dickinson, Dec. 7, 1917, "General Correspondence—1917-4," Box 24, C14.

33. Office of the Surgeon General, "Confidential Report from the War Department," "Correspondence Relating to Special Subjects" (1918), Entry 399, Box 81, NM-84, RG 165, NA. Another report asserted that the "Venereal rate in Camp Dix is rising steadily now, on account of the influx of newly drafted men." "Report of Lieutenant Mark Wiseman, Sanitary Corp, April 22, 1918," "General Correspondence (Subject File)—1918-21," Document 25345, Entry 376, Box 51, NM-84, RG 165, NA.

34. The confluence between New York City and federal efforts is not surprising. Not only did New York lead the nation in attempts to control prostitution before the war but many officials who became important in the War Department began their work in New York City. I have already discussed Raymond Fosdick's background and importance in new efforts during the war; in turn, he brought many New York reformers with him. For

example, he appointed Maude Miner, director of the New York Protective and Probation Society, to head the Section on Women and Girls, an organization under the auspices of the CTCA. Katharine Bement Davis left her position at the Bedford Hills State Reformatory to head the CTCA's Committee on Women's Work.

35. "Response to Questionnaire from Mr. Joseph Mayer, American Social Hygiene Association, October 1918," Box 4, C14.

36. "Prophylaxis Problems," Box 24, C14. See also "Venereal Disease and Work of Social Hygiene Division, C.T.C.A.," Entry 376, NM-84, Box 24, RG 165, NA.

37. "Response to Questionnaire from Mayer."

38. "Re Conference at District Attorney's Office relative to the Return of the Fleet," "General Correspondence—1917-4," Box 4, C14.

39. Raymond Fosdick to Frederick Whitin, Nov. 1917, "General Correspondence—1917," Box 4, C14.

40. Committee of Fourteen, *Annual Report, 1917–1918*, 7.

41. Frederick Whitin to Clarence Schultz, Apr. 8, 1918, (untitled file), Box 24, C14.

42. Frederick Whitin to J. Frank Chase of the New England Watch and Ward Society, July 31, 1917, "General Correspondence—1917-7," Box 24, C14.

43. "People vs. Sylvester Swezey," Dec. 6, 1917," "IR—Military Training Camps—Camp Mills II," Box 25, C14.

44. City of New York, Law Department, Bureau for the Recovery of Penalties, Nov. 2, 1917, "General Correspondence—1917-6," Box 24, C14.

45. "Response to Questionnaire from Mayer."

46. "Report of the Committee on Law and Legislation," 12, "General Correspondence—1918-4," Box 4, C14.

47. Roby, "Politics and Prostitution," 144-45.

48. Frederick Whitin to Rev. Paul Smith of San Francisco, May 29, 1917, "General Correspondence—1917-4," Box 24, C14.

49. Seabury, *Supreme Court*, 80-100.

50. Whitin to Rev. Smith, May 29, 1917. New York City began fingerprinting women convicted of prostitution on Sept. 1, 1910. See also Waterman, *Prostitution and Its Repression*, 36-38.

51. Whitin to Rev. Smith, May 29, 1917.

52. For example, see Inmate 3739 (northern African American Protestant), Box 1, Bedford.

53. Frederick Whitin to J. Frank Chase of the New England Watch and Ward Society, July 31, 1917, "General Correspondence—1917-7," Box 24, C14.

54. Inmate 2504 (northern African American Protestant), Box 4, Bedford.

55. Roby, "Politics and Prostitution," 187-90.

56. Whitin to Rev. Smith, May 29, 1917.

57. "S.S. Act; Secs. 12 & 13," Box 24, C14.

58. Frederick Whitin to Raymond Fosdick, Nov. 15, 1917, "General Correspondence—1917-1," Box 4, C14.

59. Frederick Whitin to Mrs. J. R. Strachan, Dec. 26, 1917, "General Correspondence—1917-1," Box 4, C14.

60. "IR—Brooklyn," Box 25, C14.

61. "IR—[untitled]—1917," Box 32, C14. For other examples, see report dated Mar. 10, 1918, "IR—Military Training Camps—Local Camp Conditions III," Box 25, C14; and "Saw Soldiers Drunk in Grab's Saloon," *New York Times*, Dec. 29, 1917, 6.

62. "IR—[untitled]—1918," Box 32, C14.

63. "IR—Military Training Camps—Local Camp Conditions III," Box 25, C14.

64. "IR—Military Training Camps—[untitled]," Box 25, C14. For other examples, see Frederick Whitin to Captain T. N. Pfeiffer, June 5, 1918, (untitled file), Box 24, C14.

65. Harry Kahan to Frederick Whitin, May 22, 1917, "IR—Brooklyn," Box 25, C14.

66. "IR—Military Training Camps," Box 24, C14.

67. "Raid Open Dives Run for Soldiers," *New York Times*, Dec. 3, 1917, 22.

68. "Saw Soldiers Drunk in Grab's Saloon," *New York Times*, December 29, 1917, 6.

69. "Sues Marshal for $200,000," *New York Times*, Oct. 1, 1920, 11.

70. "IR—[untitled]—1917," Box 32, C14.

71. For examples of the relationship between pimps and prostitutes in the 1920s and the prevalence of these arrangements, see "IR—Theatre and Burlesque, 1918–20," Box 32, "IR—Misc. Street Conditions, Various Boroughs, 1919–20," Box 35, "IR—1919," Box 32, "IR—1920–22," Box 34, "IR—Restricted—1930," Box 34, "IR—1921," Box 34, "IR—HK, 1921–22," Box 38, and "Investigator's Field Reports on Prostitution, Notes," Box 26, C14.

72. "IR—[untitled]—1917," Box 32, C14.

73. "IR—[untitled]—1917," Box 31, C14.

74. "IR—Military Training Camps," Box 24, C14.

75. Document 32454, Entry 376, Box 75, NM-84, RG 165, NA.

76. "IR—Military Training Camps—[untitled]" (1917), Box 25, C14.

77. Ibid.

78. Jane Deeter Rippin, "Survey of 500 Case Records," RG 165, NA.

79. "Summary of 3,000 Case Records Compared by States," RG 165, NA.

80. "IR—[untitled]—1917," Box 31, C14.

81. "IR—Military Training Camps—[untitled]" (1917), Box 25, C14.

82. Frederick Whitin to Mrs. Robert Dickinson, May 28, 1917, "General Correspondence—1917-4," Box 24, C14.

83. Ibid.

84. "IR—Brooklyn Reports, 1917–18 by Street Name, G–W," Box 32, C14.

85. "IR—Military Training Camps—Local Camp Conditions III" (1918), Box 25, C14.

86. "Re Conference at District Attorney's Office relative to the Return of the Fleet," "General Correspondence—1917-4," Box 4, C14.

87. Snow, *Clinics for Venereal Diseases*, 8.

88. Inmate 2473 (American-born white Protestant), Box 13, Bedford.

89. Inmate 2478 (American-born white Protestant), Box 14, Bedford. Another inmate also reported learning about "the cure" from "other girls." Inmate 2474 (American-born Polish and German Protestant), Box 14, Bedford.

90. For examples of prostitutes getting angry when a john asked to wear a condom, see "IR—[untitled]" and "IR—Brooklyn Inv. Reports and Related Material, 1914–15," Box 29, C14.

91. "IR—[untitled]—1917," Box 31, C14.

92. Inmate 2478 (American-born white Protestant), Box 14, Bedford. Police also ar-

rested a young Jewish prostitute for "using perverted methods of sexual intercourse." Inmate 2495 (American-born Jew), Box 14, Bedford.

93. "IR—Brooklyn Reports, 1917–18 by Street Name, G–W," Box 32, C14.

94. "IR—1920," Box 33, C14. For examples of other women who expressed concern about venereal disease in the postwar period, see "IR—Restricted—1930," Box 35, "IR—Restricted—Manhattan, Named Streets and All Avenues, 1927–28," and "IR—Restricted—G–R," Box 36, C14. Furthermore, investigators and undercover police began to find that women had condoms in their possession. "IR—Restricted—1924" and "IR—Restricted—1927–30," Box 35, C14. One woman even assured a john that she "had a Wassermann test taken kid, and it was negative." "IR—Restricted—46–49th Streets," Box 36, C14.

95. Frederick Whitin to Arthur Towne, Superintendent of the Children's Society, Dec. 3, 1917, "General Correspondence—1917-2," Box 24, C14. The Committee of Fourteen usually passed on information it gathered about prostitutes and immoral women to the Society for the Prevention of Cruelty to Children (SPCC) for action when it thought children should be taken into custody. Although the wartime records for the Committee of Fourteen contain a number of letters to the SPCC about children and prostitutes, the annual reports for the SPCC do not specifically mention cases like this and instead focus on several sensational compulsory prostitution cases involving children. It is impossible to know, therefore, if more children were removed during the war, as the committee records imply. It is possible that the SPCC simply did not use these cases in their annual reports, as they had far more interesting developments to relate.

96. "General Correspondence, 1918-1," Box 4, C14.

CHAPTER FIVE

1. "Report of the Women's Protective Officers Employed by the Mayor's Committee of Women and National Defense," "General Correspondence—1917-6," Box 24, C14.

2. "Re Conference at District Attorney's Office relative to the Return of the Fleet," "General Correspondence—1917-4," Box 4, C14.

3. "General Correspondence—1917," Box 4, C14.

4. "General Correspondence—1917-6," Box 24, C14.

5. For example, see "IR—[untitled]—1918," Box 32, and "General Correspondence—1917-3," Box 24, C14. For examples from Bedford reformatory, see Inmates 2492 (American-born white Protestant) and 2516 (American-born Russian Jew), Box 14, Bedford.

6. Inmate 2505 (southern African American Protestant), Box 13, Bedford.

7. Inmates 2484 (white Protestant), 2482 (American-born German Protestant), and 2480 (southern African American Protestant), Box 14, Bedford.

8. "IR—Military Training Camps—[untitled]" (1917), Box 25, C14. For similar evidence on the national level, see "Summary of 3000 Case Records Compared by State," RG 165, NA.

9. "Report on the Grand Central Palace," May 14, 1918, "General Correspondence, 1918-3," Box 4, C14.

10. New York also reported the youngest average. At 19.6, Massachusetts had the next lowest average age. All of the other states (Illinois, Kentucky, Ohio, Pennsylvania, South Carolina, and Texas) all reported averages in the early twenties. "Summary of 3000 Case Records Compared by State," RG 165, NA.

11. "IR—Military Training Camps—[untitled]," Box 25, C14. For other instances of the

drop in age for treating girls, see "General Correspondence—1917-6," Box 24, "General Correspondence—1918-1," Box 4, "IR—Brooklyn" and "IR—Military Training Camps—[untitled]," Box 25, and "General Correspondence, 1918-3," Box 4, C14.

12. Inmate 2516 (American-born Russian Jew), Box 14, Bedford.

13. Report of Jan. 8, 1918, "Secretary—Minutes, 1916–19," Box 84, C14. See also "Dance Halls," Box 83, C14.

14. "General Correspondence—1917-4," Box 24, C14. This file also contains other examples.

15. "IR—Military Training Camps—So Jersey Towns" (1917), Box 24, C14.

16. Report of Jan. 8, 1918, "Secretary—Minutes, 1916–19," Box 84, C14.

17. "IR—Military Training Camps—[untitled]" (1917), Box 25, C14. For other examples see "IR—Military Training Camps—Camp Mills II," "IR—Military Training Camps—Camp Mills," and "IR—Brooklyn," Box 25, C14.

18. Inmate 2499 (American-born white Protestant), Box 14, Bedford. See also Inmate 2483 (American-born white Protestant), Box 14, Bedford.

19. Girls were reported to have had sex in bathrooms ("IR—1913, June–July," Box 28), hallways ("IR—1913–14," Box 28), bushes ("IR—Brooklyn, Inv. Reports and Related Info" (1910), Box 29, and "IR—[untitled]—1917," Box 31), on the beach at Coney Island ("IR—Brooklyn/Queens-Investigators Reports 1914," Box 29, and "IR—[untitled]—1917," Box 31), and in one case, a girl's parlor when her parents were out for the evening ("IR—Brooklyn/Queens-Investigators Reports 1914," Box 29, C14).

20. Miner identified this sentiment as patriotism, commenting that American girls had "that same feeling as the girls in England, that they are giving themselves to the soldiers from motives of patriotism." "Secretary—Minutes, 1916–19."

21. Quoted in R. Alexander, *Girl Problem,* 12.

22. "IR—Military Training Camps—Camp Mills I" (1917), Box 25, C14.

23. In his article on pin-up posters and liberalism, "'I Want a Girl,'" Robert Westbrook argues that liberal democracies, which cannot ideologically (under the basic tenets of liberalism) compel their soldiers to give their lives for the state, have to rely on private issues to motivate soldiers. Pin-up posters, which offices of the federal government often distributed to the troops, implied that young men sacrificed not for abstract concepts like "democracy" or their duty to the state but instead for the women at home. The U.S. government encouraged men to feel that they fought to protect their mothers, daughters, sisters, and most especially wives, girlfriends, and fiancées. He argues that women were often seen to have a reciprocal duty to be worthy of such defense and provides fascinating examples of how individual women sent "pin-up" posters to their soldiers, therefore replacing the images of Betty Grable and Rita Hayworth with their own. My argument about soldiers, sailors, and treating girls reflects a similar negotiation over the meaning of women's patriotism and its intimate connection to their sexuality.

24. "Report of the Women's Protective Officers Employed by the Mayor's Committee of Women and National Defense," "General Correspondence—1917-6," Box 24, C14.

25. "IR—Military Training Camps—[untitled]" (1917), Box 25, C14.

26. Demuth was an American avant-garde painter. He was gay, but not openly so, and many of his paintings of sailors and other working-class men have both hidden and overt references to homosexuality and homosexual desire. Weinberg, *Speaking for Vice,* 43–113.

27. Ibid., 99–100.

28. For example, see Sanday, *Fraternity Gang Rape*; and Bederman, *Manliness and Civilization*.

29. For examples of rape during the war, see Inmates 2516 (American-born Russian Jew), Box 14, and 2508 (American-born Dutch Protestant), Box 6, Bedford. Investigators for the Committee of Fourteen also heard from local men that soldiers had raped young women. See "IR—Brooklyn" (1917), Box 25, C14.

30. "Report by Investigator JAS," June 6, 1917, "IR—Brooklyn," Box 25, C14. For other examples, see "General Correspondence, 1918-3," Box 4, C14.

31. "IR—Military Training Camps—[untitled]" (1917), Box 25, C14.

32. "IR—Military Training Camps—Camp Mills II" (1918), Box 25, C14. For other incidents of rape and statutory rape, see "General Correspondence—1917-4," and "General Correspondence—1917-1," Box 24, C14. See also Inmate 2516 (American-born Russian Jew), Box 14, Bedford.

33. Inmate 2516.

34. "IR—Brooklyn," Box 25, C14.

35. Ibid.

36. It is unclear what the meaning of homosexual relations would have been for sailors at this time. As George Chauncey has argued, in working-class culture in this period, men who took the active role in sex with other men would not be stigmatized nor would it imply anything about their sexual identity. But the investigator certainly found this activity worthy of note. Chauncey, *Gay New York*, 64–68.

37. "IR—Brooklyn," Box 25, C14.

38. Inmate 2482 (American-born German Protestant), Box 14, Bedford.

39. As one of the civilian agencies allied with the reformers in the CTCA, the YMCA produced a significant proportion of the propaganda used in the camps. It distributed posters and pamphlets, gave lectures and slide shows, and organized diversionary entertainment. Brandt, *No Magic Bullet*, 60–61.

40. In *Making Men Moral*, Nancy Bristow pursues a similar analysis of these posters. She argues that the CTCA saw the war as an opportunity to remake soldiers into reformers who would take their new morality to the rest of the country in the years following the war. Their vision of masculinity involved self-control, a powerful but athletic virility, and a single sexual double standard for both men and women. Bristow, *Making Men Moral*, 20, 29.

41. Frederick Whitin to Mrs. Robert Dickinson, Dec. 7, 1917, "General Correspondence—1917-4," Box 24, C14.

42. None of the Committee of Fourteen investigative reports found African American women in the camps socializing with military personnel, either African American or white. However, several investigations into clubs and bars near the camps reported African American women socializing with military men or working as waitresses. For example, see "IR—Military Training Camps—Camp Mills II" and "IR—Brooklyn," Box 25, and "General Correspondence, 1918," Box 4, C14.

43. Bristow, *Making Men Moral*, 139, 159, 163.

44. K. Davis, "Social Hygiene and the War II," 532–33.

45. Rippin, "Social Hygiene and the War," 126.

46. K. Davis, "Social Hygiene and the War II," 532.

47. Rippin, "Social Hygiene and the War," 126.

48. K. Davis, "Social Hygiene and the War II," 552.

49. I watched *The End of the Road* in the Audio-Visual Library of the National Archives in College Park, Maryland.

50. The Section on Women's Work made *End of the Road* to show to audiences of young girls. It proved so popular, however, that by the end of the war, the CTCA began to show it to soldiers. Federal officials felt that soldiers watching the film would have sympathy for the girls, would be likely to see them as sisters and fiancées, and thus would think twice about taking advantage of the girls around the camps. As Davis reported, "much to the surprise of everyone, it has made a very deep impression" on the troops. "Social Hygiene Division—Army and Navy Section," report dated June 4, 1918, "Correspondence Relating to Special Subjects, 1917–19," Box 81, NM-84, Entry 399, RG 165, NA.

51. Frederick Whitin to Mrs. Robert Dickinson, Oct. 4, 1917, "General Correspondence—1917-4," Box 24, C14.

52. Bristow noted a similar trend, arguing that by the end of the war, workers used criteria like dancing style rather than any actual evidence of sexual activity to assess the morality of the girls in question. Bristow, *Making Men Moral*, 130. She also argues that officials began the war intending to differentiate between prostitutes and charity girls, but that as the war progressed, they increasingly turned from "preventive work" and friendly dissuasion to repression of all women perceived to be "immoral." I do not disagree with this assessment but feel that, for New York, such a system already existed. For example, Bristow points out that part of this campaign against nonprostitutes involved building reformatories to house women who had gone astray. New York, however, had developed this analysis of sexuality and method of state punishment by the late 1880s. In 1886, New York City amended its laws to allow for the incarceration of a girl as young as twelve who "is willfully disobedient to parent or guardian and is in danger of becoming morally depraved." R. Alexander, *"Girl Problem,"* 50. By 1901, Bedford reformatory took such girls and tried to reform them. As with prostitution, New York's understanding of charity girls and wayward minors served as a model for the War Department. It is no coincidence that the most important women in the War Department's Section on Women and Girls, Katharine Bement Davis and Maude Miner, pioneered reform efforts in New York long before they signed onto the war effort. Davis served as the first superintendent of Bedford reformatory until she left it in 1914 to take a job as New York City's commissioner for corrections. Miner worked as a probation officer in the Women's Courts in the early years of the century and ran the Prevention and Protection Society.

53. "IR—Military Training Camps—[untitled]" (1917), Box 25, C14.

54. "Report of the Women's Protective Officers Employed by the Mayor's Committee of Women and National Defense," "General Correspondence—1917-6," Box 24, C14.

55. "IR—Military Training Camps—[untitled]" (1918), Box 24, C14.

56. "IR—Military Training Camps—Camp Mills II" (1918), Box 25, C14.

57. Report by Mrs. S. C. Douglass and Mrs. J. Cook, Sept. 22, 1917, "IR—Military Training Camps—[untitled]," Box 25, C14.

58. Adler, *House Is Not a Home*, 22.

59. For another example of an accelerated courtship, see Series I, Tape 34, Frieda Kahn, NYCILHP.

60. For an example of a woman who received part of her husband's pay, see Inmate 2504 (northern African American Protestant), Box 4, Bedford.

61. Several women later incarcerated at Bedford also seem to have been motivated by the military's dependent allowance. For example, see Inmate 2507 (northern African American Protestant), Box 14, Bedford.

62. "IR—Military Training Camps—[untitled]" (1917), Box 25, C14.

63. Jane Deeter Rippin, "Survey of 500 Case Records," RG 165, NA.

64. "IR—Military Training Camps—Camp Mills II" (1918), Box 25, C14.

65. Balmford, "Runaway Girls," 26.

66. "Re Conference at District Attorney's Office Relative to the Return of the Fleet," "General Correspondence—1917-4," Box 4, C14.

67. Frederick Whitin to Raymond Fosdick, June 13, 1917, "IR—Brooklyn," Box 25, C14.

68. "IR—Military Training Camps—[untitled]" (1917), Box 25, C14.

69. "Report on New Rochelle," June 17, 1917, "General Correspondence—1917," Box 4, C14.

70. "Report on Van Cortlandt Park by JAS," Sept. 20, 1917, "IR—Military Training Camps —[untitled]," Box 25, C14.

71. Report of Jan. 8, 1918, "Secretary—Minutes, 1916–19," Box 84, C14.

72. True, *Neglected Girl*, 69.

73. Ibid., 92.

74. Inmate 2473 (American-born white Protestant), Box 13, Bedford.

75. Interview 15007, Coser Data Set. See also Interview 15088.

CHAPTER SIX

1. Maria Ward Lambin noted in her report on dance halls in New York City that "as soon as dancing and liquor selling were separated, which occurred between 1910 and 1920 in various cities, it became apparent that dancing alone could make a lucrative amusement." Lambin, *Report of the Advisory Dance Hall Committee*, 16.

2. See Delacoste and Alexander, *Sex Work*.

3. Lorenz Hart and Richard Rodgers, "Ten Cents a Dance" (from the musical *Simple Simon*, 1930), in Esposito, *All Time Favorite Rodgers and Hart Classics*, 102–5.

4. The one exception to this was hostessing. Clubs in Harlem often used black hostesses to sit with white patrons.

5. Cressey, *Taxi-Dance Hall*, 3. See also Lambin, *Report of the Advisory Dance Hall Committee*, 31.

6. Cressey, *Taxi-Dance Hall*, 3.

7. Lambin, *Report of the Advisory Dance Hall Committee*, 3. See also "Women Launch a Crusade for Better Dance Halls," *New York Times*, Mar. 16, 1924, XX9.

8. In her report, Lambin distinguished between "dance palaces" that "solicit general patronage" and what she called closed halls, "which cater to male patrons only." Lambin, *Report of the Advisory Dance Hall Committee*, 1.

9. "Dance Craze Stays but Amateurs Rule," *New York Times*, Nov. 13, 1913, 20.

10. Quoted in Lambin, *Report of the Advisory Dance Hall Committee*, 30.

11. Ibid., 33.

12. According to Lambin, 60 percent of the dance palace patrons were men. Ibid., 2. An

article in the *Journal of Social Hygiene* argued that "the indecent dancing permitted and encouraged by the operators of these resorts has netted many of them large fortunes." See "News and Abstracts," 419.

13. Virginia Maynard, "I Was a New York Gun-Girl," *Sunday Mirror Magazine*, July 24, 1938, 6.

14. Lambin, *Report of the Advisory Dance Hall Committee*, 9. See also J. Kennedy, "Devil's Dance Dens," 12. Virginia Murray of the New York Traveler's Aid Society also noted the "lucrative compensation offered." Murray, "Relation of Prostitution to Economic Conditions," 318.

15. Lambin, *Report of the Advisory Dance Hall Committee*, 28.

16. Ibid., 29.

17. Ben Gould, "Dancing By," *Broadway Brevities*, Nov. 21, 1932, 6. Although members of Harlem's black middle class periodically expressed concern about the moral effects of dance halls in general, there were not enough of them for the community to see them as a serious problem. Fred Moore, editor of New York's largest black paper, the *New York Age*, organized a protest against the granting of a dance hall license in one neighborhood but took care to explain that "the growing evil of the Negro community was 'rent parties.'" "Negroes Support Dance Hall Policy," *New York Times*, June 21, 1926, 5. Rent parties were an African American urban tradition in the 1920s and 1930s. In an attempt to raise enough cash to pay the rent, hostesses would charge a small cover fee and provide a lavish spread, often of home-cooked southern food, and live music. The parties went on into the night and sometimes featured famous jazz and blues musicians. For example, see Terkel, *Hard Times*, 435–56.

18. In an interview with the *New York Times*, Lambin stated that the closed halls clustered "along Second and Third Avenues, from Fourteenth Street to Eighty-Sixth." "Women Launch a Crusade for Better Dance Halls," *New York Times*, Mar. 16, 1924, XX9.

19. "IR—Restricted—Dance Halls, 1927–30," Box 37, C14.

20. Lambin, *Report of the Advisory Dance Hall Committee*, 21.

21. J. Kennedy, "Devil's Dance Dens," 12.

22. Ibid.

23. Murray, "Relation of Prostitution to Economic Conditions," 318.

24. Kevin Mumford argues that taxi dancers and other "hostesses" were prostitutes and that as white women they benefited from the shelter of the dance halls in pursuing their trade. I found little evidence that taxi dancers prostituted. In fact, most taxi dance exchanges, even into the 1960s, revolved more around a highly commercial form of treating. However, I agree with the spirit of Mumford's analysis that work in these halls excluded black women, driving them into prostitution. In fact, my argument suggests that the prospects for black women in the sex trade were even dimmer, because exclusions from legal sex work carried far higher burdens than simple exclusion from sheltered prostitution, which, after all, was still illegal. Sex work, because it is legal, and because it does not usually involve intercourse, is far safer than any form of prostitution. Mumford, *Interzones*, 96–98.

25. Lambin, *Report of the Advisory Dance Hall Committee*, 22.

26. Quoted in Kennedy, "Devil's Dance Dens," 51.

27. Lambin, *Report of the Advisory Dance Hall Committee*, 17.

28. "Find Dance Halls Here 20% Immoral," *New York Times*, Mar. 1, 1924, 1.

29. "Taxi Dancing Girls Slaves of Lust, Must Choose Insults or Poverty," *Evening Graphic*, undated clipping in "IR—Restricted—Dance Halls" (1930), Box 37, C14.

30. "IR—Restricted—1931," Box 35, C14.

31. "IR—Restricted—Dance Halls, 1927–30," Box 37, C14.

32. Cressey, *Taxi-Dance Hall*, 42–43.

33. Report dated Nov. 29, 1919, "IR—Restricted—Dance Halls," Box 37, C14.

34. "Public Dance Halls," *New York Times*, June 22, 1926, 22. The Committee of Fourteen also commented on the difficulty in prosecuting dance halls for immorality, stating that "several raids were made by the police on some of the worst dance halls, but in each case the defendants were discharged by the magistrates on the grounds of insufficient evidence. It seems almost impossible to handle the problem through court action." Committee of Fourteen, *Annual Report, 1927–1928*, 26–27.

35. "Court Frees Girls Arrested in Raid," *New York Times*, Aug. 13, 1923, 15.

36. "30 Dance Hall Girls Freed," *New York Times*, Aug. 26, 1927, 15.

37. "IR—Restricted—Dance Halls, 1927–30," Box 37, C14.

38. Client BQ (American-born Italian Catholic), Box 74, WPA. As part of my agreement for use of these files, I assigned letter codes to identify the files. Where necessary I have changed their names to ethnically appropriate pseudonyms. Following her marriage, Marziano ran away to New York, where she stayed with several men. Her caseworker did not believe that she had prostituted.

39. "IR—Restricted—Dance Halls," Box 37, C14.

40. "IR—Restricted—Dance Halls, 1927–30," Box 37, C14.

41. Leo Rosten in his memoir described intensive competition between dancers for patrons. See Rosten, *People I Have Loved, Known or Admired*, 288–89.

42. "IR—Restricted—1930," Box 35, C14.

43. Ibid. Other young women talked dirty while dancing. One young woman told an investigator that she "want[ed] to feel how big yours is, and when you get a stiff one you could go to the toilet and jerk it off." Ibid.

44. Ibid.

45. Ibid. Middle-class reformers and researchers argued that managers required this sort of dancing. Virginia Murray wrote in an article for the *Journal of Social Hygiene* that two young women got fired from a taxi dance hall when "at the end of the first night the manager told them they 'didn't dance right,' which meant they didn't dance indecently enough, and not to return." Murray, "Relation of Prostitution to Economic Conditions," 317.

46. Lambin, *Report of the Advisory Dance Hall Committee*, 28.

47. For files that contain price information, see "IR—Inv. Reports—Misc. Street Conditions, Various Boroughs, 1919–20," Box 32, "IR—1921," Box 34, "IR—Restricted—1930," "IR—Restricted—1924," "IR—Restricted—1927–29," "IR—Restricted—1927–30," and "IR—Restricted—Misc., 1927–29," Box 35, "IR—Restricted—First Street," "IR—Restricted—46–49th Streets," "IR—Restricted—56–72 Sts.," "IR—Restricted—86–116 St.," "IR—Restricted—G–R," "IR—Restricted—Sa–Su," and "IR—Restricted—135–207 St.," Box 36, "IR—Restricted—117–134 St.," "IR—Restricted—Queens, Bklyn, Staten Is, 1927–29," and "IR—Restricted—Manhattan & Bronx—Street Conditions, 1927–29," Box 37, C14.

48. "Policewomen Find Dance Halls Quiet," *New York Times*, Jan. 28, 1930, 19. For other examples of women supporting out-of-work husbands, see Dan Davis, "Swinging Wide," *Broadway Brevities*, Nov. 21, 1932, 10.

49. "Public Dance Halls," *New York Times*, June 22, 1926, 22. A 1935 case in which a manager took a payoff to allow a dancer to leave with a client showed just how difficult prosecuting these cases could be. Although the jury found Moe Weingart guilty, city officials from the criminal courts admitted that his was "the first conviction of the kind in the city since the enactment of the law in 1910." "Employer Guilty in Taxi-Dance Case," *New York Times*, Oct. 6, 1934, 32.

50. Murray, "Relation of Prostitution to Economic Conditions," 318.

51. "Dance Hall Rules Backed by Owners," *New York Times*, Sept. 6, 1934, 21. According to one newspaper report, "the police received thousands of complaints" every year. "Employer Guilty in Taxi-Dance Case," 32. *Broadway Brevities* noted the trend in 1932, announcing that "Bway's newest treat is a Penny-a-Dance joint . . . boy! but you women are getting cheap." P. J. D., "On the Bandwagon," *Broadway Brevities*, Feb. 15, 1932, 6.

52. "Employer Guilty in Taxi-Dance Case," 32.

53. Priscilla Alexander, "Sex Work Still a Difficult Issue for Feminists," in Delacoste and Alexander, *Sex Work*, 184–230.

54. "New Police Curb Put on Cabarets," *New York Times*, Dec. 21, 1931, 18. These rules also stated that "Persons with criminal records, gangsters, racketeers, prostitutes, and the like, shall not be permitted to make a rendezvous or remain on the premises."

55. "Striking Hostesses Picket Dance Hall," *New York Times*, Dec. 14, 1934, 28.

56. For example, I found the forms of a medical inspection performed on a woman committed to Bedford reformatory in 1924. Her medical commitment read, "having been found as a result of such examination to be suffering from and infected with an infectious venereal disease, and the accommodations, facilities, and requirements of Regulation 5 of the Rules and Regulations Governing the Examination, Treatment and Isolation of Persons Affected with Venereal Disease, adopted by the Board of Health, July 23, 1918, in accordance with the provisions of Chapter 264, laws of 1918, not being provided at the home of said person, you are hereby authorized to remove said —— to —— hospital." Inmate 3722 (West Indian Protestant), Box 1, Bedford.

57. Seabury also found evidence that police routinely perjured themselves. Seabury, *Supreme Court*, 20–24, 80–100. Although the Seabury Investigation took place in 1930 and 1931, the events occurred in the 1920s, and the corruption that it uncovered had been widespread for years. Evidence from the investigative reports of the Committee of Fourteen indicated police corruption and malfeasance as early as 1919. For example, see "IR—1919," Box 34, C14. Bedford reformatory inmate case files also indicate that women may have been framed by police as early as 1923. See Inmates 3355 (American-born Russian Jew), Box 4, 3699 (southern African American Protestant), Box 14, 3507 (northern African American Catholic), Box 6, and 3377 (West Indian Protestant), Box 8, Bedford.

58. Seabury, *Supreme Court*, 20–24, 80–100.

59. "More Women Tell of Vice Case Fees," *New York Times*, July 16, 1931, 2.

60. Even though the rules and regulations of the police department forbade the use of stool pigeons, officers often used paid informants. Roby, "Politics and Prostitution," 188.

61. Ibid., 185–201.

62. Inmate 4048 (American-born Irish Catholic), Box 2, Bedford.

63. "Roosevelt Pardons Six Women 'Framed' by the Police Vice Ring," *New York Times*, Dec. 23, 1930, 1.

64. Adler, *House Is Not a Home*, 176. Adler most resented the police who would patronize her place, enjoy both drinks and women for free, and then raid it later in the evening. As she wrote, "Accepting my money, enjoying my hospitality and then paying me off with a phony raid! But I wasn't a squealer and I just had to take it." Ibid., 150.

65. Gilfoyle, *City of Eros*, 92–95.

66. There was little check on this power, as police had not had to obtain warrants to investigate prostitution-related offenses since 1913. Waterman, *Prostitution and Its Repression*, 57.

67. "IR—HK, 1921–22," Box 38, C14. For another example, see "IR—1922," Box 34, C14. Seabury also reported police breaking down doors to gain entry to prostitutes' apartments in *Supreme Court*, 91. In her autobiography, Polly Adler describes police violence as endemic. See Adler, *House Is Not a Home*, 143–53.

68. Both women were denied medical attention while they were in jail. When they came out, the doctor who treated them reported "contusions below the left eye—on the right and left arms and upper sternum—'marks above the right breast, which resembled teeth marks'—contusions on both breasts—the abdomen and upper thighs, on both inside and outside surfaces, and tenderness over the ribs in front, so that it hurt her to breathe." Seabury, *Supreme Court*, 87–88.

69. "IR—Coney Is & Queens—Inv. Rept., 1918–19," Box 32, C14.

70. "IR—1920," Box 34, C14.

71. "Vice in the City 'Brazen,' Worst in 15 Years, Reform Group Finds," *New York Times*, July 20, 1930. 1. See also Committee of Fourteen, *Annual Report, 1929–1930*.

72. Adler, *House Is Not a Home*, 198–99.

73. Client KJ (American-born Italian Catholic), Box 100, WPA. For other examples of alleged police corruption in the Women's Prison Association Files, see Clients KQ (Austrian Catholic), Box 100, T (white Protestant), Box 66, KF (southern African American Protestant), Box 99, KV (American-born Irish Catholic), Box 102, AY (American-born Russian Jew) and BB (white Protestant), Box 72, J (American-born Russian German Catholic), Box 63, ET (southern African American Irish Protestant), Box 88, JE (American-born Italian Catholic), Box 98, FN (southern African American Protestant), Box 90, and KA (Cuban Catholic), Box 99, WPA.

74. Marguerite Marsh reported that judges routinely took police testimony with no corroborating evidence in the women's court in 1939–40. Marsh, *Prostitutes in New York City*, 37–38.

75. Carl Warren, "Bondsmen Prey on Girls in Vice Cases," *New York Daily News*, Nov. 8, 1934.

76. Client FN (southern African American Protestant), Box 90, WPA. Other women indicate that police had begun to take bribes again. One southern African American woman told her social worker that "she had to pay the cop on the beat and the detective who made raids money every so often." Client ET (southern African American Irish Protestant), Box 88, WPA.

77. For examples, see Gretta Palmer, "Women's Day Court Would Aid Offenders," *New York World Telegram*, May 12, 1934; and "Social Plan Urged to End Vice Racket," *New York Times*, June 17, 1936, 48.

78. "Social Plan Urged to End Vice Racket," 48. In this period, police routinely either let customers go or required that they testify against prostitutes. In 1934, the *New York Evening Post* warned its male readers that "The law can't touch a man for buying a woman's favor, but it can send him to jail if he doesn't testify against her." "Don't Give Your Right Name!" *New York Evening Post*, Apr. 23, 1934.

79. For example, several women's clubs in the early 1920s backed legislation that would punish customers as well as prostitutes. See "Secretary—Minutes (Steno. Notes, 1925–28)," Apr. 8, 1925, Box 84, C14.

80. See Boxes 63–64, 66, 68–69, 73–76, 82, 88–90, 92–96, 99–100, and 103, WPA; "Girl Names Luciano Aides in Bid for Freedom," *New York Evening Journal*, May 15, 1936; "Back of Luciano Empire," *New York Post*, May 26, 1936; "Girls of 14, 15, Seized in Vice Raid on Hotel," *New York Daily News*, Mar. 10, 1937; and Gretta Palmer, "Women's Day Court Would Aid Offenders," *New York World Telegram*, May 12, 1934.

81. "Valentine Backs Tapping of Wires," *New York Times*, July 22, 1936, 11.

82. "Federal Agents Arrest 125 in 16 Vice Raids," *New York Herald Tribune*, Aug. 30, 1937. See also "Hoover Upholds G-Men's War on Vice throughout the Nation," *New York Daily News*, Sept. 25, 1937.

83. For example, see "IR—HK, 1921–22," Box 38, "IR—Restricted—1927–29," Box 35, and "IR—Restricted—Manhattan, Named Streets and All Avenues, 1927–28," Box 36, C14. See also Mark O'Polo, "Chink Gals Hustle; Oriental Pleasure Parlors Hide Shebas Who Offer Exotic Diversion at a Price; Opium, Marijuana and Strange Rituals Add to Orgies in Country's Chinatown," *Broadway Brevities*, May 23, 1932, 12. In this article, the author commented with surprise that the Chinese brothels did not require a card at entry.

84. "IR—[untitled]—1918," Box 32, C14.

85. In their reports, many investigators used the terms "brothel" and "call flats" interchangeably. Ruth Rosen noted this shift in *Lost Sisterhood*. She took the introduction of the term "call flat" to indicate a new system, considerably different from the elaborate red-light district brothels that existed at the turn of the century. Because many cities had clearly identified red-light districts where police and city officials tolerated segregated prostitution, Rosen's assumption is probably correct when viewed on the national level. However, since New York's brothels had been located throughout the entertainment districts of the city in the nineteenth and early twentieth centuries and were never segregated into a single identifiable district, the scattering of call flats throughout the city in the 1920s does not indicate a radical change in the organization of prostitution. Rosen, *Lost Sisterhood*, 69–85.

86. "IR—Restricted—1930," Box 35, C14.

87. For example, of the thirteen cases where an investigator provided evidence on the number of women working in a call flat, five had one or two prostitutes working there, four had three, three had either four or five, and one had six. Large-scale prostitution had simply become too dangerous for most women, prostitute or madam, to contemplate. For examples, see "IR—[untitled]—1905–10 Mostly," Box 38, C14. For the scale of nineteenth-century brothels, see Gilfoyle, *City of Eros*, 161–78, 197–243.

88. Adler, *House Is Not a Home*, 55.

89. "IR—Restricted—Edgecomb Ave–Fulton," Box 36, C14.

90. Adler, *House Is Not a Home*, 65.

91. The manager of Joe's Romanian Garden explained the benefits of his alliance with Lucille Rodgers to an investigator for the Committee of Fourteen on June 27, 1927. "She is very popular among the east-siders and has a large following," the investigator wrote in his report. "All her acquaintances patronize this place on account of her and that helps him a great deal in his business." When the investigator asked Joe if she could get him a girl, he replied that "she is the boss in that respect, and I am not responsible for what she does." "IR—Restricted—Edgecomb Ave–Fulton," Box 36, C14. For another example, see John Wallace, "Women Battle to Knockout in Night Club," *New York Daily News*, Nov. 1, 1926.

92. "IR—Restricted—1930," Box 35, C14. For other examples, see "IR—Restricted—1927–30," Box 35, C14; and Adler, *House Is Not a Home*, 60.

93. Prostitutes with pimps who worked in brothels were far more common in the 1930s than in the 1920s. For examples, see Clients BE (southern African American Protestant), Box 74, FU (American-born French Catholic), Box 90, and X (northern African American Protestant), Box 67, WPA.

94. Adler, *House Is Not a Home*, 138.

95. Wallace, "Women Battle to Knockout."

96. Inmate 2760 (southern African American Protestant), Box 9, Bedford.

97. Inmate 3336 (American-born white Protestant), Box 9, Bedford.

98. "IR—1921," Box 34, C14.

99. Client X (northern African American Protestant), Box 67, WPA. See also Adler, *House Is Not a Home*, 259–75.

100. Inmate 3759 (Russian Jew), Box 1, Bedford.

101. Inmate 4490 (American-born Russian Jew), Box 2, Bedford. For another example of a woman who fell in love with a man who later introduced her to prostitution, see Inmate 3350 (American-born white Catholic), Box 8, Bedford.

102. Inmate 4109 (American-born Hungarian Catholic), Box 9, Bedford.

103. "IR—1922," Box 34, C14. For other examples, see Inmates 4041 (American-born Irish Catholic) and 4490 (American-born Russian Jew), Box 2, and 3350 (American-born white Catholic), Box 8, Bedford. For similar evidence in the Women's Prison Association files, see Clients BM (American-born Irish Catholic), Box 74, FU (American-born French Catholic), Box 90, X (northern African American Protestant), Box 67, and JI (southern African American Protestant), Box 98, WPA.

104. The earliest reference I found to an African American woman working as a madam came in a case file from Bedford. The social worker reported that the current inmate's mother, a southern African American woman, had managed "a disorderly house" during the war. Inmate 3739 (southern African American Protestant), Box 1, Bedford.

105. The Women's Prison Association noted several cases of black women who worked in brothels managed by other black women. Located almost entirely in Harlem, some of these establishments catered solely to blacks, and some catered to an interracial trade. See Clients EF (southern African American Catholic), Box 85, FC (northern African American Protestant), Box 89, P (northern African American Protestant), Box 66, and KG (southern African American Protestant), Box 100, WPA.

106. "IR—Restricted—1927–29," Box 35, C14. See also "IR—Restricted—G–R," Box 36, C14.

107. Two African American jazz musicians also noted this trend in their interviews with Studs Terkel in *Hard Times*, 435.

108. Client CW (northern African American Protestant), Box 81, WPA.

109. For other examples of black women working as domestics in call flats, see Clients DA (southern African American Protestant), Box 82, and Q (northern African American Catholic but passing for white), Box 66, WPA. Polly Adler also employed a black manager and maid. Adler, *House Is Not a Home*, 65.

110. For the interracial street trade, see Marsh, *Prostitutes in New York City*, 176.

111. Although some white men and women undoubtedly also went into the interracial trade as managers, I found no evidence of white management of interracial prostitution in the Committee of Fourteen investigations or in the Bedford and Women's Prison Association files.

112. Adler, *House Is Not a Home*, 80.

113. "IR—Restricted—1930," Box 35, C14.

114. Polly Adler also reported extensive violence from organized crime in the 1920s in her autobiography. According to her, "Gangsters in general have a very low opinion of prostitutes," and this attitude could lead to violence. Adler, *House Is Not a Home*, 224. When one gangster asked why a prostitute worked "for this Jew-bastard," the woman retorted, "Because I like her and she's fair to us." As Adler related, "Apparently this answer annoyed Joe for he quickly jerked off his belt and began to beat her. The belt had a metal buckle and when it bit into her flesh the girl shrieked." Ibid., 81–82.

115. Ibid., 84. Describing another incident with gangsters, Adler wrote that she didn't encourage "them to come back. Too frequently, they wrecked not only the house, but my nervous system." Ibid., 80.

116. Ibid., 224.

117. "Dewey Bares Vice Terror," *New York American*, May 14, 1936.

118. "Dewey Pictures Luciano as Vice Syndicate Czar," *New York American*, May 14, 1936.

119. "Gaudy Madam Names Lucky as Vice Chief," *New York Post*, May 18, 1936; "Dewey Net Tightens on Vice Lords," *New York Evening Journal*, May 16, 1936; "Girl Reveals How Vice Ring Cheated Law," *New York American*, May 14, 1936.

120. "Luciano Ring Guilty, State Wins Hard Fight," *New York American*, June 6, 1936.

121. Adler, *House Is Not a Home*, 210.

122. Ibid., 210–24.

123. Committee of Fourteen, *Annual Report, 1930–1931*, 18. See also "IR—Restricted—1932," Box 35, C14.

124. Comparing prices to 1920s rates, the reporter asserted that "For the insignificant sum of a saw-buck, two of the prettiest femmes you'd ever want to see will put on an 'exhibition'—a show that would have cost at least two century notes back in 'the good old days.'" Peter M. Goode, "Nudes Feel Pinch!," *Broadway Brevities*, May 16, 1932, 1.

125. Murray, "Relation of Prostitution to Economic Conditions," 315. See also an article by the director of the Research Bureau for the Welfare Council of New York City, Neva Deardorff, "Measurement of Progress"; and Bowler, "Social Factors in Promoting Prostitution," 481.

126. Murray, "Relation of Prostitution to Economic Conditions," 315; Bowler, "Social Factors in Promoting Prostitution," 481; Marsh, *Prostitutes in New York City*, 123.

127. Client AM (southern white Protestant), Box 69, WPA.

128. Gretta Palmer, "Women's Day Court Would Aid Offenders," *New York World Telegram*, May 12, 1934. See also L. Simpson, "Off the Chest," *Broadway Brevities*, Dec. 19, 1932, 2; and Harold Stanning, "Loose Ladies Hustle! Pick-up Femmes Hit Trail to Scarlet Ruin; Hot Sisters Scram as Depresh Stings Morals; Vice Flares Anew as Loose Floosies Seek Easy Dough on Nation's Highways," *Broadway Brevities*, Oct. 19, 1933, 1.

129. "Back of Luciano Empire," *New York Post*, May 26, 1936.

130. Client BO (West Indian Protestant), Box 74, WPA. For another example, see Client CA (northern African American Protestant), Box 75, WPA.

131. "Girl Names Luciano Aides in Bid for Freedom," *New York Evening Journal*, May 15, 1936. See also "Girl Hates Men, Vice Jury Hears," *New York Post*, Apr. 2, 1936.

132. Client CC (white Protestant), Box 76, WPA.

133. Client ET (southern African American Protestant), Box 88, WPA.

134. Client BO (West Indian Protestant), Box 74, WPA. See also Marsh, *Prostitutes in New York City*, 129.

135. "IR—Restricted—1932," Box 35, C14.

136. Client EU (white Catholic), Box 88, WPA.

137. Client FO (southern African American Protestant), Box 90, WPA.

138. Wolcott, *Remaking Respectability*, 1–48.

139. C. Greenberg, *"Or Does It Explode?,"* 53–56, 153–63.

140. U.S. Department of Commerce, *Abstract of the Sixteenth Census, 1940*, 156.

141. K. Davis, "Study of Prostitutes," 174.

142. Waterman, *Prostitution and Its Repression*, 51.

143. Marsh, *Prostitutes in New York City*, 175.

144. Data from the Women's Prison Association support this contention. Several of the "confirmed" or "professional" prostitutes explained to their social workers that they had been caught by police because they violated their own rules about who, how, and when to solicit. Marsh, *Prostitutes in New York City*, 15. See also Clients S (white Protestant) and DU (southern African American Protestant), Box 66, WPA.

145. Marsh, *Prostitutes in New York City*, 175.

146. Ibid., 176.

147. Kinsey, Pomeroy, and Martin, *Sexual Behavior in the Human Male*, 603.

CHAPTER SEVEN

1. Cole Porter, "Always True to You in My Fashion" (from the musical *Kiss Me Kate*, 1948), in Kimball, *Complete Lyrics of Cole Porter*, 278–79.

2. Hence the always-popular lesbian joke: A man in a bar asks two women if they are "alone," to which they reply, "No, we're together." Even in groups of other women, some men assume that women in a bar are there to meet men and thus are "alone" even when they have company and express no interest in men.

3. Maureen Dowd, "The Manolo Moochers," *New York Times*, Aug. 29, 2001; and Brumberg, *Body Project*, 190.

4. Floyd Dell, "Why They Pet," *Parents' Magazine*, Oct. 1931, 18. Although this article de-

scribes petting as solely kissing and fondling, data from the Landis Papers show that it could also involve mutual masturbation and oral sex.

5. D. Smith, "Dating of the American Sexual Revolution," 426.

6. "Investigator's Field Reports" (1927), Box 26, C14. Over half of the women who identified themselves as charity in the 1920s mentioned being married, widowed, divorced, or separated. For other examples, see "IR—Restricted—Misc., 1927–29," Box 35, "IR—Restricted—Bronx" and "IR—Restricted—G–R," Box 36, C14.

7. For examples of other women who used work as a marker of identity, see "IR—Restricted—1927–30," Box 35, C14.

8. K. Davis, "Study of Prostitutes," 201.

9. "IR—Restricted—Misc., 1927–29," Box 35, C14. The Women's Prison Association case files contain similar records of older, married women requiring more material compensation for their time and sexuality. For example, see Client HE (American-born Italian Catholic and Jewish), Box 92, WPA.

10. For other women who spoke of later "compensation," see "IR—Restricted—Misc., 1927–29," Box 35, and "IR—Restricted—Hostesses," Box 37, C14.

11. For material requests before the war, see "IR—1916," Box 30, C14.

12. "IR—Restricted—1930," Box 35, C14.

13. "IR—Coney Is & Queens—Inv. Rept., 1918–19," Box 32, C14.

14. "IR—Restricted—G–R," Box 36, C14.

15. "IR—Restricted—Misc., 1927–29," Box 35, C14. There are several examples in this file.

16. Selma Brucet, "The Forgotten Woman: The Diary of a Girl Out of Work," *Broadway Brevities*, Nov. 7, 1932, 13. She also had trouble simply looking for work. At one employment agency, the manager "Told me to strip. Told him to go to hell. He said he'd help me. Came around the desk and tried to get helpful. I wasn't having any. Had quite a tussle. Must mend my dress tonight." Selma Brucet, "The Forgotten Woman: The Diary of a Girl Out of Work," *Broadway Brevities*, Nov. 28, 1932, 13.

17. "IR—Restricted—Misc., 1927–29," Box 35, C14. There are other examples in this file.

18. Client GX (white Catholic), Box 92, WPA. For other examples of this among both white and African American women, see Clients IE (white Catholic), Box 95, and BC (southern African American Catholic), Box 72, WPA.

19. Terkel, *Hard Times*, 219.

20. Bailey, *From Front Porch*, 21.

21. Modell, *Into One's Own*, 90.

22. Ibid., 90–92.

23. Ibid., 90.

24. Landis worked as the director of the New York State Psychiatric Hospital. His survey involved women categorized by psychiatrists as both mentally normal and abnormal and both married and single white women from New York. Unfortunately, he did not interview African American women, making these sorts of data for them very difficult to find. I found no significant difference between the normal and the abnormal, except that the abnormal, on the whole, had fewer sexual experiences than the normal, especially if they were single. The single women tended to be in their twenties, while the married women ranged in age from the twenties to the forties. The majority of the women were the chil-

dren of immigrants, most of whom in the 1920s and 1930s would still be in the working or lower-middle classes. In addition, many of these women had occupational histories that included factory work as well as department store and white-collar secretarial jobs. Some had been to high school, but only a few had attended college.

25. Like all the Landis interviews, this one took place between 1935 and 1937. The woman reported that she was thirty-one years old at the time of the interview, which means that her first date would have occurred between 1920 and 1922. 28N, Series III B, Folder 3, Box 1, Landis Papers. For other examples, see 43N, Series III D, Folder 4, Box 2, Landis Papers.

26. 22N, Series III B, Folder 3, Box 1, Landis Papers.

27. 36N, Series III B, Folder 4, Box 1, Landis Papers. For other examples of women who did not like the boys but wanted a date, see 37N and 43N, Series III B, Folder 4, Box 1, and 7N, Series III D, Folder 1, Box 2, Landis Papers.

28. 19, Series III C, Folder 1, Box 1, Landis Papers.

29. "Dancers Pay Piper $5,000,000 a Year," *New York Times*, Sept. 22, 1924, 1.

30. "Women Launch a Crusade for Better Dance Halls," *New York Times*, Mar. 16, 1924, XX9.

31. For example, see Bingham, *Determinants of Sex Delinquency*; and Reed, *Negro Illegitimacy*.

32. Series I, Tape 5, Chava Brier, NYCILHP. For other examples, see Series I, Tapes 6 and 7, Lena Rubin, Tape 104, Ruth Geller, and Tape 108, Henrietta Farber, NYCILHP.

33. Series II, Tapes 39 and 40, Lucrezia Grogone and Maria Vartone, Tape 2, Martina Tosca, Tapes 10 and 11, Carlotta Vina, Tapes 30 and 31, Graciella Felipelli, Tape 38, Carla Mastronari, Tapes 43 and 44, Gloria Granato, NYCILHP; Interview 25036, Coser Data Set.

34. True, *Neglected Girl*, 72.

35. Series I, Tape 41, Deborah Waxman, NYCILHP. See also Bingham, *Determinants of Sex Delinquency*, 36; and Inmate 3748 (southern African American Protestant), Box 1, Bedford.

36. 21N, Series III D, Folder 2, Box 2, 2M, 4M, and 7M, Series III E, Folder 1, Box 2, 14M, Series III E, Folder 2, Box 2, 16M and 22M, Series III E, Folder 3, Box 2, Landis Papers.

37. 2M, Series III E, Folder 1, Box 2, Landis Papers.

38. 12M, Series III E, Folder 2, Box 2, Landis Papers.

39. For example, of the forty-four Jewish women in interviewed in the Coser study, only two met their future husbands in commercial spaces, one at a dance and one at the theater, and both of these cases occurred in the 1920s. Interviews 15007 and 15023, Coser Data Set.

40. Series I, Tape 5, Chava Brier, NYCILHP. For other examples, see Interviews 15038, 15025, 15021, 15041, 15048, 15061, 15084, 15088, 15085, 15029, 15006, 15007, 15011, 15016, and 15019, Coser Data Set.

41. "Women Launch a Crusade for Better Dance Halls," *New York Times*, Mar. 16, 1924, XX9.

42. Inmate 4062 (Swedish Protestant), Box 11, Bedford. See also 4M, Series III E, Folder 1, Box 2, Landis Papers.

43. 14M, Series III E, Folder 2, Box 2, Landis Papers. In some of the Coser interviews young women said they met their mates in dance halls. For example, see Interviews 15073, 25009, 25021, 25027, and 25030, Coser Data Set.

44. Reed, *Negro Illegitimacy*, 56. For other examples of young women who became pregnant by men they met in dance halls, see ibid., 54; Bingham, *Determinants of Sex Delinquency*, 36; and Inmate 3774 (American-born Russian Jew), Box 1, Bedford,.

45. 16M, Series III E, Folder 3, Box 2, Landis Papers.

46. 12N, Series III E, Folder 3, Box 2, Landis Papers.

47. E. Smith, *Study of Twenty-Five Adolescent Unmarried Mothers*, 42. Other girls in the study provided similar descriptions; see ibid., 44.

48. 52N, Series III D, Folder 5, Box 2, Landis Papers.

49. 6M, Series III E, Folder 1, Box 2, Landis Papers.

50. 13N, Series III D, Folder 2, Box 2, Landis Papers.

51. 39N, Series III B, Folder 4, Box 1, Landis Papers. Some of the Bedford reformatory case files use similar language; for example, "Effie admits that she has been immoral but that she expected to marry the boy." Inmate 3747 (white Protestant), Box 1, Bedford. But in these cases, it is impossible to know whether the young woman actually used this language herself or whether the social worker chose this language to summarize the case.

52. Modell, *Into One's Own*, 40–41.

53. Ibid., 97–98. The increase of petting to orgasm was particularly marked for women.

54. Ibid., 115.

55. Coser, Anker, and Perrin, *Women of Courage*, 54. Coser also found that the poor were more likely than the middle class to use birth control to limit fertility.

56. Modell, *Into One's Own*, 115.

57. Ibid.

58. Tone, *Devices and Desires*, 108. The federal court of appeals followed suit in 1927, making condoms widely available across the country.

59. Merle Youngs, quoted in Tone, *Devices and Desires*, 188–89.

60. Coser, Anker, and Perrin, *Women of Courage*, 54.

61. Client DF, Box 82, WPA. For other examples of women obtaining abortions in the 1930s, see 32N, Series III B, Folder 4, Box 1, 52N, Series III D, Folder 5, Box 2, 23N, Series III E, Folder 3, Box 2, Landis Papers "Memoranda for Mr. Shelly, Mar. 1939–40," Series III A, Folder 4, Box 1, Alice Field Papers, Kinsey Institute, Bloomington, Indiana; Clients GE (West Indian Catholic), Box 91, HU (white, no religion listed), Box 94, and CT (white Catholic), Box 81, WPA.

62. Client IR (American-born Italian Catholic), Box 96, WPA.

63. Bailey, *From Front Porch*, 22.

64. Ibid., 23.

65. Ibid., 15–16.

66. Expensive gifts like jewelry implied an attempt to buy a woman's affection. In fact, most manuals preferred perishable gifts like flowers because they "left no obligation on the lady." Zelizer, *Social Meaning of Money*, 99.

67. For example, see "IR—1916," Box 30, "IR—Inv. Rep on Cabarets—1916–17" and "IR—Special Inspections—1916–17," Box 31 (which mentions both Yale and Princeton by name), and "IR—Restricted—Misc., 1927–29," Box 35, C14.

68. Moore, "Public Dance Halls in a Small City," 260.

69. Bailey, *From Front Porch*, 24.

70. Floyd Dell, "Why They Pet," *Parents' Magazine*, Oct. 1931, 18.

71. Ibid., 61.

72. Ibid., 62.

73. Interview 25048, Coser Data Set.

74. Interviews 25005 and 25001, Coser Data Set.

75. Interview 15038, Coser Data Set. For other examples, see Interviews 15040, 15053, 15065, 15073, 15012, and 15009, Coser Data Set.

76. Interview 15019, Coser Data Set.

77. Client DM (American-born Polish Jew), Box 83, WPA. For other examples, see "Memoranda for Mr. Shelly, Mar. 1939–40," Alice Field Papers; Inmates 4091 (American-born Russian Jew), Box 9, and 3759 (American-born Russian Jew), Box 1, Bedford.

78. Inmate 3735 (American-born Russian Jew), Box 1, Bedford. See also Client AD (white Protestant), Box 67, WPA.

79. For discussions of stereotypes of African American women's sexuality, see Hine, "Rape in the Inner Lives"; Freedman, "Prison Lesbian"; and E. White, *Dark Continent of Our Bodies*. For discussions of African American men's "hypersexuality," see Bederman, *Manliness and Civilization*, 1–44; and Mumford, *Interzones*, 3–18.

80. Client EM (American-born Jew), Box 86, WPA. Some parents refused to believe that their daughters would associate with black men. Outraged by such charges, one Irish Catholic woman's mother told a social worker that she "would not believe Katherine consorted with Negroes and that the workers of C.C. and Bedford were out to blacken K's name and not help her." Inmate 3773 (American-born Irish Catholic), Box 4, Bedford.

81. Historian Regina Kunzel carefully traces the academic debate over black attitudes toward illegitimacy in her book on unwed motherhood. She shows that social workers and sociologists changed their opinions about the causes of black illegitimacy in the 1920s and 1930s. Throughout the twentieth century, African Americans did have higher rates of illegitimacy than whites. In the early twentieth century, most social workers attributed black illegitimacy to the supposedly inherent immorality and hypersexuality of African Americans. In the 1930s and 1940s, academics and social workers, led by African American sociologist E. Franklin Frasier, attacked these theories, arguing instead that black acceptance of illegitimacy derived from cultural differences produced either by early African traditions or by the experiences of slavery. Kunzel, *Fallen Women*, 157.

82. Brooks Higginbotham, *Righteous Discontent*, 185–230; Wolcott, *Remaking Respectability*, 1–48.

83. Reed, *Negro Illegitimacy*, 80.

84. Ibid., 66. For other examples of southern and northern African Americans expressing shame over illegitimate pregnancy, see ibid., 56, 82.

85. Ibid., 68.

86. E. Smith, *Study of Twenty-Five Adolescent Unmarried Mothers*, 1.

87. Ibid., 63.

88. Ibid., 43. Another girl's stepfather disapproved so strongly he refused to allow her baby in the house; see ibid., 42. In her work on unwed black and white pregnancies in the 1950s and 1960s, Rickie Solinger has argued that social workers assumed that black women would not want to give up their children, that the black community accepted illegitimacy, and that black families were not interested in adoption. She found evidence that few of these assumptions were true in the 1950s, and that many young black women did

want to give their children up but were unable to do so because social workers failed to create an infrastructure for black adoption. Both Reed's and Smith's work on New York City indicate that this pattern held true as early as the 1920s and 1930s. Black women in their studies often indicated a desire to give their children up for adoption. Solinger, *Wake Up Little Susie*, 187–204.

89. E. Smith, *Study of Twenty-Five Adolescent Unmarried Mothers*, 41.

90. Ibid., 54.

91. Inmate 3458 (northern African American Protestant), Box 9, Bedford.

92. Client O (West Indian Protestant), Box 66, WPA. For another example of black parents rejecting a daughter who got pregnant out of wedlock, see Client DF (southern African American Protestant), Box 82, WPA.

93. Kunzel, *Fallen Women*, 144–77.

94. For examples of white parents opposing marriages between their daughters and the fathers of their babies, see "Memoranda for Mr. Shelly, Mar. 1939–40," Alice Field Papers.

95. Reed, *Negro Illegitimacy*, 82.

96. Client IL (southern African American Protestant), Box 95, WPA.

97. Interview 25055, Coser Data Set.

98. Interview 25023, Coser Data Set.

99. 2N, Series III D, Folder 1, Box 2, Landis Papers.

100. Bingham, *Determinants of Sex Delinquency*, 13.

101. Client CK (Italian Catholic) Box 79, WPA.

102. Client FG (American-born Italian Catholic), Box 90, WPA.

103. Ibid.

104. Steven Roberts, interviewed by author, June 14, 2004; Cora London, interviewed by author, May 10, 2001; Sandy Kern, interviewed by author, May 8, 2001; Mike Trombetta, interviewed by author, May 2, 2001. All interviews were in New York City.

105. Kern interview. Kern grew up in Brownsville, Brooklyn, in a working-class Jewish neighborhood. She described her family as poor, and her father worked as a pushcart peddler.

106. Trombetta interview. Trombetta grew up the only child of an Italian mother who had been deserted by his father when he was a baby. Like Kern, he described his family background as "poor."

107. Kern interview.

108. Brumberg, *Body Project*, 190.

CONCLUSION

1. Maureen Dowd, "The Manolo Moochers," *New York Times*, Aug. 29, 2001.

2. Stansell, *City of Women*, 89–101.

3. See Brumberg, *Body Project*, 190; and Dowd, "Manolo Moochers."

4. Kinsey, Pomeroy, and Martin, *Sexual Behavior in the Human Male*, 603.

5. For example, in 1987 the *Miami Herald* ran an article on prostitutes and HIV. It quoted Judge Morton Perry of Dade County, Florida, who asserted, "these days a man who visits a prostitute can become a victim of AIDS, and not just him but his family, his wife, his lover, his unborn children." Madeleine Blais, "Lethal Weapon," *Miami Herald*, Aug. 16, 1987. For

similar arguments about prostitutes spreading HIV to "innocent" women and children, see "Tougher Penalties for HIV Positive Prostitutes Supported," *San Francisco Sentinel*, July 19, 1990.

6. "Alleged Places of Assignation and Exposure, Brothels, Pick-up Spots, etc., as Reported to This HQ on Individual Venereal Disease Contact Reports," Box 1, Entry 39, RG 215, NA.

7. Brandt, *No Magic Bullet*, 162.

8. Ibid., 139–40.

9. Kathryn Close, "In May Act Areas," *Survey Mid Monthly*, March 1942.

10. "Relationships," Box 10, Entry 37, RG 215, NA.

11. Brandt, *No Magic Bullet*, 167.

12. Researchers discovered penicillin in 1943, but it did not become widely available for military use until 1944. Ibid., 170.

13. "Recommendations of the Welfare Council's Committee on Prostitution and the Women's Court for Improving the Procedures in Dealing with Prostitution Cases in New York City," 9, "New York," Box 7, Entry 40, RG 215, NA.

14. Judge Stephen S. Jackson, Domestic Relations Court, New York City, "Juvenile Delinquency—A Problem and a Challenge," 34, Box 7, Entry 40, RG 215, NA.

15. Lewis J. Valentine, Police Commissioner, City of New York, "Common Problems in the Apprehension of Civilian Contacts as Reported on Forms 140," 32, Box 7, Entry 40, RG 215, 32. For an example of a woman who was "forced in," see Inmate JX (Irish, age nineteen, 1945), Box 99, WPA.

16. Eliot Ness, "Rehabilitation in the Social Protection Program," 4, Box 3, Entry 44, RG 215, NA.

17. Ibid., 5.

18. For other examples of how drafting men disrupted their economically fragile families, forcing women into prostitution, see Inmates AR (southern African American, 1942), Box 71, and FW (white Puerto Rican, 1943), Box 90, WPA.

19. "Adolescence—1944" (Paper read before Church Mission of Help of the Protestant Episcopal Church, Tuesday, May 2, 1944, Stamford, Connecticut), 1, "New York," Box 7, Entry 40, RG 215.

20. Richard H. Anthony, "The Girl and the Man in Uniform," 4, American Social Hygiene Papers, Charles Babbage Institute, Social Welfare History Archives, Minneapolis.

21. Valentine, "Common Problems in the Apprehension of Civilian Contacts," 33. Another article found similar percentages of infection among prostitutes in the South. See Reynolds, "Prostitution as a Source of Infection." For estimates of venereal disease rates from the Great War, see Malzberg, "Venereal Disease among Prostitutes," 541.

22. Office of War Information, "Report on Juvenile Delinquency," Oct. 1943, "Juvenile Delinquency," Box 5, Entry 37, RG 215, NA.

23. "Alleged Places of Assignation and Exposure" (see note 6 above).

24. Office of War Information, "Report on Juvenile Delinquency."

25. Whitcomb H. Allen, "Young Camp Followers," 9, "Publications," Box 2, Entry 44, RG 215, NA.

26. Valentine, "Common Problems in the Apprehension of Civilian Contacts," 33.

27. Mrs. T. Grafton Abbot, "Report on Study of Youth Problems in Wartime," 3, "American Social Hygiene Association," Box 1, Entry 37, RG 215, NA. The title of this conclusion comes from a quotation in this document.

28. Office of War Information, "Report on Juvenile Delinquency." For fears of rising promiscuity among youth, see also Bascom Johnson, "Sex Delinquency among Girls" (Report delivered at an American Social Hygiene Conference, Nov. 1942), Box 1, Entry 43, RG 215, NA; and Grafton Abbot, "Report on Study of Youth Problems in Wartime," 2.

29. "Special Survey by the Children's Bureau Comparing the Amount of Illegitimacy in the First Three Months of 1941 and 1942," "Illegitimacy," Box 1, Entry 43, RG 215, NA.

30. Office of War Information, "Report on Juvenile Delinquency."

31. Regina Kunzel found that when the social class of unwed mother's changed, social workers changed their interpretations of the causes. Kunzel, *Fallen Women*, 144–70.

32. Grafton Abbot, "Report on Study of Youth Problems in Wartime," 3.

33. Ibid., 2.

34. Modell, *Into One's Own*, 40–41.

35. Brandt, *No Magic Bullet*, 164.

36. Ibid., 168–69.

37. Major George M. Leiby and Captain Granville W. Larimore, "A Study of Factors Allied with Venereal Disease," Aug. 1945, "Prostitution and Promiscuity," Box 9, Entry 37, RG 215.

38. Quoted in Brandt, *No Magic Bullet*, 164.

39. "Gallup Poll, November 1942," "Polls and Public Opinion," Box 8, Entry 37, RG 215, NA.

40. Some of these posters hyphenate "pickup" and others do not. I have retained the original usage.

41. For examples of the military treating women and men differently when it came to venereal diseases and illegitimate pregnancy, see Meyers, *Creating G.I. Jane*, 100–147.

42. D. Smith, "Dating of the American Sexual Revolution," 426. Elaine Tyler May found that 44 percent of the upper-middle-class white women and 62 percent of the men in the Kelly Longitudinal Study engaged in premarital intercourse. May, *Homeward Bound*, 120–21.

BIBLIOGRAPHY

MANUSCRIPTS AND ARCHIVAL SOURCES

Albany, New York
    New York State Archives
    Bedford Hills State Reformatory Inmate Case Files

Bloomington, Indiana
    Kinsey Institute for Sex Research
        Alice Field Papers
        Carney Landis Papers

Cambridge, Massachusetts
    Harvard University, Radcliffe Institute for Advanced Study, Henry A. Murray
        Research Center, Radcliffe College, Schlesinger Library
            World of Our Mothers Study of Jewish and Italian Immigrant Women

College Park, Maryland
    National Archives

Minneapolis, Minnesota
    Charles Babbage Institute, Social Welfare History Archives
        American Social Hygiene Papers

New York, New York
    Columbia University, Rare Books and Manuscripts Library
        Community Service Society Papers
        Lillian Wald Papers
    John Jay College of Criminal Justice
        Trial Transcript Project
    New York Public Library
        Rare Books and Manuscripts, Astor, Lenox and Tilden Collection
        Committee of Fifteen Papers
        Committee of Fourteen Papers
        Women's Prison Association Records
        Schomburg Center for Research on Black Culture
    New York University, Tamiment Library and Archives
        New York City Immigrant Labor History Project

Philadelphia, Pennsylvania
    Balsh Institute for Ethnic Studies
        Leonard Covello Papers

PUBLISHED PRIMARY SOURCES

Addams, Jane. *The Spirit of Youth and the City Streets*. Chicago: University of Illinois
    Press, 1972.

Adler, Polly. *A House Is Not a Home*. New York: Rinehart, 1953.

Balmford, Edith. "Runaway Girls: A Follow-up Study of Two Hundred Runaway Girls Who Have Found a Temporary Home in Waverly House." Master's thesis, Columbia University, 1923.

Bingham, Anne. *Determinants of Sex Delinquency in Adolescent Girls, Based on Intensive Studies of 500 Cases*. New York: New York Probation and Protective Association, 1923.

A Bintel Brief: Sixty Years of Letters From the Lower East Side to the Jewish Daily Forward. Compiled, edited, and with an introduction by Isaac Metzker. Foreword and notes by Harry Golden. New York: Doubleday, 1971.

Bowler, Alida C. "Social Factors in Promoting Prostitution." *Journal of Social Hygiene* 17, no. 8 (Nov. 1931): 477–81.

Chappell, George S. *Restaurants of New York*. New York: Greenberg, 1925.

Chernin, Kim. *In My Mother's House*. New York: Ticknor and Fields, 1983.

Coan, Peter, ed. *Ellis Island Interviews: In Their Own Words*. New York: Facts on File, 1997.

Committee of Fourteen. *Annual Report, 1913*. New York: Douglas C. McMurtrie, 1914.

———. *Annual Report, 1914*. New York: Arbor, 1915.

———. *Annual Report, 1917–1918*. New York: Arbor, 1918.

———. *Annual Report, 1927–1928*. New York: Arbor, 1928.

———. *Annual Report, 1929–1930*. New York: Arbor, 1930.

———. *Annual Report, 1930–1931*. New York: Arbor, 1931.

———. *The Social Evil in New York City: A Study of Law Enforcement*. New York: Andrew Kellogg, 1910.

Consumers' League of New York. "Behind the Scenes of Women's Work: A Study of 1017 Women Restaurant Employees." New York: Consumers' League of New York, 1916.

———. "Our Working Girls: How They Do It." Consumers' League of New York, 1910.

Covello, Leonard. *The Social Background of the Italo-American School Child*. Leiden: E. J. Brill, 1967.

Cressey, Paul G. *The Taxi-Dance Hall: A Sociological Study in Commercial Recreation and City Life*. New York: AMS, 1932.

Davis, Katharine Bement. "Social Hygiene and the War II: Women's Part in Social Hygiene." *Social Hygiene* 4 (1918): 525–60.

———. "A Study of Prostitutes Committed from New York City to the State Reformatory for Women at Bedford Hills." In *Commercialized Prostitution in New York City*, edited by George Kneeland, 173–237. New York: Century, 1913.

Deardorff, Neva R. "Measurement of Progress in the Repression of Prostitution." *Journal of Social Hygiene* 18, no. 6 (June 1932): 301–14.

Dillingham, William. *Importing Women for Immoral Purposes: A Partial Report from the Immigration Commission on the Importation and Harboring of Women for Immoral Purposes*. Washington, D.C.: Government Printing Office, 1909.

Donovan, Frances. *The Saleslady*. Chicago: University of Chicago Press, 1929.

———. *The Woman Who Waits*. Boston: Gorham, 1920.

Fernald, Mabel Ruth, Mary Holms Stevens Hayes, and Almena Dawley. *A Study of Women Delinquents in New York State*. New York: Century, 1920.

Ganz, Marie. *Rebels: Into Anarchy and Out Again*. New York: Dodd, Mead, 1920.

Gold, Michael. *Jews without Money*. 1930. New York: Carroll and Graff, 1996.

Goldman, Emma. *Living My Life*. New York: Knopf, 1931.

Henry, George. *Sex Variants: A Study of Homosexual Patterns*. New York: P. B. Hoeber, 1941.

Johnson, James Weldon. *Black Manhattan*. 1930. New York: Atheneum, 1968.

Kennedy, John B. "The Devil's Dance Dens." *Collier's Weekly*, Sept. 19, 1925, 12, 15.

Kneeland, George, ed. *Commercialized Prostitution in New York City*. New York: Century, 1913.

Kramer, Sydelle, and Jenny Masur, eds. *Jewish Grandmothers*. Boston: Beacon, 1976.

Lambin, Maria Ward. *Report of the Advisory Dance Hall Committee of the Women's City Club and the City Recreation Committee*. New York City: Women's City Club of New York, 1924.

Madeline. *Madeline: An Autobiography*. Introduction to the 1919 edition by Judge Ben B. Lindsey. With a new introduction by Marcia Carlisle. New York: Persea Books, 1986.

Malzberg, Benjamin. "Venereal Disease among Prostitutes." *Social Hygiene* 5 (1919): 539–44.

Marsh, Marguerite. *Prostitutes in New York City: Their Apprehension, Trial, and Treatment, July 1939 to June 1940*. New York: Research Bureau, Welfare Council of New York City, 1941.

Miner, Maude. *Slavery of Prostitution: A Plea for Emancipation*. New York: Macmillan, 1916.

Moore, Elon. "Public Dance Halls in a Small City." *Sociology and Social Research* 14 (1930): 256–63.

Murray, Virginia. "The Relation of Prostitution to Economic Conditions." *Journal of Social Hygiene* 18, no. 6 (June 1932): 314–21.

"News and Abstracts: The Taxi Dance Hall." *Journal of Social Hygiene* 17, no. 7 (Oct. 1931): 419–20.

New York Society for the Prevention of Cruelty to Children. *Annual Reports*. Vols. 18–60. New York, 1892–1934.

Owings, Chloe. *Women Police: A Study of the Development and Status of the Women Police Movement*. New York: Frederick H. Hitchcock, 1925.

Peters, John P. "The Story of the Committee of Fourteen." *Social Hygiene* 4 (1918): 366–68.

Reed, Ruth. *Negro Illegitimacy in New York City*. New York: Columbia University Press, 1926.

Report on the Committee on Amusement Resources of Working Girls (Inc.). New York: Peck, 1912.

Reynolds, Charles. "Prostitution as a Source of Infection with the Venereal Diseases in the Armed Forces." *American Journal of Public Health* 30, no. 11 (Nov. 1940): 1280–81.

Rippin, Jane Deeter. "Social Hygiene and the War: Work with Women and Girls." *Social Hygiene* 5 (1919): 125–36.

Rosten, Leo. *People I Have Loved, Known or Admired*. New York: McGraw Hill, 1970.

Seabury, Samuel. *Supreme Court, Appellate Division—First Judicial Department in the Matter of the Investigation of the Magistrates' Courts in the First Judicial Department and the Magistrates Thereof, and of Attorneys-at-Law Practicing in Said Courts, Final Report of Samuel Seabury, Referee*. Albany: State of New York, 1932.

Schoener, Allon. *Portal to America: The Lower East Side, 1870–1925*. New York: Rinehart and Winston, 1967.

Sholem Aleichem. *Tevye the Dairyman and the Railroad Stories*. Translated by Hillel Halkin. New York: Shocken Books, 1987.

Sloan, John. *New York Etchings (1905–1949)*. Edited by Helen Farr Sloan. New York: Dover, 1978.

Smith, Betty. *A Tree Grows in Brooklyn*. 1943. Foreword by Anna Quindlen. New York: Harper Collins, 2001.

Smith, Enid Severy. *A Study of Twenty-Five Adolescent Unmarried Mothers in New York City*. New York: Salvation Army Women's Home and Hospital, 1935.

Snow, William F., M.D. *Clinics for Venereal Diseases: Why We Need Them, How To Develop Them*. New York: American Social Hygiene Association, 1917.

Stone, Lee Alexander, M.D. *It's Sex O'clock*. Chicago: Marshall Field Annex, 1928.

Sussman, Sara. "A Settlement Club." Master's thesis, Columbia University, 1918.

Tappan, Paul W. *Delinquent Girls in Court: A Study of the Wayward Minor Court of New York*. New York: Columbia University Press, 1947.

Terkel, Studs. *Hard Times*. New York: Discus Books, 1970.

Terman, Lewis. *Psychological Factors in Marital Happiness*. New York: McGraw Hill, 1938.

True, Ruth S. *The Neglected Girl*. New York: Survey Associates, 1914.

U.S. Department of Commerce, Bureau of the Census. *Abstract of the Sixteenth Census of the United States, 1940, Population*. Vol. 2. *Characteristics of the Population*. Part 5. *New York–Oregon*. Washington, D.C.: Government Printing Office, 1943.

———. *Statistical Abstracts of the United States, 1923*. Washington, D.C.: Government Printing Office, 1924.

Waterman, Willoughby Cyrus. *Prostitution and Its Repression in New York City, 1900–1931*. New York: Columbia University Press, 1932.

Woods, Robert A. and Albert J. Kennedy. *Young Working Girls: A Summary of Evidence from Two Thousand Social Workers*. New York: Houghton Mifflin, 1913.

Worthington, George. "The Women's Day Court of Manhattan and the Bronx, New York City." *Journal of Social Hygiene* 8, no. 4 (Oct. 1922): 393–510.

SECONDARY SOURCES

Alexander, Ruth. *The "Girl Problem": Female Sexual Delinquents in New York, 1900–1930*. Ithaca: Cornell University Press, 1995.

Bailey, Beth. *From Front Porch to Back Seat: Courtship in Twentieth-Century America*. Baltimore: Johns Hopkins University Press, 1988.

Bederman, Gail. *Manliness and Civilization: A Cultural History of Gender and Race in the United States, 1880–1917*. Chicago: University of Chicago Press, 1995.

Bell, Shannon. *Reading, Writing, and Rewriting the Prostitute Body*. Bloomington: University of Indiana Press, 1994.

Benson, Susan Porter. *Counter Cultures: Salesgirls, Managers, and Customers in American Department Stores, 1890–1940*. Urbana: University of Illinois Press, 1986.

Bernstein, Rachel Amelia. "Boarding-House Keepers and Brothel Keepers in New York City, 1880–1910." Ph.D. diss., Rutgers, State University of New Jersey, 1984.

Biale, David. *Eros and the Jews: From Biblical Israel to Contemporary America*. New York: Basic Books, 1992.

Bodnar, John. *The Transplanted: A History of Immigrants in Urban America*. Bloomington: University of Indiana Press, 1985.

Bower, Stephanie. "The Common Commercial Flesh of Women: Representations of Prostitution in Turn-of-the-Century American Literature." Ph.D. diss., University of California at Los Angeles, 1995.

Brandt, Allan. *No Magic Bullet: A Social History of Venereal Disease in the United States since 1880*. New York: Oxford University Press, 1987.

Bristow, Nancy K. *Making Men Moral: Social Engineering during the Great War*. New York: New York University Press, 1996.

Brooks Higginbotham, Evelyn. *Righteous Discontent: The Women's Movement in the Black Baptist Church, 1880–1920*. Cambridge: Harvard University Press, 1994.

Brumberg, Joan Jacobs. *The Body Project: An Intimate History of American Girls*. New York: Vintage, 1998.

Chauncey, George. "Christian Brotherhood or Sexual Perversion? Homosexual Identities and the Construction of Sexual Boundaries in the World War One Era." *Journal of Social History* 19, no. 2 (Winter 1985): 189–211.

———. *Gay New York: Gender, Urban Culture, and the Making of the Gay Male World, 1890–1940*. New York: Basic Books, 1994.

Clement, Elizabeth Alice. "From Sociability to Spectacle: Interracial Sexuality and the Ideological Uses of Space in New York City, 1900–1930." *Journal of International Women's Studies* 6, no. 2 (June 2005).

———. "Trick or Treat: Prostitution and Working-Class Women's Sexuality in New York City, 1900–1932." Ph.D. diss., University of Pennsylvania, 1998.

Cohen, Lizbeth. *Making a New Deal: Industrial Workers in Chicago, 1919–1939*. New York: Cambridge University Press, 1990.

Cohen, Patricia Cline. *The Murder of Helen Jewett: The Life and Death of a Prostitute in Nineteenth-Century New York*. New York: Knopf, 1998.

Connelly, Mark. *The Response to Prostitution in the Progressive Era*. Chapel Hill: University of North Carolina Press, 1980.

Corbin, Alain. *Women for Hire: Prostitution and Sexuality in France after 1850*. Translated by Alan Sheridan. Cambridge: Harvard University Press, 1990.

Coser, Rose Laub, Laura S. Anker, and Andrew J. Perrin. *Women of Courage: Jewish and Italian Immigrant Women in New York*. Westport: Greenwood, 1999.

Cott, Nancy. "Eighteenth Century Family and Social Life Revealed in Massachusetts Divorce Records." In *A Heritage of Our Own*, edited by Nancy Cott and Elizabeth Pleck. New York: Simon and Schuster, 1979.

Delacoste, Frederique, and Priscilla Alexander, eds. *Sex Work: Writings by Women in the Sex Industry*. Pittsburgh: Cleis, 1987.

Diner, Hasia. *Erin's Daughters in America: Irish Immigrant Women in the Nineteenth Century*. Baltimore: Johns Hopkins University Press, 1983.

Dubinsky, Karen. *Improper Advances: Rape and Heterosexual Conflict in Ontario, 1880–1929*. Chicago: University of Chicago Press, 1993.

Dumenil, Lynn. *The Modern Temper: American Culture and Society in the 1920s*. New York: Hill and Wang, 1995.

Erenberg, Lewis. *Steppin' Out: New York Night Life and the Transformation of American Culture, 1890–1930*. Chicago: University of Chicago Press, 1981.

Esposito, Tony, ed. *All Time Favorite Rodgers and Hart Classics*. Miami: Warner Bros., 1995.

Ewen, Elizabeth. *Immigrant Women in the Land of Dollars: Life and Culture on the Lower East Side, 1890–1925*. New York: Monthly Review, 1985.

Fass, Paula. *The Damned and the Beautiful: American Youth in the 1920s*. New York: Oxford University Press, 1977.

Fields, Dorothy, and Cy Colman. *Sweet Charity: The Musical Comedy*. Miami: Notable Music, 1986.

Filene, Peter. *Him/Herself: Sex Roles in Modern America*. Baltimore: Johns Hopkins University Press, 1974.

Fine, Lisa. *The Souls of the Skyscraper: Female Clerical Workers in Chicago, 1870–1930*. Philadelphia: Temple University Press, 1990.

Fitzgerald, Maureen. *Habits of Compassion: Irish Catholic Nuns and the Origins of the Welfare System, 1830–1920*. Chicago: University of Illinois Press, 2005.

Foucault, Michel. *History of Sexuality, Volume I: An Introduction*. Translated by Robert Hurley. New York: Vintage, 1990.

Fox-Genovese, Elizabeth. *Within the Plantation Household: Black and White Women of the Old South*. Chapel Hill: University of North Carolina Press, 1988.

Freedman, Estelle. "The Prison Lesbian: Race, Class, and the Construction of the Aggressive Female Homosexual, 1915–1965," *Feminist Studies* 22, no. 2 (Summer 1996): 397–423.

———. "'Uncontrolled Desires': The Response to the Sexual Psychopath, 1920–1960." *Journal of American History* 74 (1987): 83–106.

Freeze, ChaeRan. *Jewish Marriage and Divorce in Imperial Russia*. Hanover: Brandeis University Press, 2002.

Gabaccia, Donna. *From the Other Side: Women, Gender, and Immigrant Life in the U.S., 1820–1990*. Bloomington: Indiana University Press, 1994.

Gilfoyle, Timothy. *City of Eros: New York City, Prostitution, and the Commercialization of Sex, 1790–1920*. New York: W. W. Norton, 1992.

Gilman, Sander. "AIDS and Syphilis: The Iconography of Disease." In *AIDS: Cultural Analysis, Cultural Activism*, edited by Douglas Crimp, 87–107. Boston: MIT Press, 1987.

Glenn, Susan. *Daughters of the Shtetl: Life and Labor in the Immigrant Generation*. Ithaca: Cornell University Press, 1990.

Goldin, Claudia. *Understanding the Gender Gap: An Economic History of American Women*. New York: Oxford University Press, 1990.

Goodman, Cary. *Choosing Sides: Playground and Street Life on the Lower East Side*. New York: Shocken Books, 1979.

Gordon, Linda. "Black and White Visions of Welfare: Women's Welfare Activism, 1890–1945." In *Unequal Sisters: A Multi-Cultural Reader in U.S. Women's History*, edited by Vicki Ruiz and Ellen DuBois, 2nd ed., 157–85. New York: Routledge, 1994.

———. *Woman's Body, Woman's Right: Birth Control in America*. New York: Penguin Books, 1983.

Greenberg, Cheryl Lynn. *'Or Does it Explode?': Black Harlem in the Great Depression*. New York: Oxford University Press, 1991.

Greenberg, Kenneth. *Honor and Slavery*. Princeton: Princeton University Press, 1996.

Grittner, Frederick Karl. "White Slavery: Myth, Ideology and American Law." Ph.D. diss., University of Minnesota, 1986.

Gusfield, Joseph R. *Symbolic Crusade: Status Politics and the American Temperance Movement*. Chicago: University of Illinois Press, 1963.

Hine, Darlene Clark. "Rape in the Inner Lives of Black Women in the Middle West: Preliminary Thoughts on the Culture of Dissemblance." *Signs* 14, no. 4 (1989): 912–20.

Hobson, Barbara Meil. *Uneasy Virtue: The Politics of Prostitution and the American Reform Tradition*. New York: Basic Books, 1987.

Hoigard, Cecilie, and Liv Finstad. *Backstreets: Prostitution, Money, and Love*. Translated by Katherine Hanson, Nancy Sipe, and Barbara Wilson. University Park: Pennsylvania State University Press, 1992.

Howe, Irving. *World of Our Fathers: The Journey of the East European Jews to America and the Life They Found and Made*. New York: Simon and Schuster, 1976.

Howe, Irving, and Kenneth Libo, eds. *How We Lived: A Documentary History of Immigrant Jews in America, 1880–1930*. New York: Plume, 1979.

Huggins, Nathan Irvin. *Voices from the Harlem Renaissance*. New York: Oxford University Press, 1995.

Joselit, Jenna Weissman. *Our Gang: Jewish Crime and the New York Jewish Community, 1900–1940*. Bloomington: University of Indiana Press, 1983.

Kasson, John. *Amusing the Millions: Coney Island at the Turn of the Century*. New York: Hill and Wang, 1978.

Kennedy, Elizabeth, and Madeline Davis. *Boots of Leather, Slippers of Gold: The History of a Lesbian Community*. New York: Penguin, 1994.

Kennedy, Susan Eastbrook. *If All We Did Was to Weep at Home: A History of White Working-Class Women in America*. Bloomington: Indiana University Press, 1979.

Kimball, Robert, ed. *The Complete Lyrics of Cole Porter*. New York: Knopf, 1983.

Kinsey, Alfred C., Wardell B. Pomeroy, and Clyde E. Martin. *Sexual Behavior in the Human Male*. Philadelphia: W. B. Saunders, 1948.

Kunzel, Regina. *Fallen Women, Problem Girls: Unmarried Women and the Professionalization of Social Work*. New Haven: Yale University Press, 1993.

Laqueur, Thomas. *Making Sex: Body and Gender from the Greeks to Freud*. Cambridge: Harvard University Press, 1990.

Larson, Jane E. "'Women Understand So Little, They Call My Good Nature "Deceit"': A Feminist Rethinking of Seduction." *Columbia Law Review* (March 1993): 375–471.

Lewis, David. *When Harlem Was in Vogue*. New York: Penguin, 1997.

Lunbeck, Elizabeth. *The Psychiatric Persuasion: Knowledge, Gender, and Power in Modern America*. Princeton: Princeton University Press, 1994.

Lystra, Karen. *Searching the Heart: Women, Men, and Romantic Love in Nineteenth-Century America*. New York: Oxford University Press, 1989.

May, Elaine Tyler. *Homeward Bound: American Families in the Cold War Era*. New York: Basic Books, 1988.

Meyerowitz, Joanne. *Women Adrift: Independent Wage Earners in Chicago, 1880–1930*. Chicago: University of Chicago Press, 1988.

Meyers, Leisa. *Creating G.I. Jane: Sexuality and Power in the Women's Army Corps during World War II*. New York: Columbia University Press, 1996.

Modell, John. *Into One's Own: From Youth to Adulthood in the United States, 1920–1975*. Berkeley: University of California Press, 1989.

Mumford, Kevin. *Interzones: Black/White Sex Districts in New York and Chicago in the Early Twentieth Century*. New York: Columbia University Press, 1997.

Nasaw, David. *Going Out: The Rise and Fall of Public Amusements*. New York: Basic Books, 1993.

Newton, Esther. *Mother Camp: Female Impersonators in America*. Chicago: University of Chicago Press, 1972.

Norworth, Jack, and Albert Von Tilzer. "Take Me Out to the Ball Game." In *Major Problems in American Sports History*, edited by Steven A. Reiss. Boston: Houghton Mifflin, 1997.

Odem, Mary. *Delinquent Daughters: Protecting and Policing Adolescent Female Sexuality in the United States, 1885–1920*. Chapel Hill: University of North Carolina Press, 1995.

Orsi, Robert. *The Madonna of 115th Street: Faith and Community in Italian Harlem, 1880–1950*. New Haven: Yale University Press, 1985.

Ottley, Roi, and William Weatherby, eds. *The Negro in New York: An Informal Social History*. New York: Oceana, 1967.

Peiss, Kathy. "'Charity Girls' and City Pleasures: Historical Notes on Working-Class Sexuality, 1880–1920." In *Passion and Power: Sexuality in History*, edited by Kathy Peiss and Christina Simmons, 57–70. Philadelphia: Temple University Press, 1987.

———. *Cheap Amusements: Working Women and Leisure in Turn-of-the-Century New York*. Philadelphia: Temple University Press, 1986.

Reimers, David, and Frederick Binder. *All the Nations under Heaven: An Ethnic and Racial History of New York City*. New York: Columbia University Press, 1995.

Roby, Pamela Ann. "Politics and Prostitution: A Case Study of the Formulation, Enforcement, and Judicial Administration of the New York State Penal Laws on Prostitution, 1870–1970." Ph.D. diss., New York University, 1971.

Rosen, Ruth. *The Lost Sisterhood: Prostitution in America, 1900–1918*. Baltimore: Johns Hopkins University Press, 1982.

Rothman, Ellen. *Hands and Hearts: A History of Courtship in America*. New York: Basic Books, 1984.

Sanday, Peggy Reeves. *Fraternity Gang Rape: Sex, Brotherhood, and Privilege on Campus*. New York: New York University Press, 1990.

Schwartz, Paula. "Partisanes and Gender Politics in Vichy France." *French Historical Studies* 16, no. 1 (Spring 1989): 126–51.

———. "Redefining Resistance: Women's Activism in Wartime France." In *Behind the Lines: Gender and the Two World Wars*, edited by Margaret Randolph Higonnet, 141–54. New Haven: Yale University Press, 1987.

Smith, Daniel Scott. "The Dating of the American Sexual Revolution: Evidence and Interpretation." In *The American Family in Social-Historical Perspective*, edited by Michael Gordon, 2nd ed., 426–38. New York: St. Martin's, 1978.

Smith-Rosenberg, Carroll. *Disorderly Conduct: Visions of Gender in Victorian America*. New York: Oxford University Press, 1985.

Snyder, Robert. "City in Transition." In *Metropolitan Lives: The Ashcan Artists and Their New York*, edited by Rebecca Zurier, Robert Snyder, and Virginia Mecklenburg, 2nd ed., 29–57. New York: National Museum of American Art and W. W. Norton, 1995.

Snyder, Robert, and Rebecca Zurier. "Picturing the City." In *Metropolitan Lives: The Ashcan Artists and Their New York*, edited by Rebecca Zurier, Robert Snyder, and Virginia Mecklenburg, 2nd ed., 85–189. New York: National Museum of American Art and W. W. Norton, 1995.

Solinger, Rickie. *Wake Up Little Susie: Single Pregnancy and Race before Roe v Wade*. New York: Routledge, 1992.

Stansell, Christine. *City of Women: Sex and Class in New York, 1789–1860*. Chicago: University of Illinois Press, 1982.

Takaki, Ronald. *Strangers from a Different Shore: A History of Asian Americans*. Boston: Little, Brown, 1989.

Thompson, E. P. "The Moral Economy of the English Crowd in the Eighteenth Century." In *Customs in Common*, 185–258. New York: Merlin, 1991.

———. "The Moral Economy Revisited." In *Customs in Common*, 259–351. New York: Merlin, 1991.

Tone, Andrea. *Devices and Desires*. New York: Hill and Wang, 2001.

Ullman, Sharon. *Sex Seen: The Emergence of Modern Sexuality in America*. Berkeley: University of California Press, 1997.

Van Cleve, John Vickrey, and Barry A. Crouch. *A Place of Their Own: Creating the Deaf Community in America*. Washington, D.C.: Gallaudet University Press, 1989.

Walkowitz, Judith. *City of Dreadful Delight: Narratives of Sexual Danger in Late-Victorian London*. Chicago: University of Chicago Press, 1992.

———. *Prostitution and Victorian Society: Women, Class and the State*. Cambridge: Cambridge University Press, 1980.

Watson, Steven. *The Harlem Renaissance*. New York: Pantheon, 1996.

Weinberg, Jonathan. *Speaking for Vice: Homosexuality in the Art of Charles Demuth, Marsden Hartley, and the First American Avant-Garde*. New Haven: Yale University Press, 1993.

Weiner, Lynn. *From Working Girl to Working Mother: The Female Labor Force in the United States, 1820–1980*. Chapel Hill: University of North Carolina Press, 1985.

Welter, Barbara. "The Cult of True Womanhood: 1820–1860." In *The American Family in Social-Historical Perspective*, edited by Michael Gordon, 313–33. New York: St. Martin's, 1978.

Westbrook, Robert. "'I Want a Girl, Just Like the Girl That Married Harry James': American Women and the Problem of Political Obligation in World War II." *American Quarterly* 42, no. 4 (Dec. 1990): 587–614.

White, E. Frances. *Dark Continent of Our Bodies: Black Feminism and the Politics of Respectability*. Philadelphia: Temple University Press, 2001.

White, Luise. *The Comforts of Home: Prostitution in Colonial Nairobi*. Chicago: University of Chicago Press, 1990.

Wolcott, Victoria. *Remaking Respectability: African American Women in Interwar Detroit.* Chapel Hill: University of North Carolina Press, 2001.

Woolacott, Angela. *On Her Their Lives Depend: Munitions Workers in the Great War.* Berkeley: University of California Press, 1994.

Zelizer, Viviana. *The Social Meaning of Money: Pin Money, Paychecks, Poor Relief, and Other Currencies.* New York: Basic Books, 1994.

INDEX

40, 189, 231–32, 234, 236; formation, 13–14, 38, 43, 229–33, 236; honor and, 29–30; mothers, 18–19, 27, 30–31, 156, 165–67, 169, 231–33, 235, 237, 249–58; parental authority and, 6, 13–19, 24–36, 39–43, 50, 189, 228–39, 247; sisters, 29, 38, 155–56, 249; sons and courtship, 30; violence, 30, 235, 270–71 (n. 50)

Federal government: Commission on Training Camp Activities, 117, 126; propaganda and, 122–24, 131, 142, 151, 155–68, 243, 247–58, 287 (n. 39), 288 (n. 50); repression of prostitution and, 115–25, 128, 137, 143, 198, 243–58, 281 (n. 1); venereal disease control and, 115–25, 243–58

Femininity, 48, 70, 160–68

Fosdick, Raymond, 117, 126, 174

Germans. *See* Immigrants and children of immigrants

Gifting, language of, 70, 147

Great Depression, 8; abortion and, 226–27; marriage and, 226–27; prostitution and, 179, 197, 206–11, 216–17; taxi dancing and, 192–93; treating and, 216–17

Homoeroticism, 152

Homosexuality: men and, 73, 154, 272 (n. 92), 281 (n. 5), 287 (n. 36); women and, 85, 297 (n. 2)

Homosocial: men, 48, 153; women, 29, 36, 47, 49, 53, 56–64, 75, 220–21, 270 (n. 45)

Hotels: prostitution and, 45, 69, 71, 110. *See also* Raines Law hotels

Immigrants and children of immigrants: courtship and, 2, 13–16, 25–44, 172, 225–26, 230–31, 236–38; ethnic hostility and, 19; French, 80; German, 2, 15, 29, 80, 133–34; Greek, 24; Irish, 2, 15, 29, 80, 261 (n. 2); Italian, 2, 15, 19,

25–32, 41, 43, 80, 220, 225–26, 230, 235–38, 263–64 (n. 49), 265 (n. 68); Jewish, 2, 15, 18, 21–27, 29, 32–44, 80, 102, 172, 225–26, 230–32, 265–66 (n. 93); prostitution and, 79–80, 102; racism and, 5, 229–32; treating and, 51–52; West Indian, 2, 233–34

Interracial socializing, 4, 133, 186–91; black attitudes toward, 83–84, 232, 274–75 (n. 30); courtship and, 6, 214, 230–32, 301 (n. 80); dating and, 230–32; prostitution and, 81–83, 154, 202–4, 210, 296 (n. 111); relationships and, 189, 230–32; treating and, 52, 65

Irish. *See* Immigrants and children of immigrants

Italians. *See* Immigrants and children of immigrants

Jews. *See* Immigrants and children of immigrants

Kinsey, Alfred, 17, 211, 224–25, 228–29, 260 (n. 8)

Landladies and landlords: prostitution and, 108–9, 272–73 (n. 1); respectability and, 21, 25

Lesbians, 85, 297 (n. 2)

Love: in courtship, 13–15, 19, 25, 28, 32–36, 38, 43–44, 189, 224, 228–29; in marriage, 13–14, 25, 33–35, 172

Madams: Adler, Polly, 172, 178, 194, 196, 200–202, 204–5, 277–78 (n. 70), 293 (n. 64), 296 (n. 114); black, 202–4, 208, 295 (nn. 104, 105); business practices of, 76, 91, 193, 198–204, 295 (n. 91); careers of, 76, 88–89; organized crime and, 178, 193, 198, 204–6, 296 (n. 114); pimps criticized by, 200–201; violence and, 200–201

Marriage: arranged, 25–26, 28, 32–35; choice of partner and, 26, 32–36, 40,

and, 173; race and, 6, 85, 231–35, 301–2 (nn. 81, 88); rates of, 225–27, 231–35, 247; treating and, 64

Prohibition, 128, 177, 191, 193, 204–6

Promiscuity, 14, 16, 18–25, 49

Propaganda, 122–24, 131, 142, 151, 155–68, 247–58, 287 (n. 39), 288 (n. 50); race and, 160–63

Prostitutes: as agents of the enemy, 118–19, 253–58; attitudes of toward charity girls, 69; internment of, 117–21, 125, 128, 142, 160, 243–45, 282 (n. 20); as neighbors, 102, 104, 110–11; responses of to repression, 136–43

Prostitution: business practices in, 76–77, 86–99, 137–38, 198–204; in candy stores, 98–99; as career, 76–78, 94, 140; casual, 77–78, 99, 108–13, 141, 178, 197–98, 204, 212; charity girls and, 1, 9–10, 44, 46–47, 59–60, 63, 69; children and, 76, 98, 104–7, 111, 142–43, 194, 208, 216, 244–45, 279–80 (n. 101), 285 (n. 95); in cigar stores, 98–99; clandestine, 77–78, 108–13, 140; definitions of, 1, 60; demographics of, 78–86, 209; family preservation and, 76, 105–6, 108, 208–10, 214, 244–45, 279 (n. 96); historiography of, 9, 277 (nn. 66, 70); as identity, 45, 94; independent, 89–113, 127–43, 178; interracial, 81–83, 154, 202–4, 210, 296 (n. 111); laws of New York and, 89–90, 99, 125–28; marginalization of, 3–4, 178, 193, 211, 245–46; marriage and, 65, 106, 208; men's attitudes toward, 19, 71–72, 74, 105; military personnel and, 115–25, 130, 138–42, 155, 242–58; patriotism and, 140–42; police and, 79, 88, 129–30, 137–39, 193–98, 178, 209–11; profits and, 91–92, 99, 102, 105, 109, 139, 277 (nn. 55, 56); race and, 79–86, 163, 178, 191, 202–4, 208–11, 274 (n. 15); in Raines Law hotels, 1, 9–10, 44, 46–47, 59–60, 63, 69, 108; reputation and, 57, 60, 77, 110–11, 113; respectability and, 4, 14, 22–23, 41–42, 53, 58–61, 77, 111, 113; street walking and, 6, 78, 88, 99, 129, 136–37, 178–79, 202–3, 209–10, 273 (n. 3); treating and, 3–4, 9–10, 44, 60, 108, 110–12, 211, 214–17, 240–41; venereal disease and, 19–20, 67, 79, 140–43, 242–46, 248–58, 272 (n. 72), 292 (n. 56); violence and, 115, 128, 135, 178, 193, 195–96, 200–201, 293 (n. 68); visibility of, 87, 102–4, 110, 112, 149; women in public and, 50, 64, 73, 176, 212–13, 217, 241; as work, 14, 47, 91, 110; working-class attitudes toward, 41–42, 60, 87, 104–7, 112–13; working-class housing and, 77, 90, 98–102, 107–10, 127, 280 (n. 114); World War I and, 114–43, 157, 212, 215, 243, 253

Racism, 209, 275 (n. 34); marital choice and, 4, 214, 230–32; middle class and, 81–85, 186–89, 229; prostitution and, 79–86, 202–4, 211, 274 (n. 15); working class and, 5, 229–32

Raines Law hotels, 89–98, 108, 126–36, 143, 178, 276 (nn. 47, 49), 278 (n. 73); description of, 94–98; growth of, 90; police and, 92–93; profits and, 91–92; safety and, 91–92, 97; working-class housing and, 90; World War I and, 126–37, 143

Reformers, 7, 54–55, 85, 116–28, 144–76, 181–87, 196–98, 219–20; racism and, 81–86, 186–89; social purity and, 116–28, 155–76. *See also* Committee of Fourteen; Middle class

Religion: courtship and, 4–5, 214, 230–31, 237; premarital intercourse and, 52; treating and, 51–52, 165, 168–69

Reputation: courtship and, 28–30, 37, 41–42, 236–38; dance halls and, 36–37, 58, 221–22, 269 (n. 29), 270 (n. 49); landladies and, 24–25; location of sex and, 69; premarital intercourse and, 67–68,

236–38; prostitution and, 57, 60, 77, 108, 110–11, 113; treating and, 57–59, 64, 67–68

Respectability: black working-class definitions of, 8–9, 209; black middle-class definitions of, 5–6, 81–84, 209, 230, 233–35; landladies and, 24–25; prostitution and, 4, 14, 22–23, 41–42, 53, 58–61, 77, 111, 113; sex work and, 6, 177, 192–93; treating and, 3–4, 37, 47, 58–59, 65, 171; white middle-class definitions of, 7–8, 160–68, 171; white working-class definitions of, 7–8, 18, 22, 41–42

"Ruin," 18, 23, 41–42, 59, 106

Sailors. *See* Military personnel

Seabury Investigation, 130–31, 193–96, 292 (n. 57)

Seduction under promise of marriage, 15–16, 20–25, 173, 222

Segregation: in Bedford Reformatory, 5, 275 (n. 31); in New York City, 83–86, 178, 203, 209–11, 269 (n. 23), 274 (n. 20)

Sex industry: marginalization of prostitution and, 3–4, 9, 177–93, 211, 241–42; race and, 4, 6, 177–93. *See also* Prostitution

Sex play (i.e., reaching first, second, or third base), 22, 26, 45, 66–67, 147–48, 154, 172, 188, 213, 222–25, 228–29, 241

Sexual barter and exchange, 2–3, 47–49, 52, 149, 212–13, 238

Sexual desire, 23, 67–68

Sexual double standard, 242, 248, 258

Sexuality: working-class norms and, 1–2, 10, 14, 16–17, 47, 61, 115, 145, 164, 171; working-class morality and, 12, 14, 19, 47, 111, 165, 172

Sholem Aleichem, 32–33

Sloan, John, 54, 61–62, 94–95, 99–101, 270 (n. 33), 271 (n. 61), 278 (n. 80)

Slumming, 83, 210

Socialism, 33, 38–39

Soldiers. *See* Military personnel

Speakeasies, 199–200

Street walking, 78, 273 (n. 3); dangers of, 88, 129, 179, 209–10; laws on, 99; race and, 78, 178–79, 202–3, 209–10; repression of, 129, 136–37

Taxi dancers: as innocents, 181, 184–88

Taxi dancing, 6, 9, 177–93; definitions of, 179–81, 260 (n. 14); erotic dancing and, 190–92; labor activism and, 192–93; prostitution and, 184–86, 190–91, 193; race and, 177, 186–90, 290 (nn. 17, 24); reformers and, 181–87, 190, 291 (n. 45); respectability of, 192–93; venereal disease and, 191. *See also* Sex industry

Terman, Lewis, 17

Treating: absorbed into dating, 4, 10, 115, 145, 174, 212–13, 217–28, 238–40; cheating men and, 64–65, 72–73, 187–89; courtship and, 37, 64, 74, 171, 217–28, 240–41; definitions of, 1, 3, 45, 48–49, 52, 56, 60, 70, 147; demographics of, 51–52, 147–50, 174, 269 (n. 24); historiography of, 7, 46–47; as identity, 45, 69–70, 217; language of, 48–49, 63, 238–42; learning about, 57, 61; material goods and, 70, 212, 214–17; men's attitudes toward, 71–75, 165, 215; men's control and, 75, 147, 151, 154, 176, 188, 217; middle class and, 160–76, 288 (n. 52); parents and, 37, 57, 165–67; patriotism and, 75, 114–15, 144–76, 214; premarital sex and, 47, 52, 61, 66, 213, 223; prostitution and, 3–4, 9–10, 44, 60, 108, 110–12, 211, 214–17, 240–41; race and, 51, 65–66, 187–88; reputation and, 57–59, 64, 67–68; respectability and, 3–4, 37, 47, 58–59, 65, 171; risks of, 64–67; safety and, 57; venereal disease and, 66, 160–63, 167–69, 272 (n. 72); women in public and, 50, 73, 176, 212–13, 217, 240–41; women's control and, 73; World War I and, 144–76, 188, 212

U.S. government. *See* Federal government

Venereal disease: charity girls and, 66, 160–63, 167–69, 272 (n. 72); diagnosis of, 121–22, 125, 127, 243–44; military personnel and, 114–25, 155–68, 243–58; prostitution and, 19–20, 67, 79, 140–43, 242–46, 248–58, 272 (n. 72), 292 (n. 56); rates of, 117, 121–22, 124, 245, 281 (n. 11), 282 (n. 33), 303 (n. 21); treatment of, 121–22, 125, 128, 167, 243–44; wayward minors and, 19–20, 140, 272 (n. 72)

Victory girls, 243, 245–47, 253–58

Violence: in courtship, 30, 235, 241; family, 30, 235, 270–71 (n. 50); masculine identity and, 155–60; organized crime and, 193; pimps and, 200–201; police and, 195–96; prostitution and, 115, 128, 135, 178, 193, 195–96, 200–201, 293 (n. 68); rape, 151, 153–54, 195, 239, 241, 248

Virginity. *See* Chastity

Wayward minors: blacks and, 85; definitions of, 7, 18, 51, 268–69 (n. 18); venereal disease and, 19–20

West Indians. *See* Blacks; Black women; Immigrants and children of immigrants

"White slavery," 80, 92, 198, 275 (n. 40)

White supremacy, 5–6, 229

Work, wage, 50, 76, 277 (nn. 55, 56); black women and, 8, 50, 267 (n. 8); daughters' wages and, 45, 56; freedom for women and, 29, 39–40, 49–51, 56, 61–62, 108, 112, 267–68 (nn. 9, 10); prostitution and, 47, 76, 92; as site for discussing sexuality, 57–60

World War I, 113–76; charity girls and, 113–14, 144–76, 246; national repression of prostitution and, 114–25, 212, 215, 243, 253, 281 (n. 1); organization of prostitution and, 127–43; premarital intercourse and, 225–27, 247; repression of prostitution in New York City and, 125–28, 212, 215, 282–83 (n. 34), 288 (n. 52); treating and, 144–76, 188, 212; venereal disease and, 114–43, 243, 245, 249

World War II, 9; dating and, 213; premarital intercourse and, 213; prostitution and, 242–58; venereal disease and, 242–46, 248–58; victory girls and, 243, 245–47, 253–58

Zaget, Samuel, 42

GENDER AND AMERICAN CULTURE

Imagining Medea: Rhodessa Jones and The-ater for Incarcerated Women, by Rena Fraden (2001).

Painting Professionals: Women Artists and the Development of Modern American Art, 1870–1920, by Kirsten Swinth (2001).

Remaking Respectability: African American Women in Interwar Detroit, by Victoria W. Wolcott (2001).

Ida B. Wells-Barnett and American Reform, 1880–1930, by Patricia A. Schechter (2001).

Taking Haiti: Military Occupation and the Culture of U.S. Imperialism, 1915–1940, by Mary A. Renda (2001).

Before Jim Crow: The Politics of Race in Postemancipation Virginia, by Jane Dailey (2000).

Captain Ahab Had a Wife: New England Women and the Whalefishery, 1720–1870, by Lisa Norling (2000).

Civilizing Capitalism: The National Con-sumers' League, Women's Activism, and Labor Standards in the New Deal Era, by Landon R. Y. Storrs (2000).

Rank Ladies: Gender and Cultural Hierarchy in American Vaudeville, by M. Alison Kibler (1999).

Strangers and Pilgrims: Female Preaching in America, 1740–1845, by Catherine A. Brekus (1998).

Sex and Citizenship in Antebellum America, by Nancy Isenberg (1998).

Yours in Sisterhood: Ms. Magazine and the Promise of Popular Feminism, by Amy Erdman Farrell (1998).

We Mean to Be Counted: White Women and Politics in Antebellum Virginia, by Elizabeth R. Varon (1998).

Women Against the Good War: Conscientious Objection and Gender on the Ameri-can Home Front, 1941–1947, by Rachel Waltner Goossen (1997).

Toward an Intellectual History of Women: Essays by Linda K. Kerber (1997).

Gender and Jim Crow: Women and the Poli-tics of White Supremacy in North Caro-lina, 1896–1920, by Glenda Elizabeth Gilmore (1996).

Delinquent Daughters: Protecting and Polic-ing Adolescent Female Sexuality in the United States, 1885–1920, by Mary E. Odem (1995).

U.S. History as Women's History: New Femi-nist Essays, edited by Linda K. Kerber, Alice Kessler-Harris, and Kathryn Kish Sklar (1995).

Common Sense and a Little Fire: Women and Working-Class Politics in the United States, 1900–1965, by Annelise Orleck (1995).

How Am I to Be Heard?: Letters of Lillian Smith, edited by Margaret Rose Gladney (1993).

Entitled to Power: Farm Women and Tech-nology, 1913–1963, by Katherine Jellison (1993).

Revising Life: Sylvia Plath's Ariel Poems, by Susan R. Van Dyne (1993).

Made from This Earth: American Women and Nature, by Vera Norwood (1993).

Unruly Women: The Politics of Social and Sexual Control in the Old South, by Victoria E. Bynum (1992).

The Work of Self-Representation: Lyric Poetry in Colonial New England, by Ivy Schweitzer (1991).

Labor and Desire: Women's Revolutionary Fiction in Depression America, by Paula Rabinowitz (1991).

Community of Suffering and Struggle: Women, Men, and the Labor Movement in Minneapolis, 1915–1945, by Elizabeth Faue (1991).

All That Hollywood Allows: Re-reading Gen-der in 1950s Melodrama, by Jackie Byars (1991).

Doing Literary Business: American Women Writers in the Nineteenth Century, by Susan Coultrap-McQuin (1990).

Ladies, Women, and Wenches: Choice and Constraint in Antebellum Charleston and Boston, by Jane H. Pease and William H. Pease (1990).

The Secret Eye: The Journal of Ella Gertrude Clanton Thomas, 1848–1889, edited by Virginia Ingraham Burr, with an introduction by Nell Irvin Painter (1990).

Second Stories: The Politics of Language, Form, and Gender in Early American Fictions, by Cynthia S. Jordan (1989).

Within the Plantation Household: Black and White Women of the Old South, by Elizabeth Fox-Genovese (1988).

The Limits of Sisterhood: The Beecher Sisters on Women's Rights and Woman's Sphere, by Jeanne Boydston, Mary Kelley, and Anne Margolis (1988).